The Khoisan are a cluster of southern African peoples which include the famous Bushmen, or San, 'hunters', the Khoekhoe 'herders' (in the past called 'Hottentots'), and the Damara, also a herding people. The present-day Khoisan include hunter-gatherers, pastoralists, and wage labourers. In spite of differences associated with their economic pursuits, as well as differences in language and other aspects of culture, the Khoisan peoples share features of territorial organization, gender relations, kinship, ritual, and cosmology. These represent elements of structures held in common across economic, cultural, linguistic, and 'racial' boundaries. This book focuses on these structures and the diverse forms which they take within Khoisan culture and society. It is written within the framework of regional structural comparison.

Part I examines the theoretical aspects of regional structural comparison, and the prehistory and classification of the Khoisan peoples. Part II presents an extensive ethnographic overview of Khoisan culture and social organization – the first since 1930. Part III explores facets of Khoisan society in comparative perspective, and, in particular, the complex relationships between environmental conditions, ethno-linguistic boundaries and processes of change. There are chapters on settlement patterns, politics and exchange, religious belief, and kinship.

Cambridge Studies in Social and Cultural Anthropology
Editors: Ernest Gellner, Jack Goody, Stephen Gudeman, Michael Herzfeld, Jonathan Parry

85
Hunters and herders of southern Africa

A list of books in the series will be found at the end of the volume

HUNTERS AND HERDERS
OF SOUTHERN AFRICA

*A comparative ethnography of the
Khoisan peoples*

ALAN BARNARD

University of Edinburgh

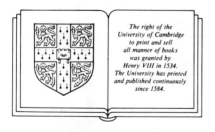

The right of the
University of Cambridge
to print and sell
all manner of books
was granted by
Henry VIII in 1534.
The University has printed
and published continuously
since 1584.

CAMBRIDGE UNIVERSITY PRESS

Cambridge

New York   Port Chester

Melbourne   Sydney

Published by the Press Syndicate of the University of Cambridge
The Pitt Building, Trumpington Street, Cambridge CB2 1RP
40 West 20th Street, New York, NY 10011, USA
10 Stamford Road, Oakleigh, Victoria 3166, Australia

First published 1992

Printed in Great Britain at the University Press, Cambridge

A catalogue record for this book is available from the British Library

Library of Congress cataloguing in publication data

Barnard, Alan.
   Hunters and herders of southern Africa: a comparative ethnography
of the Khoisan peoples / Alan Barnard.
      p.   cm. – (Cambridge studies in social and cultural anthropology; 85)
   Includes bibliographical references and index.
   ISBN 0 521 41188 2
   1. San (African people) 2. Khoikhoi (African people) I. Title.
II. Series.
   DT1058.S36B37   1992
   305.896'1068 – dc20   91-17705 CIP

18.95

ISBN 0521 41188 2 hardback   ISBN 0521 428653 paperback

S.E.

68247

The pattern is the thing
GREGORY BATESON

Contents

Part III: Comparisons and transformations

Figures and maps

Tables

Preface

This book owes much to the inspiration of the two people who, a decade and a half ago, passed judgement on my earliest, awkward attempts at regional comparison (Barnard 1976a) – Isaac Schapera and Adam Kuper. The ethnographic content and general comparative approach to the Khoisan material were foreshadowed by Schapera's *The Khoisan peoples of South Africa* (1930), and one purpose of the present volume is to bring that masterly work up to date. On the other hand, my theoretical orientation owes more to the structuralist methodology pioneered in southern African ethnography by Kuper's *Wives for cattle* (1982). A second purpose of this book is to present Khoisan ethnography in a framework comparable to that which Kuper uses for Southern Bantu ethnography. The task is similar, if more complicated due to the greater diversity of social structure among the Khoisan peoples.

None of the chapters in the present book is a reprint of any previous paper, but several include material from earlier papers. Part of Chapter 2 appeared in 'Kinship, language and production: a conjectural history of Khoisan social structure', *Africa* 58: 29–50 (1988). Sections of Chapter 8 were included originally in 'Sex roles among the Nharo Bushmen of Botswana', *Africa* 50: 115–24 (1980). Material in several chapters (especially Chapter 12) is derived from 'Rethinking Bushman settlement patterns and territoriality', *Sprache und Geschichte in Afrika* 7 (1): 41–60 (1986). Part of Chapter 14 originally appeared in 'Structure and fluidity in Khoisan religious ideas', *Journal of Religion in Africa* 18: 216–36 (1988). Chapter 15 is based mainly on material from 'Universal kin categorization in four Bushman societies', *L'Uomo* 5: 219–37 (1981); and from 'Nharo kinship in social and cosmological perspective: comparisons between Southern African and Australian hunter-gatherers', *Mankind* 19: 198–214

(1989). Chapter 16 is based on material from 'Kin terminology systems of the Khoe-speaking peoples', in J.W. Snyman (ed.), *Bushman and Hottentot linguistic studies, 1979*, University of South Africa, Pretoria (1980); from 'Khoisan kinship: regional comparison and underlying structures', in Ladislav Holy (ed.), *Comparative anthropology*, Blackwell, Oxford (1987); and from 'Kinship, language and production: a conjectural history of Khoisan social structure', *Africa* 58: 29–50 (1988).

My field research among Khoisan groups in 1974–5, 1979, and 1982 was sponsored respectively by the Swan Fund of the Pitt Rivers Museum (University of Oxford), the Hayter Travel and Research Committee and Department of Social Anthropology of the University of Edinburgh, and the U.S. National Science Foundation (BNS–8023941). Formal permission to conduct work in Botswana was granted by the Office of the President of Botswana, and I am grateful to that Office and to the other officials in Central Government, and in the districts, who allowed me the opportunity to conduct my fieldwork without hindrance. Equally, I would like to thank my informants, who so generously gave their time and offered me their friendship. To mention but a few, in Botswana I would like to acknowledge the help of Dabe, Dãse, G/uã'n//ae, Kamti, Khamai, K'uaba, Maxu, N/am//ua, N/isa, N/u, N//u'n//ae, N!ose, Sobe, Tatum, Tete, Thamku, Tshabu, Tsau'n//ae, Tshebe, /Hoha, /Homa, /Ise, ≠A≠e, //Oro, //Xidau, !Ane, !Xa, !Xoba (and their namesakes). In Namibia I would like to thank Christiaan Afrikaner, Maria Magdalena Block, Daniel Dâsab, Paulina Dâsas, Eliphas Eiseb, Josef Isaak, Josef Kahuika, Simon Kooper, Isaak Swarts, Thomas Tibott, and Jan !Goaseb. Johannes Boois, Kennedy McIntyre, and Motsame Phiri provided invaluable assistance as interpreters; my thanks to them too. I am also much indebted to the Ghanzi and Xanagas ranchers who allowed me to roam freely across their lands. Most of them, I am sure, would prefer to remain anonymous.

I am grateful to many colleagues who have contributed, both through comments on chapters of this book, and through discussions and correspondence on its issues through the many years of its preparation. It is difficult to mention their names without fear of neglecting someone, but my gratitude is due, among others, to Nick Allen, John Argyle, Megan Biesele, Kuno Budack, Alan Campbell, Peter Carstens, Liz Cashdan, Tony Cohen, Ursula Dentlinger, Tony Good, Mathias Guenther, Ørnulf Gulbrandsen, Wilfrid Haacke, H.J. Heinz, Roger Hewitt, Bob Hitchcock, Ladislav Holy, Rick Huntington, Tim Ingold, Sue Kent, Klaus Keuthmann, Adam Kuper, Jessica Kuper, Bob Layton, Richard Lee, David Lewis-Williams, Ken Maddock, Lorna Marshall, John Parkington, Nic Peterson, Beatrice

Sandelowsky, Isaac Schapera, Rosalind Shaw, George Silberbauer, Jan
Snyman, Hendrik Steyn, Jiro Tanaka, Tony Traill, David Turner, Rainer
Vossen, Martin West, Ernst Westphal, Thomas Widlok, Polly Wiessner,
Ed Wilmsen, and James Woodburn. I also acknowledge the Edinburgh
students who attended my course 'Khoisan Peoples of Southern Africa'
and thereby helped, if unknowingly, to mould this book.

Finally, as always, I owe a special debt to my parents for their unending
generosity, without which I would never have been able to complete this
work, and to Joy, for endless tolerance and support.

A note on orthography

Not least because of the 'clicks', the spelling of Khoisan words often causes problems for authors and readers alike. Some explanation of these sounds, and some other sounds found in Khoisan languages, may be helpful. I also include here a few brief comments on the usage and spellings of ethnic group names and on abbreviations used in the description of kinship systems in this book.

Clicks

Clicks are consonant sounds produced by allowing air to pass into (rather than out of) the mouth. They are combined with other consonants to form clusters, e.g., *!kh* (a palatal click followed by a *k* and an *h*). Apart from odd expressions like 'Tisk, tisk' in English and certain words in the peculiar 'mother-in-law languages' of the Australian Aborigines, clicks occur only in the Khoisan languages, two languages of East Africa (Hadza and Sandawe), and certain Southern Bantu languages, particularly the Nguni languages of the Indian Ocean coast and related dialects spoken in the southern African interior (Zulu, Xhosa, Ndebele, etc.). The latter groups acquired their click-containing vocabulary originally from Khoisan peoples.

There have been a number of attempts to put the click symbols into writing. In his catalogue of the Library of Sir George Grey, W.H.I. Bleek (1858: 6) recorded no less than 28 different *systems* that had by then been invented. He opted for the one created in 1854 by the Egyptologist, Richard Lepsius (1863 [1854]). This system, though with a 'not equal to' sign in place of Lepsius' original broken vertical line for the alveolar click, was adopted by the 1856 conference of the Rhenish Mission Society (RMS) and has remained in general use ever since. Bleek later added the 'bull's eye' symbol (a circle with a dot in the middle) for the bilabial click. The Lepsius-RMS-Bleek system (hereafter, the Standard Khoisan system) is the one I use.

The five basic clicks in this system are given below, together with their traditional labels and descriptions of their method of articulation and their sound.

⊙ Bilabial. A bilabial stop or affricate. Produced by realeasing air between the lips, often as in a kiss. Found only in !Xõ and Southern Bushman languages.

/ Dental. A dental or alveolar affricate (sometimes described as a fricative). Produced by a sucking motion with the tip of the tongue on the teeth, as in the English expression of annoyance written 'Tisk, tisk', phonetically [/ /]. Found in all Khoisan languages.

≠ Alveolar. An alveolar stop, produced by pulling the blade of the tongue sharply away from the alveolar ridge, immediately behind the teeth. A difficult sound for many people, rather in-between / and ! in sound. Found in all Khoisan languages.

// Lateral. A lateral affricate (sometimes described as a fricative). Produced by placing the tip of tongue on the roof of the mouth (the exact position varies) and releasing air on one side of the mouth between the side of the tongue and the cheek. More simply, the clicking sound film cowboys use, [// //], to make their horses go. Found in all Khoisan languages.

! Palatal, sometimes called cerebral or retroflex. An alveopalatal or palatal stop, produced by pulling the tip of the tongue sharply away from the front of the hard palate. When made with lips rounded, it sounds rather like a cork popping from a wine bottle. Found in all Khoisan languages.

The other systems still in existence include that of the International Phonetic Association (IPA) and that employed in Bantu languages. Although the remainder of the International Phonetic Alphabet is used universally, the IPA click symbols are not used today by *any* Khoisan specialist, whether anthropologist or linguist. Except in the important monograph on Khoekhoe phonetics by D.M. Beach (1938), they have never found favour with specialists. The Bantu system has been in use in Xhosa and Zulu (originally in mission schools) since the 1820s and has recently gained favour among some Khoisan specialists (see, e.g., Wilmsen 1989a). This system has the advantage of employing symbols which are readily understood by literate speakers of click-possessing languages, but the disadvantage of phonological ambiguity. Specifically, two clicks found in Khoisan languages, the bilabial and the alveolar, are not present in Bantu languages and therefore have no symbol (though, confusingly, *c*, *x*, *v* and other symbols were occasionally used in nineteenth-century Khoekhoe texts for the alveolar click). Also, the *x* in the Bantu system signifies a lateral click (// in the Standard Khoisan system), while in other systems *x* signifies a voiceless velar fricative (written with an *h* or a *g* in Bantu languages). The Standard Khoisan click symbols and their IPA and Bantu equivalents are given below. The 'bull's eye' for the bilabial click was only finally approved by the IPA in 1976 (see Pullum and Ladusaw 1986: 112), while the Beach's 'double-barred esh' still awaits official approval (1986: 143–4).

Standard Khoisan	*IPA – D.M. Beach*	*Bantu*
☉	☉	(no symbol)
/	ʇ	c
≠	ǂ	(no symbol)
//	ʖ	x
!	ʗ	q

Click consonant clusters include the click plus one or more other consonants. The specific consonants which may be used in any given language are sometimes called 'click releases', and most linguists who specialize in the study of Khoisan languages include the click proper and the release as a single click phoneme. Thus, in a given language, *!k*, *!kx*, and *!kh* might be regarded as three distinct phonemes. Clicks may also be voiced or nasalized. Voicing (the simultaneous production of a *d* or a *g* with the click) is usually indicated by writing a *g* before or after the click symbol, while nasalization (with voicing) is similarly indicated by writing an *n* before or after the click symbol. I generally write the *g* or *n* before, although in some cases (particularly in the Nama language and in citing the work of other authors) I place the *g* or *n* after the click symbol.

An additional complication concerns the practice of some German scholars of indicating voicing and nasalization by wavy lines above and below the click symbols (see, e.g., Köhler 1981). In this usage, a wavy line above a click symbol written vertically, e.g., ʇ̃, indicates nasalization (without voicing), and a wavy line below a click symbol indicates voicing without nasalization. A voiced, nasalized click is indicated in this system by the click symbol followed by an *n*, for example, |*n*. The Standard Khoisan equivalent would be *n*/ or /*n*.

Examples of click releases are given below, using a dental click series for purposes of illustration.

/ or /k	dental click with non-phonemic velar release
/q	dental click with uvular release
/' or /ʔ	dental click released on a glottal stop
/x	dental click released on a voiceless velar fricative
/x'	dental click released on a voiceless velar fricative followed by a glottal stop
/h	dental click with aspiration
g/ or /g	voiced dental click
n/ or /n	nasalized dental click (with voicing)
n̥/ or /n̥	nasalized dental click (voiceless)

Wherever relevant and possible, I have standardized the orthographic representation of non-Nama Khoisan languages according to the principles followed in my *Nharo wordlist* (Barnard 1985), without non-phonemic *k* after a click symbol. For example, Nharo *!kau* or *!au* is given in this book as *!au*. The deletion of this unconsciously articulated (but essentially inaudible) *k* is now normal practice for those linguists who specialize in Khoisan languages, and it seems sensible to follow suit in order to make comparisons between different languages easier. An exception to this rule is my retention of the spelling *!Kung*, arguably now virtually an English word. Indeed, proper nouns are generally spelled in this book according to common usage in English ethnography, rather than according to strict phonological rules (see 'Ethnic group names', below). Other exceptions occur in /Xam words. Here I follow the texts as recorded by W.H.I. Bleek and Lucy Lloyd (e.g., 1911). On Korana, I follow Engelbrecht (1936) and Maingard (e.g., 1932) in appropriate contexts. Their orthography is in general a compromise between Nama usage and the Standard Khoisan usage illustrated above.

The standard orthography of Nama or Nama/Damara differs in some respects from Standard Khoisan. Nama is, in fact, the only Khoisan language with a standardized orthography. It would be absurd to spell Nama words in any way other than the way Nama, the Damara, and other literate speakers of this language spell them, although for consistency in typefaces I do use slanted in preference to Nama's more usual vertical click symbols. Beware, therefore, that in Nama a click symbol followed directly by a vowel symbol is produced with glottal stop (which is *not* represented orthographically) between the click and a vowel. A click symbol followed by a *g* indicates not voicing but the *lack of* a glottal stop. A click symbol followed by an *n* indicates nasalization. The pronunciation of Nama clicks is illustrated below for the dental click series.

Nama orthography	Standard Khoisan orthography
/	/' or /ʔ
/g	/ or /k
/n	n/ or /n

Nama orthography was reformed in 1970 and again in 1977, but the differences between the old and new systems are very minor (*Nama/Damara* 1977). They concern mainly hyphenation and the representation of some vowels and diphthongs (e.g., the replacement of German-influenced *ei* with *ai*). In this book Nama words are given in modern orthography. Traditional spellings are included only where these are particularly relevant (e.g., in citations from early sources). Morpheme divisions are, by hyphens, only where I wish to draw attention to the meaning of specific morphemes.

Finally, it may be of interest to the non-specialist that the pronunciation of clicks in ethnic group names is entirely optional when speaking a non-Khoisan language. Acceptable anglicizations may be produced either by articulating a non-click sound of approximately the same phonological position (e.g., *p* for ⊙, *t* for / or ≠, *k* for // or !), or by ignoring the click entirely and simply pronouncing the release followed by the remainder of the word. When speaking English, I myself say *Kung* for '!Kung', *Gwi* for 'G/wi', and *Gana* for 'G//ana'. Other non-English sounds may also be anglicized. In particular, the voiceless velar fricative of Khoisan languages is often rendered in English as a voiceless velar stop (e.g., *Ko* for '!Xõ', *Kam* for '/Xam').

Non-click consonants and vowels
The remainder of sounds which occur in Khoisan languages are given in this book in standard phonetic symbols which should cause few difficulties.

A glottal stop, IPAʔ, is written as ' – as is common practice now among several Khoisan specialists. I have standardized as *kx'* the orthography of the consonant cluster written variously as *k''*, *kx''*, and *kx'*, though these other forms may be found in citations from earlier sources. I take this to be more or less the same sound in all Khoisan languages, namely a voiceless velar or glottal affricate accompanied by a glottal stop. In some Western and Central Khoe dialects, and even idiolects, *kx'* occurs in free variation with *k'*, whereas in others these are distinguished as separate phonemes (see Barnard 1985: 8).

In Khoe languages there is generally no phonemic distinction between s and ʃ (sometimes written š) or between z and ʒ (sometimes written ž). I have therefore standardized these as s and z, respectively. The actual sound generally lies in between English s and ʃ (orthographic *sh*) or z and ʒ (orthographic *zh*). Köhler's (e.g., 1966a) Kxoe ç is similar to ʃ.

Following the practice established in my *Nharo wordlist* (Barnard 1985: 7), semivowels are written as *w* and *j* where they occur initially, but otherwise take the form *u* or *i*. For example, Nharo *khwe* or *khue* is written as *khue*. My orthographic *j* is a voiced palatal central approximant, as in Afrikaans or German *ja* ('yes'), not English *judge*. The letter *y* is not used for this sound except in Eastern ≠Hoã, where I follow Jeffrey Gruber's (1973) orthography.

Vowels are represented with standard phonetic symbols. Vowel length, or 'doubling' of vowels of like value but different tone, is phonemic in some languages. In Nama this is indicated by a macron over a single vowel symbol, e.g., *sāb* (meaning 'Bushman', masc. sg.). In other languages, vowel length is usually indicated by the use of two identical symbols, e.g., Korana *saab*. D.F. Bleek's (1929a; 1956) use of the colon to indicate length, say, *sa:b*, may be regarded as standard for some languages, such as /Xam, and is used in this way by Maingard (1932) and Engelbrecht (1936) in their Korana texts. I retain it in such cases. However, I do not use this symbol in Nharo (Bleek's 'Naron'), the fieldwork language she and I have in common. Nasalization is indicated by a tilde (or in Nama orthography, a circumflex) above the relevant vowel symbol, and pharyngealization or 'pressing' by a tilde below, e.g., ≠ãã̰, a term cited by Traill (1974: 9) as one of the many ethnic self-designations for the !Xõ.

Phonemic tone is very often difficult to identify and is not indicated here unless essential. The most notorious case is the Korana, Nama, and Damara distinction between the *tarás* ('wife', 'cross-cousin', 'marriageable female joking relative') and the *tàras* ('father's sister', 'sister', 'parallel cousin', 'unmarriageable female avoidance relative'). Here, for consistency, I write Engelbrecht's (1936) Korana *táras* as *tàras* – probably, as in Nama, having low falling tone on the first syllable. This contrasts with *tarás*, which has a high rising tone on the second syllable.

Ethnic group names

To a non-specialist encountering the Khoisan literature for the first time, the variety of ethnic group names and the diversity of spellings for them may seem as daunting as the clicks. My general policy is: (1) to stick to the best-known terms when referring to well-known peoples, (2) to use self-appellations when appropriate, (3) to use as precise a designation as possible, (4) to avoid the use of prefixes and suffixes in ethnic group names, and (5) to be etymologically and phonologically accurate without being phonetically pedantic.

However, these principles are not always easy to reconcile, and decisions have to be made according to context. For example, I write 'San' and not 'Sa' as the synonym for 'Bushman', in spite of the fact that the -*n* in this term is actually a plural suffix in the language from which it is derived. To use 'Sa', although it might be in keeping with my fourth principle, would be un-English and therefore contrary to my first and fifth principles. To take another example, I frequently use 'Zu/'hoã' (singular) and 'Zu/'hoãsi' (plural) in preference to '!Kung'. This usage conforms to my second, third, and fifth principles. Although 'Zu/'hoã' is not as widely employed in non-specialist circles as '!Kung', this usage also marginally conforms to my first principle in that it is in common use among specialists, especially to designate Central as opposed to Northern or Southern !Kung. I use the plural suffix -*si* in this case, since this is common practice among ethnographers of that group. However, following my fourth principle, I avoid the Khoe suffixes -*n*, -*na*, -*qua*, etc., used by early writers in ethnic group names (e.g., 'Namaqua'). In this book I do not usually use Bantu prefixes, *Ba-*, *Ma-*, *Ova-*, etc., although I have used these when writing in other contexts, such as in Botswana government reports. In Botswana the use of *Ba-* is not only acceptable but standard English (e.g. 'Batswana', in reference either to ethnic Tswana or to citizens of the country), while elsewhere it is generally inappropriate.

Place names are also spelled in a variety of ways by different authors. In general, I follow here the form used in the country to which I refer. For example, the place name frequently spelled '≠Xade' by ethnographers is rendered here as 'Xade', to accord with spelling standardization in Botswana. The names of non-literate individuals are spelled more phonetically, with standard click symbols where appropriate, or in the manner in which their names are recorded by earlier writers.

Abbreviations

The following standard kin type abbreviations are used, especially in tables and lists of relationship terms.

F	father	M	mother
S	son	D	daughter
B	brother	Z	sister
H	husband	W	wife
P	parent	C	child
G	sibling	E	spouse
y	younger	e	elder
s	senior	j	junior

ss	same sex	os	opposite sex
ms	man speaking	ws	woman speaking
v	vocative	N	namesake

These are employed in strings to indicate specific genealogical position. For example, FBS means 'father's brother's son', FyBS means 'father's younger brother's son', FBSy means 'father's brother's son who is younger than ego'. 'Elder' and 'younger' denote real relative age, whereas 'senior' and 'junior' denote relative positions in respect of linking relatives. For example, my FyBS is 'junior' to me, though he may be either older or younger. The distinction of relative position among classificatory siblings (often including parallel cousins) is common among Khoisan peoples. Some groups make this distinction on the basis of age, and others on the basis of seniority.

Part I

The Khoisan peoples

1

Introduction

The Khoisan peoples

The Khoisan peoples are a large cluster of southern African nations. Some of them are pastoralists, others are hunter-gatherers or hunter-gatherer-fishermen, and virtually all today include individuals who work as herdsmen or labourers for members of other ethnic groups. Yet, in spite of differences associated with their subsistence pursuits, many otherwise diverse Khoisan peoples share a great number of common features of territorial organization, gender relations, kinship, ritual, and cosmology. These features are not randomly distributed; nor have they simply diffused from one group to another as single culture traits. They represent elements of structures held in common across economic, cultural, linguistic, and 'racial' boundaries. The focus of this book is on these structures and on the diversity which they take within Khoisan culture and society.

Theoretical premises
Comparison

Comparison is both a method and a theoretical concept (cf. Śaraṇa 1975; Holy 1987; Parkin 1987). For me, its theoretical importance increases when we compare not just two or three societies, but a range of similar societies, such as those which define a culture area. The kind of comparison I am interested in is what has been called 'controlled' (Eggan 1954) and more specifically 'intensive regional' (Schapera 1953) comparison.

This approach differs logically from large-scale cross-cultural studies where a 'global sample' is envisaged (e.g., Murdock 1949; Goody 1976; Ember and Ember 1983). Equally, it is very different from studies which define similarities, differences, or analogies between either whole cultures or isolated culture traits. In the latter case, comparison is merely illustrative. Examples of this type of study might include works as diverse as a short paper dealing with a single trait found in two or three societies (e.g., Radcliffe-Brown 1924) and a twelve-volume treatise on a vast array of culture traits found worldwide (e.g., Frazer 1911–15 [1890]). What is lacking in these cases are mechanisms for determining cause and effect or for defining cross-cultural variation in relational terms. Radcliffe-Brown's (1924) study of the 'mother's brother problem' posits structural relations, but only within specific societies, not cross-culturally.

In contrast, Goody's (1959) essay on the same subject focuses on two very closely related societies, in which opposite forms of behaviour between a mother's brother and his sister's son can be ascribed to differences in the rules of inheritance. Goody's study is an excellent example of controlled comparison, but it is narrow in scope. Goody sacrifices broader ethnographic coverage in order to maintain a tighter control over his comparisons. In contrast again, Nadel's (1952) 'essay in comparison' discusses witchcraft in four African societies from two different regions (two are Sudanese and two are Nigerian). Each regional pair shows both similarities of historical relationship and divergences, but comparisons between non-regional pairings also reveal features which would seem to be associated with variations in kinship, gender relations, age structures, and so on. Nadel's study is structural but only partly regional, the other part being illustrative. Nadel sacrifices an element of control in order to illustrate structural contrasts which would otherwise not be apparent.

This book is written from a specific perspective which has been labelled 'regional structural comparison' (Kuper 1979). Ideally, it entails both a structural dimension and the level of control which a regional focus can offer, though, like Goody and Nadel, one must inevitably sometimes sacrifice one in pursuit of the other. Regional structural comparison formed a major part of my Ph.D. thesis (Barnard 1976a) and parallels the development of the idea by Adam Kuper, who was my thesis supervisor. His work, exemplified by *Wives for cattle* (1982; see also Kuper 1975), has focused centrally on the politics of marriage among the Southern Bantu-speaking peoples. My own work in kinship has focused more on the relationship terminologies of the Khoisan peoples and has emphasized the notion of regionally conceived 'underlying structures', as well as historical transformations (e.g., Barnard 1987; 1988a). Indeed, the concept of a regional structure first occurred to me while I was doing fieldwork in Botswana. There I met members of various Bushman groups who described their usages of relationship terms with reference to usages in related dialects. They classify speakers of these dialects as 'kin' through the ideology I have termed 'universal kin categorization' (1978a; 1981). This necessitates a kind of structural 'translation' between the kinship systems of different peoples, and the practice in kinship is paralleled in other social spheres. My work on settlement patterns has followed a similar model, one which concerns logical possibilities of seasonal occupation, as well as ecological pressures and constraints (1979a; 1986a). Much the same is true of my work on religious ideas, where flexibility, even in individual belief, can be interpreted as operating within a great system of mythological and symbolic expression (1988b).

This book continues the approach which I used in those earlier papers. What earlier writers have described merely as cultural differences are seen here as part of the larger, regional structure of beliefs and practices – a structure of structures. To some degree, indigenous thinkers have an intuitive knowledge of this structure, as the example above shows. Just as English-speakers (even small children) know how to use nouns and verbs correctly in the English language, so too the Bushmen, Khoekhoe, and Damara know how to use, for example, religious ideas within the 'grammar' of the Khoisan religious system as a whole. This, of course, does not mean that they can always define explicitly the categories or formulate the rules of such a 'grammar'; as experts in their own cultures, they do not need to. Explication of that 'grammar' is the task of the anthropologist.

Khoisan kinship and underlying structures

A large part of this book deals with kinship. Kinship is a focal point in Khoisan society and one which is especially significant for regional comparison. This is not so much because kinship is a 'privileged system' in any of the senses specified and criticized by David Schneider (1984). It is because kinship appears to be the most fundamental area of difference between Khoisan societies, while at the same time having at its core certain principles which unite Khoisan culture as a whole.

Foremost among these principles are the classification of relatives as 'joking partners' or 'avoidance partners', their classification as marriageable or unmarriageable, and for certain relatives, as 'senior' or 'junior'. In the hierarchically arranged herder societies, it is through kinship that hierarchy is played out. Among the hunter-gatherers, it is through kinship, as well as through quasi-kin relationships of giving and receiving, that equality is defined and maintained. Although not quite a 'core symbol' in the sense of David Schneider or Roy Wagner (1986), the regional system kin classification functions as a 'core' underlying structure of social relations.

In studying Khoisan kinship, I have often found that the rigid application of traditional models drawn from other parts of the world or from anthropological, rather than indigenous discourse, obscures interesting features. An approach which takes into account similar features across societal boundaries can reveal underlying structures which add much more to our understanding of kinship than the surface structures which are the subject of conventional methods of formal analysis. Common features of kinship behaviour, for example, may be expressed terminologically in one language, but not in the language of a closely related, neighbouring group. One group may distinguish relationships by a large number of relationship terms; another may employ one term for a large number of relationships, while distinguishing jurally between different genealogical positions within the same relationship category (Barnard 1987). There have been earlier comparative studies which imply some notion of underlying structure. Radcliffe-Brown's (1913; 1930–1) comparative and theoretical studies of Australian Aboriginal social organization, Josselin de Jong's (1977 [1935]) argument for the study of the East Indies as an 'ethnographic field of study', Eggan's (1950; cf. 1955 [1937]) work on the Western Pueblos, and Goody's (1959) essay on the mother's brother in West Africa are cases in point. Yet none of these studies made explicit either the generative principles or the constraining rules which such underlying structures entail.

A few points may help to clarify my views on this subject. First, my concept of an underlying structure implies a notion of cross-cultural similarity. An underlying structure (e.g., of systems of kinship or of religious belief) is not usually unique to a people, but found in common among several peoples. It therefore differs from Kuper's (1980: 21; 1982: 155–6) notion of the underlying structure of Swazi 'symbolic dimensions', which is particular to the Swazi. Likewise, my notion of underlying structure is analogous neither to that of the 'deep structure' of a particular language, nor to that of 'universal grammar' in linguistics. An underlying social or cultural structure is neither specific to one people nor universal.

Secondly, the concept of an underlying structure is essentially an empirical one; therefore its precise extent will depend on context. One may speak of the kinship systems of the Khoe-speaking peoples as having a common underlying structure, or of those of the Khoisan peoples as a whole having a greater or more distant underlying structure. One may talk about the underlying structure of Bushman settlement patterns and exclude from this structure the settlement patterns of Khoekhoe and Damara herders, or one may wish to try to explain all these patterns within the same, larger structure. It is also possible to define underlying structures beyond a region. Variation within a given world religion (e.g., Christianity or

Buddhism) or due to its influence (e.g., in family structures) is sometimes best explained in such terms.

Thirdly, the concept of an underlying structure presupposes the contrasting concept of a surface structure. For example, surface structures include those aspects of kinship classification which are implied directly by relationship terminologies. Each speech community has its own relationship terminology structure, and, as noted above, conventional methods of analysis deal with these, while ignoring the complexities of underlying regional or other larger structures. Similarly, typologies of relationship terminology structures ('Eskimo', 'Iroquois', etc.) or descent systems (patrilineal, cognatic, etc.) entail a notion of comparability only at a surface level and frequently fail to reveal either underlying differences within 'types' or underlying similarities across typological boundaries (cf. Barnard and Good 1984: 55–7, 59–66, 104–6).

Ethnographic background
Terminology: some complications
The term 'Koïsan' (later 'Khoisan') was coined by Leonhard Schultze (1928: 211) in his biometric study of 'Hottentot' and 'Bushman' populations. He intended it as a biological label. Popularized by I. Schapera (1930), 'Khoisan' has long been taken as a cultural and linguistic label as well. It reflects a traditional, if not strictly accurate, ethnological division of the groups. *Khoi* (in old Nama orthography) or *khoe* (in modern Nama orthography) means 'person'. The Nama and Korana, the two herding peoples who have survived into the present century, use the compound *Khoekhoen*, 'People of People', as their self-appellation. In fact, *Khoe* was first recorded, as *Quena* (the *-na* is a common-gender plural suffix), by Jan van Riebeeck in January 1653 (M.L. Wilson 1986a: 252) and is found as a generic term for 'people' in most Khoe languages – i.e., those of the Khoekhoe, the Damara, and certain 'Central Bushman' groups. In Nama the term requires a number-gender suffix (*khoeb*, a man; *khoes*, a woman; *khoera*, two women; *khoeti*, three or more women; etc.). In the English compound 'Khoisan', the first syllable refers to the Nama themselves and other cattle-herding Khoekhoe or 'Hottentots'. Following established practice among linguists who specialize in Khoisan languages, I use the spelling 'Khoe' as a linguistic label or when referring to the Khoekhoe themselves, but retain the traditional spelling 'Khoi-' in the artificial compound 'Khoisan', which is distinctly a European and not a Khoisan word.

Sān is the Khoekhoe word for 'Bushmen' or 'foragers'. Unlike *khoe* it is grammatically complete. *Sān* is the common-gender plural form. *Sonqua* and *soaqua*, the forms most frequently used in seventeenth- and eighteenth-century records, are syntactically masculine plural, although they were applied collectively to women and men alike. An interesting contrasting case is the usage *k'au khoedzi* (literally 'male people', but with a feminine plural suffix), which means 'men' in Nharo, a Khoe dialect spoken by 'Bushmen'. The term 'San' is commonly employed today by anthropologists who object to 'Bushman' on the grounds that it is, in their view, a racist or sexist term. Yet, in my view 'San' is not much better; certainly it has not always had the best connotations in the language from which it comes. At times it seems to have meant 'tramps', 'vagabonds', 'rascals', 'robbers', 'bandits', etc. (see, e.g., Hahn 1881: 3). In Cape Khoekhoe dialects and in Nama it generally carried negative connotations and was applied both as a generic term (e.g., to refer to black, white, or Nama 'rascals') and as an ethnic label (to refer to Bushmen). In earlier times, it referred primarily to low-status Khoekhoe who had lost their cattle, and was only later extended to its present use (Guenther 1986a: 28–30). Nevertheless, it can be employed in Nama today as an ethnic label, in a more or less neutral sense, just as it is by English-speaking anthropologists. The problem, still, is that it is often taken as meaning non-Khoe – in spite of the fact that many foraging as well as herding populations speak Khoe and not 'San' (non-Khoe Khoisan) languages. Although 'San' is gaining wide acceptance among non-specialists, several ethnographers who formerly used it have now reverted to 'Bushman'.

Another fashionable alternative among anthropologists is 'Mosarwa' (plural, 'Basarwa'), a term borrowed from Setswana, the language of the Tswana people. Needless to say, it has some of the same problems. The usage *Basarwa* is a neologism. It has only been in existence since the 1970s. The upper-case *Ba-* prefix (that of 'people' and 'tribes') officially replaces the *ma-* (a prefix for 'things') of the traditional form *masarwa*, although most speakers, including Basarwa themselves when they speak Setswana, still say *masarwa*. The stem *-sa* is probably a loan word, related etymologically to the *sa-* of Nama *san*, while the *-rwa* is from a Common Bantu term frequently applied to indicate diminutiveness. Interestingly, white people are still designated *makgoa* (singular, *lekgoa*), perhaps in recognition of their lack of the unitary 'tribal' status which now seems to be granted, implicitly, to the scattered and diverse Basarwa peoples. The term 'Masarwa' (plural) has also been used incorrectly in some early twentieth-century writings, including colonial service reports, to refer to various specific Bushman groups (as in phrases like 'the Masarwa tribe of Bush-men'). Although 'Basarwa' is now used as the plural form in both Tswana and English-language publications in Botswana, I prefer to use the English word 'Bushman' in an international context. There sees to me no reason to prefer a Tswana word for an English one in this context.

Recently, another term has been suggested. The Argentinian anthropo-logist Carlos Valiente Noailles (Valiente Noailles 1988: 26–8), noting the use of *kua* for 'Bushman' among some groups in the southeastern Kalahari, has employed 'Kúa' as a generic term. He uses it mainly for speakers of 'Central' Bushman languages, and more specifically for the G/wi and G//ana whom he studied. The problem here is that this term already has an even more specific usage, referring not to the G/wi and G//ana at all, but exclusively to other southeastern Kalahari groups. They use it as an ethnic self-designation. Its only advantage as a generic label seems to be that it has not yet acquired any negative connotations.

Any term which is applied to low-status individuals can acquire negative connotations. The English word 'Bushmen' (from the Dutch *Bosjesmans*) has much the same history as 'San' (cf. Guenther 1986a: 31–9). The earliest recorded usage of 'Bosjesmans' is 1682, although in the early decades of contact 'Sonqua' or 'Soaqua' was more common. 'Sonqua' was replaced by 'Bosjesman' in official documents around 1770 (M.L. Wilson 1986a: 256). I am happy to allow context to determine usage, but my own preference is 'Bushman', if only because it is in common use in my own language.

In the 1970s there was a heated debate between historians Anna Boëseken (1972–4; 1975) and Richard Elphick on this issue (1974–5), with Boëseken arguing the sanctity of historical terminology in historical context and Elphick arguing that usage by historians should reflect the current and not the past situation. While in some respects I sympathize with Boëseken's position, in the case of 'Hottentot' and 'Khoekhoe' (or 'Khoi-khoi') I follow Elphick in my preference for the latter. 'Hottentot' is a term of much etymological speculation (e.g., Nienaber 1963a; 1963b); although no one knows for certain, it was probably derived from a Cape Khoekhoe dance chant in use in the late seventeenth century. In the seventeenth and eighteenth centuries, writers frequently applied the term 'Hottentot' indis-criminately to all Khoisan peoples, a practice followed in the nineteenth century by Theophilus Hahn (1881: 2–3). The later application of 'Hotten-tot' specifically to herding peoples was apparently instigated by Lichten-stein (1811, I: 248), and is common in nineteenth- and twentieth-century texts. However, it has in recent decades acquired such offensive conno-tations that it is best to avoid it totally, especially as there exists an indigenous word, 'Khoekhoe', which today is invariably preferred by the people themselves.

'Khoe' and 'San': further complications

The problem is further complicated because the distinction between Khoe and San, or Khoekhoe and Bushman, is by no means clear. For example, the 'typical Bushman' is said to be characterized by

diminutive proportions, slight habit, light yellowish skin, steatopygia, and hair in sparse peppercorn tufts; . . . and by speaking language of an isolating, non-inflectional type, phonetically remarkable for the great prevalence of 'click' consonants; and . . . by living in small nomadic bands which lead a purely hunting and collecting existence, practising neither agriculture nor pastoralism. (Schapera 1939: 69)

But as Schapera points out (1939: 69–72), there is really no such person as a 'typical Bushman'. The usual descriptions of physical characteristics seem to apply mainly to the extinct Bushmen of the Cape Province. Such well-known groups as the !Kung, who live more than 1,500 kilometres north of Cape Town, have a very different appearance. Northern and Southern Bushmen do speak isolating languages, but the Khoe-speaking Bushmen of the central Kalahari, the Okavango delta, eastern Botswana and other areas have inflecting languages, related not to those of 'typical Bushmen', but to those of the Khoekhoe.

Only Schapera's last characterization, that of Bushmen as hunter-gatherers who live in small nomadic bands, is useful for comparative purposes. Yet even if we accept this as a basic definition, there are problems. Many Bushmen who have lived at one time by hunting and gathering have now settled permanently at waterholes, where they cultivate gardens or raise livestock. I retain the word 'Bushman' for members of such groups, although in the strictest sense the word applies to their ancient and not their present lifestyle. However, I would generally not apply the term 'Bushman' to herders who have temporarily lived as hunter-gatherers. Here I am thinking of hapless seventeenth- and eighteenth-century Cape Khoekhoe who lost their cattle, and nineteenth-century Damara who fled their Nama masters and lived as foragers in the rugged hills of northeastern Namibia.

'Bushman' is much more of an odd-job word than 'Khoekhoe'. The Khoekhoe all speak closely related languages, and their culture and social organization are relatively uniform. The Bushmen, on the other hand, speak a variety of languages which are only very distantly related, or even unrelated. They are also more culturally diverse. Furthermore, 'Khoekhoe' is a word which the designants apply to themselves, whereas 'Bushman' has always been a collective term for peoples who generally have no equivalent in their own languages. It is not surprising that the widespread use of 'Bushman', or for that matter 'San' or 'Basarwa', has created problems, especially for historians and archaeologists (Elphick 1979: 4). Yet the concept of 'hunter-gatherers who live in small bands' is a helpful one, and it is best to keep some such term (cf. Parkington 1984a; M.L. Wilson 1986a: 261–4).

One final point is worth mentioning here: the ethnological status of the Damara. Schapera (1930: 3) notes that the inhabitants of southern Africa before 1652 'are customarily classified into four separate groups, known respectively as the Bushmen, the Hottentots, the Bergdama [Damara], and the Bantu'. Again, classification is 'on the basis of racial, linguistic and cultural distinctions' (1930: 3); apparently because of 'racial' differences, the Damara are excluded from the category Khoisan. Here Schapera is following the intent of Schultze's original usage, but I think this is a mistake. Culturally, the Damara are a Khoisan people. In Namibia they have long lived in close association with the Nama. Although some of their customs are borrowed from the Herero, a Bantu-speaking people, they speak the Nama language, and the essential features of their rituals, their mythology, and many aspects of their social organization, are easily identified as Khoisan.

The Khoisan peoples, then, include the Khoekhoe (Hottentots), the Damara, the Khoe-speaking Bushmen, and the non-Khoe-speaking Bushmen of southern Africa.

Ethnic classification

The intricacies of Khoisan ethnic classification will be dealt with in Chapter 2, but some further introductory comments may be useful here.

Khoe-speaking peoples include the Khoekhoe, the Damara, the Bushmen of the central Kalahari and Okavango, the Hai//om and other Bushmen of the Etosha area of northern Namibia, and quite possibly smaller groups in Angola. Similar relationship terminologies – a key defining feature of social structure – are found among all these peoples, and in each case the marriage rule is either to matrilateral or to bilateral cross-cousins. The Khoekhoe nations, who include the Nama, the Korana (!Ora) and others, traditionally hunted, gathered, and herded cattle and sheep. They lived in circular encampments which were made up of patrilineally related kin, in-married wives, and in-married husbands (often performing bride-service). Their tribes, clans, and lineages were hierarchically ranked and each tribe had its own independent, and often powerful, chief. The

Damara were once servants and blacksmiths for the Nama, and they also herded livestock. Yet many Damara in the late nineteenth century lived entirely by hunting and gathering and by stock-theft. Their encampments were like those of the Khoekhoe, but without any vestige of patrilineal organization. Their religion has both Khoisan and Central Bantu elements, as indeed does that of the Hai//om. The Khoe-speaking Bushmen, or Khoe Bushmen, inhabit the vast central region of the Kalahari desert, areas east of the Kalahari, and the Okavango swamps to the north. The desert-dwellers live by hunting and gathering, and the swamp-dwellers by hunting, gathering, and fishing. Although Khoe Bushman social organization is to some extent reminiscent of that of other, non-Khoe-speaking Bushman groups, in many respects the affinities of Khoe Bushman kinship systems are with those of the Khoekhoe. Little is known of the Hai//om, but they seem to be a hybrid group. They were probably !Kung who for some reason forsook their language and other aspects of culture for those of the Nama and Damara. Such Khoekhoe characteristics as patrilineal local organization and exogamous cross-descent name lines have been reported among them.

The non-Khoe-speaking Bushmen include the !Kung of Botswana, Namibia, and Angola, the !Xõ of southwestern Botswana, the Eastern ≠Hoã of southern Botswana, the /Xam of the Cape Province, and remnants of other Cape Bushman groups. All are, or were, hunter-gatherers. The !Kung are well known for their leisurely, loosely structured camp life and band organization, their 'Eskimo-type' relationship terminology, and their alternate-generation naming system by which kin categorization is extended throughout society. The !Xõ are less well known. They live in the harsh south-central Kalahari and are notable for their relative isolation. The little-known 'Eastern ≠Hoã' received their name in order to distinguish them from the !Xõ, who are also sometimes called '≠Hoã; the fact that they speak a different language from the !Xõ was discovered little more than a decade ago. The /Xam, who came to prominence through the folklore studies of W.H.I. Bleek (pronounced 'Blake' or [blek]) and Lucy Lloyd (e.g., Bleek and Lloyd 1911), are now culturally and linguistically extinct. The other Cape Bushman groups are also either extinct or long acculturated to Bantu and Cape Coloured ways.

Ethnographic sources and areas of study
Ethnographers bring with them their own interests, theoretical expertise, and expectations when they go to the field. The Khoisan literature is very rich in detail and varied in content, and areas of interest peculiar to

individual ethnographers have come to be associated with the respective groups those ethnographers have studied. The !Kung ethnography is richest of all, thanks to the multiplicity of fieldworkers who have specialized in the study of this people. Other groups, in contrast, are less well known and achieved more specific associations in the world of anthropological discourse. The /Xam, as I have noted, are known chiefly through folklore studies. Little is known of /Xam kinship, ecology, or political organization.

Alien influences leave their mark in the ethnographic record, and this factor too is reflected in the theoretical interests of ethnographers. The Eastern Khoe Bushmen, greatly influenced by the Tswana among whom they live, have been the subject of studies of acculturation and ethnic relations by Robert Hitchcock (1978a; 1980). Similarly, the Nharo (Naron), who share their lands both with ranchers and with subsistence herders, have been described by Mathias Guenther (1976; 1977; 1979a) within a framework of ethnic pluralism. Such studies have meant that these groups are often perceived as not only economically dependent, but also lacking in traditions and values of their own. With reference to the Nharo, Guenther (1986b) has recently tried to redress the balance by treating 'tradition' as well as 'change', but the unfortunate image of the Nharo as 'acculturated' as opposed to 'pure' Bushmen persists in the minds of anthropologists who should know better.

For the regional comparativist these disparities in theoretical interest, detail of ethnographic coverage, and degree of acculturation create problems. Yet the problems can be overcome. Simply being aware of them is a great help (Barnard 1989a).

Organization of the book
In Chapter 2, I bring to light some of the problems in the study of Khoisan society by looking in more depth at the classification of Khoisan societies and at Khoisan history (taken in its widest sense to include prehistory).

Subsequent chapters, in Part II, deal with selected societies and societal groupings in more detail. I hope that this material can serve as a summary of the findings of all those researchers who have written on Khoisan social organization. Naturally, I have been more selective with the !Kung data, which runs to many volumes, than, say, the Eastern ≠ Hoã data, which is extremely patchy. While I do not pretend to redress the balance entirely, I hope at least to give some idea of the variety of forms of social organization in existence among the Khoisan. Also important in these chapters is the comparison of the approaches and findings of different ethnographers, for example, the discrepancies between G/wi and G//ana ethnographers on aspects of G/wi and G//ana settlement patterns. Though culture may not be a 'thing of shreds and patches' (Lowie 1947 [1920]: ix–x, 441), ethnographic reports are; and part of the purpose of Part II is to sew them together in a culturally meaningful way.

The more theoretical and comparative chapters are contained in Part III. Some of these are based loosely on one or more earlier papers of mine, and others are completely new. The emphasis in all cases is on understanding Khoisan culture as regionally specific and intelligible as a whole. Culture traits are not random or merely functional elements in one culture or another. They are integral parts of a regional social structure, and differences between groups are explicable in terms of environment, subsistence, linguistic origins, diffusion, and other historical influences.

Although I have chosen to organize this book first ethnographically and then thematically, theoretical and comparative problems will emerge throughout. Many such problems stem directly from the theoretical interests of the various ethnographers. For example, the !Xõ data in Chapter 4 present an opportunity to introduce the problem of territoriality there, before a more formal discussion of the same issue in Chapter 12. H.J. Heinz, the leading ethnographer of the !Xõ, has a particular interest in this problem. His descriptions of the !Xõ as being highly territorial call for comment in the light of comparable data on the !Kung, for example, who have been described by some of their ethnographers as having highly flexible territorial arrangements.

Similar arguments apply in my decision to treat general aspects of relationship-terminology semantics in the chapter on the Nharo, the Khoisan people with whose language and culture I am most familiar, and in the section on the Eastern ≠Hoã. The separation of data from theory is difficult at the best of times, and in the case of Eastern ≠Hoã kinship, it is especially problematic. Virtually all that has been written about this people is a highly theoretical account of their relationship-terminology system. As with !Xõ territoriality, it seems appropriate to look at comparative, theoretical questions in the context of the data from which the model is drawn.

Finally, it is worth a further thought to compare my intention here with that of Schapera in his classic, *The Khoisan peoples of South Africa* (1930). Schapera, a student of both Radcliffe-Brown and Malinowski, was working in a comparative perspective entrenched in a functionalist framework. He was also writing at a time when ethnography was not perceived as theory-laden, as it is now. His book was based closely on his library Ph.D. thesis (1929), a document which, except in length, bears closer resemblance to a modern British M.Phil. or M.Litt. than a fieldwork-based Ph.D. His superb Tswana fieldwork was still to come, that being the subject of his subsequent D.Sc. degree and later monographs.

The sources Schapera had available in the 1920s were the early writings on the Khoekhoe and Bushmen (mainly travelogue), the Bleek family material (mainly on language and folklore), a few historical compilations, some German colonial ethnographies of South West African Bushmen and Nama, Winifred Hoernlé's important but relatively meagre output on the Nama, and Dornan's work on the 'Hiechware' of the eastern Bechuanaland Protectorate. His monograph concentrated on themes similar to those of the present one: kinship, the life cycle, social control, subsistence and trade, politics, religion, and magic. Some of the themes of his book, namely physical characteristics, material culture, and art, will be given much less attention here. These have now become such specialized areas that to do justice to them would require more than just one book. More importantly, they are themes which lie outside my own interest in the comparative analysis of social structure, which was indeed Schapera's main concern too. Schapera's vision of the Khoisan peoples in 1930 was one of relatively homogeneous groupings. This is perhaps the greatest difference between his monograph and mine. Whereas he could divide the Khoisan peoples into two fairly neat units – 'the Bushmen' and 'the Hottentots' – we can no longer make such a precise distinction. It need hardly be reiterated that the ethnography now available dwarfs that which Schapera had to hand many times over; this fact alone, I hope, will serve as a justification for looking again at the Khoisan in comparative perspective.

2

Ethnic classification, origins, and history of the Khoisan peoples

Classification of the Khoisan peoples

To a handful of experts the classification of Khoisan peoples is a fascinating topic. To almost anyone else the topic in its own right is unlikely to evoke any immediate reactions but confusion and bewilderment. In this chapter I hope to reduce the confusion, but first a look at some of the problems that bewilder even the experts may be of interest, even to the non-specialist.

Some problems

There are literally hundreds of ethnic group names in the Khoisan literature, and authors use the names in different ways. For example, '!Kung' (from the plural of a !Kung word for 'person', *!xũ*) is often used today in a generic sense to refer to all the speakers of !Kung languages, while nineteenth-century and early twentieth-century writers consistently distinguished the Southern !Kung or ≠Au//eisi as a separate people. They called them the 'Auen', which is ≠*au//eisi* without the clicks and with a Nama or Nharo suffix in place of the !Kung one. Also, some modern writers who speak of '!Kung' culture or society really mean that of the Central !Kung, who call themselves not *!xũ* at all, but *žu/'hoãsi* ('real people').

Some groups are referred to by several names. The group in this book called '!Xõ' are also known as !ku, !kõ, !kũ, Koon, Lala, /ŋu//en, '//ŋaʰmsa, tuu'⊙ŋaʰnsa, !xong, //nǫ, Tshasi, n̩/-u-mde, !gaokx'ate, !oʰju, ⊙wa, ⊙kha, Magong, /ŋamani, /'ŭkate, ≠ãã, ≠gẽ, ⊙ha, ≠huã, etc. (Traill 1974: 9). This is bad enough, but the problem is compounded by the fact that the last name is also applied to the neighbouring (Eastern) ≠huã or ≠Hõ̀ã. 'Eastern ≠Hoã' and 'Western ≠Hoã' are not two branches of the same ethnic or linguistic group, but linguistically distinct groups who happen to use the same word, ≠*hoã*, for 'person'.

Another problem is that each Khoisan specialist has his or her own, often idiosyncratic, spellings for the various group names, and preferences change from publication to publication. Citations would only be invidious here, but there exist three articles published during the 1970s, by three different authors, in which the designations for Khoisan ethnic groups change without explanation between the title and the text!

Over the years, some writers have reverted to artificially constructed generic names and complicated numbering systems to identify the groups and their languages. Needless to say, there is no common agreement, and individual authors have changed their systems as new data have become available (cf. Winter 1981). The word 'Khoisan' itself (like 'Austronesian' or 'Indo-European') is an artificially constructed and, for that matter, grammatically unlikely Nama compound (*khoe*, 'person'; *sā*, 'to forage' or 'forager'; *n*, common gender plural). The form 'Sakhoin' (which contains the same three morphemes but in a different order) would have better fitted the rules of Nama morphology, although what it might mean is open to interpretation (E.O.J. Westphal, pers. comm.).

Yet all these are relatively minor difficulties. The major error of most earlier writers has been their consistent and mutually exclusive distinction between 'Bushmen' and 'Hottentots'. I have already alluded, in Chapter 1, to the difficulty of making polythetic definitions of these two words. The only useful definitions of Khoisan ethnic divisions are those which are designed for a specific purpose or which employ a single or coherent set of criteria. When differentiated, the three usual sets of criteria employed are: biological (genetic), linguistic, and economic.

In June 1971, a symposium was held in Johannesburg on 'The Peoples of Southern Africa'. One aim of this symposium was to draft a uniform set of names for some of the larger ethnic divisions of the subcontinent. The conference organizers summarized the proposals as follows:

Biological entity (race or physical type): San, Khoikhoi, Negro (or South African Negro).

Language: Bushman, Hottentot, Bantu.

Economy (or way of life): Hunters (or hunter-gatherers), Herders (or pastoralists), Cultivators, Peasant-villagers, Townsmen. (Jenkins and Tobias 1977: 51)

The problem is that these writers, like others before them, glossed over the distinctions which they themselves brought to our attention.

To take first the example of the San or Bushmen: when we speak of the little yellow people as a biological or racial entity, we use the term San. When we speak of their language and, more generally, of their cultural aspects, we refer to them as Bushmen; while 'hunters' refers to them as exponents of a particular economy. (1977: 51)

Taken literally, this implies that all three sets of criteria coincide. This, of course, is not what the authors intended, but their careless usage of 'San', 'Bushmen', and 'hunters' only confirms the notion that these terms do identify precisely the same population. What we need are not new labels, but accurate descriptions of what and whom we are talking about.

It is worth while to take each set of classification criteria in turn.

Genetic classification

To a nineteenth-century expert, a 'true Hottentot skull' was 'dolichocephalic, akrocephalic, leptoprosopic, mesomeme, platyrhine, and leptostaphylinic' (Shrubsall 1898: 280), while 'Bush crania' could be described as 'subdolichocephalic, metriocephalic, orthognatic, mesomeme, platyrhine, leptostaphylinic, cryptozygous, and microcephalic' (1898: 273). Such classifications are nowadays regarded as nonsense. Modern studies emphasize fluid and inherently imprecise biological differences, which are defined in terms of genetic distance.

Genetic distance is measured by gene frequency, usually by the relative frequency of those genes whose presence or absence can be determined by simple tests, e.g., for blood factors or for the ability to taste certain chemical substances. Since this frequency differs only in quantity from one population to another, geneticists are generally reluctant to use their findings for classification as such (but see Figures 2.1 and 2.2). Instead, populations are usually placed on a multi-dimensional set of continua, for simplicity often reduced to a single continuum, with genetically similar populations closer together, and genetically dissimilar populations farther apart. However, it is important to remember that genetic proximity, even if it can be attributed to close biological relationships, does not necessarily imply a common biological origin, let alone a common cultural origin. Without corroborative historical or linguistic evidence, there is no way one can tell whether two populations have emerged from a single common ancestral stock or whether they are descended from two separate stocks who have interbred. There are in fact four possible, non-random reasons for similar sets of gene frequencies between any two populations: (1) a shared recent ancestral origin; (2) interbreeding; (3) similar selection pressures on the two populations; and (4) a lack of genetic drift since separation, due, for example, to relatively large population sizes of inbreeding groups (Harpending and Jenkins 1973: 179–80; cf. Spuhler 1973: 428). Only the last of these four possibilities is unlikely for the Khoisan.

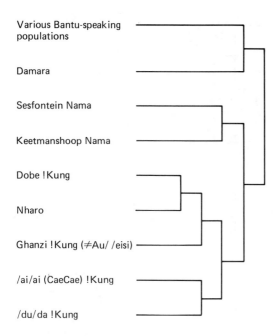

Various Bantu-speaking populations

Damara

Sesfontein Nama

Keetmanshoop Nama

Dobe !Kung

Nharo

Ghanzi !Kung (≠Au/ /eisi)

/ai/ai (CaeCae) !Kung

/du/ da !Kung

Figure 2.1 Relative minimum genetic distance linkages
Source: Based on numerical data and summary chart by Harpending and Jenkins
(1973:185)

Over a quarter of a century ago, Singer and Weiner (1963) demonstrated that both Bushman and Khoekhoe populations share a considerable amount of genetic material with other southern African groups. More recent research has concentrated on specifying the genetic distance between specific Khoisan groups. In general, genetic distance within Khoisan southern Africa shows a greater correlation with geographical proximity than with linguistic relationship or cultural similarity (Jenkins 1972: 463–91; Harpending and Jenkins 1973; Nurse and Jenkins 1977: 99–103; cf. M.L. Wilson 1986b: 19–21). Figures 2.1 and 2.2, which are based on Harpending and Jenkins' (1973: 185) statistical evaluations of various markers of genetic distance for selected populations, illustrate this point. Genetic linkage is, implicitly, a form of classification, in that a hierarchical series of (unnamed) categories is suggested. The formal principles of genetic classification are similar to those of the morphological classification in Linnaean taxonomy, where classes at each level *are* named. Yet geneticists, working more narrowly within the species level, tend to be more cautious with their labelling than are other biologists, since common origin is unprovable by genetic means alone. The very fact that minimum and maximum linkages yield slightly different classifications is a further caveat.

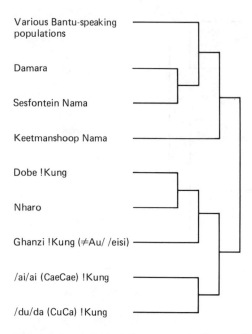

Figure 2.2 Relative maximum genetic distance linkages
Source: Based on numerical data and summary chart by Harpending and Jenkins (1973:185)

The geographical locations of the various groups are shown in Figure 2.3.

Linguistic classification

Language is, for our purposes, more useful. In many ways it is the most precise of the three methods of classification. Linguistic relationships express far less transient sets of attributes than economic pursuits, and they involve more qualitative distinctions than those suggested in studies of genetic distance. This is because, as a rule, it is possible to infer whether the common vocabulary of two given languages is due to a common linguistic origin or due to borrowing.

Rules of grammar are rarely borrowed, but are held in common between related languages. However, like genes, loan words pass from population to population. The source and therefore the direction of their borrowing can often be traced. Cognates, particularly in distantly related languages, will show evidence of sound shifts, whereas loan words will not. In languages such as !Kung and Nharo, spoken by adjacent but linguistically distant peoples, much shared vocabulary can be assumed to be borrowed (cf.

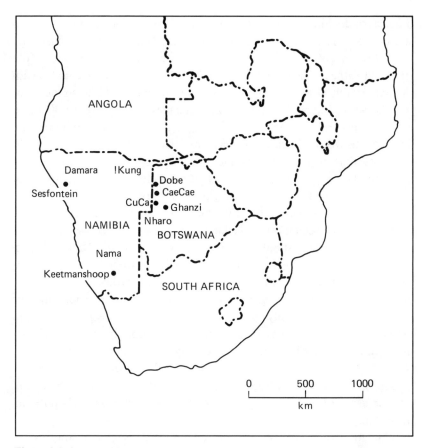

Figure 2.3 Geographical locations of selected populations

Barnard 1985: 28; 1988a: 42–3). The vocabulary which is shared by !Kung
and Nharo but not found in Nama, Korana, or G/wi, for example, can be
assumed to be of likely !Kung origin. If it were of Nharo origin, one would
expect cognates in the other Khoe languages (Nama, Korana, and G/wi), to
which Nharo is more closely related.

  Geneticists work on the assumption that the relative occurrence of
genotypes in any given population will remain constant unless disturbed
(the 'Hardy-Weinberg Law'). Of course, disturbance does occur – through
mutation, natural selection, migration, and chance. The disturbance of the
supposed steady state is what geneticists measure. Glottochronologists also
work on the basis of a constant, but in this case the constant is the rate of
change. Words are presumed to be lost from a standard set of vocabulary
items at a constant rate. Therefore it is possible, in theory, to measure the

time depth dividing any two languages which are derived from a common source, say English and German, or Nharo and Nama. The problem is that this rate may not, in fact, be as constant as traditionally believed. More specifically, the lexical diversity of the Khoe languages, when coupled with the remarkably close correspondences in grammar, could be an indicator that the rate of lexical change for these languages (and perhaps for Khoisan languages generally) is faster than for languages in other parts of the world. The reasons for this need not concern us directly here, though one might speculate that population size and other demographic factors may be involved. The important point is that specific, chronological estimates of linguistic distance need to be taken with a grain of salt.

With these principles in mind, it is possible to construct a model of the relationships between most of the languages spoken by Khoisan peoples – indeed a model which should be agreeable to both 'lumpers' and 'splitters' among Khoisan language specialists. Basically, all specialists would agree that the Khoisan peoples include speakers of numerous click-using languages which belong to some four or five language families, subfamilies or groups. The linguistically 'genetic' relationships between all Khoisan languages have yet to be established beyond question, but most specialists do assume, at least for reasons of practicality, that we can at least speak of a Khoisan phylum or superfamily. Branches of this superfamily are here loosely termed 'families', 'subfamilies', or 'groups', depending on context and the usage of writers cited. For many, such terms are merely notional devices anyway.

While modern specialists in Khoisan languages disagree to some extent in the usage of hierarchical terms of classification, they largely agree on the hierarchy of classification itself. The relationship between the Central Bushman dialects and Khoekhoe (Hottentot) was first recognized by Greenberg (1950), who grouped the two as 'Central Khoisan'; this group or family has subsequently been called by a variety of names, but its existence as a uniform entity separate from (non-Central) 'Bushman' is not disputed by any specialist in the field today. The terms I employ for this and other families are generally those agreed verbally at the sixth and final Bushman and Hottentot Linguistic Seminar, which was held in Pretoria in 1979. Summaries of the history of Khoisan linguistic classification and of the complexities of issues involved have been compiled by Westphal (1971; cf. 1962a; 1962b), Köhler (1975: 305–37; 1981: 457–82) and Winter (1981: 329–46).

Briefly, Khoisan language families or subfamilies include Khoe (also known as Khwe-Kovab or Hottentot), !Kung (Ju), Ta'a (including !Xõ),

Figure 2.4 Geographical locations of major non-Khoe-speaking Bushman groups

!Wi, and tentatively, 'Southwestern' or 'Cape' (/Xam). Eastern ≠ Hoã may well constitute a link between the !Kung and Ta'a groups (see Traill 1973; Westphal 1974). In terms of the traditional classification of Khoisan languages, formulated by Dorothea Bleek in the 1920s (Bleek 1929a; 1956), Khoe includes both 'Hottentot' and 'Central Bushman', !Kung is 'Northern Bushman', and the others represent the 'Southern Bushman' group. The approximate locations of the non-Khoe-speaking Bushman groups mentioned are shown in Figure 2.4, and the locations of the Khoe-speaking peoples are shown in Figure 2.5.

The *!Kung-speakers* include the !Xũ or !O !Kung of Angola, the Zu/'hoãsi of northern Botswana and Namibia, and the ≠Au//eisi of western Botswana. The !Kung are not a Khoe-speaking people, but their history has led them into contact with some of the Khoe groups of the central Kalahari

Figure 2.5 Geographical locations of major Khoe-speaking groups

(Barnard 1988a). In fact, the !Kung and the Khoe Bushmen appear to be genetically (in the literal, biological sense) very close (Nurse and Jenkins 1977: 102), and there are surface structural similarities in their kinship systems and other aspects of culture which cannot be attributed to chance.

The *Ta'a-speakers* are a small cluster of groups who live in the south-central Kalahari. Their land is poor, and their social and territorial organization reflects the strong social solidarity of their individual bands (Heinz 1972; 1979). Although linguistically unrelated or very distant, they are biologically closer to the Khoe-speaking populations of the central Kalahari (Nurse and Jenkins 1977: 102).

The *!Wi-speakers* are a heterogeneous and geographically scattered cluster. They include the /'Auni-≠Khomani Bushmen of the northern Cape Province (e.g., D.F. Bleek 1937a; 1937b), the //Xegwi or Batwa of the eastern Transvaal (Potgieter 1955), and remnants of 'Mountain Bushman' groups in Lesotho and surrounding parts of South Africa. The /Xam are possibly a branch of the !Wi family and possibly a separate family (the 'Southwestern' or 'Cape' family). All these groups are largely extinct as linguistic and cultural entities, although their descendants are today found within other populations.

The *Khoe-speaking peoples* are both the most numerous and the most culturally diverse. They inhabit the central Kalahari desert and Okavango swamps of Botswana, and much of Namibia. Formerly there were also Khoe-speaking groups in parts of South Africa. The Botswana peoples are mainly hunter-gatherers, and the Namibian and South African peoples pastoralists, though there are many exceptions. Thus the word *Khoe* designates the linguistic division which includes both those peoples today commonly called Khoekhoe or 'Hottentots' (the Khoe-speaking herders) and those peoples called Central or Khoe Bushmen. As a linguistic term, it also includes the languages of one or two dark-skinned peoples not commonly classified as Khoisan, viz. the Damara and perhaps the Kwadi of Angola. The Damara speak a Nama dialect, and the Kwadi speak a language which might or might not be genetically related to those of the (other) Khoe-speakers. Its precise status has yet to be determined, though Ehret (1982: 167–71) speculates a close genetic relationship between Kwadi and 'Hietsho' (more commonly known as Hietshware), an eastern Kalahari Khoe Bushman dialect, and further suggests that the Damara may originally have been Kwadi-speakers. No definitive evidence is given for either assertion.

The Khoe-speaking Bushmen are diverse as well as geographically widespread. I refer to them as 'Khoe Bushmen' in order to emphasize the fact that the members of this group are both Khoe-speakers and hunter-gatherers at the same time. Westphal's (e.g., 1962b: 5–6) term 'Tshu-Khwe', which is a compound of two words each meaning 'man', in different dialects, is to be avoided since its homonym in some of the languages has uncomplimentary connotations. In an earlier note (Barnard 1976b: 12) I suggested D.F. Bleek's (1928a: 2, 40) term 'K"am-ka-kwe' (*kx'am-ka-khue*), but since this too is often used in a derogatory way, it is also avoided here. However, I reserve the term 'Khoe Bushmen' specifically for speakers of languages Westphal classifies as 'Tshu-Khwe'. I exclude some Namibian Bushman peoples who speak Khoe languages, notably the Hai//om. The Hai//om are thought to have originated as a result of contact between the Nama and the !Kung of northeastern Namibia (Werner 1906; Fourie 1928: 83). The Khoe Bushmen of Botswana have a separate linguistic origin, a much earlier divergence from the Khoekhoe or Early Khoe. Their linguistic origins will be discussed shortly.

The Khoe languages spoken by Bushmen may be divided into several groups or subgroups. There are three modern classifications: Westphal's (1971: 378–80), based on various grammatical and lexical criteria, Köhler's (1962), based on grammatical criteria alone, and Vossen's (1984; 1988a; 1988b; 1990), based on a combination of lexicostatistics and dialectometrics (itself a combination of phonological, tonological, and semantic criteria). The difference between these classifications is not in the placement of particular languages in one group or another, but rather, in whether the languages of the Khoe-speaking Bushmen of Botswana should be considered as constituting a single group with several subgroups, or as constituting several groups. Westphal classifies them as one group ('Tshu-Khwe'; i.e., Central Bushman or Khoe Bushman), and Köhler as members of four separate but related groups (Naró, //Kanákhoe, Kxoé, and Shuákhoe). In spite of their differences in methodology, Vossen's work confirms Köhler's basic classification, but with some slight modifications. He terms his 'subgroups' and distinguishes Naro, //Ana (G//ana), Kxoe, Shua, and Tshwa, with (in his most recent work) a recognition of an especially close relationship between Naro and //Ana which might merit their consideration as a single subgroup.

On the basis of geographical, cultural, and linguistic criteria (in the case of linguistic criteria, the work of these three linguists), I classify the Khoe-speaking Bushmen, or Khoe Bushmen, as members of four divisions. The *Western Khoe Bushmen* include the Nharo, Ts'aokhoe, Qabekhoe, and N/haints'e (together, Köhler's and Vossen's Naro group or subgroup). All of these are the western Botswana peoples who have been in contact with the !Kung. In terms of social structure as well as geographical location I also include the ≠Haba as a culturally 'Western' group, although their linguistic affinities are much more 'Northern' or 'Central'. In Vossen's more recent study (see 1988b: 64) they appear to be linguistically marginal to the major divisions.

The *Central Khoe Bushmen* include the G/wi and G//ana of the Central Kalahari Game Reserve (Köhler's //Kanákhoe group, Vossen's //Ana subgroup). As Vossen's findings make clear, the Central Khoe Bushmen are closely related to the Western Khoe Bushmen, and communication is possible across the dialect boundary. The *Northern Khoe Bushmen* of the Okavango (commonly known as the 'River Bushmen', Köhler's and Vossen's Kxoe group or subgroup) are another ethnic division. Included in this division are the Kxoe, studied by Köhler himself, and other hunter-gatherer-fishers and part-time cultivators of the area.

Finally, the *Eastern Khoe Bushmen* include all the Khoe-speaking peoples of eastern Botswana (Köhler's Shuákhoe group, Vossen's Shua and Tshwa subgroups). Linguistically, the Shua and Tshwa are more distant from the Western, Central, and Northern Groups than any of these is from the others (Vossen 1990: 361–72). They have also been much influenced by Tswana culture. Conventionally, they include the Hietshware, different groups who call themselves *kua*, and the Deti (who, like the ≠Haba are somewhat difficult to pin down to a precise linguistic division). Other groups, including some who speak dialects closely related to those of the Central Khoe Bushmen, also live today in eastern and southern Botswana. In particular, large numbers of G//ana are found in eastern Botswana among Tswana and speakers of Eastern Khoe Bushman dialects. Although linguistically 'Central', in some cases these latter individuals or groups are culturally 'Eastern' and, where appropriate, will be described along with the eastern Botswana peoples.

Economic classification
On the basis of subsistence ideology, all Khoisan peoples may be classified loosely as either 'hunters' or 'herders' (Monica Wilson 1969). The 'hunters' include those whose economy, before contact with Bantu-speakers, Khoekhoe and whites, was based exclusively on hunting and gathering, or in the case of the 'River Bushmen' of the Okavango, on hunting, gathering, and fishing. The 'herders' include those peoples whose economy was based on cattle and sheep herding, as well as on hunting, gathering, and fishing. In historical times, some 'herders' have taken to a purely hunting and gathering lifestyle, for example, if their animals were lost through drought or theft; and archaeologists have recently reported significant evidence of long periods of 'hunter'/'herder' contact (e.g., S.L. Hall 1986; Smith 1986).

The word 'Bushman' is used in this book as a synonym for Monica Wilson's term 'hunters'. The ethnic division classified economically as 'herders' is here termed 'Khoekhoe' (rather than 'Hottentots'). The Khoekhoe include the Nama, the Korana, and the Cape Khoekhoe, both eastern and western. The Cape Khoekhoe apparently vacillated between herding and hunting lifestyles, depending on whether individual families or clans had access to livestock, and are largely indistinguishable archaeologically from hunter-gatherers of this area. The Korana, despite one historian's doubts of their historical existence as a single ethnic group (Ross 1975), survived as a linguistic and cultural entity into the twentieth century (Engelbrecht 1936). Their descendants are today classified by the South African authorities as 'Coloured', irrespective of their individual ancestry, and the Khoekhoe aspects of their culture have largely been lost. The Nama are the only group who remain as a cultural unit. They live mainly in Namibia, still by herding, and preserve their own, grammatically complex and richly expressive language. Nama has been a 'written' language for well over a century and today boasts a recently modernized orthography and a large number of literate speakers.

The Damara (also known as Berg Dama or ≠Nu Khoe) are usually distinguished as a separate group, neither Bushman nor Khoekhoe and therefore not Khoisan. They are typically more heavily built and darker-skinned than most Khoisan peoples and are generally believed to have a separate racial origin. Yet, as I have pointed out, 'race' is not a sufficient reason to exclude a people from a *culture* area. At one time, perhaps for centuries, the Damara worked as servants and blacksmiths for the Nama. Their language – and a good part of their culture – is virtually identical to that of the Nama. In fact, that language is known officially in Namibia as 'Damara/Nama' or 'Nama/Damara', in the recognition that it is spoken by both groups, and perhaps reflecting the fact that the Damara are now more numerous than the Nama themselves. Like other anthropologists and linguists, however, I myself prefer 'Nama' as the name of the language, just as I prefer the term 'English' for the majority language of my native United States and 'Portuguese' for that of Brazil. This usage alludes to linguistic history, and not to inter-ethnic or national politics.

For all these reasons I consider the Damara part of the Khoisan culture area neither Khoekhoe nor Bushman, but Khoisan nevertheless.

Origins and history of the Khoisan peoples
Origins of the non-Khoe-speaking Bushmen
The precise origins of the Khoisan peoples are obscure. Physical anthropologists have long argued that the Bushman (or Boskoid) 'race' once spread over all southern and eastern Africa as far north as Egypt (Tobias 1964; Jenkins 1972: 25–6), and at least one scholar has hypothesized a possible relationship between present Bushman populations and South African fossil remains some 40,000 years old (Tobias 1956a). For our purposes, the present-day Bushmen (and in particular, the non-Khoe-speaking Bushmen) can be regarded as the aboriginal inhabitants of southern Africa. Although comparisons of stone artefacts have led some archaeologists to suggest the possibility of migrations from East Africa southwards at the beginning of the Late Stone Age, perhaps 10,000 or 12,000 years ago (see e.g., Clark 1959: 166–8, 183–4), the prevailing opinion among archaeologists today is that such large-scale migrations are unlikely. As Inskeep pointed out in his classic review of South African prehistory (Inskeep 1969: 20), the diffusion of tool-making techniques is much more probable.

Beyond this, very little can be said about the origins of the non-Khoe-speaking Khoisan peoples. Late Stone Age archaeological sites are generally not distinguishable as belonging to specific modern groups. Yet through the evidence of linguistic diversity, we can assume that present groups are not descended from a recent ancestral linguistic stock. It is likely that most non-Khoe-speaking Kalahari groups have occupied their present locations for thousands of years (see Denbow 1984). There is growing evidence of displacements of hunter-gatherers by herders in the Cape from around 2,000 years ago (see, e.g., S.L. Hall 1986; Smith 1986; 1987), but there is no evidence for the migration of any such groups from south to north.

Origins of the Khoe-speaking peoples
Archaeologically, little is known about the prehistory of the Khoekhoe either. Few definite early Khoekhoe sites have been identified, and although the topic is of great interest to the archaeological fraternity, no archaeologist has yet pursued in depth the problem of Khoekhoe origins. What archaeological and physical anthropological evidence there is suggests that the ancestors of the pastoralist Khoekhoe must have been a southern African Late Stone Age people whose culture was influenced by that of the Early Iron Age farmers and metalworkers (Inskeep 1969: 24). Little has happened in the last two decades of archaeological research to alter this view substantially. Indeed, although sites containing domestic fauna are common in the Western Cape, archaeologists are still reluctant to claim them as 'pastoralist settlements' (M. Hall 1987: 3).

In contrast, early writers on Khoekhoe prehistory confidently assumed that the Khoekhoe had migrated from eastern or central Africa. Most prominent among these writers were George William Stow, who completed his work in 1880, George McCall Theal, writing at around the turn of the century, and Heinrich Vedder, writing in the 1920s and 1930s. In support of this theory, Stow (1905: 267–8 and map) relied mainly on Korana legends, on his wide general knowledge of southern African peoples, and on what now seems to have been unjustified speculation. Theal (1902: 20; 1907: 28, 36–7) and Vedder (1938 [1934]: 119–24) supported their versions of the theory by taking into account W.H.I. Bleek's belief in the supposed relationship between some North African languages and the Khoe languages known to scholars of his day. This theory, the subject of Bleek's Ph.D. thesis (1851; cf. 1869; 1872), was widely known at the time. Some textbooks still hold to the Bleek theory, in spite of the inadequacy of the evidence to support it. Through the years a number of modified versions have been put forward. For example, Schapera's (1930: 43) version suggests that the Khoekhoe may have emerged from a mixed population of East African Bushmen and 'Hamites'.

There can be little doubt that the domesticated animals owned by the Khoekhoe came from the Near East, but any migration of the Khoekhoe themselves from north of the Zambesi is now regarded as very unlikely (see M.L. Wilson 1989). A more plausible theory of migration and diffusion, one essentially consistent with Inskeep's hypothesis, can be pieced together from the work of more recent writers.

Raymond Mauny (1967: 583–9) presented archaeological evidence to suggest the diffusion of pastoralism from the Near East through Egypt and the Sudan, and subsequent migrations of pastoralists southwards along the East African highlands. According to his evidence, these migrations began about 2500 B.C. Presumably the ancestors of the Khoe peoples acquired at least some of their animals from these people or from later East African migrants sometime before the Bantu migrations (cf. Tobias 1955: 12; Epstein 1971, I: 77–8, 492–8; 1971, II: 157). Khoekhoe sheep are biologically similar to Egyptian sheep (Zeuner 1963: 180), and Khoekhoe and Southern Bantu cattle and cattle-customs resemble those of North Africa, not those of most Bantu-speaking peoples (see, e.g., Jeffreys 1968: 16–18). Indeed, some Southern Bantu cattle customs, such as the Xhosa terminology of cattle markings, are thought to have originated among the Khoekhoe (Maingard 1934: 128–9, 138); and the common Southwestern Bantu and Khoe words for 'cow' and 'sheep' (though not that for 'goat') are of Khoe rather than Common Bantu origin (Westphal 1963: 253–6; cf. Ehret 1967). It is likely that pastoral Khoekhoe society began with the acquisition of various aspects of culture, including livestock and material culture, by southern African Bushmen, from a people of northern origin.

The similarity in vocabulary between Khoe Bushman and Khoekhoe languages has been known to scholars for over a century. It was first recognized by the mythologist, linguist, librarian, trader, and politician, Theophilus Hahn (1881: 7–11), although he thought, perhaps incorrectly, that all languages spoken by Bushmen must be related to Khoekhoe. Writers continued to assume a genetic relationship between Khoe and 'Bush' languages until the 1960s, when Westphal's (e.g., 1963: 237) emphatic denials that such a relationship had been proved became quite widely accepted. Even Greenberg (1950), who had been the first to classify the languages of central Kalahari Bushmen as Khoe ('Central Khoisan') rather than Bushman, accepted the notion of a single 'click' language family. The matter of a common origin for all Khoisan languages has been much debated in recent decades, with Westphal arguing against the common origin theory and Traill arguing for it (see Honken 1977). As I have suggested above, it makes little difference whether the various non-Khoe languages really do constitute several language families, or constitute a single language family consisting of several language groups. The important point here is that the Khoe languages are distinct from the rest, and are spoken by both hunter-gatherers and herders.

Westphal's (1971: 378–82) classification of non-Bantu click-using languages of southern and eastern Africa comprises up to eight language families, including three tentative ones. Of these eight, at least one, the Khoe family, had one parent language which was almost certainly clickless. Contact between this parent language of unknown origin and another extinct language, which was click-using, gave rise to Proto-Khoe (Westphal, pers. comm.; cf. Westphal 1963: 234, 259, 264; 1980: 68–72). The click-using 'Bush' (non-Khoe) substratum is responsible for most of the common click-containing vocabulary of the modern Khoe languages, while most of the common clickless vocabulary and the grammar (pronouns, number-gender suffixes, etc. are generally clickless) are from the other language. I term this other language 'Clickless Proto-Khoe' in order to distinguish it from Proto-Khoe proper, which originated as a result of the contact between Clickless Proto-Khoe and the substratum language. According to Westphal, the Khoe languages, and especially the Khoe Bushman ones, still contain more clickless vocabulary than any of the non-Khoe ones.

Greenberg (1955 [1950]: 82–3; 1963: 67), however, takes a different view. In his argument against 'the "Hamitic" theory in its pure form', i.e., that the Khoekhoe themselves are not migrants from East Africa, he suggests that clicks are at least as frequent in Khoe words as in Bush words. His figures for the ratio of clicks to words in connected discourse are: Hietshware 16 per cent, !Kung 18 per cent, Nama 26 per cent, /Xam 30 per cent, and Korana 44 per cent. In my view, these figures are slightly misleading, because Bush languages (represented here by !Kung and /Xam) tend to be relatively isolating and Khoe languages (represented by the other examples) tend to be relatively synthetic and agglutinating. In other words, the latter have more morphemes per 'word', and the ratio of clicks to morphemes would certainly not show such a great difference between the languages. Also, in central and eastern Kalahari Khoe languages there is a tendency to drop clicks. Many G//ana, for example, pronounce the name of their ethnic group simply as *gana*. Traill (1980) has called attention to this feature, particularly in reference to the Northern and Southern Kua dialects, which are closely related to Hietshware. Northern Kua is losing two click series (phonemes with $\neq$ or !, plus click releases) and Southern Kua is losing one series (phonemes with !, plus click releases). For example, the word for 'to stay' is $n \neq u$ in several Khoe Bushman dialects, but *niu* in Northern Kua. The word for 'giraffe' is *n!abe* in most dialects, but *gabe* in Northern and Southern Kua and *nabe* in G//ana (see Vossen 1984; Traill 1980; 1986).

The divergence of the Khoe-speaking peoples

Until fairly recently, what all theories seem to have taken for granted is distinct 'hunter' and 'herder' populations, the latter possessing both sheep and cattle. Current thinking on this is more sceptical. For example, a west coast route for the introduction of sheep by the Khoekhoe some 2,000 years ago, and a later east coast route for the introduction of cattle by Iron Age (presumably Bantu-speaking) people is one intriguing possibility. This gets around the notion of a migration of people, suggesting instead the diffusion of goods (Parkington 1984b). Furthermore, if we accept the probability of intensive hunter–herder interaction throughout the last 2,000 years (see, e.g., Wilmsen 1989a), we might imagine that it would be difficult to distinguish Khoekhoe from neighbouring Khoe-speaking groups until well after the divergence of the languages (cf. Marks 1972; Parkington 1984a). Nevertheless, the groups we know today have originated somehow; and at least some migrations, though perhaps not in large groups (as was previously assumed), must have occurred. With this in mind, let us return to the vexed problem of later migrations of the Khoe-speaking peoples.

While granting that the 'Hamitic theory' is not the answer, most authorities regard it as likely that the Khoe-speaking peoples are the product of a common origin and subsequent dispersal from somewhere north of their present locations. There are in fact several theories of Khoe migration from a point of origin or dispersal in central Africa. Stow (1905: 249 and map) and Cooke (1965), among others (cf. Willcox 1966; Jeffreys 1968: 23–4), suggested a route westwards from around Lake Malawi, north of or through the Okavango to present-day Namibia and then to the Cape. The most prominent of Stow's contemporaries to oppose this view was J.M. Orpen (1964 [1908]: 20–5). This Irish-born writer and politician had been a legislator in the Volksraad of the Orange Free State Republic, the Cape Parliament, and the Legislative Council of Rhodesia, as well as the administrator of Basutoland. Quite naturally, he favoured a migration through some of his constituencies, and this is what he suggested – with groups turning inland from an east coast route. D.F. Bleek (1928a: 66; 1929a: 11) tentatively considered the possibility of a more southerly route than that which Stow had suggested, westwards through the central Kalahari, into Namibia. Westphal (1963: 263; 1980: 71), in contrast, has suggested a Khoe Bushman divergence westwards into the Kalahari and a southern route (through Botswana) for the Khoekhoe migrations.

Bleek, Cooke, and Westphal alike tried to account for the existence of Khoe- or 'Hottentot'-related languages among Botswana Bushmen, but in fact only Westphal's theory accounts for the precise linguistic relationships of the different Khoe-speaking peoples. Cooke's theory, based mainly on the distribution of rock paintings, was (in the absence of applicable genetic data) accepted as probable by Jenkins in his thesis on genetic linkages (Jenkins 1972: 468–73). There no doubt could have been some pastoralist migration along this northerly route, but it is unlikely that this was the main route. Given the sequence of Khoe divergence that both Bleek and Cooke propose – Khoe Bushman, Nama, and Cape (including Korana) branching off from the mainstream in that order – Nama should stand linguistically between Khoe Bushman and Korana. In fact, the Korana language has long been known to be intermediate between Khoe Bushman and Nama in every respect (see Maingard 1932: 152–3; 1957: 69–71; 1963; Westphal 1963: 251). The relationship between Khoe Bushman, Korana, and Nama is more than sufficient evidence for the probability of a Khoekhoe migration through South Africa itself, either along the coast or inland, to the Cape. The alternative is to suppose that Korana diverged from the ancestral language of the Khoe Bushmen later than Nama. Yet even this would not account for the common vocabulary of Nama and Korana (i.e., that not shared with Khoe Bushman), let alone the common Khoekhoe pastoralist culture of the Nama and Korana peoples.

Elphick (1977: 3–22; 1985: 3–22) has outlined some of the arguments for each of these theories and, citing historical comparisons of more recent migrations, has also come to the conclusion that Westphal's theory makes the most sense. However, his interpretation of the Khoe dispersal hypothesis does differ slightly from Westphal's. Westphal holds that the Khoe Bushmen diverged from the ancestors of the Khoekhoe, and moved to their present location from Zimbabwe or eastern Botswana. Elphick assumes that the Khoe Bushmen occupied at least some of their present locations in Botswana first, and that the Khoekhoe migrated south with their livestock from these areas. Elphick's schematic map (1977: 16; 1985: 16) illustrates their migration from the Okavango region, apparently through the central Kalahari. However, in view of the harsh environment of the central Kalahari, the southward migration almost certainly would have taken place to the east, more or less as Westphal suggests. This was in fact

Elphick's original intention (Elphick, pers. comm.), as his text, if not his map, makes fairly clear (1977: 17–18; cf. Ehret 1982: 169).

Following Westphal and Elphick, we may assume the likelihood that at least some of the ancestors of the Khoe Bushmen migrated from or through what is now Zimbabwe or eastern Botswana and settled in what is now western Botswana. According to glottochronological estimates by Köhler (1966a: 147) and Ehret (1982: 165) this divergence took place about 2,000 years ago, though, as I noted above, such estimates should be treated warily. The immediate ancestors of the Khoe Bushmen may have been speakers of the 'Bush' substratum language, and perhaps the clients of the Clickless Proto-Khoe-speaking herders; or they may have been a tribe of herders themselves. There is no way of knowing. Yet it is interesting to note that the Khoe Bushman word for 'cow' (*gue*, as opposed to Nama *goma*) has undergone one of the sound shifts which distinguish Khoe Bushman from Khoekhoe. This indicates that the word has not been reborrowed from Nama in recent times but has been in continuous use, at least among one Khoe Bushman group, since the Khoe Bushman dispersal (Westphal, pers. comm.). This in turn suggests that cattle may have been known in southern Africa before the Khoe Bushmen diverged from the Khoekhoe, and perhaps adds support to the view that the Clickless Proto-Khoe-speakers were a herding people.

After the Khoe Bushman divergence, the ancestors of the Khoekhoe moved slowly southwards and acquired further click-containing vocabulary from one or more 'Bush'-speaking peoples (see Westphal 1963: 259; Köhler 1966a). From a subsequent area of dispersal – Westphal (1963: 251) suggests 'the general area between and south of Prieska and Upington' – the Nama moved northwards and acquired more click-containing lexical stock from an additional 'Bush' substratum. Just where the Damara fit in is not at all clear. No one knows what language they spoke before they came into contact with the Nama. It is commonly assumed that the distinctive 'Bush' substratum of Nama is from the language of a now-extinct, physically 'Bushman' people, but it seems to me not implausible that the speakers of this substratum language were the ancestors of the modern Damara. Ehret (1982: 168, 170) suggests alternatively that the Damara were Kwadi-speakers, and this too is a possibility. Admittedly Occam's razor is only one step removed from pure speculation, but to suggest any other theory of Damara origins than these is to postulate both a language without a known population and another population without a known language (see also Chapter 11).

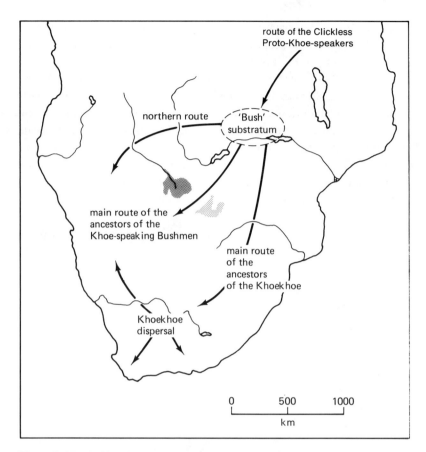

Figure 2.6 Probable migration routes of the Khoe-speaking peoples

After the Nama divergence, the ancestors of the other Khoekhoe nations either dispersed or moved southwards again. Stow's belief (1905: 267–315) that as a unified people the Korana migrated from near Cape Town to the interior after Dutch settlement was never fully accepted by the Korana specialist, L.F. Maingard (see Maingard 1931: 487–8; 1932: 106–14). Maingard's proposal that the Korana may have trickled into the Upper Orange River region in small, independent groups seems to be borne out by more recent archival research by Ross (1975), while Elphick (1985: 19–20) has added his support to the view that the Korana occupied their historic location near the Orange before Khoekhoe migration to the Cape. There is an interesting indigenous explanation, cited by Elphick among others, which might shed some light on the problem. According to a very old

Korana gentleman interviewed by Wuras (1929: 290) in the mid-nineteenth century, Korana legends told that all the Khoekhoe once lived at a place called 'Chei am *aub' (apparently *xai-am kx'au-p*, perhaps meaning something like 'virile man'), between the Vaal and Orange Rivers. After a quarrel, said the old man, the Khoekhoe divided. One group (presumably the Nama) moved down the Orange, one group (the Cape Khoekhoe) went south, and 'the greatest and richest tribe', the Korana, remained at Chei am *aub. Naturally, such an account would have to be treated with some scepticism were it not for the fact that it coincides so neatly with the linguistic evidence. My view is that migrations took place in both directions. The origin of the Korana, still a mystery, will be taken up in Chapter 9.

The linguistic prehistory of the Khoe-speaking peoples and their probable migration routes are illustrated in Figure 2.6.

Part II

A survey of Khoisan ethnography

3

The !Kung

Introduction

The !Kung consist of three main ethno-linguistic groups: the Central !Kung of Botswana and Namibia, the Northern !Kung of Angola, and the ≠Au//eisi, or Southern !Kung. In her comparative dictionaries of Bushman languages, Dorothea Bleek (1929a; 1956) designated these groups NII, NIII, and NI respectively (the initial *N* identifying these as 'northern' Bushman languages). Several anthropologists and linguists now use the indigenous designation *Zu/'hoãsi* ('real people', also spelled *Ju/wasi*), or the short forms *Zu* or *Zhu* ('person'), or *Zu/'hoã* ('real person', singular), to designate the Central !Kung. The !Kung proper, in a sense, are actually the Northern !Kung, the only group who use the term !Kung (*!xũ*, another word for 'person') as an ethnic self-appellation. The ≠Au//eisi are distinguished from the '!Khũ' or 'Kung' in early ethnographic accounts, but there is no question that their relationship to the others is close enough to consider them a branch of the same 'people'. Following current practice among ethnographers who have worked with them, I retain the indigenous plural suffix -*si* in 'Zu/'hoãsi' and '≠Au//eisi' when using these terms as plural nouns.

Traditionally, these three labels identify indigenously defined dialect areas, but they also correspond roughly to cultural units and environmental zones (see Figure 3.1). It is difficult to estimate the !Kung population. In total, they may number as many as 25,000 or even 30,000, although most estimates given in anthropological accounts as well as official censuses are much lower (cf. Marshall and Ritchie 1984: 14–28; Gordon 1986a). The largest group is certainly the Central !Kung, though the Northern !Kung are scattered across a larger land area.

The !Kung are the best known of all Khoisan peoples. They are also

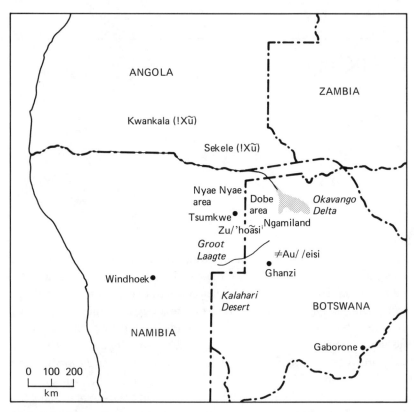

Figure 3.1 !Kung dialect areas

among the most studied, and best studied, of any ethnic group in the world. Ironically, this concentration of interest in one Khoisan people has hidden the wider ethnographic context of !Kung society as but one among many Khoisan societies. Equally, the fact that virtually all modern research among the !Kung has been carried out in only two adjacent and similar areas has contributed to a misguided view that these areas are the only ones in which !Kung live. When anthropologists speak of 'the !Kung', they almost invariably mean the Central !Kung.

Due to the theoretical interests of many who have worked with the !Kung, readers of !Kung ethnography are too often left with the mistaken impression that these people lived until recently in splendid isolation both from other Bushman groups and from non-Bushmen. It is as if culture contact there were unknown or likely to lead only to contamination of the 'purity' of the foraging lifestyle. In reality, !Kung in all areas have long lived in contact with other Bushman groups, as well as Ambo (Ovambo), Herero,

Tswana, and other Bantu-speaking peoples. They have shared their land and traded with these groups for centuries (Gordon 1984; Wilmsen 1986; 1989a; Barnard 1988a).

Ethnographic studies of the !Kung

Early ethnographers include Lebzelter (1928; 1928–9) and D.F. Bleek (1928b) in the north, and Passarge (1907) and Kaufmann (1910) among the ≠Au//eisi. Yet their work (summarized in Schapera 1930) has long since been overtaken by superb studies by the Marshall family, Richard Lee, and many others.

In 1950, Laurence Marshall retired from a career in engineering and business which had included such successes as the development of radar and the early 'radar cooker' (microwave oven). He took his son John to the Kalahari in that year and returned for a second trip in 1951 with his wife Lorna and daughter Elizabeth. Between 1950 and 1961 members of the family made eight expeditions to the Kalahari. Laurence confined his own published ethnographic observations to photography. John became a film maker and has since documented in that medium both traditional practices and the rapidly changing way of life of the Zu/'hoãsi. Elizabeth wrote a bestselling book on the family's travels and the peoples (G/wi and Zu/'hoãsi) they encountered (Thomas 1959), while Lorna, a graduate in English literature, wrote up the more systematic ethnography. She concentrated her studies in what she came to call the Nyae Nyae area of western Namibia (!Kung *n//hwã!ai*, Herero *Onyainyai*). The results were published in the journal *Africa* (Marshall 1957a; 1957b; 1959; 1960; 1961; 1962; 1969). These papers, apart from those on religion, were later included in her book *The !Kung of Nyae Nyae* (1976), and a further book on belief and ritual is planned.

In 1963–4, Richard Lee conducted his doctoral research with the Zu/'hoãsi of the Dobe area of Botswana, immediately across the border from Nyae Nyae. He too has returned many times for further fieldwork. Many of his students too worked at Dobe (see Lee 1979a), and we now have detailed data on that area for a period of over twenty-five years.

Lee's early inspiration was the cultural ecology of Julian Steward (especially Steward 1955). His exemplary dissertation on !Kung ecology (Lee 1965) was richly quantitative and provided significant input in the development of Marshall Sahlins' concept of 'the original affluent society' (Sahlins 1974 [1968]: 1–39). Since then, Lee has adopted an explicitly Marxist stance and acquired interests in such issues as class relations and state formation. Nevertheless, most of his !Kung work remains in the

Stewardian tradition. His publications include a multiplicity of articles and two important books, *The !Kung San* (1979b), which includes the bulk of his ecological findings, and *The Dobe !Kung* (1984).

Students of Richard Lee and Irven DeVore (DeVore accompanied Lee on two of his early field trips) include several who have made great contributions to Khoisan ethnography. Lee and DeVore have edited a collection which contains important papers by a number of them (Lee and DeVore 1976), but much of the more specialized work has been published elsewhere. Among the latter are Biesele on symbolism, and communication (e.g., 1978), Draper on gender and socialization (1975a; 1975b; 1978; cf. 1972), Howell on demography (1979), Katz on the medicine dance (1982), Shostak with the biography of a !Kung woman (1983 [1981]), and Yellen on ethnoarchaeology (1977). A more recent collection, dedicated to Lorna Marshall, has been published in the 'Quellen zur Khoisan-Forschung' series (Biesele 1986).

Since the start of the fieldwork by Lee and his students, others have come upon the scene. Two who deserve special mention are Polly Wiessner (1977; 1982) and Edwin Wilmsen (1986; 1989a). Both had a background in archaeology, and both began their research with the !Kung at CaeCae (also spelled /Ai/ai, /Xai/xai, Xaixai, or Kai Kai), near Dobe, in 1973. Wiessner concentrated initially on material culture and later on reciprocity. Since 1973, Wilmsen has probably spent more time in northwestern Botswana than any foreign fieldworker. He favours an approach which takes greater notice of the centuries of contact the !Kung have had with Bantu-speaking peoples, and one which more vociferously counteracts the popular image of the !Kung as pristine, 'stone-age' hunter-gatherers. Recently, Robert Gordon, a Namibian-American anthropologist, has contributed to the debate on Bushman history through extensive archival research on !Kung and Hai//om relations with outsiders (e.g., Gordon 1984; 1985; 1986b; 1989). The debate between these so-called 'revisionists' (e.g., Wilmsen and Denbow 1990) and those who, in contrast, might be labelled 'traditionalists' (e.g., Solway and Lee 1990), has implications well beyond Khoisan studies and should keep anthropologists arguing for many years to come.

There is a separate Portuguese tradition of scholarship on the !Xũ of Angola. This includes various works in Portuguese and French by the Alsace-born missionary Carlos Estermann (summarized in Estermann 1976 [1956]: 1–19), by anthropologists António de Almeida and Maria Emília de Castro e Almeida (summarized in Almeida 1965), and by ethnologists Carlos A.M. de Oliveira Santos (Oliveira Santos 1958) and Manuel Viegas Guerreiro (Viegas Guerreiro 1968), among others. This tradition will be touched on only briefly here, as its emphasis has been on physical anthropology and material culture rather than on social organization. Nevertheless, Viegas Guerreiro's account is especially interesting for its comparative treatment of !Xũ ethnography (including both his own work among the Kwankala and that of Oliveira Santos among the Sekele) in the light of earlier studies of other Bushman groups.

Subsistence resources and settlement patterns
Zu/'hoã subsistence and settlement
The specifics of Zu/'hoã subsistence strategy have been documented in a vast series of publications, especially by Richard Lee (see especially Lee 1968a; 1969a; 1973; 1979b). Nearly all !Kung areas are blessed with relatively large supplies of water and plant resources, and the eastern Zu/'hoã region, where Lee has worked, is probably the best of these. The people of this area have the advantage of over a hundred species of edible plants, providing a varied and nutritious diet throughout most of the year. Chief among these is the mongongo or mangetti (botanical name, *Ricinodendron rautanenii* Schinz; !Kung name, //"xa [Lee's orthography]). Mongongo trees grow several metres tall, and from their branches produce a highly nutritious nut. Lee (1979b: 184, 191–2) mapped thirty-five large mongongo groves, some extending for 15 kilometres, over sand dunes and along ancient dry riverbeds. They do not grow at all in the calcrete soils around Ghanzi (≠Au//ei country) or in areas where flooding occurs, and are found in few parts of the Kalahari outside the !Kung areas. Mongongos ripen around April, in the early part of the dry season, but can be gathered virtually the whole year round (Lee 1979b: 188–90). Collecting is done by both men and women, and bands frequently camp in the groves in order to exploit their maximum potential. Other major food items include two additional nutritious 'nuts' – the morama (technically a bean, *Bauhinia esculenta*) and the marula (*Scherocarya caffra*). All these are eaten roasted, cooked directly in the fire.

There are permanent waterholes in Zu/'hoã country, and during the winter dry season each band camps at one of these (see, e.g., Marshall 1960; 1976: 156–200; Lee 1976 [1972]; Yellen 1976). Bands number on average some 25 people or more. Often several bands, as well as small groups of Herero and Tswana pastoralists, will share the same permanent waterhole. CaeCae, for example, has a Zu/'hoã population of about 220 and a Herero and Tswana population of about 40 (E.N. Wilmsen, pers. comm.). Some Zu/'hoãsi do remain at their permanent waterholes all year round, but most bands move away during the summer wet season in order to exploit seasonally available water and plant resources within overlapping band territories (termed *n!ore* [sing.], *n!oresi* [pl.]). At this time of year, Zu/'hoãsi get their water from pans and tree trunks, where it collects as a result of rainfall. Areas of plentiful plant resources can be utilized by more than one band, while areas of poor resources are not exploited at all. There is also considerable movement of individuals from camp to camp at all times of year, and this movement is intensified during the wet-season period of dispersal.

Among the Zu/'hoãsi, there are two main levels of social organization: the band and the nuclear or extended family (see, e.g., Marshall 1976: 156–200). Families, though, are not territorial units; they do not exploit separate, owned domains. Although band membership is flexible, bands generally include closely related people, each related by blood or marriage to a core group of brothers and sisters.

Recently there have been some changes in anthropological thinking about the Zu/'hoãsi, partly in response to political pressures and partly as a consequence of new field data. Anthropological descriptions of the Zu/'hoãsi as 'nomadic', with 'flexible band membership' and 'a lack of territoriality', have been used, in both Botswana and Namibia (when under South African control), to justify claims that Zu/'hoãsi have no traditional notion of land tenure. Yet fieldwork in the past decade has suggested a more territorial model of the traditional settlement pattern which is consistent with Zu/'hoã attempts to remain longer at their dry-season camps. Wilmsen's (1982: 102) historical re-evaluation of Zu/'hoã social structure suggests a continuity of residence, by core band members and their descendants, of well over a hundred years (see also Wilmsen 1986; 1989a: 158–94; 1989b). This model is supported by Wiessner's (1977: 265–347; 1980) evidence that changes in band membership, when seen over a long period of time, tend to be only temporary, e.g. for the purpose of long-term visiting or bride service.

Since the early 1960s Zu/'hoã territorial organization has greatly changed. In Botswana, bands tend to spend much longer at their dry-season waterholes than in the past. In the early 1960s they were spending about three-quarters of the year dispersed in the wet-season camps and one-quarter of the year aggregated. Later in the decade the ratio was reversed. Many Botswana !Kung groups were spending nearly three-quarters of the year aggregated at the waterholes and depending more and more on Herero and Tswana residents for their livelihood (Lee 1979b: 368; cf. 1972a; 1972b; 1972c; 1972d [reprinted in Lee 1976]). This pattern is the opposite of what one would expect if the amount of rainfall were the determining factor, as the rainfall was considerably greater in the latter period (see, e.g. Lee 1976 [1972]: 80–2). In the 1970s significant attempts were made to bring development projects, including two schools and a shop (to buy in handicrafts as well as sell other goods), to the !Kung of western Botswana. The impetus for these projects came from Botswana government, but their implementation was initially in the hands of anthropologists. The Kalahari Peoples Fund, a small charity founded in 1973 by a group of anthropologists, was in the forefront of these activities.

In Namibia, the situation has been more drastic, though there have been signs of improvement in the last few years. In 1970 a Bushman 'homeland' was established by the South African government. This reserve included only part of the land traditionally inhabited by Namibian Zu/hoãsi along the Botswana border, and much of the more westerly area originally designated for the reserve is uninhabitable. The establishment of the reserve led to the construction of a school and an administrative camp at Tsumkwe (also spelled 'Tshum!kwi'). In 1978 the South African Defence Force (SADF) added a military camp and began recruiting Zu/'hoãsi as soldiers (Lee and Hurlich 1982; see also Lee 1988a). Many individuals have since given up hunting and gathering in order to live from the earnings of the military camp, and the population there is now too large to engage successfully in traditional subsistence techniques. John Marshall, Claire Ritchie, and Megan Biesele have spent several years trying to encourage the development of cattle husbandry in order to help the Zu/'hoãsi to regain control over their economy (see Marshall and Ritchie 1984: 123–57). Their efforts have been at least partly successful, although in the 1980s they did meet with strong opposition from South African wildlife officials and the SADF. The South African authorities wanted to restrict subsistence to traditional hunting techniques in order to develop a game reserve, partly as a buffer between areas controlled by the South West Africa People's Organization (SWAPO) and the remainder of Namibia (Gordon 1985). In March 1990 Namibia became independent, and the future offers prospects for more enlightened development in the Zu/'hoã area.

!Xũ subsistence and settlement

The northernmost !Kung live outside the Kalahari sand system in a forested area of southeastern Angola. According to Dorothea Bleek (1928b: 106), their self-designation is !o !kũ (more accurately, !o !xũ), 'forest people'. They are also known locally as Kwankala (Vakwankala) and Sekele (Vassekele) (see Almeida 1965: 1–11; Viegas Guerreiro 1968: 54–6). They have lived in close association with Ambo (Ovambo) and other Bantu-speaking cultivators and pastoralists for centuries. Indeed, at least one of these terms, *kwankhala*, is simply Ambo for 'any peoples they consider poor, uncivilized or that wander from place to place' (Andy Shikesha, quoted in Ritchie 1987: 33). From the Bantu-speakers who gave them such names, the Northern !Kung have learned to cultivate crops and herd goats and cattle (Viegas Guerreiro 1968: 123–8). Some groups also fish with nets and spears (1968: 120–3). Although clientage has been common in recent decades, in the 1920s D.F. Bleek encountered small, apparently independent, hunting-and-gathering bands of two to six men with their wives and families (Bleek 1928b: 109). Ironically, Schapera (1930: 78–9) attributed the small size of the bands then to their reliance on Bantu-speaking patrons. Estermann (1976 [1956]: 4) reported that in the 1950s some !Xũ were still following a foraging way of life, but that from March to May, when wild food is scarce, !Xũ women and girls would assist neighbouring Bantu-speaking cultivators in their winter harvests in exchange for handfuls of grain and flour (cf. Viegas Guerreiro 1968: 129–41).

In the 1970s and 1980s, their country was a battleground between government troops of the Movimento Popular de Libertacão de Angola (MPLA) and guerrillas of the União Nacional de Independéncia Total de Angola (UNITA), supported by South Africa. The extent of damage to the !Xũ way of life is not yet possible to assess. No ethnographer has done intensive fieldwork in this area since the start of the Angolan civil war in the 1970s.

≠Au//ei subsistence and settlement

At the other end of !Kung country live the ≠Au//eisi. They are frequently called by other versions of this term, such as ≠xau//eĩ, //k"au-//en, or (by early ethnographers) *Auen*. They are known locally as *Makaukau*, a Bantu corruption of the same term.

The ≠Au//eisi occupy land adjacent to and overlapping that of the Nharo. They share their land not primarily with Bantu-speakers but the white ranchers, mainly Afrikaners. Permanent white settlement began in 1897, when settlers from the Cape Colony arrived in what is now the Ghanzi farm block of western Botswana. The descendants of these settlers live there to this day and raise cattle for Botswana's large export trade in beef (see Russell and Russell 1979). The northern areas of the block are the traditional lands of ≠Au//eisi groups who in the nineteenth century migrated between Zu/'hoã country, the Groot Laagte, and the area of the modern farm block. Judging by linguistic evidence and by obvious !Kung traits in the kinship systems of the Nharo, Ts'aokhoe, and ≠Haba, contact between the !Kung and the Khoe Bushmen is ancient. The direction of borrowing seems to be mainly from the ≠Au//eisi (or other !Kung) to the Western Khoe Bushmen (Barnard 1988a: 42–4), though some data in D.F. Bleek's (1956) dictionary cast doubt on this assumption (see 'Kinship and marriage', below). Today, as in the past, many individuals move freely between the Dobe area and the Ghanzi ranches. Although they still hunt and gather for much of their subsistence, relative overpopulation, by both humans and livestock, prevents the ≠Au//eisi from being able to follow a lifestyle based more on their traditional hunting and gathering pursuits (Childers 1976: 19–20, 53–8).

Kinship and marriage
The kinship system of the Zu/'hoã !Kung is widely known among anthropologists. What is less well known is that this system is by no means typical. Indeed, the !Kung are virtually unique among Khoisan peoples for their 'Eskimo'-type terminology structure which, like the English one, classifies parallel and cross-cousins by one set of terms, and distinguishes siblings. Their custom of classifying through the 'name relationship' is also well known to students of anthropology, but it too is unknown among most other Khoisan groups.

Relationship terminology
What follows is a simplified account of !Kung, and particularly Zu/'hoã, relationship terminology usage. I shall draw mainly on the descriptions of Marshall (1957a; 1976: 201–86; cf. Fabian 1965), Lee (1984: 56–86; 1986), and Wilmsen (1989a: 171–80; 1989b: 54–8), concentrating at first on those aspects of the system on which all three authors agree. Wherever possible, I shall use Snyman's (1975) orthography.

In its idealized form, the terminology is simple. The !Kung classify relationships as either 'joking' or 'avoidance'. These anthropological labels do not necessarily characterize typical behaviour between individuals, but they have come into standard use. More importantly, they offer the mechanism for comparison between Khoisan systems which utilize equivalent named or unnamed categories through which more precise relationships are defined. The technicalities of this will be reserved for Chapter 15.

Joking and avoidance terms alternate generationally. Grandparents (who are joking relatives) are called by terms with the stem *!u* or *tun* (*txũ*, according to Wilmsen). Father and mother (who are avoidance relatives) are called *ba* and *tae* respectively, while uncles are termed *txũ*, and aunts, *g//a*. Elder brothers are *!o*, elder sisters, *!ui*, and younger siblings of either sex,

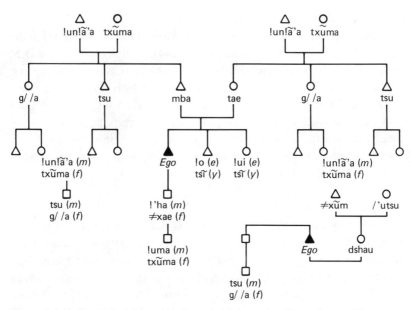

Figure 3.2 Zu/'hoã kinship terminology: basic structure for male ego (!Kung specialists disagree on terms for female ego)

tsĩ (here joking/avoidance categorization depends on whether one is of the same or opposite sex). Cousins (joking partners) are called by the same terms as grandparents, or by diminutive forms of these terms. Sons and daughters are *!'hã* and *≠xae* respectively, while nephews and nieces are termed as uncles and aunts. Grandchildren are socially equated with grandparents and cousins, and are termed accordingly, using diminutive forms when addressed directly. In general, diminutives are constructed by adding the suffix *-ma* (meaning 'small' or 'young') and, where necessary, by dropping the suffix *-!ã'a* ('big' or 'old'), which is generally applied to grandparents and other senior relatives. A more complete list of referential terms is given in Table 3.1, and the basic structure of consanguineal usage is illustrated in Figure 3.2.

When the name relationship is brought in, complications begin. Even so, these complications are actually quite straightforward when we realize that the underlying principle of alternating generations remains. All !Kung are named after senior relatives, in a pattern which alternates between father's and mother's sides of the family. A namesake, especially the specific one from which a given !Kung derives his or her name, is, by definition a close joking partner. Ideally, the first-born son is named after his father's father and the second after his mother's father; but what if I am the third son? If

Table 3.1 *Zu/'hoã relationship terms*

Marshall	Lee	Wilmsen	denotata
!gun!a	*!kun!a*	*!un!ã'a*	Marshall, Lee: PF, PGS, CS, namesake Wilmsen: PF(ms), PM(ws), PGS(ms), PGD(ws), namesake (stem: *!gu*, *!ku* or *!u*)
!guma	*!kuma*	*!uma*	Marshall, Lee: CC Wilmsen: CS(ms), CD(ws) (stem: *!gu*, *!ku* or *!u*)
tŭn!ga	*tun!ga*	*txŭg!a*	Marshall: PF(ws), PGS(ws), CS(ws) (all as variants of *!gun!a* for woman speaker), ZH, EB Lee: ZH, EB Wilmsen: PF(ws), PGS(ws), CS(ws), ZH, EB, potential H (apparent stem: *tun* or *txŭ*)
tŭn	*tun*	—	PM, PGD, CD, BW(ms), WZ
tsu	*tsu*	*tsu*	PPF, PB, GS, PGCS, CCS
tsuma	*tsuma*	*txŭma*	Marshall, Lee: GC(ms) Wilmsen: PM(ms), PGD(ms), CD(ms), potential W (stem: *tsu* or *txŭ*)
//ga	*//ga*	*g//a*	PPM, PZ, GD, PGCD, CCD
//gama	*//gama*	—	GC(ws) (stem: *//ga*)
ba	*ba*	*mba*	F (stem: *ba*)
tai	*tai*	*tae*	M
!go	*!ko*	*!o*	Marshall, Lee: Be Wilmsen: Be, and alternative term for some distant affines
!kwi	*!kwi*	*!ui*	Marshall, Lee: Ze Wilmsen: Ze, and alternative term for some distant affines
tsĩ	*tsin*	—	Gy
!ha	*!ha*	*!'hã*	S
≠khai	*≠hai*	*≠xae*	D
!hoa	*!kwa*	*!hõa*	H
tsau	*tsiu*	*dshau*	W
≠tum	*≠tum*	*≠xŭm*	Marshall: EF, DH Lee: EF Wilmsen: EF, DH, and some distant affines
/utsu	*/otsu*	*/'utsu*	Marshall: EM, HZ, SW Lee: EM, HZ Wilmsen: EM, HZ, SW, and some distant affines
n!unba	*n!unba*	*!unba*	Marshall, Lee: CEF Wilmsen: CEF, and some distant affines (stem: *n!u* or *!u*)
n!untai	*n!unta*	*!untae*	Marshall, Lee: CEM Wilmsen: CEM, and some distant affines (stem: *n!u* or *!u*)

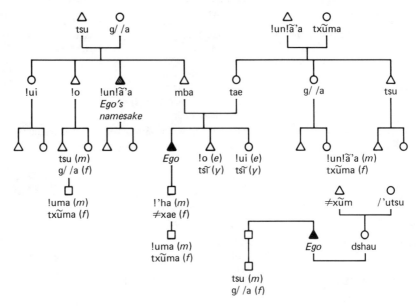

Figure 3.3 Zu/'hoã kinship terminology: an alternative structure (ego named after his father's brother)

my older brothers already bear the names of our grandparents, I will usually be named after an uncle instead. In this instance, my namesake-uncle will be, by definition, my *!u!ã'a* or 'grandfather' (the term means literally 'name-elder'), and his siblings will be classed as my 'siblings'. By the rule of alternating generations, his parents will be termed as if members of my parents' generation. Thus collateral terms alternate generationally, both upwards and downwards, with cousins classified as 'uncles/nephews' and 'aunts/nieces', with nephews and nieces as 'cousins/grandchildren', etc. On the opposite side from that where my name comes, classification retains the basic structure described earlier. Figure 3.3 illustrates a case where I am named after a father's brother.

The ≠Au//ei and Northern !Kung terms recorded by Dorothea Bleek (1924: 62, 64–5) reveal a very similar pattern. In addition to presenting the terms themselves, Bleek gives some intriguing asides: the suggestion that *!ku* or *!kũ* 'means "kinsman" or "namesake"'; and that *mama* (recorded as a term of address by Marshall and by Wilmsen) is used reciprocally between grandparents and grandchildren and 'seems to be a term of affection' (1924: 62). She also notes the etymology of *ma* as a diminutive, *!na* as meaning 'big, grown up', and ≠*ga* as 'old, worn out', and she suggests that the ≠Au//eisi among whom she worked, in the Nharo–≠Au//eisi–Nama borderland, employed Nharo terms (1924: 63). The two examples she gives, however, seem to me to be Common Khoe (/*wiakwe* for 'brother-in-law') and Nama (//*kũ* for 'greatniece' [classificatory child]), respectively. Indeed the former term may be partly a loan translation: /*wi*-, Khoe for 'in-law'; -*a*-, the !Kung transitional morpheme; -*kwe*, the !Kung morpheme of reciprocity (cf. Snyman 1970: 150–1).

This raises an interesting problem worthy of some reflection, at least among Khoisan specialists: how did so many early ethnographers come to record Khoe-derived terms among the !Kung? In Bleek's posthumous *Bushman dictionary* (1956), there are some eighty such terms (including variant transcriptions) from the more northerly !Kung dialects. She had culled these terms from her own notes and from the works of Viktor Lebzelter, Hans Schinz, J.H. Wilhelm, Heinrich Vedder, Lucy Lloyd, and C.M. Doke. Among them are *ai* ('mother', also noted by Wilmsen in the form *aiya*, 'own mother'), *sau* and *zau* (for 'wife', perhaps a semantic shift from the Nama or Nharo term for 'mother'), *sau-!a* (grandmother), /*ui-sau* and *kui-sau* (mother-in-law), /*we* and /*wi* (in-law), *auba* (here having the Nharo meaning 'father', rather than the Nama meaning 'husband'), and *di !gas khe* (for 'my sister'), as well as a few more doubtful ones. Astonishingly, apart from *ai* none of these terms has been recorded in the published works of more recent writers.

Marriage

Among the Zu/'hoãsi, boys marry between the ages of 18 and 25, and until recently girls have married as young as 12 or 16. First marriages are arranged by parents, and typically initiated by the mothers of the prospective bride and groom. Marriage prestations, called *kamasi*, are exchanged between prospective parents-in-law (Lee 1984: 75–7). These gifts are said to 'seal' the marriage (see 'Politics and exchange', below). 'Marriage by capture', reported by early ethnographers, still occurs. Yet like 'giving away the bride' in Western societies, its significance is largely ceremonial (see Lee 1984: 77–9).

There is some disagreement among ethnographers about the prohibited degrees of relationship. The prohibitions recorded by Marshall (1976: 253–9) are the most extensive. They include all first, second, and third cousins; affines of the parents' and children's generation, and spouse's siblings' spouses (though spouse's siblings and siblings' spouses are permitted); stepparents and stepchildren; and parents' and spouse's parents' namesakes, children's and children's spouses' namesakes, and (reciprocally) namesakes' parents, namesakes' children, and namesakes' opposite-sex siblings. There is no substantial disagreement about steprelatives and name relatives, but other ethnographers record different rules concerning the marriage of cousins and the logic behind the classification of affines. According to Lee (1984: 75), first and second cousins are prohibited. His discussion of affinal classification is consistent with Marshall's.

According to Wilmsen (1989a: 177–80), there is no prohibition *per se* on marriages between cousins, although first-cousin marriage is often pre-cluded because of namesake links. When grandparents give their names to more than one set of grandchildren, cousins often turn out to be termino-logical 'brothers' and 'sisters'. Second and third cousins, according to Wilmsen, are precisely those who *are* marriageable. The marriageable category is *txũg!a* or *txũma*, which Wilmsen translates loosely as 'cousin'. These are defined as all those opposite-sex, same-generation individuals descended from one's parents' parents' siblings or parents' parents' par-ents' siblings. Barring name restrictions, they include everyone whose parents are termed *tsu* or *g//a*. After ego's marriage, his or her spouse's parents, and a host of other relatives previously termed *tsu* and *g//a*, become ≠*xũm* and */'utsu* ('spouse of *tsu*'). Likewise, after one's child's marriage, one's child's spouse's parents are termed *!unba* ('name-father') and *!untae* ('name-mother').

I am inclined to accept the rules noted by Wilmsen as comprising the best representation of the system. Nevertheless, Marshall's (1976: 261) sugges-tion that there are 'three degrees of approval of marriages: preference, permission and toleration', makes much sense, while Wilmsen's 'prescrip-tive'-type diagrams (1989a: 172–3) are very misleading indeed. The !Kung do not practise 'prescriptive marriage' in Rodney Needham's (1973) sense. In terms of degree of formalization, the !Kung system stands in between the classic 'prescriptive' systems (e.g., those of South India), and the classic 'non-prescriptive' ones (e.g., the English), but closer to the 'non-prescrip-tive' end of the scale (cf. Barnard and Good 1984: 100–4). On the jural level, the !Kung system has also been likened to 'Crow–Omaha' alliance struc-tures in its use of name lines to restrict the choice of spouse (1984: 106), but in the light of Wilmsen's evidence there may be good grounds for reconsidering the problem.

For the ≠Au//eisi, Kaufmann (1910: 156–8) reports that marriage was only permitted after initiation, and that premarital sexual relations were rare. Interestingly, he also suggests that polygyny was not uncommon in places where food supplies were plentiful, but that monogamy was the norm where resources were scarce. Bride service and initial uxorilocal residence are practised among all !Kung groups, and among the ≠Au//eisi,

men hold the initiative in marriage arrangements (cf. Shostak 1983 [1981]).
≠Au//ei marriage prohibitions are not recorded, but true 'marriage by
capture', including capture of foreign girls as wives, is said to have occurred
(Kaufmann 1910: 154).

For the Angolan !Kung, Viegas Guerreiro (1968: 231–2) mentions
prohibitions against marriage to consanguineal kin on both sides of the
family, but does not give details on how far these prohibitions extend. D.F.
Bleek (1928b: 112) states, rather loosely, 'Some of the married couples were
cousins, but the majority were unrelated, as far as they knew'. Marriage
sometimes takes place before puberty, though such spouses are regarded as
in a nebulous social category (Viegas Guerreiro 1968: 233–4). Among the
Kwankala, initial uxorilocal residence and bride service are the norm (1968:
243–4). Polygyny is permitted among both the Kwankala and the Sekele as
long as certain conditions, including agreement of the first wife, are met
(1968: 244–8). D.F. Bleek (1928b: 111) suggests that the Angolan !Kung
'have mostly two or three wives'. Divorce is permitted, notably on grounds
of adultery (Viegas Guerreiro 1968: 253–4).

Childrearing and socialization
The !Kung are well know for their tolerant attitude towards their children.
From the time they can walk, children, especially girls, are taught by their
mothers to gather plant foods. Boys learn, from their peers and from older
boys, how to stalk and kill game. Children of both sexes play together, and
adults of both sexes take part in socializing the youngsters. The egalitarian
nature of their society fosters co-operation rather than competition
(Draper 1978).

Relatively sedentary !Kung exhibit a number of differences from more
nomadic !Kung. Children raised in a sedentary environment do more work,
travel further from their homes, and interact more with those of similar sex
and age, and less with those of the opposite sex or with older or younger
people, than do those who are nomadic (Draper 1975b; Draper and
Cashdan 1988). Perhaps most significantly, sedentary Zu/'hoã adults spend
less time with their children, and interaction between the children themselves tends to be less in caretaking and more in peer-group activities
(Draper 1975a). When Zu/'hoãsi cease their seasonal migrations, sexual
differentiation increases. Women tend to stay at home more, while men are
more likely to stay away from home, even if only looking after herds
nearby. Lee (1984: 137; cf. 1981 [1978]) suggests that this tendency may
mark the beginning of women's subordination.

Politics and exchange

The maintenance of social order has been an important theme in !Kung ethnography for many years. Lee (e.g., 1972c; 1972e; 1976 [1972]; 1979b: 333–400) has tended to concentrate on the resolution of conflict and the notion of 'ownership', including corporate ownership of land, as vital forces in !Kung social organization. Important papers by Marshall (1961; reprinted in Marshall 1976; and in Lee and DeVore 1976) and Wiessner (1982), on the other hand, emphasize the formal rules for sharing of such things as meat and tobacco. These papers also document the gift-giving networks which function to redistribute property and bind individuals in quasi-kin relationships across vast areas of the northern Kalahari.

In his key text, Lee (1979b: 333–400) places particular emphasis on relations of production as determinants of Zu/'hoã politics. Zu/'hoãsi have no formal political structures. Rights to land and resources are inherited bilaterally, and kinship bonds provide a framework for both production and political organization. The core group of kinsmen within each band are known as the *kx'ausi* (owners) of the *n!ore* (band territory). Membership of this group is retained as long as a given individual continues to reside in his or her territory. When people wish to camp within a territory or use its resources, they seek permission of the 'owners'. The term *kx'au-n!a* (big owner) is applied to the nominal head of the band (Marshall 1976: 191), but people tend to avoid this term as a self-appellation, for fear of being regarded as putting on airs (Lee 1979b: 344). Membership of the core group, seniority of residence, age, and personal qualities are all factors in ascribed leadership, but boastfulness and attempts to dominate are strongly discouraged (Lee 1979b: 344–6; see also Lee 1969b; reprinted in 1984: 151–7).

Marshall (1976: 287–312) emphasizes the significance of sharing for maintaining co-operation within the band, and between bands. !Kung society is characterized by strict rules of meat sharing. Through these, !Kung distribute the proceeds of the hunt to successful hunters, unsuccess-ful hunters, and non-hunters alike. Hunters lend arrows to each other, and the 'owner' of the kill is the owner of the killing arrow even though it will have been shot by another hunter. The owner shares his meat with the other hunters, with his affines, with the members of his band, and often with members of other, nearby bands too. Those who receive meat then distribute it to their families, to name relatives, and to others. Tobacco and other consumables are also widely shared, and it is almost inconceivable for a !Kung to eat or smoke alone. However, plant foods are shared much less extensively. In general, each family procures its own.

Marshall also comments on the exchange of non-consumables, but she leaves much unsaid about the precise mechanism of these transactions. Some twenty years after Marshall's fieldwork, Wiessner took up the problem and succeeded in uncovering a wide network of exchange (Wiessner 1977; 1982; 1986). This has come to be known by the !Kung term *hxaro*, which means roughly 'giving in formalized exchange'. By the time of marriage, the average !Kung will have between ten and sixteen *hxaro* partners, including close kin, as well as distant relatives and friends, spread over wide areas (Wiessner 1982: 72–4). Underlying the *hxaro* system of delayed, balanced reciprocity is an assumption that these gift-giving partners exist in a state of mutual generalized reciprocity of rights to water and plant resources (1982: 74–7).

Non-*hxaro*, formalized gift-giving occurs at betrothals, at weddings (when parents of the bride and groom exchange presents), and when a baby has its first haircut (when the person after whom it is named offers a gift) (Marshall 1976: 309). The former two, which involve gifts between inter-marrying families, are termed *kamasi*. These coexist with obligations of bride service on the part of the groom (see Lee 1984: 75–6). The historical relation between !Kung and Nharo marriage practices is not known, but it is interesting that the same term (in its Nharo form, *kamane*) describes a more elaborate set of gift-giving obligations among the latter people, who do not, or no longer practise, bride service (see Chapter 8).

In addition to exchange within !Kung society, there has long been trade contact between !Kung and Bantu-speaking peoples, as well as with Nama and Damara, and with other Bushman groups. The evidence is extensive (e.g., Gordon 1984; Wilmsen 1982; 1986). Incoming trade items have included a variety of iron and copper utensils, wooden bowls, tobacco, coffee, glass beads, and even cowrie shells; while outgoing goods have included, among other things, ostrich feathers and eggshell beads, and animal hides and horns. According to Gordon (1984: 207), all of Zu/'hoã country and beyond 'seems to have been crisscrossed with well-developed trading networks' (Gordon 1984: 207). Implicit in the accounts of Gordon and Wilmsen is an assumption that other recent ethnographers have been blinded by their desire to see the !Kung as isolated remnants of primitive purity untouched by wider economic structures. Through archaeological as well as documentary evidence, we now know that exchanges, of many kinds, have linked the !Kung and other Bushmen with the outside world for more than a millennium (Denbow 1984).

Religion
The deities and spirits
The !Kung universe is inhabited by a great god, a lesser god, their wives and children, and the spirits of the dead. The distinction between these beings, however, is not always clear, and several of the names of the deities are held in common between more than one being. This is not uncommon in Khoisan religion, and may reflect both linguistic and conceptual ambiguity (Barnard 1988b; see also Chapter 14).

The Zu/'hoãsi of Nyae Nyae call the great god ≠Gao!na (Old ≠Gao). In addition to this term, which is his 'earthly name' (i.e., a name found too among human !Kung), ≠Gao!na also bears seven 'divine names'. Each of these divine names – Hishe, Huwe, Kxo, !Gara, Gani ga, ≠Gaishi≠gai, and //Gauwa (Marshall's orthography) – is also shared with the lesser god (see Marshall 1962: 223–6). The first three names may be derived from terms in other languages (cf., e.g., the Nharo divine name Hiesheba). The fourth, fifth, sixth, and seventh names are terms for medicinal plants believed to grow in heaven (E.N. Wilmsen, pers. comm.). The lesser god (whom Wilmsen calls the 'Administrator', as opposed to the 'Creator') has no earthly name. According to Marshall, he is usually called //Gauwa (more accurately G//ãũa), a common term in several Khoisan languages for 'God', 'Devil', or the spirits of the dead. The wives of the great and lesser deities alike are called by these same divine names, but with the feminine suffix -di appended – Hishedi, Huwedi, etc. In addition, the great god's two wives bear the earthly names Khwova!na and //Gow (Marshall's orthography) and are also addressed by various respect terms. Indeed, some of the names of the deities are semi-taboo and are themselves uttered only with respect or, by some Zu/'hoãsi, not at all.

The religious beliefs of the northern groups would seem to be similar to those of those to the south, but there are some differences. The Kwankala call their deity //Nava or //Gawa, and the Sekele use the term !Ga (Viegas Guerreiro 1968: 97–8, 127; his orthography). Both Estermann (1976 [1956]: 7) and Viegas Guerreiro (1968: 127) report that tilling the soil is regarded as contrary to the world order established by //Gawa, but they say little about the implications of this for adoption of agriculture by Angolan groups. Like many other Khoisan groups, Angloan !Kung also revere the moon (/ui). According to one of Estermann's informants: 'The moon is like our god. When it appears, we greet it, saying, "Little Father (or Little Mother), you have come to visit us"' (Estermann 1976 [1956]: 12). There is a notion that the moon is the place where the spirits of the dead reside (Estermann 1976 [1956]: 13). Although the idea 'moon worship' has long since been jettisoned by Khoisan ethnographers, the Northern !Kung, like the Cape Khoekhoe and the //Xegwi of South Africa, seem to envisage the moon as a manifestation of the deity. This fact, along with the widespread use of the term *g//ãũa* and its derivatives across southern Africa, is an interesting and significant testament to the unity of Khoisan religion (cf. Chapter 14).

In addition to the deities and spirits proper, !Kung belief maintains a constellation of mythological beings (see Biesele 1975; 1976). Of some fifty distinct folktales collected by Biesele among the !Kung of Ngamiland, about half belong to 'mythical time', and the other half are concerned with the isolated activities of various additional characters. The former selection is a body of interconnected, bawdy material that displays the relationships and attributes of Kauha (Biesele's spelling for *G//ãũa* or *//Gauwa*, identified as the trickster 'God' rather than as 'Devil') and his associates. These associates include (in Biesele's orthography) his sons Kan//ka and !Xoma, his brother-in-law !Ko!kotsi/dasi ('eyes-on-his-ankles'), and his apparent daughter-in-law, the enigmatic !Xo//kamdima (possibly meaning 'beautiful antbear maiden'), also known as !Kxodi ('elephant girl'). The latter part of Biesele's collection includes mainly animal fables. However, it also includes two important tales which are widespread among Bushman peoples and, to my mind, clearly 'mythological': the story of the Moon and the Hare, which explains the origin of death, and the story of the division of the world between hunter-gatherers and herder-farmers (Biesele 1976: 321–3; cf. Guenther 1989: 50–4, 65–8, 71–5). We shall return to the Moon and the Hare in Chapter 5.

N/um and the medicine dance

The most important ritual for the !Kung, and indeed for all Bushman groups, is the trance or medicine dance. This has been described in some detail by Lee (1968b), Marshall (1969), and Katz (1976; 1982). All three authors emphasize the fact that the dance is a community enterprise stemming from the egalitarian principles of !Kung society, and all three suggest that the dance promotes psychological well-being.

The medicine dance is about the use of *n/um* to achieve *!ia* (commonly spelled *!kia*). *N/um* has variously been translated as 'medicine', 'energy', or 'power'. The term can be used to describe most anything from herbal medicines to menstrual blood, from a tape recorder to the vapour trail of a jet plane (Lee 1984: 109). In the context of the medicine dance, *n/um* is harnessed within the stomach of a medicine man or woman and made to 'boil'. 'Boiling' induces *!ia*, or 'trance', and through trance one can use his power (most often it is men who do so) to cure the sick. Learning to achieve trance requires years of training and practice. Percentages are difficult to estimate and there are disagreements among ethnographers, but possibly as many as half adult male Zu/'hoãsi, and many females as well, are capable of it. The ≠Au//eisi also have a reputation for their trance skills, but the Zu/'hoãsi are invariably credited with the greatest abilities.

Lee (1968b: 39–41) lists five phases of the trance performance. The first is the 'working up' phase. This is characterized by long periods of singing and clapping on the part of women of the group, and dancing on the part of men. The second phase involves entering trance. Dancers may concentrate on trying to achieve a trance state, or may assist others in obtaining it. Trance is usually achieved, either suddenly or gradually, after some 30 to 60 minutes. Lee called the third phase 'half death', an unfortunate phrase which has stuck in the literature. In my view, this phase is best described as metaphorical death; indeed, it is called 'death' (not 'half death') in several Bushman languages. The trance performer collapses in a state of high physical and mental strain. He, or indeed she, may hallucinate. He will tremble with tension, shriek and moan, and have to be assisted by other dancers, who will rub his body to keep it warm. By no means all trance performers are capable of attaining this heightened phase of trance, and in my experience of both !Kung and Nharo trance performers, curing is thought to be possible without it.

The fourth phase is what Lee terms 'active curing'. This lasts perhaps an hour, and several such curing performances, by one or more medicine men, can occur through the night. In this phase, the medicine man places his hands on each and every person present, though sick people are singled out for special treatment. This practice has the effect of binding the group as a whole and makes participants of everyone, including ethnographers (Lee 1968b: 53; Marshall 1969: 379–80). The final phase is the return to normal. Sometimes this is slow in coming. The most memorable dances last not only all night, but through the next day and the following night. A change of personnel is possible, but the action may continue as each achieves trance, cures, and collapses in exhaustion.

N!ow

One of the most interesting peculiarities of !Kung belief is *n!ow* (Marshall 1957b). This is not to be confused with the Nama notion of *!nau*, which refers to a state of ritual danger at times of individual crisis (see Chapter 10). Rather, *n!ow* is primarily a force which influences the weather. It is present, at all times, in each human being and in certain large animals.

Individuals acquire their *n!ow* before birth. Different informants gave

Marshall slightly different explanations of its origin, but they agreed that it is formed in the womb or implanted there by the Great God. There are two types: 'good' or rain-bringing *n!ow* and 'bad' or cold-bringing *n!ow*. When a child is born with good *n!ow*, it rains. When a child is born with bad *n!ow*, the weather turns cold. The significance of human *n!ow*, in fact, seems to be largely confined to the time of birth. The only exception recorded is that a child born with good *n!ow* may later be asked to urinate in the fire or burn some of his or her hair, in order to make it rain. Although the notion of *n!ow* perhaps bears more resemblance to a Western superstition than a theological concept, the act of rain-making in this manner is not as odd as it may seem. Rain itself is the object of superstitious belief, when, for example, !Kung avoid use of the proper term for 'male' (heavy) rain, *!ga !go*, but talk freely of 'female' (gentle) rain, *!ga di* (Marshall 1957b: 232–3; Marshall's orthography). Equally, the rain is associated with hair in the sense that, in the ≠Au//ei as well as in the Zu/'hoã dialect, rain clouds are said to be 'the rain's hair', *!ga-k''wisi* (D.F. Bleek 1956: 374; Bleek's orthography).

Animals which possess *n!ow* are the giraffe, eland, gemsbok, kudu, hartebeest, and wildebeest. When a Zu/'hoã hunter kills one of these, its *n!ow* is released. In a complex interaction with the *n!ow* of the hunter, it creates a rainy or cold condition in the weather. Marshall (1957b: 239) compares these ideas to rain-making customs among other Bushman groups, specifically the burning of horns as appeasement to the Rain being in a /Xam myth (Bleek and Lloyd 1911: 193–8). Drawing on Marshall's data and on these /Xam notions, Vinnicombe (1972: 200) has postulated similar constructs in her symbolic analysis of South African rock art, an interpretation at least partly supported by Lewis-Williams (1981a: 87; see also Chapter 5). While *n!ow* as such may be unique to the !Kung, it does nevertheless bear at least a marginal relationship to the complex of beliefs about the rain which are spread throughout southern Africa.

Initiation ceremonies

In the past, the !Kung practised both male and female initiation, though these rites have been on the wane since the 1950s. Louis Fourie's (1928: 92) description of the ≠Au//ei boys' ceremony, quoted verbatim by Schapera (1930: 124–5; cf. Kaufmann 1910: 141–2), is relatively well known, if not particularly intelligible. On the first day, the boys were given no food or water but subjected instead to the 'smoke of the "devil's" fire' and 'the "devil's" urine'. On the next day, their skin was blackened, and they danced hour after hour, with little food or water. The third day was much the same. On the fourth, they walked through a water-filled pan, gathered veld food, and, in the evening, were 'introduced' to G//aua. Then they ate honey which he had brought. On the fifth day, they were cleaned up and permitted to move about the camp, as long as they did not speak to unmarried women. Thereafter, each day was spent in tests of hunting skill. Those boys who passed the tests were tattooed with meat from their own kill. Viegas Guerreiro (1968: 218–21) gives a similar account of initiation among the Angolan !Kung, while ethnographers of the Zu/'hoãsi (e.g., Lee 1979b: 235–40) emphasize the hunting-magic aspect of initiation.

Lee (1979b: 238–9) describes the tattooing in detail. In a performance he observed, a mixture of charred herbs and fat was rubbed into ten tiny cuts made in the skin, on the initiate's breastbone. Then further cuts were made on the left side of the chest, the left side of the belly, under the left scapula, at five separate locations on the left arm, and finally, between the eyes.

Female initiation, not observed by any modern ethnographer of the Zu/'hoãsi, is said to have been dominated by the Eland Bull Dance, performed at the time of a girl's first menstrual period. This ceremony is widespread throughout the Kalahari, perhaps reaching its most elaborate form among the Nharo and the Hai//om (see Chapters 8 and 11). Dorothea Bleek (1928a: 23) described the form of the ≠Au//ei female initiation as having the same form as the Nharo one. The initiate was placed in a hut and attended by women of the band, while all the men had to leave the area. There was one exception, the man who represented the eland bull. Wearing horns and dancing in a step which mimicked the movements of this animal, he would 'chase' the women around the fire and hut. The initiate took no active part in the ceremony, but the other women, lifting their skirts behind them as they danced, represented female sexuality, in opposition to the powerful 'medicine' of the eland bull (cf. Barnard 1980b: 117–18; Lewis-Williams 1981a: 43–67). Among the Angolan !Kung, tattooing much like that found in male hunting rites was also performed (D.F. Bleek 1928b: 122; cf. Schapera 1930: 118–22; Viegas Guerreiro 1968: 221–31).

Some comparisons between the male and female ceremonies are revealing. For the Zu/'hoãsi today, the ritual tattooing of the boys might best be regarded as hunting magic, rather than 'initiation' (cf. Barnard 1979b: 70; 1980b: 117–18). Yet in a wider context, hunting *is* something to be 'initiated' into, in the sense that it marks the primary identity of an adult male. Just as the female ceremony signifies a woman's roles as a potential wife and mother, the male rites among the Zu/'hoãsi acknowledge a man's hunting prowess. Other Bushman groups, notably the !Xõ and the western Nharo of the 1920s (see Chapters 4 and 8), perform or performed month-long ceremonies of dancing, instruction, hunting, and ritual tattooing. The patterns of the tattoos on the body are virtually the same among all these groups. Interestingly, among the G/wi, ritual tattooing of the chest, shoulders, and thighs follows not only a young man's first kill, but also a young man's first trance performance (Silberbauer 1965: 89, 99), thereby marking a different aspect of 'manhood'.

4

The !Xõ and Eastern ≠ Hoã

Introduction
The !Xõ, defined broadly, are a widely scattered people. As noted in Chapter 2, they call themselves by an extraordinary variety of names. !Xõ is the most widely used term, though ≠ Hoã is common in the east and Tshasi in the south. Dorothea Bleek (1929a; 1956) knew the westernmost !Xõ as the /nu //en or SVI (Southern Bushman linguistic group, language number six). This group lived along the Upper Nosob River (also spelled Nosop or Nossop) in what is now Namibia. Her *masarwa* or SV are also closely related, while the /nusan or SVIa language, studied by J.G. Kroenlein in 1861, is now known to be quite distinct (Traill 1974: 10–11).

The Eastern ≠ Hoã (hereafter, ≠ Hoã) are only very distantly related, but live in close proximity to the !Xõ on their southeastern boundary. As they were only 'discovered' (i.e., discovered not to be !Xõ) in the early 1970s, very little is known about them anthropologically. In the Kweneng district, some ≠ Hoã live in association with members of the Khoe-speaking groups studied by Vierich (1977; 1982a; 1982b) and Motzafi (1986). These groups will be discussed in Chapter 7. In this chapter, my remarks on the ≠ Hoã will be confined to a brief look at the relationship terminology system recorded by the American linguist, Jeffrey Gruber (1973). This is virtually the only ethnographic material which exists on the ≠ Hoã *per se*.

The !Xõ
Research among the !Xõ
The !Xõ are known to the outside world mainly through the M.A. thesis (1966) and subsequent publications of H.J. Heinz (e.g., 1972; 1978a; 1979; Heinz and Lee 1978). As a parasitologist at the University of the Witwaters-

rand, Heinz decided to study parasitic diseases affecting Bushmen. He made his first trip to the Kalahari in 1961 and soon became more interested in !Xõ culture than in parasitic diseases. He already had a Ph.D. in parasitology, so he decided to submit his findings on the !Xõ as an M.A. thesis. This thesis (Heinz 1966), as detailed as many Ph.D.s, is our main source on !Xõ social organization.

No other ethnographer has studied the !Xõ in any depth, but several German scholars have completed specialist studies, particularly in ethology (notably Eibl-Eibesfeldt, e.g., 1972; 1974a; 1975; and Sbrzesny 1976). Their work is not often cited in reference to Khoisan ethnographic issues, partly because it is less accessible in English-speaking countries than other works which touch on similar themes (e.g., Shostak 1983 [1981]), and partly because it stands outside the tradition of social or cultural anthropology as this is commonly understood. For the latter reason also, it will not be examined in any detail here.

The South African linguist, Anthony Traill, has made the !Xõ language his primary research interest. While linguistic studies also fall outside the scope of the present book, a few facts are of interest. Like !Kung, !Xõ is a somewhat isolating, somewhat inflective language. Yet it is much more complex than !Kung, and has a number of grammatical features of great fascination to specialists (see, e.g., Traill 1974; Dickens 1977; Dickens and Traill 1977). Among other things, !Xõ seems to possess more phonemes than any other language in the world. Astonishingly, the dialect studied by Traill (1977a; 1977b; 1979a; 1985) has eighty clicks, thirty-nine non-click consonants, and at least forty-four vowels (excluding diphthongs and tone contrasts). Zu/'hoã, by comparison, has some forty-seven clicks, forty-one non-click consonants, and thirteen vowels (Snyman 1975). The high number of clicks in both cases results from the practice among Khoisan specialists of counting the click releases as integral parts of the click phonemes. In addition, !Xõ possesses the bilabial click series ⊙, ⊙ ′, ⊙w, etc., which is not found in any !Kung or Khoe dialect. There is also a degree of dialect diversity among the !Xõ which makes communication difficult except within relatively small but scattered speech communities. Not surprisingly, !Xõ has attracted much attention from linguists, while the social scientists who have worked with this people have employed largely observational approaches.

The !Xõ environment

The !Xõ live in one of the poorest environments of the Kalahari. Large game is less prevalent there than elsewhere in the Kalahari, vegetable foods

are sparse, there is no staple equivalent to the mongongo exploited by the
Zu/'hoãsi, and permanent natural waterholes are few in number. Their
traditional lands are also occupied by Kgalagari herders who have been in
the region for centuries, and some Nama who are refugees from the wars of
the German occupation. These herding groups seem to have little direct
contact with !Xõ, in contrast to the situation among either the !Kung or the
Khoe-speaking peoples of eastern Botswana. This is partly due to the fact
that the land is so poor. It cannot easily sustain either large herds of
livestock or a high density of hunter-gatherer subsistence activity.

The !Xõ also have fewer natural water supplies per land area than the
Bushmen of almost any other area. The only exception is the very dry
southern Kalahari area of Kalahari Gemsbok National Park, the home
of the 'Auni- ≠ Khomani (see Chapter 5). Today, the eastern part of !Xõ
territory is well stocked with water, thanks to the main trans-Kalahari
road, which runs through it. The road is used for the transportation of
livestock from the ranching areas of Ghanzi to the abattoir at Lobatse, in
southern Botswana. It is marked by a line of boreholes, each of which has
become the focal point of a !Xõ band or cluster of related bands.

Figure 4.1 shows the locations of the peoples and places discussed here. It
is based on a variety of sources (cf. Heinz 1966: 93 and maps; 1979: 467, 471;
Traill 1974: 9–25 and maps). Heinz and Traill include more detailed maps
of !Xõ band cluster locations and dialect areas, respectively. The boundary
between Eastern and Western !Xõ dialect areas is based on Traill's findings.

Like members of other Bushman groups, the !Xõ have a considerable
knowledge of their environment. Botanical and zoological knowledge is
not specialized, but held by every !Xõ adult (see Heinz and Martini 1980;
Heinz and Maguire n.d. [1974]). Heinz and Maguire, working with just one,
female informant, were able to record the names and uses of 206 of 211
plants species they collected. Their informant displayed little concern with
plant physiology, but a thorough understanding of practical matters such
as availability and use value.

Spatial organization
According to Heinz (1966: 11), all !Xõ 'have the feeling that they have
common ties', which they do not share with members of other Bushman
groups. However, their primary identity is that of their location or territory
rather than that of simply being !Xõ (Traill 1974: 8–9). Relations between
!Xõ of different areas are friendly, but characterized also by formality and
reserve. Within !Xo society there are three levels of social organization,
each of which seems to be associated with a territory. These comprise the
band cluster, the band, and the family.

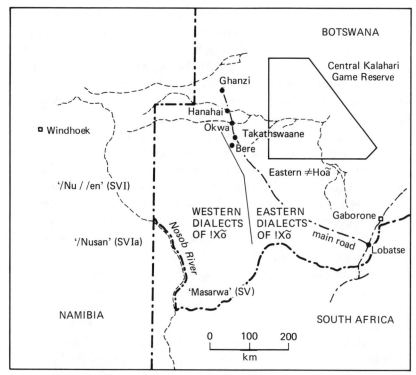

Figure 4.1 !Xõ country

The largest unit is the band cluster. Heinz (e.g., 1966: 91–4; 1979) uses the term 'nexus', with either 'nexus' or 'nexuses' as the plural. I prefer 'band cluster', particularly as a designation for a population group as opposed to its territory. Each band cluster has a 'group name' or *miate*. These often designate simply location. ≠ Oa ⊙'ani means 'People of the East'; and so on. Yet in reality, there is no single 'People of the West', as this term is used to contrast related dialect and band cluster areas in different !Xõ areas. Some !Xõ groups, though, do have more specific and evocative names. One of the names for the Okwa !Xõ is Gau ⊙'ani ('People from the Soft Sand'), while their neighbours from Takathswaane are known as /E !Um ⊙'ani (People That Follow the Eland') (Heinz 1966: 93; 1979: 467–8; Traill 1974: 24; cf. Figure 4.1).

Band cluster boundaries are in many cases identical with the dialect boundaries. Members of different bands of the same band cluster recognize their common kinship through intermarriage or through descent from common ancestors, while kinship ties between members of different band clusters are not traceable (Heinz 1966: 11; see also 1979: 466–7). Thus those who share the same band cluster membership refer to each other as *ŋ /u tu* ('my people'), and members of other band clusters are called *a /u tu* ('your people'). In contrast to the !Kung, who have overlapping territories (though of band and not cluster level), the !Xõ have clearly defined band cluster territories, with strips of no man's land between them. These strips separate each band cluster from neighbouring ones and prevent incursions into alien hunting grounds.

Each band cluster is divided into some two to seven bands. Bands are smaller than those found among some other Bushman groups (Heinz 1966: 93–4; 1979: 468). A typical !Xõ band has between 30 and 45 members, and the largest band observed by Heinz in the early 1960s had a population of 60 (Heinz 1966: 52). The band is composed of a group of families who habitually camp together and who are linked through ties of consanguinity or by name links. Although the !Xõ lack the system of name transmission found among the !Kung and Western Khoe Bushmen, they nevertheless have a notion that a person may join a particular band if he or she happens to bear the same name as someone living there (Heinz 1966: 50). Sometimes more than one band will camp together, in which case they will still be separated by a space of a hundred metres or more (Heinz 1966: 53).

The smallest social unit is the family. Unusually for Bushmen, the !Xõ seem to regard the family, as well as the band cluster and the band, as a territorial unit. Although by right all band territory may be used by any family of the band, in practice each family exploits its own area within the band territory. Similarly, although each band collectively owns the resources of its territory, with permission members of different bands of the same band cluster may hunt within each other's band territories.

Territoriality

In comparing the !Xõ nexus or band cluster to supra-band groupings within other Bushman areas, Heinz (1966: 91–2) sets out to establish the widespread existence of the band cluster as a political unit. However, as his own description makes clear, the !Xõ band cluster is far more important than comparable units (if indeed such units can be identified) among the !Kung or the G/wi. In my view, these latter Bushman societies do not have anything quite comparable at all. The Nyae Nyae area of Zu/'hoã country is not a political unit and has no boundary to distinguish it from other Zu/'hoã areas or even from ≠Au//ei or !Xũ areas. Heinz's comparisons were evidently designed to validate his own ethnography by appealing to its apparent lack of uniqueness. Instead of arguing that the !Xõ are more territorial than other Bushman groups, Heinz maintains that because he found the !Xõ more territorial than other ethnographers have found their Bushman groups, the other ethnographers underestimate territoriality.

My present view is that, whereas the !Kung are probably more territorial than some of their ethnographers described them, the !Xõ are probably not as territorial as either Heinz or I (Barnard 1979) have previously suggested. Certain aspects of their apparent 'territoriality' are clearly manifestations of kinship principles. Whereas the !Kung now seem to be more 'territorial' than previously regarded, the !Xõ seem to be not so much concerned with territory, but with group membership. The 'territoriality' which they exhibit may be characterized as group solidarity played out in spatial terms, rather than an explicit notion of resource or boundary defence (Barnard 1986a: 48). For example, the vast majority of !Xõ marriages are contracted within a band cluster; but if a marriage is made between two people of different band clusters, each partner in theory remains a member of his or her own natal band cluster for life. This ethnographic observation can be interpreted either in terms of territoriality or in terms of a strong kinship principle. Heinz's descriptions (especially 1972; 1979) lean towards the former interpretation. This view could be coloured by his belief that Bushmen are territorial by the very nature of their foraging lifestyle, if not by the innate tendency towards territoriality which he ascribes to humans in general.

Economic and political relations

In spite of the detailed accounts of social relations in Heinz's work, there is no mention of any gift-giving mechanisms quite comparable to the *hxaro* system of the !Kung. It is tempting to suggest that he ignored them, but if he is correct, the apparent lack of such relations among the !Xõ may be a factor contributing to the relative isolation of their kin groups. Heinz's (1966: 29–32) description of rights in property deals mainly with the rules of inheritance and with gift-giving within the family.

Objects of Western origin, such as cups, bowls, and iron pots, are the joint property of husband and wife. Household property of the husband is said to belong to the wife after marriage, and vice versa, though very personal items, such as clothing, jewellery, and bows and arrows, are excluded. Items which are not joint property are inherited by children, at the discretion of the parent who bequeaths them. Gifts are given within the family throughout life. Gifts from parents-in-law remain the property of the recipient. Those exchanged between husband and wife revert to the respective donor's parents after the recipient's death, if he or she dies young. This property is in turn passed down to the elderly heir's 'closest joking partners' (1966: 32), presumably their grandchildren.

Economic groups are formed on an *ad hoc* basis (Heinz 1966: 149–52). Women tend to go out on gathering trips as individuals, but they gather firewood and water communally, as is the case among other Bushman groups. Ideally, hunting is done by two or more men together. !Xõ men also prefer to drive cattle in groups of two men, no matter what the size of the herd. Sometimes trading expeditions of half a dozen men travel to neighbouring bands to exchange skins and other objects for tobacco or money.

In his major publications, Heinz has frequently spoken of the existence of headmen, though their precise function is not entirely clear. For example, in explaining the fusion of two bands whose numbers have been depleted, Heinz (1972: 409) says: 'All cases of this nature entail detailed discussion between the old members of each band, during the course of which a certain degree of leadership is exercised by the headman.' In most Bushman societies, band headmanship reflects seniority, but in the !Xõ case, it seems to reflect kin connections. It is normally inherited patrilineally, though a weak headman is not necessarily recognized, and certainly not followed, if he fails to live up to the reputation of his lineage (Heinz 1979: 468–9).

On the other hand, ritual authority is vested in the hands of elders, who may also be headmen. Unlike headmanship, which operates at band level, ritual authority is a matter for the band cluster as a whole. It is appropriate for the oldest headman of a band cluster to lead the dance ceremonies of the male initiation rite (Heinz 1979: 469–70). The accumulation of wealth is also respected, independently of political and ritual authority. Whereas politics and ritual are the domain of men, in recent times wealth is often under the control of women (H.J. Heinz, pers. comm.).

Family life

While not as obvious to the observer as the band, the family represents a significant unit of sharing and of common residence. Even so, children over the age of ten usually sleep in separate huts with other unmarried boys or girls – each sex having its own bachelor hut within the camp (1966: 19). The fire is the defining focus of the family and household, and children of all ages join their parents to share meals in common.

The rules of seating at the family fire are less rigid than among some other Bushman groups, but generalizations can be made. The wife sits with her back to the hut, and her husband next to her. Children usually sit near their parents, with same-sex siblings together. Visitors sit facing the sleeping place. Otherwise, individuals may sit almost anywhere, regardless of joking or avoidance status. The exception is a man's mother-in-law. She will not come near the main fire. Instead, she will make a separate fire near her daughter, and others may join her there, while her husband sits with their daughter's husband and other relatives at the main fire (1966: 20).

Spouses are on close terms. Like other joking partners, they may quarrel openly without fear of being taken too seriously. However, accusations of adultery or of negligence in looking after small children can result in violence. Men have authority over their households though 'hen-pecked' husbands are not rare (Heinz 1966: 22). Both polygyny and polyandry are permitted, though infrequent, and a polygamous family will share a common identity as a family (1966: 18). One !Xõ man married to three wives claimed that though all slept together within the same hut, he would lie between a different pair of wives each night (1966: 33).

Upon divorce, the wife returns to her father's band, and the husband, if performing bride service in the band of his wife's parents, may return to his own band (Heinz 1966: 38). Brothers and sisters maintain relations of affection and responsibility over each other in spite of the technically 'avoidance' relationship between them. Their bonds are, in a sense, closer than those between husband and wife (1966: 181). Indeed, the family, along with the band cluster, is one of the two most durable units of !Xõ social structure. In contrast, bands may split as a result of quarrels, and undesirable members, with their families, may be expelled (1966: 38, 90).

The !Xõ do not practise adoption in any formal sense, but orphans are taken in by their mother's relatives. If parents are unable to feed their children, other relatives may feed and care for them. A baby whose mother has died or has no milk may be fostered by an individual other than a close relative, and in this case payment, in the form of a skin or a wool blanket, is expected. The elderly are customarily taken in by younger relatives when no longer able to provide for themselves. As is typical in Khoisan society, the sharing of vegetable food defines active membership in a domestic unit, while meat is shared throughout the band as a whole (Heinz 1966: 34–5).

Naming

The !Xõ do not have a !Kung-type naming system. Nevertheless, there do seem to be some rules of name-relative exogamy, and names are passed between relatives. Most names have no recognizable meanings, and they are sex-specific (Heinz 1966: 153–8).

Ideally, the first-born child is named by its maternal grandparents. In effect, this means that the child will bear its mother's father's or mother's mother's 'first name'. The paternal grandparents similarly name the second-born child of a couple. After the first two children, the parents may name their own offspring and usually choose the names of relatives with whom they have friendly dealings. A child may not be named after its own parent.

Apart from 'first names', two other types of name are found: nicknames and band cluster names. Little is said about nicknames. Band cluster names are apparently added to first names and are derived from the band cluster name of the relative whose first name one shares. Formerly, according to Heinz's informants, band cluster names defined exogamous units, but this is no longer the case (1966: 155–6). In the case of the children of exogamous marriages, even full siblings may possess different band cluster names (1966: 229).

Heinz is unspecific about the exact nature of name-relationship rules of behaviour, but he does suggest that they are not taken as seriously as those of consanguineous or affinal relationships (1966: 157). Name relationships do not override consanguineous or affinal ones. Certain name relatives are apparently forbidden as spouses, and common names are sometimes avoided in order not to limit the child's future marriage prospects (1966: 155).

Religious beliefs and practices
Like most Khoisan peoples, the !Xõ recognize two deities, one being good and the other a mixture of good and evil. The good deity is Gu/e, sometimes referred to simply as *kxe aa*, 'the old man'. This is a common term of respect, which may also be applied to humans and to the second deity. Little is known about Gu/e, and various opinions are found as to his nature. Some of Heinz's informants said that he is married and has children. One claimed that Gu/e's children lead Bushman hunters to their prey, while Gu/e himself collects the spirits of the dead. One woman said that Gu/e collects only male spirits, while his wife collects the female ones. One denied that it is known whether Gu/e is male or female, and none were able to describe the deity's appearance. It seems to be generally agreed that Gu/e is the creator of humankind, but the details are a subject of indigenous theological controversy (Heinz 1975a: 20–2). The second force is called /Oa. He is generally believed to have been created by Gu/e. Some described /Oa as Gu/e's 'boy' or 'younger brother', and it is said that the two are in a joking relationship (Heinz 1975a: 22–3).

Although they perform no sacrifices and make no offerings, the !Xõ frequently address prayers to Gu/e. They do not pray to /Oa, but they believe that he may either help Gu/e to save life or act as an independent agent of sickness and death (Heinz 1975a: 21, 22–3). The !Xõ have little to say about the heavens. They deny that the stars are spirits. They have little to say about the sun or moon, except that the moon is good 'because it gives light and keeps the night cold' (1975a: 25). One informant said, very unusually for a Khoisan cosmologist, that the sun is 'male' and contraposed to the 'female' rain, which falls as the moon's urine (1975a: 25). The description, nevertheless, indicates a lesser degree of personification than these heavenly elements typically have among other Khoisan peoples.

Each person has a spirit or soul (/aa). This spirit resides in the chest and departs from the body upon death. Spirits of the dead live in the sky, or, according to some !Xõ, in both the sky and the earth. Those who commit suicide become 'dust devils', but there is no belief in any other animate forces in nature (Heinz 1975a: 23–4).

As with all Bushmen, the medicine dance is the central rite of their religious practice (see Heinz 1975a: 27–9; Eibl-Eibesfeldt 1974b). Yet the !Xõ are unusual in their claim that the singing of their medicine men is a 'prayer' (Heinz's word) to Gu/e. The form of the dance is virtually identical to that of the !Kung. The dance is held as much for relaxation and enjoyment as for purposes of curing illnesses, and the !Xõ seem to hold less regard for its effectiveness as a cure than do other Bushmen. They envy the Nharo for their superior abilities in performing trance cures, just as the Nharo themselves envy the !Kung.

While the !Xõ medicine dance is important, it is not particularly distinctive. In contrast, the male initiation dance and associated ceremonies are more distinctly !Xõ. They are perhaps the most elaborate rituals recorded among Khoisan peoples. At the time of Heinz's early fieldwork, male initiation was an affair kept secret from women and from uninitiated boys. Yet it involved large numbers of men, from several bands of the same cluster. Men's gatherings lasted from April (the truffle season) to July, though the details of such gatherings are not entirely clear from available accounts (see Heinz 1966: 125–6, 146–7). What is clear is that the ceremonies lasted only about four days, much shorter than similar rites reported among other groups by earlier writers (e.g., Passarge 1907: 100–3). Typically, the dance site would be more than a kilometre from the nearest camp. The ceremony could involve a host of officials – teacher, tattooer, fire-maker, etc. – though sometimes one man performed all these tasks, and any !Xõ male could take on the task of summoning others to hold the initiation. Men hunted during the day and ate at night, but meat was forbidden to the initiates. An elder would instruct the boys in mythology, magic, marital etiquette, and the 'danger' associated with menstrual blood. The ceremony also involved tattooing and the teaching of hunting skills. The initiation dance itself, known as the *tsoma* (Heinz uses the spelling *chomma*), has unique music and dance steps. However, although associated with the secret initiation of young boys, the *tsoma* could be performed in the presence of women, when the men returned to their communities. After the dance ceremony, the initiates would be reminded of their names and reintroduced to the women of their bands. The 'power' of the new initiate was so strong that he had to look through handfuls of grass at each of the women, lest his direct gaze cause them to wither away. He would then dispense herbal medicines enhanced by his ritual potency (Heinz 1966: 125–34; 1978b).

The !Xõ have little knowledge of herbal cures, but they perform ritual tattooing (Heinz 1975a: 29–30). This is done for three purposes. For luck in hunting, they rub the carbonized skin of a duiker or steenbok into parallel cuts in the forearm. For general good health, they use charcoal from the *n!u* tree (*Lonchocarpus nelsii*), scratched into rows of cuts on the back. To relieve pain, they tattoo the afflicted part of the body with carbon. Additionally, a medicine called *tso* is tattooed into, or rubbed onto, the back of a medicine man to increase his powers. This *tso* is identified by Heinz as *Cammiphora pyracanthoides*, though in Nharo and other Khoe Bushman dialects, a similar term, *tsho*, is employed for all kinds of 'medicine'.

A !Xõ burial

Heinz (1986) describes in some detail a !Xõ burial which he witnessed in 1974. The man responsible for performing the burial first selected a shady site. The men present dug a rectangular pit, oriented north–south, and hollowed out a burial chamber. This chamber was dug into the eastern wall of the pit. The body of the deceased, wrapped in a blanket, was lowered horizontally and placed on its side in the side chamber. The head was put on a pillow and made to face west. The grave was then covered with grass and branches, and two vertical poles were erected to mark the grave. Each person present, including women and children waiting some distance from the grave, filed past the grave and threw some sand into it. A third pole was then placed horizontally between the two vertical ones. The father of the deceased prepared a purifying medicinal liquid in which those who had had contact with the corpse washed. Finally, branches were placed over the grave and the men who had performed the burial sat to say a short prayer and then departed, flicking their hands in the air.

Heinz (1986: 34–5) draws attention to the fact that !Xõ burial practices resemble those of the !Kung, but with some differences. Both groups orient the face towards the west, but the !Kung place the body with the head to the south, whereas the !Xõ place it with the head to the north. The !Kung surround the entire area of the grave with a thornbush fence, whereas the !Xõ place branches directly onto the grave. In place of the prepared medicine of the !Xõ, the !Kung use plain water for washing themselves after the ritual.

The Bere project

It is difficult to speak of the !Xõ without considering the influence of H.J. Heinz, either as an ethnographer or as a development engineer. Unfortunately, his work in setting up the Bere project is glossed over in his autobiography (Heinz and Lee 1978), but the reports on its early progress make interesting reading (Heinz 1970; 1973; 1975b; Wily 1973a; 1973b; 1976).

Bere is a !Xõ settlement in the !Um ⊙'ani band cluster territory, south of Takathswaane. Heinz established livestock rearing at Takathswaane in 1969, and by 1971 moved a number of Takathswaane families to a new settlement at Bere. From the start of the scheme, Bere had its own borehole, well away from the main Ghanzi–Lobatse road. Various companies put up funds, and white volunteers from South Africa, Austria, and West Germany arrived to help in the construction of permanent buildings. At Heinz's instigation, !Xõ families from Okwa were invited to join the scheme too. The only requirement was that they each owned at least one cow. At that point, with two bands of different geographical origin, Bere was declared a 'closed' settlement.

From early on in the project, a shop and a school were built. Each was a success in some sense, but each also marked the onset of unanticipated difficulties. The shop was run by Heinz's !Xõ wife, N/amkwa, who, because of her status and her financial skills, soon found herself in a difficult position in the community. The school became the preserve of a young New Zealander, Liz Wily, who proved to be an excellent teacher. Yet her ideas were at odds with Heinz's. Heinz had explicitly set up Bere on capitalist principles, while Wily appeared to espouse the principles of Maoist China. Their well-known quarrel resulted in Wily leaving the scheme and being appointed Botswana's first Bushman Development Officer, later Basarwa Development Officer (see also Chapter 13).

Today, Bere is run by the Botswana government. The school is a success with the children, as it has always been, though it is fair to say that the !Xo are neither successful capitalists nor Maoists. The greatest problem with the

Bere scheme has always been the reluctance on the part of the !Xõ residents to invest the time required to keep herds of animals. The small scale of livestock ownership also militated against subsistence by herding. Heinz was right that the Bushman economics is predicated on individualism as much as on collectivism, but individual ownership of very small herds (often one beast per family) does not permit sufficient sales of livestock for the accumulation of capital. Development planners have learned from the successes and failings of Bere, and Bushmen in other parts of the Kalahari are today taking to livestock rearing, beekeeping, and horticulture as a result (cf. Wily 1982a).

Relationship terminologies of the !Xõ and Eastern ≠ Hoã
The !Xõ terminology
All !Xõ classify each other as either 'joking' or 'avoidance' relatives. Joking relatives are free and intimate in their dealings with each other, while avoidance relatives maintain a greater emotional and physical distance. The !Xõ relationship terminology is presented in Figure 4.2. Joking terms include ≠e, //am, same-sex ⊙xa and ≠xan, and ŋ/ŋ. Avoidance terms include all the others. The distinction between ⊙xa and ≠xan is made on the basis of seniority and not simply age. When applied to parallel cousins, these terms distinguish the relative ages of ego's and alter's parents, rather than the relative ages of ego and alter themselves. Only joking partners, specifically those termed ≠e, are marriageable.

The terminology is interesting because of its application of the rules of joking relationship categorization. It is the only known system for which Silberbauer's 'principle of congruent triangles' (1972: 311; 1981: 144–6) holds true for all kin types except opposite-sex siblings (Heinz 1966: Fig. 30). In other words, when tracing links either through the generations or through spouses, a joking partner's joking partner is always a joking partner, a joking partner's avoidance partner is always an avoidance partner, an avoidance partner's joking partner is always an avoidance partner, and an avoidance partner's avoidance partner is always an avoidance partner. Thus, unusually, cross-cousins (the children of joking partners) are classified as 'avoidance'. In a number of other Bushman societies (e.g., the G/wi, Silberbauer's example), the rule holds true for all kin more distant than first cousins, but not for first cousins themselves.

Only four rules are needed to generate the system: (1) same-sex sibling equivalence, (2) opposite-sex sibling non-equivalence, (3) spouse equivalence, and (4) adjacent generation non-equivalence. These rules may be applied in any order, and it is because of this fact that cross-cousins are avoidance partners. In fact, they are termed as 'children' – more accurately,

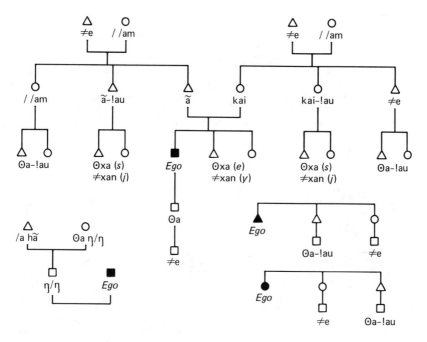

Figure 4.2 !Xõ kinship terminology: basic structure
Terms for female ego (bottom right) are not recorded ethnographically, but are here inferred from the internal logic of the system.

'classificatory children', ⊙ *a !au.* ⊙ *a* means 'child', and the suffix -*!au* means 'step', 'extended', or 'classificatory'.

The Eastern ≠ Hoã terminology

When Jeffrey Gruber (1973) recorded the Eastern ≠ Hoã terminology, he apparently had no idea of its significance in comparative perspective. From the lack of sociological detail, he seems equally unconcerned with the meaning of the terminology for the ≠ Hoã, except in a narrow linguistic sense. Yet from Gruber's point of view, both the terminology itself and his own very unusual analysis of it, in a journal devoted solely to transformational generative grammar, reveal his concerns as very different from ours. For him, this terminology illustrates fundamental properties of language. For me, on the other hand, it illustrates a novel twist to the underlying structure of Khoisan kinship specifically. Here, I will simply present the terminology structure and make a few observations in relation to the !Xõ terminology. A fuller comparative analysis must wait until Chapter 15, where the essentials of both Gruber's transformational generative analysis and my reinterpretation of his data are presented.

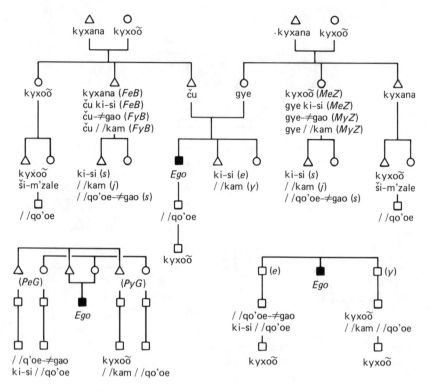

Figure 4.3 The Eastern ≠Hoã terminology

Figure 4.3 represents my own genealogical model of the terminology. This is quite different from Gruber's presentation, but it preserves the data and illustrates them in a form comparable to that which I use for relationship terminologies generally. This should make comparisons with other terminologies, including the !Xõ one, quite easy.

The ≠Hoã terminology distinguishes parallel and cross-relatives. In this aspect, it resembles both the !Xõ terminology and the Kgalagari terminology, from which the term *ši-m'zale* is derived. Cross-cousins may be called either *ši-m'zale* or *kyxoõ*. Cross-cousins do not share categorization with 'classificatory children', as among the !Xõ. Rather, the usage of the term *kyxoõ* follows the pattern of the !Xõ term ≠*e* ('grandparent, 'grandchild', etc.). The dual classification of parents' same-sex siblings as both 'grand-parents' (*kyxoõ* and *kyxana*) and 'parents' siblings' is a further caveat, and one which must await comparative treatment in the light of data on other Khoisan peoples, to be presented in Chapter 15. As among the !Xõ, relative seniority of siblings is distinguished terminologically. This is quite unusual for Bushmen, for whom real relative age is generally more important.

5

The Southern Bushmen

Introduction

The various Southern Bushman peoples are diverse and scattered. They have contributed substantially to the genetic and linguistic makeup of South Africa's majority population, but in recent centuries they have been very few in number. Their way of life was already subject to pressure of warfare and assimilation at the time their existence was first recorded, by transient explorers and government agents (e.g., Burrow 1801–4; Lichtenstein 1928–30 [1811–12]; and John Campbell 1815; 1822). Schapera (1930) and Stow (1905) presented distillations of the early travellers' reports, but the details of Southern Bushman life and customs are nevertheless sparse in comparison with what is known anthropologically of other Khoisan peoples.

What we do know of the Southern Bushmen comes partly from these accounts, but much more comes from in-depth studies of the few remnant populations which have been available to Western scholars. The tradition of 'scientific' ethnography among the Southern Bushmen began in the middle of the nineteenth century. Indeed, the classic 'Bushman' of European imagination was not a Bushman of the Kalahari. He was a Cape Bushman – or rather, a caricature of a Cape Bushman – physically paedomorphic and steatopygous, and intellectually mystical and animistic. These stereotypes are perpetuated today through the works of Sir Laurens van der Post (e.g., 1958; 1961; van der Post and Taylor 1984) and others. Although the ethnographic data behind such stereotypes was good for its time, it is nevertheless poor on most aspects of social organization and biased towards mythology and folklore. There is also a wealth of rock art in the Southern Bushman region. This has received much attention since the late nineteenth century and is today an area of extensive and theoretically interesting research. My treatment of Southern Bushman mythology and

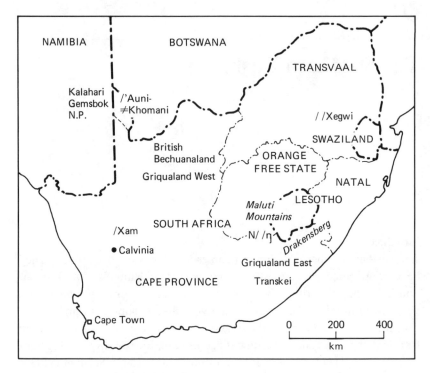

Figure 5.1 The Southern Bushmen

rock art here will only scratch the surface of available material. My main concerns will be in trying to understand the social and symbolic structures suggested by the material, and in the comparison of these to aspects of culture of other Khoisan groups.

Figure 5.1 shows the location of the major recorded Southern Bushman groups and some relevant geographical features. It should be noted that I use the term 'Southern Bushmen' here in a sense slightly different from that of Dorothea Bleek (e.g., 1956), in that I exclude the well-known !Xõ and their neighbours the Eastern ≠Hoã, dealt with in the last chapter.

The /Xam

There is no question that by the end of the nineteenth century the best known of all Bushman populations was the /Xam (Dorothea Bleek's linguistic group SI). According to Bleek and Lloyd (1911: 144), /Xam, more fully /Xam-ka-!kui, was a term used among Cape Bushmen to mean 'Bushman' in a general sense. Considering the linguistic diversity of Bushman peoples, I doubt if it could have had such general applicability, unless we grant that /*Xam-ka-*≠*kakken* really does mean 'any Bushman language' as opposed to 'the /Xam language'. Today /*Xam* invariably denotes the speakers of this particular language, whereas !*kui* (in the form '!Wi') denotes the language group to which they belong.

Until the middle of the nineteenth century, the /Xam inhabited several areas of the northwestern Cape Colony, south of British Bechuanaland. Their best known representatives lived near Calvinia, only 300 kilometres northeast of Cape Town. They were already dying out at the time ethnographers first encountered them. White farmers had ruthlessly hunted them down as early as the beginning of the eighteenth century, and the culture which remained was in the hands of a depleted and denigrated population.

Research on the /Xam

In 1870, Wilhelm Bleek, then curator of the library of the distinguished ex-governor of the Cape, Sir George Grey, was given the opportunity of his lifetime. Twenty-eight Bushman prisoners had been sent to work on the breakwater in Cape Town harbour. Bleek persuaded the new governor, Sir Philip Wodehouse, to allow him to take a few of the Bushmen to his home to work as his servants and serve as his informants. Bleek and his sister-in-law, Lucy Lloyd, spent the next few years recording thousands of pages of folklore, mythology, and other texts from a succession of /Xam informants. Six main informants – five men and one woman – provided Bleek and Lloyd with the bulk of their material. At least one of them, //Kabbo, was almost certainly a medicine man, and he provided splendid information on magic as well as myth. Most of the transcriptions were done by Lloyd, who continued the work after Bleek's untimely death in 1875 (see Spohr 1962; Thornton 1983). This material, which is housed in the J.W. Jagger Library of the University of Cape Town, is the source of the published /Xam narratives (Bleek and Lloyd 1911; D.F. Bleek 1923; 1931–6; 1936). More recently, it has provided the basis for a detailed interpretive and structural analysis of /Xam society and myth by the British linguist, Roger Hewitt (1986).

The following account is based mainly on Hewitt's reconstructions from the unpublished Bleek and Lloyd texts.

An outline of /Xam social organization

Eighteenth- and early nineteenth-century accounts of the /Xam indicate an isolated, semi-nomadic lifestyle, with bands of between eight and thirty people, and sometimes larger aggregations for hunting or defence against marauding whites (Hewitt 1986: 25–6). Families had both summer and winter residences and owned waterholes in each of one or more 'estates' (D.F. Bleek 1923: vii).

Each spring or pool in that dry country had its particular owner and was handed down from father to son with the regularity of an entailed estate. Many families owned more than one water, had summer and winter residences, to which they resorted as the growth of the field supplies or the movement of the game necessitated. (1923: vii)

The implication is that inheritance of these estates was patrilineal, though this is wisely disputed by Hewitt (1986: 26–7). Group membership was probably inherited bilaterally, and could also be acquired through marriage. I suspect that Bleek's phrase 'father to son' may simply be an androcentric way of saying 'generation to generation'. Like most Bushmen, the /Xam were monogamous, and their practice of postmarital residence was ambilocal. Not unexpectedly, there seem to have been no wedding ceremonies. More surprisingly though, there is no recorded evidence of bride service, or of marriage or childbirth gifts. It is very possible that these were not in existence among the /Xam, either because they had disappeared at the time of field research or because they had never existed. It is also possible that they were missed or dismissed as not being of much relevance by ethnographers. Indeed, Dorothea Bleek missed these things among the Nharo during her fieldwork with them in the early 1920s (see Chapter 8), and Winifred Hoernlé similarly failed to record details of marital exchange among the Nama two years later (see Chapter 10).

Happily, the /Xam naming rules are recorded. A baby would be named by its parents after the place where it was born or after either the child's physical features or those of one of its parents (Stow 1905: 103). Later, a child might informally receive, in addition to this 'little name', a new name, which would gradually replace the original one (Hewitt 1986: 29–30).

There is no evidence of male initiation rites, but ceremonies were held to mark a girl's first menses (Hewitt 1986: 279–86). The girl was secluded in a hut specially built for the purpose, and only her mother was permitted to attend her. The period of seclusion lasted until the following new moon, and the girl was allowed only limited supplies of water and only small amounts and certain kinds of food. The girl's family also reduced their food intake during this period. Even after her release from confinement, the girl was subject to strict food and even language taboos (she was not allowed to refer to some species of animal except by their 'respect names'). These taboos lasted until her marriage. Further taboos accompanied menstruating women in general, and there is extensive evidence in the Bleek and Lloyd texts to indicate both the extreme ritual danger of women in this condition, and an association between menstruation and !Khwa, the /Xam deity.

Gathering was generally done by women and children, and hunting by men, sometimes in the company of their sons. Old women had special responsibility for caring for children, especially when the children were ill. When necessary for survival of the group, old people might be left behind during transhumant migrations, while younger members of the community went ahead to find water or food. Sometimes the old died before the others could return with provisions (Hewitt 1986: 31).

In hunting, men used bows and arrows poisoned with animal and vegetable extracts, and various kinds of pitfalls and traps. Large game was cut up where it fell. Arrows were shot by their owners (apparently not lent, as with Kalahari Bushman groups), and though meat was shared, the owner of the killing arrow generally took the skin. /Xam men also fished the Orange and other rivers with funnel-shaped traps and bone-tipped harpoons (Hewitt 1986: 32–3). Though plant gathering was done by women, honey collecting was exclusively the province of men (1986: 34–5). Ownership of a beehive was indicated by a pile of stones placed nearby. Men also collected ants' chrysalids, which were a popular food.

Networks of trade (and possibly gift-giving) existed beetween /Xam groups and with Khoekhoe and Bantu-speaking populations, though data on these exchanges and on gift-giving are sparse (Hewitt 1986: 36). Meat was shared according to participation in the hunt and through complex rules (see, e.g., Bleek and Lloyd 1911: 274–85). Various accompanying food taboos are also recorded (see, e.g., Bleek and Lloyd 1911: 270–5; Hewitt 1986: 38).

Music and dancing were important aspects of /Xam social life. Some dances were performed by women, but most involved only the men. The women provided accompaniment by clapping and drumming. Dances were performed after a successful hunt, at the first thunder storm of the rainy season, and at the initiation of a group of medicine people (Hewitt 1986: 39–40). The general term for 'medicine person' was *!gi:xa* (plural, *!giten*), though various more specific terms designated specialists in rainmaking, diagnosis and treatment of illnesses, by means of induced snoring and trance, and by physical substances. Both men and women could be *!giten*. As among Kalahari Bushman groups, some medicine people had the ability to change themselves into other forms, such as birds or jackals. Some too had powers over particular species of game and could use these powers either malevolently or for good, e.g., in denying or aiding hunters in their quest for meat (D.F. Bleek 1931–6: *passim*; Hewitt 1986: 287–99).

/*Xam mythology*

As I have remarked, /Xam thought is known primarily through the studies of the Bleek family. These formed the nucleus of Schapera's (1930: 160–201) summary of Bushman religion and magic, though Schapera did not deal directly with mythology or folklore as a theme in itself. Yet, since the topic is of such great importance in the history of Khoisan studies, and indeed to the /Xam who told the myths to Bleek and Lloyd, a brief look at the context and content of some of the recorded narratives is in order.

The fundamental context of the tales as we have them is as written texts. Some are less than 100 words, but most are between 400 and 1,000 words in length. The problem in gauging the linguistic register of these tales is that, without a knowledge of the /Xam language, it is very difficult to tell the degree to which they represent real speech, and the degree to which their retelling by the Bleek family has cast them in an English idiom different from the intended one. The Bleek translations tend to be very literal. What they indicate is that /Xam folklore, like the folklore of other Bushman groups, had a matter-of-fact character about it. The choice of word and phrase often seems to me to reflect primarily the childlike image of the Bushmen in the eyes of Dorothea Bleek (e.g., 1923: [ix]; 1928a: 42–3). In some cases, tales have been shortened 'by leaving out wearisome repetition' (D.F. Bleek 1923: [v]). Whether this is an ideal method of translation or not, repetition is a stylistic device even in ordinary speech among many Khoisan peoples. Through their folklore, the /Xam expressed their thoughts about the nature of the universe. The fact that they did it in plain language, with tales that often seem to have more in common with Aesop's Fables than the high mythology of the ancient Greeks, is no reason to suppose that the tales do not express a deeper meaning than that which appears on the surface. To me, they often seem to express meaning at more than one level simultaneously.

/Xam narratives tend not to be set in an ancient or other-wordly time. They are set in the recent past, in places not much different from the world of the storytellers themselves. They tell of encounters between humans and animals, between humans of different ethnic groups, and between mythological animals. A secular concern with encounters between !Xõ foragers and Korana marauders is apparent in some (e.g., D.F. Bleek 1929b: 309), but most of the tales do have a more 'mythological' basis.

In arranging the chapters of *Bushman folklore* (Bleek and Lloyd 1911), Lucy Lloyd divided the narratives into two categories: 'Mythology, Fables, Legends, and Poetry', and 'History (Natural and Personal)'. The first category includes chapters on 'The Mantis', 'Sun and Moon', 'Stars',

'Other Myths', 'Animal Fables', 'Legends', and 'Poetry'. The latter includes 'Animals and their Habits . . .', 'Personal History', and 'Customs and
Superstitions'. Hewitt (1986) largely follows this pattern. I prefer Mathias
Guenther's (1989: 36–8) simpler typology: 'Creation', 'Primal Time', and
'The Trickster', but with the proviso that 'primal time' be taken as simply
non-present-oriented time. These three categories clearly reflect the most
common themes of the tales, though specific tales may lie in more than one
of the three. Trickster stories are of special interest throughout the Khoisan
region for the ease with which they can be manipulated. Tricksters are
found both in narratives of 'primal time', notably /Kaggen the Mantis, and
in tales of recent times, where Bushmen themselves may act as tricksters.
The classic 'fairy tale' motif, though present in Khoekhoe and Damara
collections (e.g., S. Schmidt 1980), is absent from the Bushman repertoire.
Nevertheless, isolated elements of this motif (magical flight, quests, etc.) are
found within specific Bushman tales (cf. Guenther 1989: 38).

What is most striking about all this is the uniformity of Bushman
folklore. Guenther's typology is presented in a book of folktales from both
the /Xam and the Nharo. In his typology, Guenther (1989: 31, 34) hints at
the 'dual creation', an idea common to a greater or lesser extent in all
Khoisan belief systems. After the first creation, the original animals and
humans were undifferentiated by species and lacking in their defining
attributes (in the case of animals) or customs (in the case of humans). In
myths of this type, the characters represented by animal species names can
just as well be taken as human. The second creation entailed a transformation, whereby animals and humans acquired their salient characteristics.

One key myth of the second creation, shared by /Xam, Nharo, Khoekhoe, and Damara, is the story of the Moon and Hare, or the origin of death.
Wilhelm Bleek (1875: 9–10) regarded this as a 'Hottentot myth' borrowed
by the /Xam and other Bushmen. Sigrid Schmidt (1980: 242–3) has
encountered over forty variants among various Khoisan groups, and it now
seems virtually pan-Khoisan in its distribution. The /Xam version presented in *Bushman folklore* (Bleek and Lloyd 1911: 56–65) begins with a
prayer to the Moon – an unusual twist. In the myth proper, the Hare's
mother is found, apparently dead, but really only sleeping. The Hare cries,
and the Moon becomes annoyed at this and slaps him, splitting the Hare's
lip. Later, it is revealed that the Hare represents humankind. If the Hare
had accepted the Moon's insistence that his mother was only sleeping,
humanity would resemble the Moon in having perpetual life. Since the Hare
contradicted the Moon, he, and humanity, have acquired death. The rarer
myth that follows this one in Bleek and Lloyd's collection, 'The Moon is

Not to be Looked at When Game has been Shot' (1911: 66–9), is one I also encountered among the Nharo. The permutations of Moon and Hare myths, as well as taboos concerning the moon, are varied, but the basic structure as presented above is very widespread throughout Khoisan southern Africa. Indeed, the Western notion of 'the man in the moon' has its counterpart in Khoisan belief as 'the hare in the moon'.

/Kaggen

To the /Xam, the deity is represented by /Kaggen, the Mantis. /Kaggen is variously responsible for the creation of the Moon and the animals, and for the maintenance of human sociality. Unlike the Moon, he is not prayed to. He is a trickster figure, but one with the power to bring the dead back to life and to change himself and other animals into different forms (see Bleek and Lloyd 1911: 1–37). There are other deities too, notably !Khwa, the Rain (also associated with the Eland and with the preservation of menstrual taboos), and //Khwai-hem, the All-Devourer. The latter is a monster who eats everything in sight. His daughter the Porcupine was adopted by /Kaggen to save her from this fate. Her son the Ichneumon, in turn, acts as /Kaggen's adviser and sidekick.

The exploits of these beings can be read in any number of collections. What is of greater theoretical and comparative interest here is the nature of /Kaggen himself. It is puzzling that so few Western writers admit in Bushmen the ability they would ascribe to the theologians of the European Dark Ages – the ability to express divine mystery in ambiguous words. Since 1966, at least five writers have questioned the idea that the /Xam believed that the High God and the praying mantis were one and the same thing, saying that the Bleek family merely confused the /Xam word for 'God' with that for the insect. As David Lewis-Williams (1980: 20) suggests, this homonymous fallacy gets us nowhere in understanding the complexities of /Xam belief. Yet, whereas Lewis-Williams says, somewhat mystically, '/Kaggen neither is nor is not a praying mantis', I prefer a more obvious but also non-homonymous interpretation.

In my view, /*kaggen* is *both* the word for 'mantis' and the name of the /Xam God. The /Xam God takes the form of a praying mantis, and his name may designate either a mantis, in secular terms, or God, depending on context. The polythetic nature of the term is not unlike that of *n!adiba* in Nharo, which means both 'sky' and 'God'. In the /Xam case, further ambiguity may lie in the fact that the Mantis is an oracle (the point emphasized by Lewis-Williams). To a /Xam, the praying mantis may be *the* Oracle. To borrow a Christian idiom, the Oracle and Mantis are of 'one substance'. The homonymic interpretations of Schmidt (1973), Gusinde (1966), and others cited by Lewis-Williams are highly implausible. There is no phonological evidence one way or the other, but the semantic equivalence of the /Xam Mantis and the /Xam God is, by my reading of the Bleek family texts, virtually undeniable.

The //Xegwi

The //Xegwi (Bleek's SIII) of the eastern Transvaal are one of the least known of the Khoisan peoples. The major source on this group is a short monograph by E.F. Potgieter (1955). This includes a thirty-one-page description of //Xegwi culture by Potgieter, a twenty-nine-page sketch grammar of their language by D. Ziervogel, various plates, and a genealogy of all //Xegwi of 'pure descent' alive in the Lake Chrissie area in 1955, as well as their spouses and immediate ancestors. Only sixty-six living individuals, several of them non-//Xegwi (mainly Swazi), are included in Potgieter's genealogical table.

The term Potgieter uses for the //Xegwi is Batwa, a word found in several Bantu languages to mean simply 'Bushman' (Zulu *acaThwa*, Sotho *Baroa* or *Barwa*, Tswana *Masarwa* or *Basarwa*, etc.). The local Swazi call them *amaNkqeshe*, *amaNgqwigwi*, or simply *amaBusmana* (Potgieter 1955: 2). It is said that earlier //Xegwi spoke both their own language and Southern Sotho. From hints in his text, it seems likely that the //Xegwi communicate amongst themselves in the Swazi language and that Potgieter too used this language as the medium of his fieldwork.

A fair portion of Potgieter's account is anecdotal in the extreme: 'Mr Edward van Zyl maintains that he was present when his father detained a Batwa man, shortly after 1880 on the farm Goedhoop 131 . . .' (Potgieter 1955: 5). Nevertheless, this short monograph contains among the most concise *Notes and queries*-style summaries of exotic customs to be found in any Bushman ethnography. It is honest and, almost surprisingly, to the point. As a study in acculturation, it also tells us something about the impact of black and white civilizations on the red peoples who inhabited South Africa.

Potgieter's (1955: 8–9) description of the settlement patterns and family life of the //Xegwi is rather vague. In former times, //Xegwi lived in grass and mat shelters, in caves, and on reed platforms on lakes and pans in the aquatic locale. Monogamy was the general rule, and parents and small children would occupy a single hut, while post-pubescent boys and girls would live in separate shelters. In some cases, single families lived in isolation. On the white-owned farms of Potgieter's time, similar arrangements prevailed. In some cases, parents and married sons occupied adjacent huts, while married men often cared for their aged parents and widowed or divorced sisters. Huts were either clustered together or arranged in rows, and some stood in close proximity to the kraals of Swazi farm employees. Not surprisingly, trade between the Swazi and the //Xegwi pre-dates European contact (Potgieter 1955: 25–6), and seems to have involved the exchange of ostrich feathers (from the //Xegwi), for grain and metal tools.

The life cycle

At the time of Potgieter's fieldwork, there were no small children in the community, but he recorded statements from his informants about the practice of medicinal rites to aid in childhood development (Potgieter 1955: 9–10). The head of the newborn child was smeared with medicines in order to make the soft parts of the skull close up. The infant and its mother were then secluded from men for a few days. After this, the women would take the child to a place where lightning had struck and cut its skin just above the navel, so that blood dropped on the spot. The child was brought home and given an enema, so that 'the bird of the heaven' (i.e., the lightning) would be driven out. This was regarded as necessary for the proper healing of the navel. At the age of six or seven, the child would have its ears pierced in order to ensure that it 'would obey its parents' (1955: 10).

The //Xegwi practised both male and female rites of transition. There are hints of male and female 'age groups' (Swazi or Zulu *izintanga*) being formed in association with such rites (Potgieter 1955: 16–17), though the mechanism for their recruitment is difficult to explain since the rites are individual and not collective affairs. The male rite took place at the time of a boy's first nocturnal emission. He would wash in the nearest water and inform his father of the occurrence. His father would then prepare a hot, medicinal liquid. In the presence of all the adult males of the community, the boy would dip his fingers in the liquid and lick them. This was said to protect him 'against dangerous results from contact with females' (Potgieter 1955: 10). The female rite took place at a girl's first menstrual period. She too would wash and inform her mother. The girl would then be covered in a kaross and squat in her mother's hut, while her mother's younger sister or another woman would beat a drum. At dusk, women and girls would dance, clap, and sing a menstruation song (1955: 11). Marriage was permitted at any time after these rites had taken place.

Marriages could be contracted with anyone except siblings and parents' siblings. Statements were also made to Potgieter (1955: 11) indicating that marriages should be outside the Swazi family name or lineage (*isibongo*), although such marriages did occur at the time of his fieldwork. Residence is reportedly always virilocal; a young married couple would live in a newly constructed hut near the hut of the man's father. Although in recent times livestock was used, traditional bridewealth consisted of a blesbok ram trapped in a game pit, or a bird, specifically a stork, goose, or korhaan. The game was trapped at full moon and had to be delivered to the home of the girl's parents while the moon was still round (Potgieter 1955: 11). The reasons for this peculiar custom are obscure, but associations between the full moon, fertility, and good fortune generally, are part of the wider Khoisan cosmology.

Intriguingly, //Xegwi are said to have buried their dead facing west in former times, and north in recent times (Potgieter 1955: 4, 17). This earlier custom is widespread among Kalahari Bushman peoples and may reflect a pan-Bushman notion of the rising of the spirit with the setting of the sun, while the latter custom is found among the !Kung (see, e.g., Heinz 1986: 34–5; Roos 1931). In some cases the dead were buried in their huts, which were afterwards burnt or abandoned. Abandonment of such huts and campsites is the custom among some Kalahari Bushman groups today, and the dead and death are tabooed among Bushman peoples generally (cf. Fourie 1928: 95). Among the //Xegwi, burial customs in the 1950s otherwise mimicked those of the Swazi (Potgieter 1955: 17), but at the full moon after the month of burial a feast was held, with purification rituals involving washing of the relatives, as well as singing, instrumental music, and dancing. This event was a happy occasion and seems to have celebrated a release from the solemnity which accompanied the funeral proper and its month of mourning (1955: 17–18).

//Xegwi religion

The religion of the //Xegwi was monotheistic or possibly ditheistic. Potgieter describes /A'an, the supreme being, as 'creator of heaven and earth and the giver of many good things'. In former times it was believed that the spirits of the dead would reside with this being in the heavens, and in Potgieter's time the term /a'an was in use among Christian //Xegwi for their God. There was also a notion of /a'an 'e la tleni (/A'an the small), a lesser being who assists the creator god (Potgieter 1955: 29). The moon (klolo) too was credited with supernatural intervention as provider of food, though it is doubtful whether Potgieter's (1955: 29) claim of 'a former more systematic worshipping of the moon' can be sustained (see also Chapter 14).

Other Southern Bushmen

Of the many Southern Bushman groups which have roamed the interior of South Africa, very few survived into the present century. Those which did survive did so only as remnant populations, and these are now virtually absorbed into the other population groups. In this section, I want to examine the data on the intermingled /'Auni (Bleek's SIV) and ≠Khomani (Bleek's SIIa) groups, often called simply the /'Auni-Khomani, and the 'Mountain Bushmen', at least some of whom warrant the name 'People of the Eland', or N//ŋ. The latter are known primarily through archaeological evidence of their rock art and through archaeological investigations into their subsistence base and settlement patterns. Related archaeological studies of Western Cape groups will be touched on in Chapter 9.

The /'Auni- ≠ Khomani

The /'Auni- ≠ Khomani were the subject of intensive investigations by a number of scholars in the early part of the twentieth century, and especially in the 1930s. The journal *Bantu Studies* devoted two issues, numbers 10(4) and 11(3), to these investigations. The key papers were those by the anatomist, Raymond Dart (1937a; 1937b). While the second is of less relevance here, the first of his papers is important as the major description of a /'Auni- ≠ Khomani settlement.

The settlement studied consisted of a population of 77, living in 11 huts. Most were of the ≠Khomani 'tribe', but the linguistically related /'Auni with whom they had intermarried were fully integrated into the community. The members of the community were otherwise closely related, though unfortunately Dart's concern with the biological notion of 'inbreeding' overshadowed his discussion of kinship, in the social anthropological sense (1937a: 165). Nevertheless, Dart refers to the people as having a 'patriarchal hospitality', by which newly married couples lived with the girl's father's family. Unmarried men lived with their male 'cousins' and their wives, while widowed men lived with their deceased wives' sisters and their husbands. Children, after infancy, seem to have been 'customarily' taken in by their grandparents.

Children were named after their relatives (1937a: 170–1). Some children bore the names of their parents, and others their grandparents, but naming after an 'uncle', 'aunt', 'great-uncle', 'great-aunt', etc., was preferred. I have been unable to find any particular pattern in Dart's genealogies. Moreover, his suggestion that the Bushman names he recorded are the same as or similar to those of the !Kung and therefore 'of great antiquity' (1937a: 171) cannot be sustained.

Many of the papers included in the *Bantu Studies* collection are now seriously outdated, but others are deserving of interest, even today. Musicologist Percival Kirby's (1936b) fine study of /'Auni and ≠Khomani musical practice and form remains one of the most detailed such studies carried out on any Khoisan people. This is complemented by an interesting, but less reliable paper on ≠Khomani games, play, and dances, by the linguist C.M. Doke (1936). The music performed is characterized by a recognition of partials in the harmonic series of stringed instruments, and an ability to use these to construct comparable pentatonic and other modes in singing. /'Auni and ≠Khomani music was also characterized by simple phrasing, a preference for triple time (or duple time triply subdivided), part hand-clapping as an accompaniment to singing, and harsh tone production in vocal performance. All these features are typical of Khoisan music in general, which has since become the subject of a number of little-known studies (see, e.g., Kirby 1936a; England 1968; Marshall 1976: 363–81; Westphal 1978; Rycroft 1978; Brearley 1984; 1988).

The dances were more unusual. Doke (1936: 469) describes a highly stylized 'baboon dance', consisting of grooming and leap-frogging, in imitation of the behaviour of baboons, and 'obvious sexual movements' by a male performer in respect of female dancers. This seems to have no serious ritual implications, and therefore differs greatly from medicine or eland dances recorded among other Bushman groups. He also describes a 'wedding dance' (1936: 470) re-enacted for his benefit shortly after the wedding of a middle-aged couple, but this again was mundane in its content. The groom's party danced the groom towards a dance ring between his hut and his bride's, while the bride's party did the same for her. The two parties met in the middle and were danced, several times, towards the groom's hut, where they were finally welcomed by the women of that group. The 'induction dance' (1936: 470–1) is the most intriguing, as, according to Doke, it was held in order to incorporate new members into the community. Yet it is not quite clear from the description whether this was a regular occurrence or simply the acting out of the arrival of a newcomer in dance step. I suspect the latter; the ritual element one might expect in such performances is lacking, and to my knowledge the dance has no counterpart elsewhere among Bushman groups. In contrast, Dorothea Bleek (1937a: 257–8) records a /'Auni text on female initiation which is much more typical of Bushman ritual. This includes seclusion of the initiate for two days during her first menstruation, attendance of the girl by her grandmother, dancing by men (the 'eland bull' is not mentioned), and finally, the tattooing of the girl by her grandmother.

H.P. Steyn visited the /'Auni-≠Khomani area in 1982 and 1983 and found a remnant population still hunting and gathering there (Steyn 1984). Some still identified themselves as ≠Khomani, though all members of the community then spoke Nama. His description of hunting practices indicates sparse resources but probably a loose notion of territory. In the past, Steyn's informants claimed, they lived in small, scattered groups in the summer and aggregated on the Nosob River in the summer. They lived extensively on tsama melons and hunted mainly gemsbok (their favoured quarry) and smaller, non-migratory game.

The 'Mountain Bushmen'

The 'Mountain Bushmen' and related groups, of Lesotho, Natal, Griqualand East, and the Transkei, were well known to travellers and administrators of the late nineteenth century. Yet at that time they were dying out, and their way of life seems to have been dominated by raiding neighbouring peoples for livestock. Over the past thirty years, there has been considerable archaeological research in these areas, both mountainous (where populations survived to a later date) and more low-lying (see, e.g., H.J. Deacon 1976; Parkington 1984b). Several archaeologists have applied regional-comparative approaches. These utilize ethnographic analogy, often coupled with historical materialism, for example, to suggest changes in gender relations over time (Mazel 1989) or the distribution of systems of gift-giving analogous to *hxaro* among the !Kung (Wadley 1989). In one especially interesting study, Wadley (1987: 17–33) analyses archaeological data and micro-environmental (mainly botanical) evidence for seasonality in the Magaliesberg of the southern Transvaal. She concludes that, of five logical possibilities, transhumance from grassland occupation in the spring and summer to bushveld occupation in the autumn and winter is the most likely pattern of settlement (cf. Barnard 1979a; Chapter 12).

Other modern accounts of 'Mountain Bushmen' vary in style and quality, from reminiscences on rock art and early writers (e.g., Ellenberger 1953; How 1962) to detailed archival studies (e.g., Wright 1971). Patricia Vinnicombe's *People of the eland* (1976) combines the best of both styles. The Bushmen of the Maluti Mountains and the Drakensberg may indeed have been 'people of the eland', for they knew themselves by this term. The word for 'Bushman' in Southern Bushman dialects, sometimes wrongly glossed 'home people' ('home' being a homonym of 'eland'), has been recorded as //ŋ, //ŋ !kwa, //ŋ !kwi, with plurals //ŋ !ke and //ŋ degan (D.F. Bleek 1929a: [v], 25; 1956: [vii], 611; cf. Schapera 1930: 32). By analogy with /Xam (from /Xam-ka-!kui), I propose to call them simply the N//ŋ – with the click pronounced. For those not used to clicks, an acceptable anglicized pronunciation might be 'eng' or [eŋ].

We know that the N//ŋ also focused their 'deepest aesthetic feelings' and their 'highest moral and intellectual speculations' on this animal (Vinnicombe 1976: 353), but not enough can be salvaged from the sources to give much description of their social organization. There are no southern African rock painters alive today. The last, a man called Mapote, probably died in the Maluti Mountains in the 1930s. Nevertheless, a brief look at their rock art and the studies which have been made of it can be revealing. In particular, it is important to consider the theoretical approaches in rock art studies, as well as the content of the rock art itself.

Rock artists and rock art studies in southern Africa
Vinnicombe (1986: 275–9) has identified at least two distinct phases in the history of southern African rock art studies. She labels these the 'antiquarian' phase and the 'detached quantification' phase. A third, unnamed phase may be implicit in her argument, but in any case is obvious as a growing tendency in rock art studies. We might call this one the 'symbolic' phase.

The first, long phase characterizes rock art studies as practised until the late 1960s, and the approach still has its few adherents. Research, as often as not carried out by gifted amateurs rather than professionals, focused on techniques, classification, and chronology. Results were generally framed in Eurocentric terms. Prominent writers in this tradition include George William Stow, a geologist by profession, who as early as the 1860s was using rock art as a clue to understanding population movements (see Stow 1905: 22–40 and map; Stow and Bleek 1930; cf. Chapter 2); and Alex Willcox, a quantity surveyor, who in the 1950s pioneered the use of colour photography to copy rock paintings (see, e.g., Willcox 1956; 1963). In the spirit of this approach, Willcox (1963: 16–17) warned his contemporaries to resist the temptation 'to go into the details of Bushman culture further than is relevant to the interpretation of the rock art and beyond what is necessary to indicate the character of these people'. Although naive in some respects, the antiquarian approach has at least alerted scholars that the rock art of the subcontinent is diverse in style and content. Early work, notably Stow's, distinguished the 'sculptors' or 'engravers', who lived generally in the central parts of the subcontinent, from the 'painters', who lived mainly in the east and south. Stow held that the former group long ago migrated into the subcontinent by an easterly route, while the latter took a westerly route. It is now known that petroglyphs (both true engravings and 'peckings') are widely distributed along the supposed route of Stow's 'painters' in Namibia. Later work has focused on rock art zones and even 'schools' of painting, and attempts have also been made to associate such schools to specific lithic industries and ethnic groups (see, e.g., Rudner and Rudner 1978). For example, the widely distributed 'Formal' school of rock painting (static and stylized human figures, with naturalistic, sometimes polychrome, animal figures) has been linked with the 'Wilton' group of Late Stone Age lithic industries. The 'Cape Schematic' school (crude, finger-drawn, monochrome figures and geometric designs) is said to be associated with the more recent 'Smithfield B' industry. The 'Dynamic' school, whose numerous paintings of eland and other animals grace the caves of the Drakensberg, is equated more specifically to those Bushmen whose remnant populations were known to white travellers in the late nineteenth century.

By the 1970s, archaeological practice had changed direction. New 'scientific' approaches paved the way for intensive quantitative techniques. Vinnicombe (1967) and Tim Maggs (1967) provided important early examples, but the detached quantification phase is best exemplified in parts of later, book-length works by Vinnicombe (1976), Harald Pager (1971), and David Lewis-Williams (1981a). All these works are based on the definition and quantification of broad figurative styles or the generic activities of the figures painted (dancing, hunting, etc.). More recent work in this tradition, notably Tilman Lenssen-Erz's (1989) analysis of Pager's Brandberg material, places equal emphasis on the detail of specific features of the anatomy, posture, and background scenery relating to a figure. He sees these as 'syntactical' elements which, when combined in a painting, make up action analogous to that which may be described in speech. This radical form of objectification is, to some extent, a reaction against the radical symbolic approach which emerged out of quantitative studies. There is a considerable overlap between the earlier 'soft' quantification approach and the symbolic approach. Lenssen-Erz, explicitly in the spirit of Harald Pager, is simply taking a step back to the early days of the quantification phase, then moving ahead by a different route from the others.

In the 1970s and 1980s, as I have implied, interest grew in looking behind mere quantification towards a more symbolic approach. This symbolic approach draws on both social theory (French structuralism, semiotics, etc.) and ethnographic analogy. Vinnicombe's work is very much in this stream (e.g., 1972; 1976). In *People of the eland* (1976), she uses a combination of documentary sources and rock paintings to try to reconstruct the culture of the N//ŋ. At first glance, this is not unlike Stow's idea 'of collecting material enough to compile a history of the manners and customs of the Bushmen, as depicted by themselves' (Stow in a letter to T.R. Jones [1870], quoted in Lewis-Williams 1981a: 15). The difference is that Stow regarded rock paintings as expressions of the everyday life of hunting peoples, or at least real events in their lives, whereas to Vinnicombe they are the expression of the religious symbolism of an eland cult.

The most vociferous proponent of the new approach is David Lewis-Williams, who has published extensively on the subject (see, e.g., 1981a; 1981b; 1982; 1983a; 1983b; 1984; 1986; Lewis-Williams and Loubser 1986). His version of the approach is predicated on two controversial notions: that Bushman rock art is primarily concerned with depiction of trance perform-ance, and that there exists a cultural unity between extinct rock-painting populations, the /Xam story-tellers, and the !Kung he has visited in northwestern Botswana. One inherent danger in work of this kind is in implying that Bushman thought is monolithic. Yet, while others have exaggerated the uniformity of Bushman symbolism (e.g., McCall 1970), Lewis-Williams and his associates, in their more recent work, have been careful not to fall into this trap. One, Thomas Dowson (1988), has explicitly tried to tackle the problem of individuality in the rock art, and its relation to the assumed wider cognitive system from which the work of idiosyncratic artists has emerged. Further warnings about the symbolic approach have recently been issued, though only implicitly, by Mathias Guenther (1990). He remarks, quite correctly, that Bushman mythology and rock art seem to occupy two quite separate domains of expression, and that ritual is linked to art rather than to mythology. Most recent work on the comparison between these domains has indeed concentrated on ritual and art, whereas previous generations of writers have sought in vain the connections between /Xam myth and prehistoric painting.

The relationship between the quantitative and the symbolic approaches is interesting. It was the awareness of the quantity of eland and trance performances depicted in the paintings which first alerted scholars to the importance of symbolism. Yet the trend is now away from quantification and towards ethnographic analogy. As Lewis-Williams notes, in two of his recent papers:

Many surveys of Southern African rock art have depended almost entirely on amassing numerous measurements for each depiction, but numerical listings of features which may or may not be significant tell us nothing about the meaning of the art. (Lewis-Williams 1983c: 249)

When we started to take all this [comparative] information seriously we discovered somewhat unexpectedly that, far from being simply narrative or decorative, the rock art was associated with the activities of San medicine people, or shamans, who [among the !Kung] today number about half the men and a third of the women in any camp. (Lewis-Williams 1988: 2)

The linguistic associations of people, eland, and the dance are also intriguing. One might reflect on the fact that, while the N//ŋ inhabited the mountainous areas of eastern South Africa and Lesotho, this same term, //nĩŋ or //nĩ has been recorded as 'eland' as far north as Angola, while //ŋ means 'dance' in /Nu//en or western !Xõ (D.F. Bleek 1956: 619; Bleek's orthography). The Zu/'hoãsi have three different word's for 'eland', n! (the most literal term), *dabba* (a woman's respect term for the animal, especially in reference to female initiation), and *tcheni* (Lewis-Williams 1981a: 14, 46; Lewis-Williams' orthography). *Tcheni*, the men's respect word, is more literally translated as 'dance'.

Southern Bushman relationship terminologies
The /Xam terminology
Hewitt (1986: 28) remarks, 'Such kinship terms as were collected [among the /Xam] are incomplete and based mainly on vocabulary sources rather than on any actual observations of kinship as a system of obligations and affiliation within the group'. Although this is true, there are sufficient data for us to ascertain the basic structure of the terminology; and a few isolated details of kinship rules and behaviour have been recorded.

The terminology structure is illustrated in Figure 5.2. Essentially, this terminology is descriptive, in that there are specific, compound terms for most genealogical relationships. I have included in the figure all the salient terms recorded in Bleek's (1924: 57–62) discussion of /Xam kinship usage. Some additional terms or usages are reported in her *Dictionary* (1956: *passim*), but as often as not these appear to be either erroneous, variant, or peculiar plural forms recorded by earlier researchers.

Apart from its descriptive character, the terminology does include a few generic terms, such as //kã and //kaxai, and !kõiŋ and !koite. The classificatory terms //kã, for males, and //kaxai, for females, were employed in address for siblings, parallel cousins, and cross-cousins alike. There was no prohibition on cousin marriage of any kind, and no specific class of kin were terminologically defined as potential spouses. The terms !kõiŋ (grandfather) and !koite (grandmother) could be used as address for any senior person, regardless of kin relationship. Likewise, all older women were called *xoakengu* (mothers). A peculiar distinction was made between 'real'

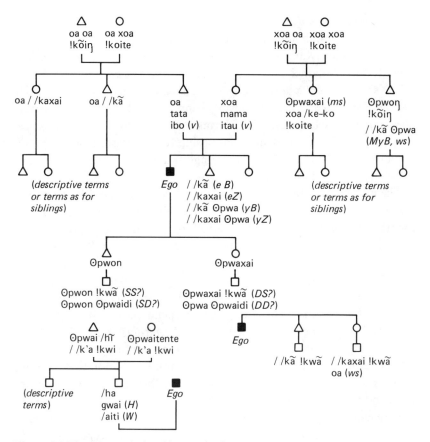

Figure 5.2 The /Xam relationship terminology

(*kwokwan*) grandparents (a man's mother's parents or a woman's father's parents) and 'lent' (/*xwobe*) grandparents (a man's father's parents or a woman's mother's parents). This distinction may reflect Khoe influence, for implicit in it is a shadow of the cross-descent name line system of the Nama and Korana (cf. Chapters 9 and 10). Indeed, the word /*xwobe* is related to words for 'lend' or 'borrow' in many Khoe dialects (e.g., Nama /*khuwi*, G/wi /*obe*, Nharo /*hoba*).

    D.F. Bleek (1924: 59) remarks that there was a close relationship between a woman's siblings, of both sexes, and her children, and Hewitt (1986: 28) deduces from circumstantial evidence a joking relationship between grandparents and grandchildren. Beyond this, little can be said about /Xam kinship rules or behaviour.

The //Xegwi terminology

The //Xegwi terminology (from Potgieter 1955: 13–16) is similar in its structure. As in /Xam, terms tend to be descriptive: e.g., *aa aa* means literally 'father's father' and is distinguished from *xwa aa*, 'mother's father' (cf. /Xam *oa oa* and *xoa oa*). However, Zulu and Swazi terms were also in use in Potgieter's time, presumably employed when informants were speaking in these languages. Such terms tend to follow the more classificatory usage of Southern Bantu relationship terminologies (e.g., *mkhulu* is employed for 'grandfather'). One English-derived Bantu term occurs, *u-aanti* (meaning 'father's sister').

The indigenous //Xegwi terms are given below, together with borrowed forms which occur within indigenous usage. The primary terms are: *aa* (F), *xwa* (M), ⊙*wari* (C), ⊙*ung* (S), ⊙*wake* (D), //*a* (B), //*ake* (Z), *klo ki e* (H), and *n/a* (W). Secondary terms include: //*a 'e la* //*kxee* (older B), //*a 'e la tleni* (younger B [*tleni* is Bantu-derived]), *xwa* //*ake* (MZ), *xwa* //*ake 'e la* //*kxee* (MZe), *xwa* //*ake 'e la tleni* (MZy [*tleni*, again, is Bantu-derived]), and *xwa* //*ake klo* (MZH). Terms for MZC and FBC are not given by Potgieter, but those for FBC and MBC are: //*oni* (FBC [a unique term]), //*a* (FBS [the same as for B]), //*ake* (FBD [the same as for Z]), *mzala ki e* (MBC [*mzala* is a Bantu term]), *malume* ⊙*wari* (MBC [*malume* is a Bantu term]), //*ii* (MBS [a unique term]), and /*ale* [MBD [a unique term]). In addition to descriptive terms, the term *nkhloli* is used in //Xegwi for 'brother-in-law', 'sister-in-law', and for their spouses.

Potgieter (1955: 16) says virtually nothing about the sociological implications of the terminology or about kinship behaviour, except that fathers, fathers' brothers and a woman's elder brothers are treated with respect. A man's mother-in-law is the object of great respect, but more freedom is permitted in relations with his father-in-law. Potgieter hints that the rules of conduct 'are often no longer observed', and cites the fact that older relatives were in his time frequently addressed by name rather than relationship term.

My suspicion is that the descriptive form of the //Xegwi terminology, and of Southern Bushman terminologies generally, reflects a loose principle of social classification and a related lack of constraint in matters such as marriage prescriptions, joking/avoidance distinctions, or universal kin classification. In this respect, the Bushmen of South Africa seem to have differed markedly from those of the Kalahari. In spite of Potgieter's claims, there is no evidence that these differences are a direct result of contact with Bantu-speakers or Europeans. The Bantu languages possess terminology structures which are formally equivalent in a number of respects to Central

Kalahari Bushman ones, and not to those of South African Bushmen. European languages with which Bushmen have come into contact are, broadly speaking, more comparable to Northern Kalahari Bushman languages.

The /'Auni terminology

To say anything at all about the /'Auni terminology is really scraping the ethnographic barrel. Nevertheless, a few words on the kinship terms given in Dorothea Bleek's (1937b) /'Auni vocabulary list may be worth while for comparative purposes.

Most of the terms recorded are those for primary kin. The terms for other relatives may be divided into three categories: those which imply descriptive usage, those which are more classificatory, and those which are apparently erroneous. Ignoring the last category, most are descriptive. For example, /ke/ke, given for 'grandfather', means literally 'father's father'. There are two distinctive classificatory terms in Bleek's list: /kãĩ, given as 'cousin, relative'; and txõ, given as 'brother-in-law, husband's brother'. The latter is interesting, as it resembles phonologically one of the most common Western Khoe Bushman terms, that for the joking category which includes cross-cousins and nephews and nieces, among others (see Chapter 8). Another, //amaro, is defined as 'niece, cousin's child', and it may also be a classificatory term. Other terms are obvious cognates to those of /Xam and even !Xõ, notably ⊙pwa for 'child', ⊙pa for 'son', and ⊙pwa:xe and ⊙pxwe for 'daughter'.

Finally, at the risk of scraping right through the barrel, I might add that Dorothea Bleek (1956: 308) once recorded a ≠Khomani term for (female) 'cousin', namely /ke:ki. This apparent generic term, however, is probably equivalent to the word variously transcribed as /keiki or /keikji in ≠Khomani and /ge:k in /'Auni, and meaning 'woman' or 'wife'. Why it is here recorded for 'cousin' is unknown.

6

The G/wi and G//ana of the central Kalahari

Introduction

The G/wi and G//ana, or Central Kalahari Bushmen, are among the most isolated of Khoisan peoples. They were unknown in Dorothea Bleek's time, but speak a language of her 'Central Bushman' type (e.g., Bleek 1942), related more to the languages of the herding peoples than to those of the Bushman groups described thus far. As suggested in Chapter 2, this relationship is very distant, and the G/wi and G//ana have probably lived in their traditional habitat for many centuries if not millennia.

Theirs is the Central Kalahari Game Reserve (C.K.G.R.), which lies in the eastern Ghanzi District of Botswana. In *The harmless people*, Elizabeth Marshall Thomas (1959) describes her family's encounters with the G/wi (whom she calls the 'Gikwe') in the 1950s. Since then, ethnographies by Silberbauer, on the G/wi of the C.K.G.R., Tanaka and Valiente Noailles, on mixed or undifferentiated G/wi and G//ana groups in the same area, and Cashdan, on eastern G//ana and related groups in Botswana's Central District (east of the Reserve) have made them famous. Cashdan's material will be treated mainly in Chapter 7, as eastern G//ana now form part of the complex of interacting ethnic groups in the Central District. Our concern in this chapter will be with the G/wi and with those G//ana who live in close association with them in the Reserve (see map, Figure 6.1).

The proper names for the G/wi and G//ana are *g/uikhoena* and *g//anak-hoena*, literally 'G/wi people' and 'G//ana people'. Their languages are called *g/uikz'uisa* and *g//ana-di-damsa*, or 'G/wi speech' and 'the G//ana tongue'. Although the forms 'G/wikhoe' and 'G//anakhoe' are in use, I prefer the shorter terms 'G/wi' and 'G//ana'. The latter are the terms favoured by most ethnographers and are by far the more common in both primary and seondary ethnographic literature. As far as I am aware, the

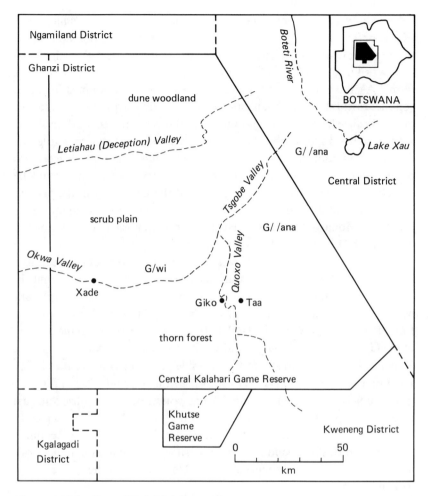

Figure 6.1 The Central Kalahari Game Reserve

term *g/wi* has no specific meaning other than in reference to the G/wi themselves, but *g//anakhoena* has been translated 'people of the well', in reference to isolated water resources in the southeastern C.K.G.R. (Cashdan 1977: 2).

Studies of the G/wi and G//ana
The G/wi came to prominence in the 1960s through the work of Ghanzi District Commissioner and Bushman Survey Officer, George B. Silberbauer. He served for six years in those posts, spending some three years of that period, beginning in 1958, among the G/wi of Xade pan (also known as

≠Xade or ≠Kade, from its G/wi pronunciation, and often anglicized as 'Kade' or [kadi]). This pan became the site of Silberbauer's borehole, in the south-central part of the Reserve. At least until the late 1970s, the Xade area was known colloquially among Ghanzi Bushmen as 'Silberbauer's farm'. As Bushman Survey Officer, Silberbauer was commissioned to conduct research on Bechuanaland's Bushmen in general, but for reasons of practicality he chose to concentrate on the G/wi and to work in short-term stretches. In retrospect, his decision was a wise one, for very little was then known about this people. His important *Bushman survey report* was published by the Bechuanaland government in 1965. Before his research he had studied anthropology and linguistics at the University of the Witwatersrand, and afterwards went on to teach anthropology and complete his Ph.D. at Monash University. He has since published one important monograph (1981) and other works on the G/wi.

Jiro Tanaka began his fieldwork in 1966. His book, which bears the Japanese title *Busshuman*, was published in 1971, and a revised English-language edition, translated as *The San*, appeared in 1980. Other relevant works in English include summaries of his early findings (1969; 1976), an English–G//ana–G/wi wordlist (1978a), a comparative study of the ecology of the G//ana and the Mbuti of Zaire (1978b), and a comparative study of Kalahari hunter-gatherers and the Rendille pastoralists of Kenya (1982). His Japanese publications cover much the same ground. Coming from a primatological background, Tanaka has concentrated on observational studies. Comparisons between Bushmen and other African hunter-gatherers, between Bushmen and other desert-dwellers (such as the Rendille), and between Bushmen and non-human primates are common in his work and in the work of his students at Kyoto University and the University of Tokyo.

In the 1970s and 1980s Carlos Valiente Noailles led a group of field-workers who studied various aspects of settlement, social organization, and religion. They made eleven expeditions to the Kalahari in this period, of which six (between 1977 and 1987) were to the C.K.G.R. The results are summarized, often directly from fieldnotes, in Valiente Noailles' *El circulo y el fuego* (1988). They offer the opportunity to update information given by Silberbauer and Tanaka, especially on population dynamics. Although Valiente Noailles refers to the people he studied as 'Kúa', in terms of the more usual classification of Bushman groups they are G/wi and G//ana rather than Kua proper (see Chapter 7).

Other ethnographers who have done studies of G/wi and G//ana social organization and subsistence activities include Tanaka's students

Kazuyoshi Sugawara (e.g., 1984; 1988a; 1988b) and Masakazu Osaki (e.g., 1984). The great strength of these more recent fieldworkers is their concentration on the minutiae of cultural detail, especially behavioural aspects, on topics in which research is still lacking on any Bushman group. My own contact with G/wi and G//ana has been largely in the Ghanzi farm area, where I had the opportunity to examine G/wi and G//ana kinship terminologies in the light of comparative data on the indigenous Nharo and Ts'aokhoe (see Chapters 8 and 17), and, to a lesser extent, in the Central District (see Chapter 7).

Habitat and settlement
The 'traditional' G/wi settlement pattern
The Central Kalahari Game Reserve was established in 1961, at Silber-bauer's instigation. It extends over some 52,600 square kilometers: an area somewhat larger than Belgium, The Netherlands, Denmark, or Switzerland. It includes three diverse environmental zones: in the north, a zone of sand dunes with many species of trees and shrubs and large herds of migratory game; in the central area, a zone of flat bushveld; and in the south, a more heavily wooded zone. Only the southern and central zones contain enough edible plants to support permanent occupation. The south and east, where there is mopane forest, are the best for human habitation, while the central area is excellent hunting territory. The short grass found near pans there affords the hunters the ability to stalk game under cover. Rainfall in the Reserve is lower than in !Kung country, but rather higher than in /'Auni-≠Khomani territory. It is nevertheless sparse and sporadic, varying from 170 to 700 millimetres per year. The average in the years 1961 to 1971 inclusive was measured at about 392 millimetres (Tanaka 1980: 21). Most rain falls in December, January, and February.

From data given by Silberbauer (1981: 192–3), it appears that in the early 1960s (at the end of a long period of drought) G/wi band territory sizes were about the same as !Kung ones, while their population was somewhat larger than among the !Kung. The six bands surveyed by Silberbauer ranged from some 457 to 1,036 square kilometres, with an average size of about 780 square kilometres. The populations recorded ranged from 21 to 85, with an average of 57 people per band and a population density of about one person per 14 square kilometres.

More interestingly, G/wi settlement differs from !Kung settlement in two important ways (Barnard 1986a: 45–6). In the first instance, the G/wi settlement cycle is, in a sense, the reverse of that of the !Kung. In the second, the G/wi aggregating and dispersing units are of a much smaller order. The

!Kung aggregate, several bands together, in the dry season and disperse as band-sized units in the wet season; whereas the G/wi disperse into family units in the dry season and aggregate as band-sized units in the wet season. During the dry season, each G/wi family unit moves to a different part of its band territory and its members obtain water from plants or from the bodies of animals hunted. This is necessary, since in G/wi country there is no surface water at this time of year. A !Kung-style aggregation would be impossible for the G/wi in the absence of a permanent water supply. During the wet season, each band aggregates and migrates around its territory in order to exploit seasonal food and water supplies, including patches of water-bearing tsama or mokate melons (see Silberbauer 1972: 296–7; 1981: 246). These usually persist for some time after all surface water has dried up. Clearly the differences between !Kung and G/wi settlement are not merely the result of ideology, nor the result of environmental determinants alone. They are the result of a complex interplay between ideology and micro-environmental factors (cf. Keenan 1977).

Silberbauer (e.g., 1981: 166–7; 1982: 28–9) draws attention to yet another unit of social organization, which he terms the 'cliques'. I prefer the designation 'family cluster', a unit of two or more families who build their huts near each other in a wet season camp. Valiente Noailles (1988: 140) records the phrase *itse ka //aesi* ('our family') for such a unit and contrasts it with *kika //aesi* ('my family'), the domestic unit (cf., e.g., Nharo //*ai-sa*, 'home'). Tanaka (1969; 1980: 127–35) also makes extensive reference to what he calls 'clusters of families'. He compares them to the core kin groups of a !Kung band. In contrast to Silberbauer, who views them as ephemeral, Tanaka stresses their enduring quality as units of kinship, and views them in terms of their developmental cycle. One might reasonably ask whether in fact Silberbauer's 'cliques' and Tanaka's 'clusters' do refer to the same sort of unit at all. The fact is that groups cluster and disperse according to the movements of the band, and residential units have aspects of both kinship and political principles at their core (see 'Politics', below). The precise nature of family clusters as enduring groups seems to be difficult to establish, but as among the !Kung, they may represent groupings which form, dissolve, and reform, over great lengths of time.

G//ana settlement and migration in the eastern C.K.G.R.

The settlement pattern and territorial organization of the G//ana of the eastern Reserve is similar in a number of ways (see Cashdan 1977; 1980a; 1984a; 1984b). Groups disperse in the dry season and aggregate in the wet season. The difference is that the annual cycle for many individuals also includes travel to better-watered areas outside the Reserve. These trips involve interdependence of kin and affines; there is no system comparable to that of the !Kung, with mutual rights between gift-giving partners (see Cashdan 1984b: 326–7). Cashdan (1984a: 450–2) has documented long-term mobility between base camps for a period of more than 120 years. This indicates that the exact locations have changed through time, but that G//ana groups have inhabited the same general areas of the eastern Reserve throughout the last century.

Of equal importance is her documentation of overlapping territories (1984a: 452–3). The G//ana base camps Cashdan intensively studied, Molapo and Totwe, are the central locations of two large band territories. These territories overlap not because of a lack of boundary precision, but rather because individuals have specific rights within territories. There is a strong patrilineal bias in the inheritance of land rights among men, and through a tendency toward virilocal residence, women usually claim rights in the territory of their husbands (1984a: 449–50). In the preliminary report on his early research, Tanaka (1969: 14) also noted overlapping ranges, perhaps partly accounting for his later suggestion (1980: 121) of a 'vagueness of territoriality' related to the constant travel of individuals between camps. On the whole, I favour Cashdan's explanation as the most plausible, particularly in view of her intensive study of territoriality in the region.

A schematic representation of eastern C.K.G.R. G//ana settlement, based on descriptions and maps by Tanaka (1980: 78–81; 116–27) and Cashdan (1984a; 1984b) is shown in Figure 6.2.

Changes in subsistence and settlement patterns
Many changes have taken place in the Reserve since the time of Silberbauer's fieldwork (see Silberbauer 1982). With migration of several G//ana bands into the Reserve in the late 1960s, the settlement pattern became more flexible. Then with the severe drought of the late 1970s and early 1980s, many Central Kalahari Bushman bands migrated, at least seasonally, to areas east, south, and west of the Reserve. Large numbers of these people moved out to take advantage of borehole water and food distributed through Botswana's drought relief programme (see also Chapter 7).

At the time of Silberbauer's fieldwork, the population of the C.K.G.R. was probably around 2,000 (see Silberbauer 1965: 14). In Tanaka's time it was about 1,000. At least half of these people made Xade part of their territorial range, though the permanent population of the Xade areas remained at around 200 throughout the late 1960s and early 1970s (Tanaka 1980: 25, 81). In 1976 the permanent population was reported to be about

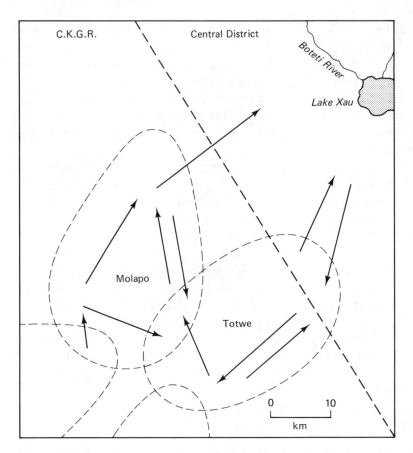

Figure 6.2 Schematic representation of G//ana migrations in the eastern Central Kalahari Game Reserve

1,200, of whom 57 per cent were Bushmen and 43 per cent were Kgalagari (Valiente Noailles 1988: 18–19; cf. Murray 1976). Cashdan's (1984a: 445) estimate of the G//ana population of the eastern part of the Reserve, around 800 in 1976 to 1977, is consistent with this figure. In 1978, as the drought worsened and inhabitants began to move out of the Reserve, the total population was said to be barely 600 (Valiente Noailles 1988: 19).

The Kgalagari are the oldest existing Bantu-speaking inhabitants of Botswana, having entered the southern part of the country probably centuries before European colonization. In the Reserve, each Kgalagari group has its own recognized territory (known as a *lefatshe*, plural *mafatshe*) and maintains patrilineal kin-group-based councils (singular *lekgota*, plural *makgota*). According to Valiente Noailles, the Kgalagari territories are regarded as 'traditional', and have long been used as their hunting areas (see Valiente Noailles 1988: 175–87; cf. Cashdan 1984a: 449–50; Cashdan and Chasko 1976). These groups, living mainly in the south and east of the Reserve, were largely ignored by the earlier ethnographers. Indeed, Silberbauer's study of Kgalagari–Bushman relations (Silberbauer and Kuper 1966) was carried out nearly 300 kilometres away, on the Namibian border. The relationship between the Bushmen and Bantu-speaking inhabitants of the Reserve has never been fully explained in the literature, but it is likely that there is some overlap between the categories 'G//ana' and 'Kgalagari'. The G//ana tend to speak both their own and the Kgalagari language; and it is common belief, both among the G//ana themselves and members of other ethnic groups, that the G//ana originated as a result of intermarriage or concubinage between Bushmen (presumably G/wi or their close relatives) and Kgalagari.

At the start of the drought of the late 1970s, there was only one functioning borehole in the Reserve. This was at the location known to the G/wi and G//ana as !Koi!kom, in the Xade area. It was sunk by Silberbauer in 1959. By the 1970s, it was becoming overcrowded with members of several bands who had no traditional history of living in that area, though through alliance networks other bands may have had rights to use Xade country in the past. Such alliances were formed on the basis of ties of intermarriage and reciprocal rights to exploit each other's territorial resources (Silberbauer 1965: 52; 1972: 302–4), but in the decades since Silberbauer's fieldwork such rights had become rather imbalanced. Silberbauer himself always removed the borehole pump when he left the Reserve, in order to prevent a population explosion and the spread of disease which he felt would probably follow (George Silberbauer, pers. comm.). Due partly to the great expense involved, his solution to the problem – the drilling of some fifteen boreholes in all parts of the Reserve (see Silberbauer 1965: 134–5, 136) – has never been effected.

Coupled with changes in territorial use have been changes in subsistence strategy. Around 1979, the people of Xade were being taught to grow crops by an agricultural assistant dispatched by the Remote Area Development office (Tanaka, Sugawara, and Osaki 1984: 9; Osaki 1984: 49). This had little immediate impact in this drought-stricken area. The borehole was inefficient, and the crops, mainly maize and beans, had to compete for both water and space with recently introduced goats and donkeys. More significant were the hunting activities of the residents. Osaki (1984: 52–6) reported an enormous amount of hunting on horse and donkey in the early 1980s. This included both individual, one-day hunts on horseback with an iron-tipped spear, and group expeditions of six or seven people on donkeys and horses, with the donkeys being used mainly for transport. The latter method generally takes about a week and, unlike the former, is pre-arranged. The trend started in the 1970s, when there were a few horses at Xade, but by the time of Osaki's fieldwork equestrian hunters had assumed virtual dominance over an enlarged Xade area in the southwestern part of the Reserve. In the five months from September 1982 to January 1983, 91 large animals (mainly gemsbok and eland) were killed by hunting from horseback, as compared with only three by bow and arrow, and one by dogs and spear. Osaki does not give details for all animals killed, and his category 'large animals' (and specifically, 'large artiodactyls') is somewhat ambiguous. Nevertheless, it is possible to make a rough comparison with the details recorded by Silberbauer (1965: 30; cf. 1972: 286; 1981: 205). In the same months of 'an average year' of the early 1960s, Silberbauer found that 13 large animals had been killed, out of an annual total of 60 such animals and a much higher take (in terms of meat content) of small game. The small game in Silberbauer's total included an annual total of 168 small antelope (springbok, duiker, and steenbok), 161 birds, 227 springhare, 295 rodents, 440 tortoises, etc. The result of the use of horses and donkeys has been a greatly expanded hunting area, specifically a diamond-shaped territory about 100 kilometres from north to south and some 60 kilometres east to west at its widest point. This is almost double the size of the area mapped by Tanaka (cf. Tanaka 1980: 17; Osaki 1984: 55). There has also been an increase in large game hunting and a decrease in small game hunting. It is doubtful whether there has been much increase in the amount of meat eaten. The consumption of meat in Silberbauer's time was higher than among the !Kung; and !Kung meat consumption, as some of the !Kung ethnographers like to point out, is higher than that of Texans.

Cashdan (1984b: 317–19) has noted the use of water storage facilities at three G//ana 'home base' locations in the eastern part of the Reserve. These home bases are made possible in the first place by seeding areas for the production of marotsi melons. These water-bearing fruits are similar to the better-known tsama melons, but much larger. In a good year, enough marotsi melons can be stored to keep an entire band supplied with water until August, the height of the dry season, with some left over for the few people who may wish to remain at home base until the spring rains. Some G//ana even add to their water-storing facility by the use of steel drums, while others prefer to follow the tradition of escaping to areas outside the Reserve where water is more plentiful.

All these changes are regarded by some observers as irreversible, but such a conclusion could be premature. The G/wi and G//ana have long taken temporary residence at farm boreholes and Tswana cattle posts, and band alliances do allow for the temporary changes in the residence of even entire bands, should this be necessary or desirable (cf. Silberbauer 1972: 296–7; 1981: 178–80). In 1987, Valiente Noailles (1988: 49–50) recorded the central locations of eight traditional Kgalagari and Bushman territories in the C.K.G.R., and noted five wells with potable water, as well as pans. Populations were varied, but none were high (1988: 78–9). Xade then had a population of 25 males and 27 females. Giko (a site rich in tsamas and other vegetable resources, some 80 kilometres east-southeast of Xade) had 17 males and 28 females. Taa (20 kilometres east again, and just one kilometre from a diamond prospecting camp) had eight males and four females. The populations of each settlement included both old and young people. The data were gathered in February and March, when G/wi and G//ana are traditionally aggregated in band units.

Like the !Kung, the G/wi and G//ana are under pressure to adapt to changing international priorities. A recent danger, now averted, was the threat posed by wildlife officials in Botswana to remove the inhabitants of the Reserve and resettle them in the Kweneng District, south of the C.K.G.R. and west of the Khutse Game Reserve. The irony is that in spite of their names, at least the former 'game reserve' was created as much for the Bushmen as for the animals it protects. After independence, understandably, the policy of keeping a reserve for one population group alone was overturned as being too much like the iniquitous pursuits of Botswana's southern neighbour (cf. Ramsay 1988). The compromise, effected in 1990, seems to be that inhabitants of the Reserve may stay as long as hunting is carried out by traditional means (see also Chapter 13).

It is ironic that a reserve set up specifically for Bushmen might have been denied to them because of the words 'game reserve' in its name (particularly since the impetus for the removal came from the European Community, which imports beef from Botswana). Game populations suffered greatly in the drought of the early 1960s, again in 1970, and in more recent times. Non-traditional hunting techniques were part of the problem, but they do not seem to have been the main concern of wildlife experts with an interest in preserving the habitat for animals. Lack of water in grazing areas and lack of grazing near water resources, along with fences preventing annual migrations across the desert, are probably more important factors in the declining population of ungulates (see Owens and Owens 1984: 294–303, 319–21). In 1982 diamond prospecting began in the C.K.G.R., and this too is a cause of some concern (see Valiente Noailles 1988: 104–9). A commission was set up in 1985 to consider the future of the Reserve, and matters are still under debate. According to Survival International, the population of the Reserve is now less than 1,000, and it would seem not unreasonable that a territory the size of many European countries should be able to support both such a number of its indigenous human inhabitants and the wildlife for which the fencing represents as great a threat as hunting.

Politics

We are fortunate to have an excellent overview of the G/wi political process (Silberbauer 1982), from which the present account is mainly drawn (see also Silberbauer 1981: 167–78; Tanaka 1980: 107–10; Valiente Noailles 1988: 138–9, 164–9). Silberbauer's paper on this subject was originally presented at the (First) International Conference on Hunting and Gathering Societies, held in Paris in 1978, and it remains the finest discussion of Bushman politics in the ethnographic record. It refers to an ethnographic present of the early 1960s.

The political process is centred on decision-making at the band level. To some extent, politics is a seasonal preoccupation, alternating with the dispersed, family-oriented lifestyle which characterizes G/wi social structure during the winter and early summer. With seasonal aggregation, family autonomy is replaced by the consensus politics of the band. The band was, and indeed still is, the primary territorial unit. It is united by common ties of kinship and a common identity. While close kinship to existing band members is regarded as the primary basis of claims to band membership, other ties bring in non-G/wi and even non-Bushmen as band members. In David Turner's (1978) terms, band membership is defined by both kinship confederational and locality incorporative principles (see Chapter 12).

Any adult or adolescent member of the band can be involved in decisions affecting the band as a whole. Discussions of band movements and disputes concerning individuals (e.g., marital disputes) seem to be the main subject matter of G/wi politics. The parties involved in disputes bring their cases either to the entire band or to those band members who wish to be involved. Arguments are made, and people make known their views, either explicitly, through discussion, or more tacitly, through gestures or facial expressions. Leadership emerges, but authoritarian decision-making is unheard of. Co-operation is highly valued, even where agreement cannot be reached.

The byword of Bushman politics in general and G/wi politics in particular is consensus. In Silberbauer's (1982: 31) words: 'Consensus is not unanimity of opinon or decision. In much the same way as egalitarian does not mean equality, concensus is not a synonym of democracy . . . As the etymology of the word suggests [consensus] is arrived at when people consent to judgement and decision.' Power lies not in the ability of individuals to force a consensus, but in their perceiving the mood of the band and compromising and creating opportunities to have their goals realized when the time is appropriate (1982: 34).

'Cliques' or family clusters are often formed in the normal process of band segmentation, but are perhaps best regarded as functions of aggregation. Silberbauer (1982: 28–9) uses this term to describe clusters of households who build their shelters close together in the autumn and winter camps and stand allied in activities and viewpoints. These 'subunits of agreement' are seemingly ephemeral. As camps are broken and re-formed monthly, the family clusters break up, and new ones are made.

G/wi and G//ana kinship

We know a great deal about G/wi kinship, thanks especially to Silberbauer's masterful writings on the subject (especially 1972: 304–21; 1981: 142–66). I shall draw primarily on these here, but partly also on my own knowledge of G/wi and G//ana groups in the Ghanzi ranches. Page references to Silberbauer's work are mainly to *Hunter and habitat* (1981), although the same material is found in several other publications (1961; 1963; 1965: 62–93; see also Tanaka 1980: 93–135 *passim*; Valiente Noailles 1988: 140–1).

Kinship nomenclature

The G/wi and G//ana have a system of kinship nomenclature which is typical of those of the Khoe-speaking peoples. It differs substantially from that of the !Kung and the /Xam, but has some structural elements in common with that of the !Xõ, notably the distinction between cross and parallel cousins. The G/wi and G//ana, however, do not regard cross-cousins as fictive 'children'. Rather, in common with other Khoe-speaking people, they classify cross-cousins as potential spouses.

The terminology structure is simple. The G/wi and G//ana terms I recorded are illustrated in Figures 6.3 and 6.4. Apart from the specific terms illustrated in the figures, there is a category 'avoidance relative', *!ao*, and the term for 'joking relative' is simply this term in the negative, *!ao-kjima* (G/wi) or *!ao-tama* (G//ana). All relatives, and indeed everyone with whom a G/wi or G//ana has long-term contact, may be classified by one or the other of these two terms (with appropriate number-gender suffixes to indicate sex), and by an ordinary 'kinship term' indicating the more specific category.

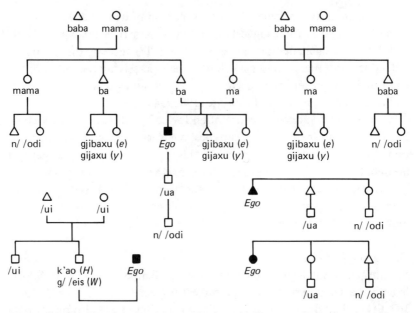

Figure 6.3 The G/wi relationship terminology (suffixes *-ma* [masc.] and *-sa* [fem.] omitted)

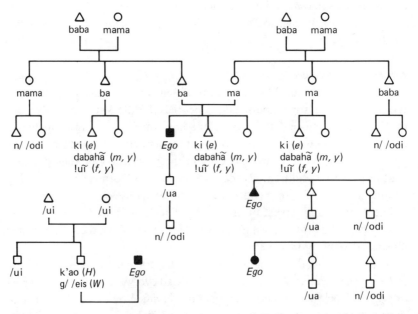

Figure 6.4 The G//ana relationship terminology (suffixes *-ma* [masc.] and *-sa* [fem.] omitted)

These are modified by number-gender suffixes (*-ma*, masc. sg.; *-sa*, fem. sg.; etc.). Normally, the prefix *ki* ('my') is also found before the terms. The details of categorization are discussed, in comparative perspective, in Chapters 15 and 16.

G/wi and G//ana know their kin relationship to a wide variety of individuals, and the system operates as a 'universal' one (Barnard 1978a), with everyone being classified by everyone else with some relationship term. They lack any system comparable to the !Kung one for bestowing names on children. G/wi and G//ana babies are named with ordinary G/wi or G//ana words which designate events occurring around the time of birth. For this reason, of course, outsiders are not given G/wi or G//ana names, but keep their own. Tanaka, for example, is known among them by his surname, while Silberbauer is called by a phonetic approximation of his first name. In the absence of the naming system, individuals trace their relationship to others through their genealogies. If that fails, then friendship links can be used as fictive 'joking' links. This is what happens in the case of anthropologists, among others.

Marriage and children

G/wi marriage is a flexible arrangement. At the time of Silberbauer's fieldwork, most G/wi married very young, between seven and nine for a girl, with boys being some seven years older (Silberbauer 1981: 149–50). Of 73 marriages analysed by Silberbauer, all were between individuals who claimed to be of the *n//odi-ku* relationship, although only eight were between cross-cousins. *N//odi-ku* may be translated literally as 'GRAND-RELATIVES to each other', with the capital letters defining this as a category of the underlying structure of Khoe kinship (Barnard 1980a; 1987; see Chapters 8, 15 and 16). This is the 'correct' marriageable category. The choice of a spouse within this category is largely up to the individual, although this is subject to parental approval. Courting is generally initiated by the boy, while the girl's parents keep an eye on him with a view to testing his suitability as an in-law.

There is no marriage ceremony as such (but see 'Initiation ceremonies', below). Rather, G/wi 'marriage' is marked by the use of the relationship terms *kxaoma* or *k'aoma* (husband) and *g//eisa* (wife). Silberbauer does not record exactly when affinal terms for parents and children-in-law come into use, but does refer to changes in behaviour in anticipation of 'joking' partners becoming 'avoidance' (Silberbauer 1981: 151). This happens, for example, if a man marries his real MBD. Before the marriage, his MB belongs to the JOKING category *babama* (senior GRANDRELATIVE); and after marriage, as a father-in-law, he belongs to the AVOIDANCE category /*uima* (AVOIDANCE IN-LAW).

Marriage is initially uxorilocal, and bride service is practised (Silberbauer 1981: 152–4). This phase may last as long as ten years. It may be terminated at the wife's initiation, or after the couple have their first child. The uxorilocal phase of marriage traditionally served as much for the education of the girl by her mother as it did for the service of the boy to his in-laws. Any G/wi marriage may be dissolved by either husband or the wife, and the children of a divorced couple are said to remain, ideally, with their father (1981: 156–8). This may reflect a 'patrilineal bias' like the one Cashdan has noted among the G//ana. Polygyny is known among both G/wi and G//ana (cf. Tanaka 1989), and members of these groups were virtually the only polygamous men I encountered in my own surveys of Bushman households in the Ghanzi ranches.

The socialization of children is a group affair. Both parents, as well as the child's siblings, grandparents, and others, take part (Silberbauer 1981: 162– 5). From the time a child learns to talk, its teaching is split between two groups: the domestic unit, and a play group consisting of children up to six or, sometimes, ten years of age. Opposite-sex siblings maintain formal 'avoidance' relationships, at least from puberty, but remain close. In a group of siblings, strong bonds are forged between those contiguous in relative age (e.g., the first and second born, the second and third, and the third and fourth) as well as between those of the same sex (1981: 165–6).

Initiation ceremonies

In common with Khoe-speaking peoples generally and in contrast to non-Khoe-speaking Bushmen, the G/wi give emphasis to female over male rites of initiation.

Female initiation marks a girl's transition to womanhood (see Silberbauer 1963; 1965: 83–9; 1981: 151–2). At the time of the girl's first menstrual period, she is secluded in a specially constructed hut and attended by her mother. At the first sign of menarche, the girl's husband will have moved out of their marital hut to the bachelors' area, beside a tree in the centre of the camp. He will not hunt until the ceremony is over. Nor will he leave his weapons behind, for fear that his wife, in her 'impure' condition, might touch them. When his wife's menstrual flow is over, he returns for the ritual tattooing, which is performed by women of the band. Normally, the boy is the only male present. Both the girl and her husband have their heads shaved and receive medicinal tattoos in matching patterns of short lines. They are then 'inoculated' with blood from each other's wounds.

The ritual tattooing, according to Silberbauer (1981: 151), serves to stress the mutual dependence of husband and wife. He views G/wi female initiation as part of marriage. On the other hand, the contrast with other Khoe-speaking peoples is interesting. Among these other peoples, a girl's first marriage follows rather than precedes initiation. Among the Nharo at least, it is a girl's grandmother (or other joking relative) rather than her mother who is responsible for the girl's well-being during the ceremony. The G/wi custom of tattooing both parties is unusual and may represent a concatenation of female and male ceremonies kept separate among other Khoisan peoples. Among other peoples, men alone receive tattoos at initiation, and women's tattooing is confined to beauty treatment and to incisions for the application of medicines for specific ailments.

The equivalent boy's ceremony is rather low-key (see Silberbauer 1965: 89). Although Silberbauer describes it as a 'puberty ceremony', it is probably best regarded simply as hunting magic rather than a puberty ceremony proper. Boys between twelve and fifteen are taken into the bush by older men. The men tattoo the boys by making small incisions on the arms and scapulae and rubbing burnt roots into them. The boys then dance, and each boy proves his hunting skills by tracking an animal and staying out overnight alone in the bush. This ceremony has nothing to do with marriage, which may be contracted either before or afterwards. Ritual tattooing also follows a G/wi's first trance performance (Silberbauer 1965: 99), itself an 'initiation' into the world which comprises G/wi spirituality.

G/wi religion

As far as can be ascertained from the ethnographic record, the religious beliefs of the G/wi and G//ana are very similar. Little is recorded of specifically G//ana religion, so I shall draw mainly on Silberbauer's G/wi material here.

Gods and spirits

The Creator God is N!adima (Silberbauer 1981: 51–4). He set the heavenly bodies on their paths and made the seasons, with their cycles of wet and dry periods. He can withhold or give rain to particular areas, but is generally remote. Though he knows the wishes of his creatures and may grant them assistance, he is not in communication with them. G/wi have no notion of prayer or worship, in the general sense of most Western or Eastern religions. They do have a mythological tradition which is related to that of the /Xam and other groups (cf. Valiente Noailles 1988: 216–21), a fact which perhaps lends some plausibility to Laurens van der Post's (1961: 139–233) famous re-telling of /Xam myths in a central Kalahari setting.

The term *n!adima* in its secular sense means 'sky', and the sky is the dwelling place of N!adima and his wife N!adisa. Humans and other mammals are their 'children'. Little is known about life in the heavens, but it is said that N!adima and his family do not kill to eat, but live from the plentiful water and vegetable resources of his dwelling place (Silberbauer 1981: 52). Unlike other Khoisan peoples, the G/wi of the central desert have no notion of 'heaven' as the dwelling place of human spirits after death.

G/wi believe too in a Great G//amama or G//auama who 'lives everywhere and nowhere' and travels among the stars and in whirlwinds across the land (Silberbauer 1981: 54). To the G/wi, G//amama is evil and casts invisible arrows down upon women. The poison of these evil arrows passes from the women to men and children of the bands. During autumn band aggregations, G/wi perform medicine dances to combat G//amama's evil. There are differences of opinion about the relationship between N!adima and G//amama. Some of Silberbauer's informants claimed that they are each aspects of the same supernatural being. However, most seem to regard them as opposing forces of good and evil. N!adima is good and largely inactive in the world, and G//amama is evil and relatively active, notably as an agent of death. There is little in the way of mythology to explain anything of their nature or of their activities. (Silberbauer 1981: 54–6; Valiente Noailles 1988: 221–9.)

The dead become spirits, g/amadzi or g//amahare (Silberbauer 1981: 112–14; Valiente Noailles 1988: 230–4). These spirits live not in the sky, but in an underworld otherwise described only by a series of circumlocutions. Spirits are liberated from their bodies when their corpses decay, and burial sites are avoided because of the danger that they bring, especially to those whom these spirits knew and loved in life. There is no communication between the living and the dead, and all spirits of the dead are said to be malevolent by nature.

The medicine dance

The medicine dance of the G/wi is much like that of any Bushman group, but there are peculiar twists. Eibl-Eibesfeldt has filmed both !Xõ and G/wi medicine dances, and his descriptions of these and of the beliefs behind them are interesting (cf. Eibl-Eibesfeldt 1974b; 1980). Among both !Xõ and G/wi, the dance is thought to protect people against evil. In the !Xõ dance, the male performers touch the women as they dance past them, and in so doing they draw evil from these women into their hands. This occurs before the first performer goes into trance. The G/wi dance starts in much the same way, with women forming a cluster around the fire and men dancing around them, but the belief behind the curing is more precise. The G/wi believe that the invisible arrows shot by G//amama or by human enemies have lodged in women and children, who offer less resistance than men. These arrows must be extracted by a medicine man in trance, who sucks them out with his mouth and pulls them with his hands, before he ritually throws them away.

Silberbauer's (1965: 97–101; 1981: 175–7) description is very much the same, but he reports that a medicine man will draw out the evil, rather than the 'arrows' themselves, before trance. The pain of this evil lodges in his chest. One of his supporters will then 'shoot' him with a snap of the fingers. After being 'shot', he collapses in unconsciousness, and then awakes in trance. Unlike some Bushman peoples who have numerous, named dances, the G/wi have only two: the Iron Dance and the Gemsbok Dance. Their form is identical. The difference between them is that 'iron' (/anu) or 'gemsbok' (/xoma) medicine, respectively, is said to be the source of the trance performer's power. A medicine man will hold each neophyte by the hips when teaching him to dance, and 'shoot' the young man with one or the other kind of medicine.

Valiente Noailles' (1988: 235–43) description, presented through his own questions and answers to informants, emphasizes, first, the more specifically curative aspects of the dance, and secondly, the unity of G//amama and the g//amahare. Tanaka (1980: 113–15) suggests that the evil spirits themselves lodge in women, to be absorbed into the bodies of men before trance. These accounts are not as contradictory as perhaps they may seem. They do emphasize slightly different aspects of the medicine dance, but in fact they differ less than explanations I recorded among the Nharo, where trance itself can be explained in various ways (Barnard 1979b: 72, 75). The differences are consistent with the idea of a flexible or fluid belief system, which among the Khoisan in general operates at an individual as well as a societal level (cf. Chapter 14).

Ecology and worldview

Finally, it may be revealing to look more explicitly at Silberbauer's theoretical orientation, in contrast to those of other writers. Whereas Tanaka and his students take the Western–Japanese scientific worldview for granted, Silberbauer does not. On a scale from absolutist to relativistic approaches, Tanaka would fall towards the absolutist end; Lee and Heinz, and to a lesser extent Marshall and Wilmsen, also towards that end of the scale, while Silberbauer alone gives pride of place to the interplay between the G/wi and scientific worldviews.

Silberbauer (1981: 258–304) describes the G/wi in terms of a 'socioecosystem' which includes both the scientific worldview and the G/wi one. The G/wi ideas of nature are not seen as incidental to the outsider's scientific description, nor as identical to it. Western science is discussed for its explanatory value, both where it agrees and where it conflicts with the G/wi worldview. The picture Silberbauer paints is a dialectical one, neither positivistic nor relativistic in any narrow sense, but enriched by the interplay between the two forms of thought as these are played out in his discussions (cf. Blurton Jones and Konner 1976; Guenther 1988).

7

The Eastern and Northern Khoe Bushmen

Introduction

The boundary between the Central, and the Northern and Eastern, Khoe Bushmen is not a precise one, on either linguistic or cultural grounds. Yet like the colonial administrator, the comparative ethnographer must draw his heuristic lines on the map, and the boundaries of the Central Kalahari Game Reserve are as logical as any (see Figure 7.1). Indeed, this comparison is not as facetious as it may seem, for to a great extent these lines today do demarcate the degree of Tswana influence on the populations concerned. While the Bushmen of the C.K.G.R. have seen relatively little of the world until recent times, those of the eastern Ngamiland, the Central District, and the Kweneng (cf. Figure 6.1) have all been involved in extensive trade networks, and many have lived in close association with non-Khoisan groups for well over a century.

The culturally defined 'Eastern Khoe bushmen' comprise a number of groups scattered from the Kweneng District of Botswana in the south to Ngamiland in the north. Most live in the Central District, often as clients of Bantu-speaking people, including Tswana, Kgalagari, Kalanga (a group closely related to the Shona of Zimbabwe), and, more rarely, Herero. The cultural (as opposed to linguistic) distinction between Central and Eastern Khoe Bushmen is a nebulous one, and I include among 'Eastern' groups some G//ana who have migrated from the C.K.G.R. to take up a more settled life among the cattle herders to the south and east. The salient characteristics of 'Eastern' groups, in this sense, are their association with herding peoples and their high degree of cultural and spatial hybridization. Yet in a linguistic sense, the Eastern Khoe Bushmen proper (excluding the G//ana and some groups in the south) may be defined by dialect, specifically by the usage of *tshua* or *shua* for 'person', rather than *khoe*. (Compare, for example, the ethnic group names G//ana*khoe* and Hie*tshware*.)

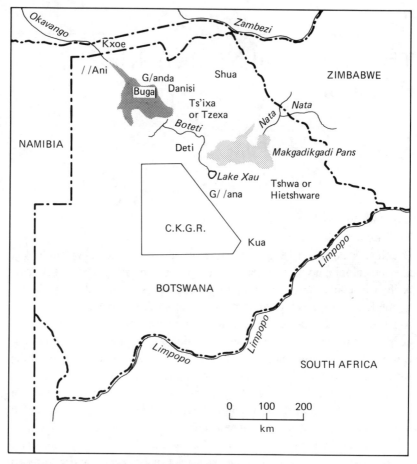

Figure 7.1 Major Eastern and Northern Khoe Bushman linguistic groups and their territories (the names //Ani, Buga, G/anda, Deti, and G//ana generally take the suffix *-khoe*, 'person')

The Northern Khoe Bushmen are those of the Okavango and surrounding regions. They live by fishing, as well as by hunting and gathering. In contrast to the Eastern groups, many Northern Khoe Bushmen live in areas which are tsetse-infested and consequently where livestock rearing is impractical. Linguistically, they resemble the Central Khoe Bushmen, whereas the Eastern groups (apart from those who use *khoe* for 'person') are more distinct.

Other, similar, groups – neither Eastern nor Northern in any strict sense – include pockets of Khoe-speakers in Angola, and perhaps the Kwadi. Such groups are similar explicitly in their long association with Bantu-speakers and their common possession of such otherwise non-Khoisan customs as totemism and circumcision. The Kwadi will be treated briefly at the end of this chapter, though I do not without considerable qualification refer to them as 'Khoe Bushmen'.

Research on Eastern and Northern Khoe Bushmen

The classic ethnography of the Eastern Khoe bushmen is that of Samuel Shaw Dornan, Irish Presbyterian missionary, surveyor, and amateur anthropologist and linguist. Born in 1871, Dornan went to South Africa during the (Second) Anglo-Boer War and stayed on to work in Basutoland, Rhodesia, Bechuanaland, and South Africa. Of particular relevance to us is his work on the 'Tati Bushmen' (Hietshware) and other groups of eastern Bechuanaland, conducted mainly during his fifteen-year residence in Rhodesia. The results of this research include an important paper on the Hietshware language (Dornan 1917) and a large portion of his mistitled monograph, *Pygmies and Bushmen of the Kalahari* (Dornan 1925: 65–207).

After Dornan, concern was expressed about the practical question of relations between the Bantu-speaking majority and the Bushman minority. Three enquiries, by government (Tagart 1933), church (London Missionary Society 1935), and the League of Nations (Joyce 1938), were soon established. The L.M.S. report is of the greatest historical interest, consisting primarily of a 16-page reply to the Tagart report by Chief Tshekedi of the Bamangwato, plus questions and answers to him and other Bamangwato leaders by members of the Society. The Tagart report had been critical of Bamangwato treatment of Bushmen living among them, and Tshekedi tried to dispel the notion that they had been enslaved or otherwise mistreated. Tshekedi explained, among other things, the contractual hunting arrangements by which Bushmen and Bamangwato hunted together, on what was considered Bamangwato land. Bushmen served as trackers and received meat from the hunt, while the Bamangwato received the skins. Tshekedi also explained at some length the Tswana custom of *mafisa*, by which a cattle owner leaves his stock with another person to look after, and gives in return the right to take milk, the right to eat the meat of any which die naturally, and the right to use them in ploughing. The system is still prevalent, and today includes the right to keep calves produced during the arrangement.

In 1937, a further 'influential committee' was set up, consisting of representatives from the administrations of the Bechuanaland Protectorate, South West Africa, and the Union of South Africa, as well as academics, 'to ensure the preservation of the Bushmen as a separate race'

(Schapera 1939: 68). After meeting several times in Cape Town, the committee resolved that an expedition was unnecessary. Sufficient written material was already in existence, they decided, if only someone could read it and summarize it in convenient form. Isaac Schapera was duly appointed, and his 'memorandum' to the committee was published in the journal *Race Relations* (Schapera 1939). Schapera's general assessment of the relations between Bushmen and other peoples (1939: 78–9) was that contact between blacks and Bushmen, particularly in the Eastern Khoe Bushman area, had 'on the whole been less disastrous' than contact between whites and Bushmen elsewhere.

Following Schapera, there was a time gap of several decades before research again began in earnest. Fieldworkers preferred to concentrate on the more isolated, seemingly exotic, groups of western Botswana and nothern Namibia. George Silberbauer was appointed Bushman Survey Officer in 1958, twenty-one years after the idea of a 'Bushman survey' had been floated, but he too chose to work with an 'exotic' group. Only in the late 1970s was extensive work again carried out among Eastern Khoe Bushmen. Elizabeth Cashdan (e.g., 1979; 1985; 1986a; 1986b; 1987; Cashdan and Chasko 1977), Robert K. Hitchcock (e.g., 1978a; 1980; 1987; 1988a; Hitchcock and Ebert 1984), and others ultimately did extensive survey work in this area. Cashdan has concentrated on trade, settlement patterns, and migration, including the migration of G//ana from the Central Kalahari Game Reserve (e.g., Cashdan 1984a; 1984b), while Hitchcock, who spent many years as a government officer in Botswana, has concentrated on economics, demography, and development issues. Both have paid close attention to relations between groups and to comparisons between Bushmen and non-Bushmen of the area. To the south, Helga Vierich (e.g., 1977; 1982a; 1982b), Pnina Motzafi (e.g., 1986) and Susan Kent (e.g., 1988; 1989a; 1989b; Kent and Vierich 1989) have analysed the social and economic life of mixed Tswana, Kgalagari, and Bushman settlements in a similar vein.

The Kalahari fringe area has also drawn the attention of archaeologists, notably James R. Denbow and Edwin Wilmsen (e.g., Denbow and Wilmsen 1983; Denbow 1984; see also Denbow and Campbell 1986), and linguists, including Anthony Traill (1986) and Rainer Vossen (1988a; 1988b; 1990). Their work will be touched on only briefly here, but of great significance is the fact that it does point to contacts between hunter-gatherer and herder-cultivator populations extending back over several centuries. This means that the Bushmen of the Kalahari fringe may be regarded not so much as recently acculturated, but as possessing a hybrid culture of some antiquity. Recent archaeological findings suggest a long period of contact and a clear association with the Great Zimbabwe culture, beginning over 1,000 years ago (E.N. Wilmsen, pers. comm.).

The Northern Khoe Bushmen were noted by Siegfried Passarge (1905), who passed through the Okavango area in the late 1890s, and Franz Seiner (1909; 1910), who was there in 1905–6. More recently, Clive Cowley (1968) has ventured through the area. H.J. Heinz has done extensive work on the Northern Khoe Bushmen, but his valuable overviews, compiled in the late 1960s and early 1970s (Heinz n.d.), are as yet unpublished. The Northern Khoe Bushmen have been the major focus of interest of the linguist, Oswin Köhler. He worked in South West Africa, as it then was, in the 1950s, and between the years 1959 and 1989 made nineteen expeditions to the Kxoe of southeastern Angola, northern Botswana, and the Caprivi Strip. The huge task of publishing his ethnography entirely through Kxoe texts (with German translations and footnotes) has begun. The first of several proposed volumes under the general title *Die Welt der Kxoé-Buschleute* appeared in 1989, with a lengthy introduction, a grammar, superb photographs, and 400 pages of text on the subject of relations between the Kxoe and other ethnic groups. Köhler's more conventional ethnographic accounts include studies of attitudes towards illness and curing (1971a; 1978), hunting magic (1973), mythology and religious belief (1978–9), the concept of 'freedom' among the Kxoe (1976), social change (1966b), the origins of cultivation as revealed through vocabulary and oral literature (1986), and other aspects of oral history (e.g., 1984). His linguistic work is better known (e.g., 1966a; 1971b; 1981), and indeed much of his ethnographic work relies heavily on linguistic data.

Ironically, in spite of all this early and recent work on the Khoe Bushmen of the Okavango and eastern Botswana, we have relatively little data on many aspects of their society. It was for so long assumed that they were merely 'acculturated' Bushmen that few ethnographers have described them in terms of a traditional lifestyle. There is no doubt that the Eastern groups long occupied an important position in southern Africa's precolonial trade networks. Today their economic life, including aspects of trade, are virtually the fully described facets of their social organization.

Eastern and Northern Khoe Bushmen and their economic base
Ethnic and linguistic classification
At least thirty Eastern and Northern Khoe Bushman groups are reported in the ethnographic and linguistic literature. This is hardly surprising, given that they are prone to classifying themselves by area of habitation and

totem, rather than by language. They are spread over a wide area and are interspersed with larger, non-Khoisan populations, and some groups have probably lived in this area for over two millennia.

Most of the Eastern and Northern Khoe Bushmen are fully integrated into the economic milieu of the wider, Bantu-speaking society. Many especially in the north, are dark-skinned, and in appearance as well as in genetic makeup, similar to the black populations which surround them. The genetic evidence suggests discrete 'black' and 'red' populations (as they occasionally designate themselves), rather than a gradual distinction between the two (Nurse and Jenkins 1977: 4; cf. Chasko *et al.* 1979). Nurse and Jenkins (1977: 108) have further noted that the distribution of 'Khoisan-speaking Negroes coincides with an area of infestation by the tsetse fly'. In other words, the hunter-gatherer-fishermen live where cattle cannot. Still, this does not explain how they came to speak the languages they do. Westphal (1963: 260) cites legends among Bantu-speakers of 'small groups of primitives' who lived by hunting and gathering, lacked chiefs, and even fire. Cashdan (1986a: 152–3) suggests that such groups may also be ancestors of the present-day Khoe-speaking Bushmen of northern and eastern Botswana, excluding the G//ana who have migrated eastwards from the Central Kalahari Game Reserve.

Vossen (e.g., 1990), following Köhler (e.g., 1981) classifies the Eastern Khoe Bushmen as *Tshwa* (including Tsua or Hietshware, and Kua) and *Shua* (including Ts'ixa, Danisi, Deti, and other groups loosely called 'Shua'), and the Northern Khoe Bushmen as *Kxoe* (including Kxoe, //Ani, Buga or Buka, and G/anda). The G//ana who inhabit parts of the geographically 'Eastern' areas are of course linguistically 'Central' or even 'Western-Central' (Vossen's *//Ana* or *Naro-//Ana* group). Although there certainly are linguistic and cultural differences, the greatest differences are found in subsistence techniques, in associated economic pursuits, and in settlement patterns. These are not necessarily correlated with language, but are related to the micro-environmental factors, modes of exploiting the various micro-environments, and degree and kind of association with the local non-Khoisan populations.

Our main concern in this section of the chapter will be with the Deti-speakers (and some G//ana-speakers) of the Boteti or Botletle River area, and the linguistically related but otherwise quite different groups (apparently Shua and Tshwa-speakers) inhabiting the Nata River area to the east. Only these groups have been studied in sufficient detail from the point of view of general social organization, and in particular, subsistence and exchange. Indeed, these facets of Eastern Khoe Bushman life are among the most distinctive and interesting to be treated in the ethnographic literature on Khoisan economics generally.

Subsistence and trade: hunter-herder-cultivator interaction

Hunter-herder-cultivator interaction has been prevalent in many distant parts of southern Africa for centuries (cf. Schott 1964: 178–283), but the eastern Kalahari fringe area has achieved special prominence due to the size and economic importance of the Bushman population there. Two detailed studies have been made of Eastern Khoe Bushman economic organization, Cashdan's Ph.D. dissertation, 'Trade and reciprocity among the River Bushmen of northern Botswana' (1979), and Hitchcock's widely circulated government report, *Kalahari cattle posts* (1978a). Cashdan's dissertation and subsequent derivative works (1986a; 1986b; 1987) are particularly relevant here, in that she uses the method of controlled comparison to account for differences in patterns of trade and reciprocity between the two eastern, river-dwelling Khoe Bushman groups which she considers.

Like the neighbouring Bantu-speaking populations, the Eastern and Northern Khoe Bushmen are herders as well as hunters. They also till the soil for grain production, and fish in the rivers which run through their lands. Dornan (1925: 106–9) noted that the Bushmen of the Boteti and the Okavango, like the Cape Bushmen, fished by use of stone dams and baskets slung from the narrowest points of the dams. They also used barbed spears and nets, and fished from raft and canoe as well as from the shore. All these techniques are still in use along the Boteti and in the Okavango. Herding, cultivating, and fishing all require an investment of time and labour beyond what is required in a typical hunting and gathering society. In James Woodburn's terms (e.g., 1980; 1982a), these Eastern and Northern groups practise a delayed, as opposed to an immediate-return economy.

Some groups, especially along the Boteti and around Lake Xau, have long engaged in extensive trade activities, for meat, skins, metal, and manufactured goods. Cashdan (1987) has argued that this trade is based on the local advantages of the Boteti area. She also suggests that the nature of trade there has altered through time as a result of changing conditions, including increases in population and changes in mobility over the last century or so. Trade becomes more advantageous to professional traders when general population mobility decreases and habitat diversity increases. This is precisely what has happened in this area. The inhabitants' former practice of sporadic and long-distance trade has evolved into a system of short-distance trade, with non-Bushmen occupying the floodplain, and the Deti and other Bushmen of the area engaging as local traders.

One characteristic of the Eastern Khoe Bushmen which distinguishes them from most Kalahari groups is the degree to which they have taken to delayed-return modes of economic activity. This includes not only trade, cultivation, fishing, and pastoralism, but also storage of resources. In the late 1970s especially, such storage activities were prevalent in the eastern C.K.G.R., where G//ana and Kgalagari alike stored water as a buffer against risk (Cashdan 1980a; 1980b; see Chapter 6). They are typical of the Nata River area as well (Cashdan 1985). In both these areas, the expanded storage of resources has resulted in increases in economic inequality and social differentiation.

In other areas where sedentization has occurred rapidly within the past two or three decades, notably in the Kua and ethnically mixed areas south of the C.K.G.R., there have been similar but more unfortunate results (see, e.g., Kent 1989a; Kent and Vierich 1989). Economic deprivation and consequent internal strife, inter-group problems, and fighting have increased. The level of violence is greatest among *recently* settled groups, precisely because individuals not used to a sedentary lifestyle are unable to release their tensions as they would in a more nomadic existence (e.g., by a shouting match or superficial fight, or through seasonal group fission). Susan Kent (1989a) distinguishes the form of violent behaviour found among recently settled groups from that of long-term sedentary Bushman populations, the latter form being less intense. Nomadic violence, it seems, disappears after time, but the process of sedentization, and particularly the speedy occurrence of permanent settlement, has deleterious social affects. These rival the economic gains which might be made as a result of the simultaneous transition to agriculture.

Settlement patterns

Settlement patterns in the two areas studied by Cashdan differ from each other and from those of the Kalahari groups (Cashdan 1979: 93–113; cf. Chapter 12). The situation in the Boteti area approximates the traditional Tswana pattern, where there is a distinction between the 'village', the 'lands', and the 'cattle post'. About half the population are ethnic Bushmen, and most of the rest are Kalanga. Virtually all the Kalanga of this area have their main residence at one of three villages in the valley. The Bushmen, in contrast, live mainly at cattle posts, where they look after the cattle of other residents, and keep some, through *mafisa* relationships. Ethnic groups occupy separate settlements, and mobile populations of G//ana move freely between this area and the C.K.G.R.

The Nata River area is very different. The residents of this locality are mainly Bushmen, though there are minority populations of Kalanga and Tswana. The Bushmen here live a more settled existence than those of the Boteti area, in what, in Tswana terms, are essentially 'cattle post' locations. Boteti groups are concentrated along the river, whereas Nata groups tend to be more evenly distributed. The reason is simple: the Boteti valley is centred on a floodplain, which is estimated to be six times more fertile than the Nata area (Cashdan 1979: 123; 1987: 125). The people of Nata rely much more on rainfall for water for their fields. The Nata River itself has high banks and does not often flood. The surrounding land is a wooded, less desert-like place on the whole, but with no especially fertile zones within it (see Cashdan 1979: 74–93). In each case, micro-environmental conditions determine the patterns of settlement and population movement.

In Northern Khoe Bushman areas, the situation more closely resembles that along the Boteti, although here too there are local differences (cf. A.C. Campbell 1976; Köhler 1989). Migration patterns depend on seasonal flooding, which takes place in the *dry* season. This results from the previous wet season's rain in the source areas of the Okavango, in central Angola. The dry season is the best time for hunting, since the surface of land is reduced. The *wet* season is a time when, due to seepage, more land is above the water line and the surface area of the water is reduced. Consequently, it is best for fishing. The various Northern Khoe Bushman groups share their territorial resources with a number of Bantu-speaking groups, including the Mbukushu (who subsist primarily by agriculture), the Yei (the archetypal fishermen of the Okavango), and, to a lesser extent, Tswana, Kgalagari, and Herero herders of the western and southern fringe areas of the Okavango Delta. To some degree, each of these groups occupies a different ecological niche. 'River Bushmen', as their informal name implies, tend to be concentrated along the banks of Okavango River itself and the main water channels of the Delta, as far south as Maun. The 'River Bushmen' Cashdan describes are found from there southwards, along the Boteti, in a continuous line of habitation.

Kinship among the Eastern and Northern Khoe Bushmen
Totemism
The most unusual feature of Eastern and Northern Khoe Bushman kinship, from a Khoisan point of view, is the existence of totemism. The majority of the Eastern groups are associated with totemic animal species, which often are taboo as food to the group concerned, and which identify exogamous units which Dornan calls 'clans'. These are probably

patrilineages of very short span, though Dornan (e.g., 1925: 67–70) seems to use the term 'clan' both for a descent line and for a larger, cognatic local group. The totems themselves are not associated with specific territories or ritual sites, but small totemically named groups may claim given locations in the manner of cognatic kin groups elsewhere in the Kalahari region. The origin of these totemic groups has been in dispute for some time. Dornan (1925: 161; cf. 1917: 53) implies that totemism may be Bushman in origin, though 'not highly developed', when compared with the practices of Bantu-speaking peoples or more particularly with those of Australian Aborigines or American Indians. Schapera (1930: 85), on the other hand, interprets Dornan as suggesting the now conventional theory that the totems were Bantu in origin and borrowed, presumably relatively recently, by the Bushmen – a view he apparently shares. Cashdan (1979: 41–2) puts forward a strong argument that totemism is aboriginal to both peoples. As she notes, the totems of the Eastern Khoe Bushmen are not found among the Tswana or other Bantu-speaking peoples with whom they are in contact, these Bantu-speaking groups have no tradition of totemic exogamy, and the oldest Bushman informants claim totems as ancient representations of their groups. The fact that they are found far and wide in the Okavango and the eastern Kalahari fringe area suggests to me a further reason to accept their early origin. However, the fact that they do not occur among other Khoisan groups implies that they are not as old as Khoisan, or even specifically Khoe, culture and language. Therefore, the most likely explanation is that they originated indigenously, or were borrowed after the divergence of the Khoe-speaking peoples but before the arrival of the Tswana in the lands north of the Limpopo. This view is consistent with the notion of long-term Bushman–Bantu contact in eastern Botswana, as suggested, for example, by Denbow (1984).

Today, totemism is found widely in the Central District and the Okavango. Totemic species include a strange assortment of wild and domesticated animals. Among those noted by Cashdan (1986a: 147) are eland, impala, zebra, hare, hippopotamus, elephant, crocodile, lion, ostrich, monkey, dog, cow, and 'heart of goat'.

Marriage and naming

The Eastern Khoe Bushmen of Dornan's time married upon payment, by the groom to the prospective father-in-law, of the skin of a freshly killed animal (Dornan 1925: 124–5). This animal had to be killed by the suitor. If the prospective father-in-law accepted it, his daughter was deemed to be married. Among one Bushman group of Southern Rhodesia (as it then was), a young man would lay gifts at the feet of the prospective father-in-law. He would then be sent to kill a large game animal in order to prove his worthiness as a husband. These customs, as Dornan (1925: 126–7) notes, are similar to those in other Bushman areas.

Heinz reports a number of variant marriage practices among the Bugakhoe (literally 'River People') and related Northern groups (Heinz n.d.). Among the /Xokhoe Bugakhoe, he reports tests of hunting skill on the part of prospective grooms, followed by gift-giving practices very similar to those among Dornan's Rhodesian groups. The gifts exchanged include a tortoise shell and a skin. Residence is virilocal from the beginning of marriage. Among the G/andakhoe (also considered a branch of the Bugakhoe), marriages are sometimes arranged between infants. After puberty, when the parties are ripe for marriage, there are elaborate ceremonies involving a two months' residence in the bride's camp (without sexual intercourse), then the return of the groom, with his bride, to his own village, where he shows her off in front of his old bachelors' hut. There the bride is stripped and rubbed with oil, then bedecked with presents from her new husband. After this, the newly married couple return to the wife's people, and the man's father-in-law may require special tasks to be performed. Among the Okavango River //Anikhoe, cattle given by both bride's and groom's people may be slaughtered for a wedding feast, and bridewealth of an ox or a goat is paid at the birth of the first child. Many men of this group have more than one wife, whereas the Swamp //Anikhoe (to the south) are generally monogamous. All these groups distinguish parallel from cross-cousins and 'prefer' marriage to the latter. Most groups seem to have institutionalized virilocal residence as the norm, sometimes after bride service; and marriage is marked by mutual gift-giving, bridewealth, or bride service, depending upon local custom and the relative wealth of the members of the community. Inheritance of land and of other things, according to Heinz, is generally in the male line, though some goods, including firearms, are passed first to a man's wife and, after her death, to their sons.

The naming practices of the groups mentioned by Heinz are interesting. The eldest of a group of G/andakhoe (Bugakhoe) siblings bears the name of one of his or her parents' siblings; the second-born, the name of a cross-cousin; and the third, the name of a parent. A Tzexa bears the name of his or her paternal grandparents, father, or father's sibling. Among other groups, names are bestowed rather as among the G/wi (see Chapter 6). Children 'fear' their same-sex siblings and 'joke' with their grandparents, but there is no association of particular names with anyone's set of egocentric relationship terms.

Relationship terminologies

No detailed study of any Eastern or Northern Khoe Bushman relationship terminology has been made. Nevertheless, what details exist enable us to make the assumption that the structure of known terminologies is essentially similar to that of Khoe-speaking peoples generally, and resembles especially those of the G/wi and G//ana.

Cashdan (1986a: 171) records the Tshwa terms from Nata as follows (Cashdan's orthography, with my hypothetical transcription in square brackets): *baba* (FF, MF, MB), *mama* (MF, MM, FZ), *ba* (F), *chaba* (FeB [*tshaba* or *tsaba*]), /*oba* (FyB), *mara* or *mera* (M), *chama* (MeZ [*tshama* or *tsama*]), /*uma* (MyZ), *chaxo* (eB, FeBS, FeBD, MeZS, MeZD [*tshaxo* or *tsaxo*]), *damaxo* (yB, FyBS, FyBD, MyZS, MyZd), *kwinke* (Z), and *njira* (FZS, FZD, MBS, MBD [more accurately rendered as *ndzira*, probably derived from Tswana *ntsala*, 'cross-cousin', 'kinsman', 'friend', etc.]). The terms for children, nephews, nieces, and grandchildren are not recorded. Assuming that the structure is consistent with that of other all Khoe-speaking peoples, one may confidently expect that *njira* or *ndzira* refers to any junior cross-relatives (i.e., that it would include opposite-sex siblings' children, and children's children), and that whatever term is applied to children (almost certainly a cognate of G/wi or G//ana /*ua*) is also applied to same-sex siblings' children. The structure of the terminology, with my orthography, is shown in Figure 7.2.

I have taken Cashdan's descriptions literally. Nevertheless, my suspicion is that 'seniority' distinctions between *damaxo* and *chaxo* (*tshaxo*) may in fact refer to the real relative ages of ego and alter rather than to their seniority, as defined by the relative ages of their parents. This would be more consistent with the Khoe Bushman structure generally. The term *kwinke* is possibly related to Nharo or indeed western G//ana, !*uĩ*. Clicks are commonly dropped in Eastern Khoe dialects, and I have found !*uĩ* in use among G//ana in the Ghanzi area for 'younger sibling'. If this is a related term, its occurrence here could indicate longstanding borrowing, possibly from !Kung in both areas (cf. Barnard 1988a: 42–4). Certainly, the usage of any term for 'sister', undistinguished for relative age or relative sex, is peculiar for a Khoe terminology. By analogy with G/wi and G//ana usage, it would seem likely that *damaxo* and *chaxo* (*tshaxo*) refer to elder and younger same-sex siblings, while *kwinke* refers to opposite-sex siblings. In

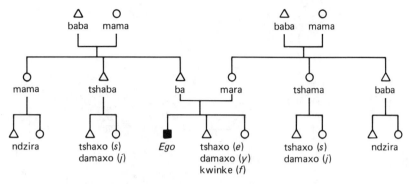

Figure 7.2 The Tshwa relationship terminology: partial representation (number-gender suffixes omitted)

other words, the terminology cursorily recorded by Cashdan is highly consistent with expectation, but only if male ego is assumed.

As far as is known, the structure of the Northern Khoe Bushman terminologies is identical to that of the Eastern ones, and the terms themselves are virtually the same too. The Bukakhoe and Kxoe relationship terminologies are illustrated in Figure 7.3. My sources are a discussion of Kxoe kinship vocabulary by Köhler (1966a: 164–5) and unpublished Bugakhoe relationship term charts by Heinz (n.d.). More complete lists, including variant usages within the PARENT/CHILD category, are given in Table 16.2 (Chapter 16).

Religion and ritual

The Kxoe recognize a deity named *Kxyani*, who is divided into male and female forms (Köhler 1978–9). The male Kxyani is responsible for the animal kingdom, and the female Kxyani is associated with the earth and the fertility of the bush. She is the subject of many Kxoe myths and is addressed as *Dixahe* or 'Owner'. The Moon is also a symbol of fertility, and hunters pray to him for good fortune in their activities (Köhler 1973). The evil deity, or evil aspect of Kxyani, is called *Conakū*. He is the 'Master of Illnesses'. Kxoe medicine men perform medicine dances, divination, and sometimes, it is said, evil magic. Both the activities of Conakū and those of human sorcerers can be countered by the knowledge held by practitioners of good medicine (see Köhler 1971a: 319–21).

Modern writers have little to say about the religion of the Eastern Khoe Bushmen, apart from the fact that such groups are associated with totemic species. Dornan (1925: 147–54), however, did record some details of the religious notions of several groups. Of special interest is his report of one

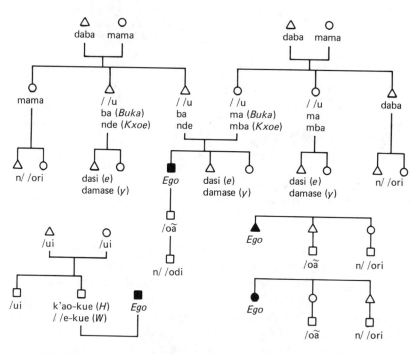

Figure 7.3 The Bukakhoe and Kxoe relationship terminologies: probable genealogical usage (number-gender suffixes omitted)

band along the Tuli River (in what is now southwestern Zimbabwe). They sang a song which went: 'Thora come to the help of Huwe' (Dornan 1925: 150). Dornan interprets this as referring to a Great God, Thora, and a lesser benevolent spirit Huwe, which in turn he sees as analogous to Khoekhoe notions, presumably of Tsûi-//goab and Haitsi-aibib respectively (see Chapters 10 and 14). These deities do battle with the evil spirit he labels *Gaua*. Dornan was on the right track, but unfortunately his attempt at regional comparison was too feeble to allow us to tease out any more details about the Eastern groups he worked with, or to see any further pattern in his data.

Dornan (1925: 54, 136–7) also notes the existence of several dances, including an 'Eland Bull Dance'. From his descriptions of many aspects of Bushman culture it is often difficult to determine which group possesses which custom, but it does seem likely that this dance was indeed an Eastern and not a G//ana, G/wi, or Nharo one. It seems to have been performed by men, who carried fly whisks and painted their faces. I suspect it was an ordinary medicine dance which he saw, and not an 'Eland Bull Dance' in the sense in which this term is applied by other Bushman groups. Elsewhere, dancing 'eland bulls' are decidedly part of female initiation rites. It should perhaps be added that Dornan did complain that the Bushmen were reluctant to perform their dances before strangers. On one such occasion when they did, Dornan tried to go to sleep just two hours into the dance, but the noise was too much and he had to stop the festivities, 'very much to the annoyance of the performers' (Dornan 1925: 137). Samuel Dornan (1925: 158–60) also reports an annual circumcision of boys who are about the age of twelve, and a simultaneous girls' ceremony involving perforation of the clitoris. Such operations were apparently performed collectively in sex-specific groups. Dornan even suggests that these practices were ancient among the Bushmen generally and that they were borrowed by the Bantu-speaking peoples, but this is highly unlikely, to say the least.

The Kwadi: a Khoe-speaking people of Angola

Finally, brief mention should be made of the apparently Khoe-speaking people of Angola. These are variously known as Kwadi, !Kwa/tsi, Cuepe, Ovakwepe, Coroca, or Kuroka. In Portuguese, they are usually called either *Cuepe* or *Corocas* (e.g., by Estermann 1956: 51–62). The latter is a generic, ethno-geographical term, which sometimes designates other peoples as well. I call them *Kwadi*, as this is the term now firmly established in the linguistic literature (e.g., Westphal 1971; Köhler 1981; Ehret 1982), though there is still some debate about what language group they actually represent. The prevailing opinion today is that Kwadi is – or was – a Khoe language, but not one which is closely related to that spoken by the Nama, Damara, and Hai//om. Nor is their language closely related to the Khoe Bushman dialects of the Okavango. The only evidence of a specific linguistic relationship between Kwadi and another Khoe language suggests that its affinities are, if anything, with the most geographically distant of all Khoe-speaking peoples, the Hietshware (Ehret 1982: 167–71; Figure 2.5). Their relationship to neighbouring groups is obscure. Estermann (1976 [1956]: 20–1, 37) suggests that the black peoples of southwestern Angola, including the Kwadi and the adjacent Kwisi, may be biologically related to the Damara, though their language is distinctly different. Indeed, the Kwadi are said to be of 'mixed Khoisan and Kwisi origin' (1976 [1956]: 37; cf. Almeida 1965: 27–9). The Kwisi today speak a Bantu language, and the original language of the Kwadi appears to be virtually extinct.

The Kwadi are very poorly described in the ethnographic literature, but they merit mentions in the works of Correia (1925), Estermann (1956: 51–62; or 1976 [1956]: 36–47), and Almeida (1965: 25–40). From the available accounts, it seems that the Kwadi were in the past very numerous. They seem to have been in their present location for some time, as they receive passing comments in the works of at least one sixteenth-century navigator (Duarte Pacheco Pereira), a seventeenth-century historian (A. de Oliveira de Cadornega), and an eighteenth-century adventurer (João Pilarte da Silva), all of whom encountered them, or heard from people who did, near the mouth of the Coroca River (Estermann 1976 [1956]: 38–40). Da Silva reported them as having cattle, but not cultivation. By the time Estermann came upon them in the 1930s, not only were they becoming assimilated into the milieu of southwestern Angolan culture generally, but they seemed to be dying out. In the 1950s, largely as a result of tuberculosis, only a few families were left. Nevertheless, Estermann did salvage some knowledge of this unfortunate people, as did António de Almeida, who visited them in 1955, and it is very possible that something of their culture survives today in the Coroca River area. I shall therefore describe their cultural attributes in the present tense.

The Kwadi womenfolk have long grown crops of millet, yams, and beans, and in recent times maize. The main pursuit of their menfolk is herding and they possess cattle, sheep, and goats. Unlike the Damara, they did not traditionally forge iron, and they had no indigenous pottery (Estermann 1976 [1956]: 43). In these respects they resemble the Bushmen of southern Angola. However, like the Bantu-speaking peoples of the area, they practise circumcision and other forms of body mutilation (see Almeida 1965: 32–6). Male initiation involves an elaborate, group circumcision ceremony, normally carried out in the bush on pre-adolescent boys. The surgeon is always a Kwadi and not an outsider. Additional, individual initiations in the style of the neighbouring Himba people are also reported (Estermann 1976 [1956]: 43). Female initiation does not involve body mutilation, but does require elaborate ceremonies. These include 'hiding' the girl in the bush, shortly *after* her first period, then carrying her back to her parents' hut. According to Estermann (1976 [1956]: 44), this is done by boys. After she reaches the village, her father kills an ox by suffocation, then presents the meat to the girl for a blessing. She is forbidden to eat this or any other meat during the initiation, but others present may share in it. Both men and women dance and sing at this time. On the fourth day, the initiate is anointed with butter, dressed in new clothes, and adorned with beads. These specific practices resemble those of neighbouring Bantu-speaking peoples more than they do those of the Khoisan peoples.

In the past, polygyny was widespread and marriage was strictly Kwadi-endogamous (Almeida 1965: 36). Estermann (1976 [1956]: 44–5) describes a very curious wedding ceremony which is quite unlike any other Angolan one, and more like that reported, for example, among the Nharo (D.F. Bleek 1928a: 33–4). In the Kwadi case, the bride is taken to the bush by the boys and girls of her family, who 'fight' with members of the groom's family when they have caught up with the party. The groom's family then 'capture' the bride and take her to the hut of her future husband. On the next day, dancing and feasting begin. The groom supplies the ox, but the bride is forbidden to eat any. On the fourth day, the bride's prospective sisters-in-law take their brother's clubs and place them near the hut, then ask the bride to lift them. She is then brought to a cow, which she ritually milks (Estermann does not explain the symbolism). After a meal, the marriage is consummated.

Estermann (1976 [1956]: 46) claims that 'clan organization' (presumably matrilineal) is recent, and that a woman's possessions are inherited by her eldest brother, and a man's by his eldest sister's son. The aboriginal religion of the people would seem to bear some resemblance to that of neighbouring groups, though terms for the deity (*Suk!ude*; cf. *Suku*, the term found in neighbouring Bantu languages) and the spirits of the dead (*/ovisika*) do contain click consonants which could indicate a Khoisan origin (cf. Estermann 1976 [1956]: 46).

Not enough is known to the outside world about the Kwadi for us to be sure of the origin of very many of their customs at all. Yet a thorough study of this fascinating people might tell us a great deal about the assimilation of ideas across the culture-area boundary, and even about the acculturation process in the abstract. For many years, southern Angolans have been forced to witness the deplorable actions of foreign forces. Now that peace seems at last to have come, it may be possible to ask Kwadi themselves, or their descendants, about their ways of life – both those of today and those of the past. We could have much to learn from them.

8

The Nharo

The Nharo and their neighbours

The Nharo live in the western part of Botswana's Ghanzi district, between the !Xõ, to the south, and the !Kung, to the north. The Nharo number at least 6,000. Guenther (1986b: 1) has put their number at 9,000, including 5,000 in Botswana and 4,000 in Namibia. By Guenther's estimates, the total is nearly one-fifth of the entire Bushman population, which he gives as 55,000. Their first prominent ethnographer, Dorothea Bleek, called them *Naron* (the final *-n* being a common gender plural suffix), and indeed *Naro-* is a phonologically more precise form than *Nharo*. I prefer *Nharo* myself, as it is more common, and indeed not entirely inaccurate, since, as Traill (1988: 157) has noted, the *h* 'reflects the breathy voice that can accompany the initial low-toned syllable'.

In most Nharo areas there is a relatively good water supply, due partly to their locations along Ghanzi ridge. This is a mixed sedimentary and volcanic formation some 100 to 150 kilometres wide, with much water-trapping limestone. It runs across the Kalahari, with the main road from Maun and Sehitwa to Sandfontein at its centre (see Figure 8.1). Since the 1890s the Nharo have had to share much of the eastern part of their country (the Ghanzi farm block) with white, and more recently black, ranchers. A separate ranching area (the Xanagas block) lies to the west, on the Namibian border. Most of the ranchers here are of mixed white–black ancestry, and some are part Nama. Areas to the south of the farm blocks and between the blocks are shared between the Nharo and Bantu-speaking subsistence herders, including Kgalagari, Tswana, and Herero (see Silberbauer and Kuper 1966). The Kgalagari entered the territory in tribal groups in the early nineteenth century, while the Herero population (coming in smaller groups) and the Tswana (coming mainly as individuals and

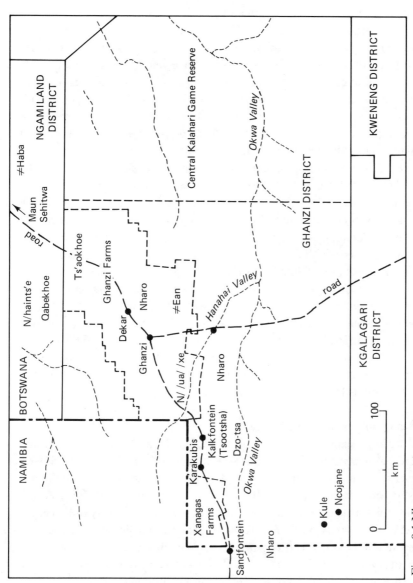

Figure 8.1 Nharo country

families) have migrated there since the arrival of the white settlers (see Gillett 1969; Kuper 1970: 6–13).

To the northeast of the Nharo, in the northernmost parts of the Ghanzi farm block and southern Ngamiland, live the Ts'aokhoe and some smaller groups, notably the Qabekhoe and N/haints'e. These smaller groups may in fact simply be branches of the Ts'aokhoe or even of the ≠Haba (see Westphal 1971: 379–80). Today the Ts'aokhoe, and to some extent also the ≠Haba, a linguistically Northern or Central Khoe Bushman group with some linguistic affinity with Nharo (Vossen 1988b: 67–9), live together with Nharo 'squatters' and ranch labourers on many northern farms. The Ts'aokhoe probably number about 1,000, and the other groups seem to be smaller still. All these groups are culturally very similar; Gary Childers (1976: 30), not without good cause, treats the Ts'aokhoe as just the northernmost Nharo band cluster. From an outsider's point of view, this classification is the most obvious one, although both the Nharo and the Ts'aokhoe prefer to see themselves as separate peoples. Together, the Nharo, Ts'aokhoe and ≠Haba, and possibly smaller independent groups, are exponents of what I have termed 'Western Khoe Bushman' social structure (Barnard 1980a: 112–13, 117–18, 121–4).

Since data on the smaller groups are very scant indeed, I shall concentrate here specifically on the Nharo, and mainly on two Nharo areas. These are the south-central area, which the Nharo call N//ua//xe, and the north-eastern area. The former is my own primary fieldwork site, and the latter is where Mathias Guenther has worked. The other areas are culturally similar, although contact with Kgalagari and Herero is greater and that with whites is less.

Ethnographic studies of the Nharo

At least six explorer-authors passed though Nharo territory in the late nineteenth century, and of these Schinz (1891) and Passarge (1907) recorded in passing some notes on Nharo social organization (cf. Galton 1853; Andersson 1856; 1861; Baines 1864; Chapman 1868). However, the title of first true ethnographer of the Nharo belongs properly to Dorothea Bleek. Her 67-page book, *The Naron* (1928a), was the first monograph ever devoted to the general ethnography of a single Bushman people. She spent about seven months in 1920 and 1921 based at Sandfontein, on what is now the Botswana/Namibia border. Her material, although meagre by modern standards, figures prominently in the pages of *The Khoisan peoples of South Africa* (Schapera 1930).

Subsequently, there followed a period of decline in Khoisan ethno-

graphic studies. Bleek herself went north to do fieldwork among Angolan
!Kung and East African Hadza. It was not until after her death in 1948 that
any detailed work was taken up among any Kalahari Bushmen, and not
until 1968 that work again began among the Nharo. In the latter year,
Mathias Guenther began his studies of farm and mission Nharo in an
eastern area of the Ghanzi farms. He wrote his Ph.D. on the pluralism and
implicit ethnic conflicts of Ghanzi society (Guenther 1973), and has since
produced a large number of books, reports and articles on the plight of the
Bushmen, especially Nharo, in this district (e.g., 1974; 1975a; 1976; 1977;
1979a; 1986c). Guenther has also written extensively on other topics, most
notably Nharo religion (e.g., 1975b; 1979b; 1981a; 1983) and has produced
a major ethnographic study of the Nharo (1986b).

In 1969, H.P. Steyn began his studies of nomadic western Nharo groups
near Kalkfontein. He is one of very few South African anthropologists
active in the study of Khoisan society (as opposed to Khoisan languages,
biology, health, etc.). Steyn's Khoisan interest has focused on Nharo
subsistence and economic relations (e.g., Steyn 1971a; 1971b; 1981a), and
he has also written two short popular books on the Kalahari Bushman
peoples (1981b; 1985).

I started fieldwork with the Nharo in 1974. Apart from comparative
studies, my field research with the Nharo has included studies of kinship
(e.g., Barnard 1976a; 1978b), gender (1980b), settlement patterns (1980c),
ethnobotany (1984, 1986b), ritual (1979b), and cosmology (1980e) I have
also written a monograph on the Nharo language (1985). The dominant
foci of my comparative studies have been kinship (see Chapters 15 and 16)
and settlement patterns (Chapter 12).

To date, no ethnographer has studied the Ts'aokhoe or the ≠Haba.
Westphal (1971: 379) locates them between Ghanzi and Sehitwa, but no
independent record of them exists in other linguistic or ethnographic work.
I believe I once encountered a group who called themselves N/haints'e
living in a settlement of some five huts in a densely wooded area of southern
Ngamiland, some 20 kilometres west of the Maun–Ghanzi road. However,
being lost at the time, I stopped only to ask directions before proceeding
back to the road which had eluded me.

Subsistence and settlement

Nharo country is rich in water resources, which are the basis of both
traditional territoriality and recent changes in settlement patterns. Before
the ranches, the seasonal cycle was probably similar to that of the central
!Kung. From the early accounts (Passarge 1907: 31–2; D.F. Bleek 1928a: 4–

5; Schapera 1930: 77, 92), it seems that the Nharo used to spend the dry season camped at large permanent waterholes. Sometimes more than one band would share a waterhole. They could remain at these camps all year round, as they generally do today, or they could disperse. Dorothea Bleek (1928a: 4–5) described the people she encountered as living in band settlements of three to twenty huts. Families would move about the territory of their 'horde', or band cluster, according to the availability of food resources, both plant and animal, in the proximity of each waterhole. In the summer wet season, families, and perhaps larger groups, would scatter to outlying areas. Some would move to the area south of the limestone ridge, to the Okwa and Hanahai valleys. There they could live off the seasonal water and plant resources and exploit the large game which inhabit that territory. Seasonal water supplies are available from around November or December, when the first rainwater collects in depressions in the sand. In the autumn, tsama melons are available. In the past they supplied the needs of many Nharo, just as they have for the G/wi and G//ana further east. Migrant Nharo would probably not have had to return to their permanent waterholes until about June or July.

Nharo still follow this pattern to some extent, but the majority of the population now live permanently at ranch boreholes in the Ghanzi and Xanagas farm blocks (cf. Barnard 1980c: 137–8; 1986a: 48–50). Some live too at Kgalagari cattle posts and villages, and nearly all Nharo supplement their traditional means of subsistence with either goat-herding, occasional wage labour, or both. The increased demand for water, especially by the commercial ranchers, has caused a sinking of the water table in recent decades. Natural waterholes were plentiful in the late nineteenth century, and were probably more numerous than in any other part of the Kalahari. Today these have largely been replaced by farm, government, and district council-owned boreholes.

Like the !Xõ, the Nharo are divided into bands and band clusters. The band (*tsou-ba*) is the primary unit of social organization, and the band cluster (*n!u-sa*) is a larger territorial unit. In fact *n!u-sa* is more accurately translated as 'band cluster territory', or sometimes even 'territory' in a more general sense. Each of these is named and consists of a recognized membership. In Bleek's time, each band cluster occupied a large territory, with several waterholes and precise boundaries which were rarely crossed except for trade. Today, the boundaries are less precise, but the band clusters remain important units of self-identity.

All members of the band cluster, both men and women, collectively 'own' (*kau*) the resources of the territory, although today legal title to Nharo lands is held by cattle-ranchers, in the case of lands within the farm block, and by the Botswana government, in the case of the lands to the south. In the traditional Nharo view, the right of ownership was given by God to their ancestors, the 'Oldest Parents', and is inherited bilaterally by persons of both sexes. The bands are far less permanent than the band clusters. A band may include any member of the band cluster who takes residence at the band's waterhole or anyone who has married into the band. N//ua//xe is essentially endogamous, but some marriages to non-N//ua//xe people and to non-Nharo do occur. Band locations are named, and it is really the location, rather than the group, which is stable over time. Each band, or aggregate of two or three bands sharing the same waterhole, can be identified by this name. Every Nharo has a band which he or she considers as his or her own, although generally a few months' residence would have to be anticipated before band membership is recognized.

The central Nharo do not migrate in band-sized groups. Thay move from location to location freely, either as visitors or as new residents. Evidence from oral tradition suggests that until the latter part of this century the Nharo tended to disperse to outlying seasonal water resources during the wet season and aggregate at the permanent waterholes in the dry season. More recently, with the acquisition of goats and the greater dependence on the ranchers for their livelihood, Nharo have tended to stay closer to permanent sources of water. Bands number from eight to over forty individuals, and often today, as in the past, two or three bands will use the same permanent waterhole or borehole. The distance from settlement to waterhole or borehole normally varies from about 30 to 100 metres. Occasionally, the distance is much greater. One band I encountered was living 3,000 metres from its borehole, and the water was transported by donkeycart.

Political organization is not highly developed. The oldest male band member is called the //eixaba (headman) and his wife is the //eixasa (headwoman), though these titles do not necessarily imply any particular authority over the others. Band membership is highly flexible; individuals change band membership many times in the course of their lives. In earlier writings, I have remarked that band cluster boundaries did not seem to be clearly defined, and had seemingly broken down due to the incursion of non-Bushman groups into their territories. Although a flexibility character-istic of recent changes in Central Kalahari Bushman settlement patterns seems to have become the norm, there is recent evidence for marked social boundaries between separated Nharo groups now residing at the govern-ment settlement scheme at Hanahai (Barnard 1986a: 49–50). In 1982 at

Hanahai, I discovered remarkably strict social, if not geographical, boundaries between members of different Nharo band clusters. Residing at this settlement are representatives of two Nharo band clusters – the N//ua//xe people and the ≠Ean people – as well as smaller numbers of members of other Bushman and non-Bushman groups. In 1982 the two groups had been at Hanahai for about three years and numbered just under a hundred souls each; in general they included individuals who had left the Ghanzi ranches (to the north) in search of a more independent life, but who maintained close ties with members of their own band clusters within the ranches. Hanahai itself is at the eastern edge of the traditional N//ua//xe band cluster territory, a few kilometres from ≠Ean country. Each such group lives separately, they have little social contact with each other, and individuals from different groups buy and sell (rather than share) the meat they acquire by hunting or herding. The N//ua//xe people claim to know few of the ≠Ean people by name and are frequently unaware even of the existence of other Nharo band clusters on their opposite, western border, about 40 kilometres away.

To the northeast, in ≠Ean country, the Nharo settlement pattern has undergone gradual but considerable changes in recent years. The first permanent white settlers arrived in that area in 1898, but the most drastic changes seem to have occurred since the early 1960s, just after the system of land tenure was changed from leasehold to freehold. This was a period when the farms were in a state of expansion. Many farms were being fenced for the first time, a better quality of livestock was brought in, engine-pump boreholes were introduced, and farmers began to pay their workers in cash, rather than entirely in kind. The newer farmers also increased the density of livestock, brought in high-velocity rifles (and killed off much of the game), and hired Kgalagari and Tswana herdsmen in preference to the indigenous Nharo. The results of these changes can be summarized very simply: first, the Nharo who had by this time become part-time herdsmen were put out of work in favour of the Kgalagari and Tswana; and secondly, those Nharo who wished to continue their traditional economic pursuits could no longer find adequate vegetable resources or game animals in the area (Silberbauer 1974). The extreme over-abundance of boreholes, in turn, led to the formation of smaller and smaller bands – sometimes only a single nuclear family at each borehole – and to increased migration of individuals and families within the northeastern farming area (Barnard 1980c: 143–5).

In contrast, certain more traditional areas such as N//ua//xe and Dzo-tsa, near Kalkfontein, still possess permanent natural waterholes which support large aggregations (often more than one band each) all year round

(Barnard 1980c: 139–41). If we were to take this pattern as the norm for the Nharo as a whole, we could describe Nharo settlement, at least relative to most other Kalahari Bushman groups, as 'permanently aggregated'. Bands do disperse, but only in order to form new groups, or for individuals and families to join up with existing bands nearby.

Property and exchange

The concept of ownership is expressed in Nharo by the word *kau*. This may be used as either a verb, 'to own', or a noun (with an appropriate suffix), 'owner'. Yet the concept is more reciprocal than that connoted by the English notion of 'ownership'. Sometimes its meaning is best expressed in English though by reversing the subject and object. It might be more accurate to think not so much of 'I own this land', but 'I belong to this land, and this land belongs to me'. The most usual way of saying this in Nharo, without the word *kau*, could be translated literally as 'This land, mine it is'.

With this proviso, the Nharo can be said to 'own' property in various ways. Land is owned collectively by those who have inherited a right to use it. A hut or a fire is owned by a family or other domestic unit who share it. Movable property is owned only individually, but, as among the !Kung, is given in formalized exchange through a network of individuals both near and far. People are also 'owned' by their senior kin. In particular, grandchildren are said to be 'owned' by their grandparents (see 'Kinship', below).

The system of formalized exchange is designated by the term *//aĩ*, normally used as a verb meaning 'to give in exchange', and some in a reciprocal construction, *//aĩ-ku*, 'in a gift-giving relationship to each other'. The notion is identical to the !Kung idea of *hxaro*. The word *hxaro* is not found in Nharo, but the concept can be expressed in !Kung through a term apparently related to the Nharo one (Wiessner 1982: 66). The !Kung word is *//hai*, which Wiessner translates as 'to hold', or figuratively, 'to be responsible [for the other person]'. Among both !Kung and Nharo, gifts are exchanged in a system of delayed, balanced reciprocity, which expresses mutual solidarity between each binary set of gift-givers. Any movable, non-consumable item may be given in a *//aĩ* relationship. Common items of exchange include clothing, weapons, tools, cooking utensils, and trade goods, such as pots and tobacco pipes. Even dogs and donkeys are exchanged. Gifts are made only upon request, and *//aĩ* partners may either accept or reject requests. Reciprocity is never immediate, for that would imply that the relationship is ended; the delay keeps it alive.

These formalized networks of giving may, as among the !Kung, imply mutual rights to use land. Certainly, they suggest rights to share in various consumable goods, such as tea, coffee, sugar, tobacco, and soap, when these are available. Though they are often exchanged especially between //aĩ partners, consumable goods are not themselves considered //aĩ goods. They are much more widely distributed and some are shared with the band as a whole. Meat, in particular, is widely shared both within the band and beyond its boundaries.

Work and leisure
The sexual division of labour
It is the wife's duty to gather veld food for her family, usually in the morning, to fetch water whenever needed, and to collect firewood, usually in the late afternoon. Women also do most of the fire-tending, cooking, hut-building and child-rearing, although these tasks may be shared among men as well. The men, supposedly, are the hunters, but if a hunt is unsuccessful, a husband will almost certainly gather at least some veld food on his return journey from the hunting grounds. This is not for fear of starvation, but from anticipation of his wife's annoyance at his lack of success. Men and boys also take primary responsibility for preparing skins and sewing them together. As such, making clothes was formerly men's work (see Bleek 1928a: 9), but today, since cloth garments have now become commonplace, each individual generally makes his or her own clothes.

This in theory is the division of labour, but in fact almost any work activity except hunting may be done by members of either sex. Given that hunting is as much sport as work, especially now that many Nharo herd goats or receive meat rations from their employers, women and older children tend to work more than most men. But this certainly does not mean that a wife cannot order her husband about; on the contrary, it is her usual excuse for doing so!

Women have control over the vegetable food gathered, and they distribute it within the co-residential group and its visitors. The co-residential group is most commonly a nuclear family, but often will include grandparents or grandchildren (sometimes in the absence of the middle generation), or other kin groupings. Men have the prestige of being considered good hunters or good honey-collectors, but again it is often women who distribute the food. Meat is shared not only with members of the co-residential group but also with neighbours and distant kin, even if they live in a different band.

Hunting is usually done in groups of two to five men. They hunt with bows and poisoned arrows, with long hooked sticks, or with hunting dogs

Table 8.1 *Means of subsistence of Ghanzi
farm Bushmen (data from Childers 1976)*

farm labour (wages and payment in kind)	38
food gathering	28
food sharing	8
herding own livestock	7
cultivating	6
craft making	5
hunting	4
other (including leather work)	4

and clubs, depending on which species are sought after. Poisoned arrows are generally reserved for bigger game such as kudu and gemsbok, and only adult males may touch the arrows. As among other Bushman peoples, arrows are lent to others, and the owner of the killing arrow is considered the owner of the meat. Nevertheless, all meat is shared according to participation in the hunt and kin relationship to the participants. If they are present or live in a nearby band, the owner's parents-in-law receive the best meat from the hind legs of any animal killed. Among the !Kung (Marshall 1961: 240; 1976: 298) and the !Xo (Heinz 1966: 43), the same custom is associated with bride service.

Ranch labour

In 1976 an American Peace Corps volunteer conducted a survey of the Bushmen of the Ghanzi ranches. Although the final report (Childers 1976) is sketchy and inaccurate in many respects, the field study nevertheless was interesting in its thoroughness. Childers tried to interview not merely a sample, but *all* of the 4,500 Bushmen believed to live in the Ghanzi block. His main interest was in subsistence economics.

According to Childers (1976: 52) 38 per cent of subsistence is derived from farm labour and 28 per cent from food gathering (see Table 8.1). Interestingly, the next-largest category presented is food sharing (8 per cent), though this figure probably makes sense only in relation to individual recipients rather than farm Bushmen as a collectivity (including, of course, those who give more than they receive). The most surprising find is the very low figure for hunting (4 per cent), but this can, with little doubt, be accounted for by a reluctance on the part of Bushmen to admit to taking animals on their employers' land. As Guenther (1986b: 155) points out, the Nharo generally hold the belief that *all* hunting is illegal, even the taking of a small tortoise or mongoose. Some hunting activity is almost certainly hidden in Childers' 'food sharing' figure. Though precise figures are not available, it is fair to say that Guenther (working in the farms), I (working on the southern fringe of the Ghanzi block, where hunting is carried out on state lands as well as in the block), and Steyn (working in the state lands to the southwest) have all found much more hunting activity than is suggested in Childers' report.

Leisure activities

As Sahlins has shown in his essays on 'the original affluent society' and underproduction in the domestic mode of production (Sahlins 1974 [1972]: 1–99), hunter-gatherers spend considerably less time in subsistence pursuits than small-scale cultivators. Much of their 'work', in any case, is considered enjoyable when compared to wage labour or cultivation. This relates particularly to hunting activities, which bring in little food but are socially important for men and boys, and which indeed define the 'Bushman' identity in reference to an outside world in which hunting is less important and cattle are what counts in the quest for social status. Herding and planting, as well as wage labour, increase work effort.

Time not spent in work activities of any kind includes that spent in camp, as well as time spent visiting. Women and men sit by their fires and those of their neighbours through the day, and especially at night. Story-telling is common, especially at night (see Guenther 1989). Many people play musical instruments: the foot bow for women, the mouth bow and *segaba* (a one-stringed fiddle) for men, and the *dengu* (thumb piano) for members of either sex (see Brearley 1984; 1988). The time spent in talking, including arguing, is considerable, lasting the majority of a person's waking hours. Among the Nharo, it is perfectly acceptable to be engaged in more than one conversation at the same time, though discussions are limited to those sitting at the same fire. It is impolite to converse with individuals sitting at another fire a few metres away.

Visiting is of great importance. This allows for //*aï* exchange, trade of consumables, the maintenance and expansion of kinship and friendship links, and ultimately, flexibility in residence patterns. Visiting (designated by the verb *dara*) is ideologically distinguished from residence (designated by the morpheme //*ai*, 'home'; e.g., in //*ai-kue*, 'at home'). Yet individuals generally possess rights to change band residence according to places they regularly visit, as these are defined as those where other links of kinship are maintained. Visiting thus serves social and economic functions beyond the individual desires of people to keep in touch and the satisfaction of their wanderlust.

Kinship
Sex and marriage
Marriage, as Dorothea Bleek (1928a: 33) perceptively noted, is 'nominally by capture'. Expressed from the point of view of a male ego, the word for 'to marry' also means 'to take' (*se*). Often others, both male and female, will aid in the mock-capture of a girl, or try to prevent it. According to custom, a man must 'take' his woman, and the rules of etiquette require that she be 'taken' with some difficulty. Men, asserting their supposed dominance, chase women; yet the women, either by keeping out of reach or by giving in, as they choose, control the situation. Bleek records an intriguing girls' game which mocks this custom:

Two young girls go off in dance step and hide behind a bush; these are the brides. Two older girls with sticks over their shoulders follow their spoor, seize them and drag them away, these are the bridegrooms. The brides scream and struggle, whereupon two other players rush up, shake their fists at the grooms and try to release the brides. These are the brides' mothers. The bridegrooms push the mothers aside and walk off dragging the brides along by one arm. The other arm the young girls throw over their heads, pretending to weep. When they have gone far enough to demonstrate a successful capture, the game ceases. There is no singing in this game. (D.F. Bleek 1928a: 20)

In fact, girls, and adult women too, may make it quite clear that they wish to be chased, if not 'captured', e.g., by quickly lifting their skirts towards their husbands or anyone else they fancy, and then running away. Another popular form of amusement is to sit by the evening fire and make sexual advances towards someone of the right kin category (or occasionally of the wrong kin category), in order to provoke reciprocation. If the pass is reciprocated, the display of affection is withdrawn and directed towards another person. If someone takes the game too seriously, reciprocating the reciprocation, this person risks the possibility that his or her partner will break the cycle and expose the aggressor as the weaker of the two. What is interesting is that in this particular form of sexual interaction the roles of men and of women are precisely the same.

Marriage is a gradual process, and there is no absolute distinction between the boyfriend/girlfriend relationship and the husband/wife relationship. Guenther (1968b: 199–204) emphasizes the idea of 'trial' marriages, expressed through the verb /hoba (Guenther gives /robe; cf. G/wi /obe), 'to borrow'. Any boy and girl who maintain exclusive or near-exclusive sexual rights over each other can be said to be *k'au* (husband) and *g//ais* (wife). Often a young couple will take residence in the hut of a mutual joking partner before building their own hut. Even before this time, they will probably have begun to share food and the girl might have asked the boy for a token gift, traditionally a large tortoise, to signify their relationship. Affinal terminology may be employed any time after a couple first have sexual intercourse, but it will not generally be continued after the couple separate unless they have enjoyed exclusive sexual rights over each other for at least a few months. This stage is not reached until the boy is about eighteen and the girl is about sixteen (rather later than among other Bushman groups).

Marriage and childbirth prestations, *kamane* (always grammatically plural, i.e., ending here in -*ne*), mark the change in the disposition of rights over individuals. A similar notion is found among the !Kung, who use the equivalent term, *kamasi* (see Chapter 3). *Kamane* or *kamasi* are conceptually distinguished from ordinary gifts, *abane* in Nharo. The Nharo claim that every marriage should be confirmed by a gift from husband to wife, and perhaps another to the wife's mother, if she insists. Any marriage which produces children, including a second marriage, should similarly be confirmed by a small feast and a series of prestations at the birth of the first child. Traditionally, the husband must kill a steenbok, the meat of which is served to his in-laws and the skin of which is cured and presented to his wife, who will use it to carry the baby and all subsequent children of the marriage.

The Nharo say they are 'owned' by their grandparents. Therefore, to secure 'ownership' of his wife a man must in theory make prestations of virtually any non-consumable goods, first to his wife's mother's mother and then to his wife's father's mother, when the first child is born. Yet as these are the child's great-grandparents, it is unlikely that they will still be living. In this case, the prestations go to the wife's mother's mother's husband or wife's mother's siblings and to the wife's father's mother or wife's fathers's siblings, regardless of their kin categories. A final prestation is made by the wife's father to the husband's mother. The Nharo are not very specific about its function, but it could be argued that this gift exists to establish primary 'ownership' over the newborn baby, and later children, for the wife's mother. An idealized representation of the cycle of marriage and childbirth prestations is illustrated in Figure 8.2.

The Nharo are essentially monogamous, and levirate and sororate do not exist as rights. Adultery is a crime against one's spouse and against one's adulterous mate's spouse. If discovered, it results in verbal and physical abuse by the victims of the crime and their sympathizers. A male offender risks confrontation primarily from his lover's husband, and a female from her own husband. It is usually men who are most angry.

Divorce is easy at any stage of marriage and for members of either sex.

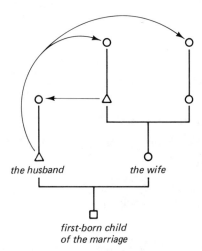

the husband   the wife

first-born child
of the marriage

Figure 8.2 Idealized representation of the cycle of marriage and childbirth gifts (*kamane*)

Children living with their parents may remain with either their mother or their father, but will remain with their mother if she demands them. All movable property is individually owned. However, a hut is built as the property of both husband and wife. After divorce it is generally the wife who keeps it. Divorces can be temporary, and former spouses maintain good relations. Only sexual rights and place of residence are necessarily affected, and the marriage prestations are not returned.

The semantics of kinship and the system of kin categories

As with all known Khoe kinship systems, there are two levels of categories: higher and lower (Barnard 1980a; 1987). Table 8.2 shows the classification of kinsmen and the usage of relationship terms within these categories, and Figure 8.3 illustrates the classification of close consanguines and affines diagramatically. The basic terms are *g//ai-* and *!au-* (for the JOKING and AVOIDANCE categories respectively), and *tsxõ-*, *!uĩ-* (*ki-*, if older than ego), *khue-*, *g//o-* (usually */ua-*, if younger than ego), and */ui-*. All of these can be used egocentrically, with prefixes *ti-* (my), *tsa-* or *sa-* (your), etc., and suffixes *-ba* (masc. sg.), *-sa* (fem. sg), etc. *Mama-*, a synonym for *tsxõ-*, never takes a prefix; nor do *aisa, auba, sauba* or *sausa*. They are commonly used in copular constructions, e.g., *Ti-tsxõ (xa-)si-'i*, literally 'My *tsxõ* she is'. They may also be used reciprocally, e.g., in the phrase *tsxõ-ku*, '*tsxõ* to each other'. The category of spouses is designated reciprocally not with the morpheme *khue*, but with *se*, 'to take' or 'marry'. The category of siblings is designated reciprocally by the morpheme *!uĩ*.

Table 8.2 *Nharo kin categories*
CATEGORY (and genealogical usage)
Nharo term, gloss (and linguistic usage)

Joking

g//ai	joking relative
!au-tama	non-avoidance relative, literally 'feared-not'

GRANDRELATIVE (PP, PosG, PosGE, PosGC, osGC, CC, N, GRANDRELATIVE's namesake, spouse's JOKING RELATIVE, etc.)

mama	grandrelative (takes no prefix)
tsxõ	grandrelative
tsxo-/ua	junior grandrelative (optional usage)

JOKING SIBLING (ssG, PssGCss, JOKING SIBLING's namesake, etc.)

ki	older sibling (literally 'old')
!uĩ	younger sibling

SPOUSE (E, EssG, ssGE, SPOUSE's namesake, etc.)

khue	spouse (literally 'person')
k'au	husband (literally 'male')
g//ais	wife (literally 'female')

Avoidance

!au	avoidance relative, literally 'feared'

PARENT/CHILD (P, PssG, PssGE, C, ssGC, PARENT/CHILD's namesake, etc.)

g//o	parent or adult offspring (literally 'to bear')
au	one's father (takes no prefix)
ai	one's mother (takes no prefix)
sau	someone else's parent (takes no prefix)
/ua	child (literally 'small')

AVOIDANCE SIBLING (osG, PssGCos, AVOIDANCE SIBLING's namesake, etc.)

ki	older sibling (literally 'old')
!uĩ	younger sibling

AVOIDANCE IN-LAW (spouse's AVOIDANCE relative)

/ui	spouse's relative (in Nharo, nomally used only for spouse's AVOIDANCE relative)

In order to define common categories among different kinship systems, I use English labels in upper-case letters. The categories of one system may be ideologically comparable to the categories of another, without necessarily identifying exactly the same sets of genealogical relationships (cf. Chapters 15 and 16). In addition to the higher level categories JOKING and AVOIDANCE, there are in the Nharo system six lower level categories, GRANDRELATIVE, JOKING SIBLING, SPOUSE, PARENT/CHILD, AVOIDANCE SIBLING, and AVOID-ANCE IN-LAW. Each of these designates a wide range of genealogical positions. 'SPOUSE' (upper case), for example, refers to a category which includes one's actual husband or wife, plus other, classificatory husbands or wives, whereas 'spouse' (lower case) refers specifically to one's actual

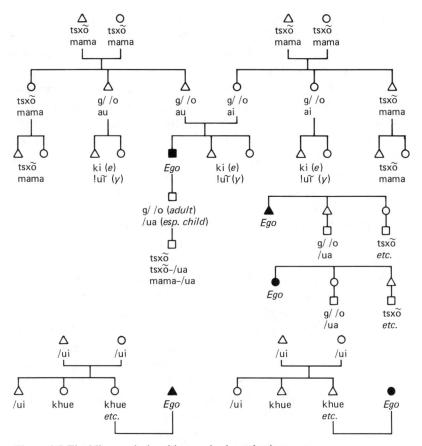

Figure 8.3 The Nharo relationship terminology: basic structure
All terms take suffixes -*ba* (masc.) or -*sa* (fem.). All terms except *au* (*ba*) and *ai* (*sa*) and *mama* (-*ba*, -*sa*) take possessive prefixes, e.g., *ti-tsxõba* ('my *tsxõ*', masc. sg.).

spouse. These category names thus have a formal validity which is not easy to express either in spoken Nharo or spoken English but which describes accurately the underlying structure of terminology usage.

A Nharo classifies every fellow Nharo he meets, both as a member of one of the higher level categories, and as a member of one of the lower level categories. On the higher level, *g//ai* and *!au* are mutually exclusive. *G//ai* has no other meaning, though in Nharo, G/wi, and other Khoe Bushman languages, *!au* means literally 'to fear' (cf. !Kung *!au*, 'to refuse'). On the lower level, the category designated *!uĩ* is, except in certain special circumstances discussed below, mutually exclusive of all other lower level categories. *Khue* (category SPOUSE) is mutually exclusive of *tsxõ* only when it applies to real spouse. According to jural rules, one can marry only a *tsxõ*, after which he or she becomes a *khue*. Other lower level categories are mutually exclusive only when their non-exclusiveness would disrupt the necessary dichotomy on the higher level; otherwise one can belong to two categories at the same time. Spouse's categories are transformed into categories of one's own. Upon marriage, all one's spouse's *g//ai* become one's own *tsxõ*, and all one's spouse's *!au* become one's own */ui*. Some Nharo do use a compound */ui-tsxõ* to talk about their spouses' GRANDRELATIVES, but, unlike in G/wi, for example, */ui* is not otherwise used for JOKING relatives. Former spouses are called *//uẽ* (literally, 'to divorce'), and the term *ti-//uẽ-ba* or *-sa* may, if one wishes, be considered an additional 'relationship term' within the GRANDRELATIVE or SPOUSE category.

Within the *!uĩ* categories, elder and younger are distinguished respectively by the egocentric relationship terms *ti-ki* (my elder 'sibling') and *ti-!uĩ* (my younger 'sibling'). *Ki* means literally 'old'. Relative age here is not of structural significance, in that relationships traced through an older 'sibling' (real or classificatory) are the same as relationships traced through a younger one. Yet, whereas relative age is not of structural significance, relative sex is, both in defining the JOKING/AVOIDANCE relationship between 'siblings' and in defining the relationships of those whose genealogies are traced through them. For this reason it is formally necessary to distinguish as two separate categories JOKING SIBLING and AVOIDANCE SIBLING.

The category *khue* also contains two non-reciprocating terms, but these distinguish only real sex. Since ego is always of the opposite sex as his or her *khue*, the distinction of relative sex cannot occur; only relative, and not real sex, is of structural significance in the Nharo relationship terminology. The sex-aspecific relationship term is *ti-khue* (with the suffix *-ba* or *-sa*), and the sex-specific terms are *ti-k'auba* (literally, 'my male') and *ti-g//aisa* ('my female'). The term *khue*, in its most general sense, means person and is cognate to Nama *khoe*. In its relationship term sense, it has the primary meaning 'spouse'.

The naming system

The Nharo name their children in much the same manner as the !Kung. In fact, many Nharo names are also !Kung names, and it is highly likely that the system was borrowed from the !Kung some centuries ago. There are differences, however. Whereas among the !Kung fathers name their children, among the Nharo grandparents or other senior GRANDRELATIVES give their own names. There is no rule of precedence about who should name the first child, except that the first set of grandparents to arrive after the birth of a child will do the honour. If both sets are present, there may be an argument about which name should be given, but once the naming occurs the child will keep its name for life. The naming of subsequent children of the marriage alternates between father's and mother's sides of the family. Names are passed from senior GRANDRELATIVES (grandparents and cross-uncles and aunts) to junior ones. Unlike the situation among the !Kung, there is no conflict of category since all those who may give names will stand in the same, GRANDRELATIVE relationship to the recipients. There is no special relationship between name-giver and name-receiver; all namesakes are GRANDRELATIVES and are thought of as close relatives. 'Namesake' (which in formal genealogical descriptions I abbreviate to 'N') is effectively a single degree of genealogical distance from ego.

The classification of relatives depends on proximity of relationship, and kinship is extended through 'namesake' as well as other links. For example, three links are closer than two. If alter is both male ego's MBD and his ZN, the latter relationship takes precedence and she is classified as his 'sister' or AVOIDANCE SIBLING (*ki* or *!uĩ*) rather than a GRANDRELATIVE (*tsxõ*). In the case of two means of reckoning giving the same number of degrees of distance, the order of precedence is affinal links first, then consanguineous ones, and then relations through namesakes. For example, if the same individual is both my WBS and my ZSN, the former line of reckoning would have to take precedence, and he would be my AVOIDANCE IN-LAW (*/ui*), not my GRANDRELATIVE (*tsxõ*). Of course, conflicting categorization can exist without further rules. When each of two people classifies the other as belonging to a different category, usually the one whose reckoning requires fewer genealogical steps will categorize the other, who will reciprocate appropriately. Sometimes, as among the !Kung, an older person will categorize a younger, who will reciprocate within the category given. In other cases, a conflict may arise, though this is only important if the two individuals are of opposite sex. Sometimes a pair will 'cheat' and apply whatever category they wish to apply, provided at least one has appropriate genealogical (including namesake) links to justify the classification (for further details, see Barnard 1978b: 616–20).

Through all these rules, it is possible for a Nharo to trace his or her relationship to everyone else in Nharo society, and to non-Nharo who are given the privilege of bearing a Nharo name. These names are said to be 'God-given', and are sex-specific and normally without meaning in the Nharo language. In contrast, nicknames are 'man-given' and are words in the Nharo language which describe some aspect of a person's appearance or character. The combination of these sets of names, plus infixes to indicate

relative age, allows the facility to distinguish individuals without the
necessity for surnames, although descriptions in terms of kin relationships
and places of origin are employed where necessary. The infixes are placed
between the name and an otherwise optional gender suffix, e.g., Dabe-*ki-ba*
(old Dabe), Dabe-*g//o-ba* (sexually mature Dabe), Dabe-/*ua-ba* (young
Dabe).

Ts'aokhoe, N/aints'e, and ≠ Haba kinship

The Ts'aokhoe have never been the subject of any intensive anthropological fieldwork. What we do know of them indicates that they are very similar
to the Nharo. Indeed there are no differences at all between the Nharo and
Ts'aokhoe kinship terminologies, either in the relationship terms themselves or in the categorical system of relationships they collectively identify.
The N/haints'e, according to E.O.J. Westphal (pers. comm.; cf. 1971: 379–
80), employ the same system of personal naming as the !Kung, Nharo, and
Ts'aokhoe, though ethnographically nothing else is known of them.
Indeed, they may be a branch of the ≠ Haba.

It is worth stressing that, linguistically, the ≠ Haba are not Western
Khoe Bushmen at all but Northern or Central. Their closest linguistic
relatives are the Bukakhoe, G/anda, and //Anikhoe of the Okavango, and
the G/wi and G//ana (Vossen 1988b: 67). Vossen's ≠ Haba informants are
those of the Ngamiland–Ghanzi District boundary, directly south of
Maun. A small number of Nharo are found in that area too, but the ≠ Haba
I encountered live well within the Ghanzi ranching area. There, at least,
they interacted closely with Nharo and Ts'aokhoe. They possessed the
!Kung-Nharo naming system, which would indicate at least a few generations of contact with the !Kung, or with Western Khoe Bushman groups.
The ≠ Haba I asked claim exactly the same rules of naming precedence as
the Zu/'hoãsi: FF, MF, etc., for boys, and FM, MM, etc., for girls (cf.
Marshall 1976: 223–5), while the Nharo and Ts'aokhoe simply alternate
between father's and mother's sides of the family. The fact that the ≠ Haba
are linguistically 'Central' rather than 'Western' Khoe Bushman comes out
clearly in the set of relationship terms which I present in Chapter 16 (Table
16.2). In particular, they employ the term *gabaxu* for all SIBLINGS. Apart
from indicating a Central Khoe lexical allegiance, this term marks the only
structural difference between the ≠ Haba and the Nharo-Ts'aokhoe terminologies. Equivalent to Nharo and Ts'aokhoe *ki* and *!uĩ*, the term is
employed for all SIBLINGS, not just younger ones. This is a very minor
structural distinction, but it is highly unusual for Khoe languages. In all
important respects, the structure of terminology usage (most notably the

terminology for GRANDRELATIVES) follows a Western rather than a Northern or Central pattern.

Religion and ritual

The Nharo God is usually termed N!adi-ba. As with the cognate term in G/wi, this is also the word for 'sky' in a secular sense. His wife or wives are called N!adi-sa (the same term, feminine singular) or N!adi-sara (feminine dual), but these are used only rarely, such as to describe as separate entities the 'mothers' of N!adiba's 'children' the Moon and the Sun (see Chapter 14).

N!adiba is believed to be the creator of the world. He is the being who established the customs of the Nharo, through their ancestors the 'Oldest Parents' (*Ka-je-n G//o-dzi*). The *Ka-je-n G//o-dzi* (the phrase is syntactically feminine but includes men and women alike) are distinguished conceptually from the *g//ãũa-ne* (common gender plural), who are the evil spirits, or spirits of the dead. All Nharo become *g//ãũane* when they die, and it is in the nature of the dead that they are 'evil', no matter how good they were in life. After a person's death and burial, contact with his or her spirit is avoided. The dead are rarely mentioned by name, and Nharo are afraid of the spirits. Spirits are said to visit the living, though these spirits are not thought of as the spirits of specific people that individuals knew in life.

The medicine dance, trance, and possession

Although the spirits are evil, their presence can be called upon in medicine dances, where they are forces for good. Nharo medicine men claim that the evil they remove from the bodies of those present at the dance either is thrown to spirits outside the dance circle, or, unusually, is dissipated through the body of the medicine man, who himself is voluntarily possessed by a spirit. Otherwise Nharo medicine dance, in form and indigenous explanation, is identical to those of neighbouring Bushman groups. Medicine dances are frequent (at least every month or so, and in some areas much more frequently), which is typical among relatively sedentary Kalahari Bushmen. Individual curing ceremonies are held too, especially when a member of the community is seriously ill.

I witnessed one case of involuntary spirit possession in 1975 (see also Barnard 1979b: 76–7). As far as I know, this is the only one recorded among any Khoisan group. One evening when women were singing and clapping, an elderly woman was 'possessed' by a passing spirit. She began to scream and shout obscenities. Others in the group tried but failed to calm her, and after about half an hour they built a fire in the centre of the camp. There, one of the men present quickly went into trance himself, by voluntary spirit possession. After about twenty minutes of intense effort, he successfully 'pulled' the evil spirit from the woman's body. During this time he placed his hands not only on the possessed woman's body, but also, for a short while, on the shoulders of each person present. Afterwards, the woman who had been possessed ran off into the bush. When she returned, a few minutes later, the evening went on as usual, almost as if nothing had happened. At the risk of sounding tritely functionalist, it was clear to me at the time that this unique event was handled effectively because of a common set of ideas about the ways in which spirits operate, and an apparent acceptance of the efficacy of the medicine dance in promoting good and dispersing evil. That is still my view. I was the only non-Nharo present, but had been at this site for some time and knew the inhabitants quite well. I believe that my own presence was entirely unrelated to the event.

Initiation rites and hunting magic
In Dorothea Bleek's time, the western Nharo indulged in lengthy male, group initiation rites involving seclusion in the bush, dancing, ritual tattooing, and the teaching and testing of hunting skills (Bleek 1928a: 23–5). The central Nharo among whom I worked either do not, or no longer, have male initiation in this sense. What they do have is a simple and optional ceremony to bring success to young hunters (Barnard 1980b: 117). This involves ritual tattooing, but little else. Young men receive two small cuts between the eyes, and sometimes cuts on the right wrist, right elbow, right upper arm, back, and left upper arm. The cuts between the eyes are made by a medicine man, but often the young man's wife or another woman makes the cuts on his arms and back. The Nharo claim that these tattoos help the hunter to 'see' better and shoot his bow more accurately. Many Nharo men do not go through the ceremony; those who are successful hunters or who do little hunting simply do not need to. Unsuccessful hunters may go through it more than once.

Young women, however, do go through an initiation ceremony at menarche (see Barnard 1980b: 117–18), for the Nharo are the archetypical performers of the Eland Bull Dance. Dorothea Bleek (1928a: 23) witnessed a ceremony which had two 'eland bulls' and regarded this as the norm. I have seen one Eland Bull Dance and had others described to me, and in all cases with which I am familiar there was only one such figure. The ceremony is normally held at the hut of the initiate's maternal grandmother or some other senior GRANDRELATIVE, and it lasts for several days. During this time, the girl sits alone in the hut and faces the wall. She is attended by women of the band. These women stay by the fire outside the hut and talk, not to the girl, but only to each other. The only man allowed near is the elderly 'eland bull'. Periodically, he joins the women and 'chases' them in dance step in a large figure-of-eight, with one loop around the hut and fire, and the other in the area beyond the fire. The women lift their skirts to expose their buttocks to the 'bull', and he puts his fingers above his head in the sign of the eland (as used in hunting sign language). He is always of the GRANDRELATIVE or *tsxõ* kinship category to the initiate (the marriageable category), but by virtue of his age, never marriageable himself. At the end of the celebrations, the female GRANDRELATIVE who waits on the girl gives her a gift, and from that point onwards she is free to take lovers or to marry.

Conclusion

The Nharo have been in contact with commercial ranchers for longer than any existing Kalahari Bushman people. Yet they retain much of their culture, even in the interior of the ranching area. The viability of their continued existence as a cultural group depends on their ability to determine their own lifestyles. To a large measure, they have been able to do this because they are the majority population in the Ghanzi farms and areas to the immediate south. Many Nharo herd their own livestock, and some grow crops. As with so many other Bushman groups, their future probably lies in animal husbandry. Their land is too poor for large-scale cultivation.

The remainder of the ethnographic part of this book deals with the Khoekhoe-speaking peoples. These include not only the Khoekhoe, but also the Damara and some hunter-gatherer groups of Namibia. The likenesses between these groups and the Nharo, and other Khoe-speaking Bushmen, should make us aware of the degree to which it is not possible to regard the Bushmen alone as defining a 'culture area'. The complications in distinguishing Bushman from Khoekhoe, and Damara from Bushman highlight the necessity of viewing Khoisan culture as a coherent if not a uniform entity.

9

The Cape Khoekhoe and Korana

Introduction

Schapera (1930: 44–50) divided the Khoekhoe into four ethnic divisions: the 'Cape Hottentots', 'Eastern Cape Hottentots', 'Korana' or '!Kora', and 'Naman' (Nama). More recent archival research suggests that the Eastern and Cape 'Hottentots' might best be considered a single people, the Cape Khoekhoe, and that three subdivisions were distinguishable within this group in historical times: Western, Central, and Eastern Cape Khoekhoe. According to historian Richard Elphick (e.g., 1985: xvi-xvii), each of the three subdivisions occupied their own ecologically and socially distinct regions. Another major ethnic division, the Einiqua, is mentioned in some of the early sources (especially Wikar 1935 [1779]), but ethnographically, virtually nothing is known about them except that they lived along the River Orange, to the east of the Korana (see Figure 9.1).

The Korana are the historic inhabitants of the northeastern Cape Province. It is doubtful that they can still be said to exist as an ethnic group, as in the course of the last two centuries their descendants have slowly become absorbed into the Baster, Griqua, or 'Coloured' population of the area (see Chapter 10). Nevertheless, their raiding activities were recorded by eighteenth- and nineteenth-century travellers, and their origins have become the subject of much debate among historians. More significantly, remnants of their culture survived in the memories of living individuals until at least the early part of the twentieth century. These remnants offer intriguing clues not only to the reconstruction of earlier ways of life among the Korana themselves, but also for the understanding of deeper structures of Khoisan society in general.

The late prehistory of the Cape

After thousands of years of occupation, settlement on the western Cape coast seems to have ended, for a time, not long after 8000 BP. Reoccupa-

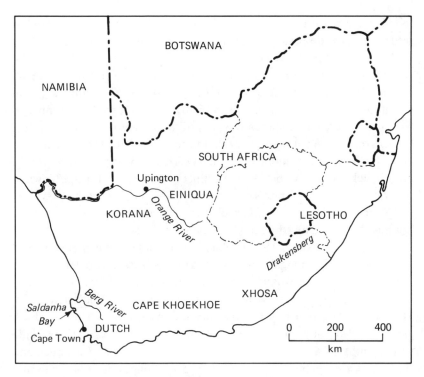

Figure 9.1 Locations of the Cape Khoekhoe (*c.* 1700), Einiqua (*c.* 1800), and Korana (*c.* 1800)

tion, presumably by the ancestors of later Bushman groups, began 4300 years ago and continued until the colonial period (Parkington 1987: 16–17). Virtually all areas of the Cape were occupied by hunter-gatherers, and the coastal Bushmen included shellfish in their diet. These coastal Bushmen are also known in the literature as the Strandlopers (literally 'beach-rangers'). Their linguistic affinity is not known, but they seem to have engaged in transhumant settlement of the coast. The Khoekhoe and the early Dutch settlers called these groups *Sonqua* (literally 'San', masc. pl.). About the time of the arrival of the Khoekhoe, the coastal Bushmen altered their settlement and subsistence strategy from one based on the large-band occupation of open areas and the hunting of large game towards the more intensive utilization of rock shelters, in small groups, and a foraging-based economy. The presumption is that the Khoekhoe took over areas previously utilized by hunter-gatherers and forced the latter to retreat to more isolated, high-ground coastal locations (Manhire 1987: 118–27).

The Khoekhoe probably arrived in the Cape some 2,000 years ago. Evidence of pottery and domestic stock dated at 2000 to 15000 BP has been found in the western and southern Cape, though interestingly, the oldest secure dates for domestic stock (sheep or goats) in the northern Cape are 1200 to 1100 BP (Klein 1986: 7). Some have suggested that coastal Khoekhoe groups were transhumant, but the details of transhumance are sketchy. According to Andrew Smith (1984), the Cochqua, a group encountered by Simon van der Stel in 1658, probably spent the autumn and winter in the area of Saldanha Bay; moved to the southeast, inland to the Berg River, in the spring (October); and returned northwards, then west along the Berg, in the summer (February). This circular pattern continued after Dutch settlement, but with a southern swing towards Cape Town in the spring, for trade. Smith's hypothesis has been contested by Tim Hart (1987) on the grounds that archaeological evidence to support it is simply not possible to obtain (though Hart himself has tried).

Clues to relations between Khoekhoe and other groups in prehistory can be found through analogies with events in the historical record (cf. Manhire 1987: 124). In the 1840s and 1850s, there was fierce raiding in 'Nomansland', on the fringe of the Drakensberg. Bushmen and disaffected Khoekhoe were at that time indistinguishable to Cape government agents. Both groups raided cattle from horseback and undoubtedly mixed socially (Vinnicombe 1976: 64–7). These known contacts between Khoekhoe and Bushmen are probably just the last instances of a long period of friendly and unfriendly contact between various groups in the northeastern Cape and Natal. Indeed, such contacts included blacks as well. Whole Khoe-speaking groups seem to have been incorporated as Nguni (southeastern Bantu) clans (Louw 1986: 160). Nguni languages (e.g., those of the Xhosa, Zulu, and Swazi) have also borrowed much click-containing vocabulary from Khoe and non-Khoe Bushman languages, while Sotho languages (the other main branch of Southern Bantu, including Southern Sotho, Tswana, and Kgalagari) have not. This Nguni vocabulary contains extensive Khoe material, including terms for herding practices, cattle markings, etc. (see, e.g., Louw 1979; 1986). Links between Khoe-speaking Bushmen, as well as Khoekhoe, cannot be ruled out. No systematic study has yet been done, but there is evidence, in Zulu, of Khoe vocabulary found in Nharo but not in Khoekhoe (John Argyle, pers. comm.).

What all this suggests to me is that, before the colonial period, a number of diverse groups inhabited present-day South Africa. It is possible that some were speakers of some previous, unknown non-click language, but there is no evidence of this. We do know that some were 'Bush'-speakers (in the sense of Westphal [1963]), some were Khoe-speakers, and some were Bantu-speakers. The Khoe-speakers, who arrived in the area after the non-

Khoe-speaking Bushmen but before the Bantu-speakers, included *both* hunter-gatherer and herder populations. Khoe-speaking herders who lost their livestock could easily become 'Bushmen', and vice versa. This is precisely what happened in colonial times (see e.g., Marks 1972; Schrire 1980); the later equation of ethnicity with the hunter/herder boundary is, arguably, an invention of European commentators, and even anthropologists in particular. For this reason, if no other, it is important to consider the Khoekhoe and the Bushmen as members of a single 'regional' unit, separate from the other (black and white) peoples of the subcontinent.

The Cape Khoekhoe in the colonial period
The first permanent European settlement in South Africa was by members of the Dutch East India Company in 1652. At this time, the Cape was the home of a pastoral population which became known as the Cape Khoekhoe. The Cape Khoekhoe included Khoekhoe-speaking inhabitants of the area from the Cape Peninsula proper to the Great Fish River. Not a great deal is known about them, although their culture has been the subject of much speculation over the last century or so.

Sources on the Cape Khoekhoe
Among the more interesting pieces of research on this people, G.S. Nienaber (1960; 1963b), a professor of Afrikaans, compiled wordlists from the works of the Dutch colonists and later works of travellers in the interior; L.F. Maingard (1931; 1934) speculated on their tribal history; and Richard Elphick (1977; 1979; 1985) described their contact with the Dutch and their eventual cultural demise, which took place not long after a devastating smallpox epidemic in 1713. Elphick's thesis on Khoekhoe–Dutch interaction in the Cape was published as *Kraal and castle* (Elphick 1977) and subsequently revised and reprinted as *Khoikhoi and the founding of white South Africa* (Elphick 1985). I shall cite here from the revised edition. Other historians have specialized in the long periods of warfare which followed, among them Susan Newton-King (1981) and V.C. Malherbe (1981), who have written specifically on the Khoekhoe 'rebellion' in the eastern Cape. Sadly, it is mainly in the accounts of such events that details of Cape Khoekhoe activities are to be found, though little of comparative ethnographic interest can be reconstructed from them (cf. Szalay 1983).

In addition to modern reassessments of early-contact Khoekhoe society, there are important early texts which have been published or reprinted in the present century. These include Schapera's collection *The early Cape Hottentots* (1933), which gives the Latin and Dutch accounts of three early

Dutch writers with English translations. Further details are known through the brilliant eighteenth-century monograph by Peter Kolb (also known as Kolbe or Kolben), *Caput Bonae Spei Hodiernum*, Volume I. This volume was published in German in 1719, Dutch in 1727, English in 1731, and French in 1741; and a German translation of the abridged French edition appeared in 1745. The most readily available version is a facsimile reprint of the 1731 edition (Kolb 1968). This edition, 'done into English from the original by Mr Medley', is not particularly reliable as an exact translation of Kolb's words, but is of very high standard among ethnographies of the time for both detail (including illustrations) and readability. In fact, Peter Kolb – by training and profession a mathematician, meteorologist, astronomer, court clerk, and schoolmaster – seems to have found his true calling as an ethnographer. His report is highly sympathetic to the objects of his study, and at times amusing as well as informative.

Cape Khoekhoe custom and social structure

We know only the outline of Cape Khoekhoe social structure, but from what we do know it seems that Cape tribes were similar in internal relations to those of better known Khoekhoe groups, i.e., the Nama and Korana (see, e.g., Dapper 1933 [1668]; Ten Rhyne 1933 [1686]). Descent, which determined group membership, was patrilineal, and precedence was established within tribes, clans, and lineages by primogeniture. Tribal and kin group organization was hierarchical, with chiefs at the top of the hierarchy (Kolb 1968 [1731]: 84–7). Chiefship was hereditary, but a chief's authority was held in check by his council, consisting of the 'captains' – also a hereditary office – of all the clans under his authority. *Kaptein* or *captain* is the traditional term in Dutch, Afrikaans, English, and as a loan word, German, for a clan leader among the Khoisan groups. As the military association of the term suggests, Khoekhoe captains (as well as chiefs) were war leaders. They also decided the outcome of civil disputes among their subjects and punished criminal offenders. At the time of Dutch settlement, each Cape Khoekhoe captain wore a 'tiger' skin (in southern Africa, the term refers to any of several indigenous species of small cat) as a mark of his office. For some reason, the Dutch soon saw fit to replace these symbols with their own – staffs of office made of wood and brass. These and government-issued replacements continued in use in the northwestern Cape long after the end of Dutch control, and, very possibly, may still be found there in the hands of families of aristocratic Khoekhoe descent.

Cape Khoekhoe groups were mobile and unstable. Camp size was variable and depended on the availability of resources, the local patterns of seasonal mobility, and the need for defence against raiders. Early writers record settlements of twenty or fewer huts, and settlements of over a hundred huts. The population density was high, in both people and cattle, when compared to later Khoekhoe habitats in the interior (Carstens 1969: 96–7). Kin ties were more important to the Cape Khoekhoe than geographical territory. Indeed, they displayed rather more interest in kinship than the Dutch felt obliged to record. Dutch officials were taken aback by questions as to their own ancestry and whether their chief 'was also of high descent' (Elphick 1985: 43), and they left virtually no details of kinship customs except records of chiefly succession.

The most notorious ceremony of the Cape Khoekhoe was the excision of one testicle of every male child at or before puberty. This was reported in some detail by Kolb (1968 [1731]: 112–18) and mentioned in passing by other early writers. Excision was denied by some nineteenth-century scholars, though Schapera (1930: 71–2) accepted it as likely that the practice did exist and later died out. I am inclined to believe it existed among specific Cape groups, but never more widely. If it did occur, it seems to have had something to do either with the prevention of the birth of twins (Kolb's explanation) or as an aid to faster running (the more general opinion)!

No record of female initiation practices survives, but male initiation was apparently an elaborate, individual affair (Kolb 1968 [1731]: 119–24). As Cape Khoekhoe adult men ate separately from women and children, male initiation granted a boy the right to eat with the men. The ceremony involved daubing the initiate with fat and soot, ritual urination on him by the elders, and the killing, cooking, and eating of a sheep. The celebrated practice of urinating on the initiate seems, by Kolb's account, to have conferred good luck and fertility, though comparison with the ceremonies of other Khoekhoe groups suggests it may be related to the notion of 'washing' away the boy's adolescence (cf. Schapera 1930: 279–85).

We know a little of Cape Khoekhoe marriage practices, though only enough to arouse speculation about how these compare to those of other Khoekhoe groups. According to Grevenbroek (1933 [1695]: 198–9):

When a girl becomes of marriageable age and ripe for a husband, a suitor from a neighbouring village, but never from the same one as his beloved . . . purchases her from her parents at the lowest price for which he can get her. Through this old established custom it is secured that she is betrothed to a stranger [*alienigenae*] and not to one of the same stock [*non gentilitio eam*]; the risk of incest is met, and the danger of illicit union . . . avoided.

Grevenbroek goes on to liken Cape Khoekhoe marriage, probably incorrectly, to female servitude. To me, his statement on courtship, bridewealth, and the prohibition of marriage to individuals of 'the same stock' is consistent with Khoekhoe custom in general. I take this phrase as excluding clan members as potential spouses and enjoining marriage to members of other clans, with compensation being claimed for the loss of the productive labour of a female clan member. If rules applying in other Khoekhoe groups also apply here, she would still have rights in her natal group, particularly over her brothers and their children, but she would invest her labour in the household of her husband and her children (cf. Kolb 1968 [1731]: 148–58, 160–1).

Each newborn baby is washed in cow-dung, dried in the sun, and then smeared with fat and powdered with buchu, prior to being named (Kolb 1968 [1731]: 141, 146–8). Buchu (this South African English word is derived from Cape Khoekhoe) consists of the crushed leaves of particular species of fragrant plants, and is still used in Bushman 'perfumes', in bush 'tea', and (by whites) in 'medicinal' brandy. Among the Cape Khoekhoe, buchu was used on both the newborn baby and its mother, and women also powdered themselves after menstrual seclusion. In these instances it was used as a means of purification, perhaps in a sense loosely analogous to the use of urine in male initiation.

Kolb (1968 [1731]: 90–111) was less sympathetic to religious aspects of Khoekhoe culture than to other customs, but does give a moderately informative account. According to Kolb – more specifically Medley's translation of Kolb – the Cape Khoekhoe recognized a supreme deity, but prayed to the Moon instead. Possibly the moon is best seen here simply as a manifestation of the supreme deity, though a distinction between the High God and the Moon is explicity suggested in Medley's translation (see Chapter 14). The Khoekhoe have long been considered moon-worshippers, and Kolb's account does not go very far to dispel this view. Full moon was a time of celebration among the Cape Khoekhoe, just as today it is the most common time for medicine dance performances among the Kalahari Bushmen.

The Korana
Historical and ethnographic sources

At the time of *The Khoisan peoples* (Schapera 1930), sources on the Korana were thin in comparison to those on the Nama. Indeed, Schapera declared that: 'The only Hottentot people whose social organization is at all well known are the Naman of South-West Africa' (1930: 223). His discussion of Khoekhoe social organization is highly dependent on Hoernlé's articles on the Nama, published in the 1910s and 1920s. Korana social organization was assumed to have been similar, and Schapera drew occasionally on the historical accounts of George W. Stow (1905) and George McCall Theal

(1907; 1919), who generally followed Stow, for such information. Stow, a geologist by profession and an historian by inclination, spent many years with the Korana in the late nineteenth century. His Korana ethnography is exceptionally idiographic and tucked into a long volume on the history of South Africa (Stow 1905: 267–315).

Fortunately, Korana studies did not end there. In the 1930s two able scholars made the Korana their special interest: L.F. Maingard (especially 1932; 1962; 1964) and J.A. Engelbrecht (1936). Both Engelbrecht and Maingard were linguists by training who, not without some success, dabbled in ethnography, folklore, and history. Engelbrecht was a South African who held academic posts at Pretoria and Stellenbosch. Maingard was a Mauritian who settled in South Africa and became Professor of French at the University of the Witwatersrand. Neglecting his appointed area of study further, Maingard later ventured to the central Kalahari and produced seminal studies in the comparative linguistics of the Khoisan, and particularly the Khoe-speaking, peoples (see Maingard 1957; 1958; 1961; 1963).

Engelbrecht is our primary source. He studied the existing social structure and the memory culture of the Korana who lived in the northern Cape Province in the 1920s and 1930s. His scholarly study, *The Korana* (1936), is based partly on this work and partly on earlier accounts. It remains the most definitive text on the people and includes a large amount of historical detail, as well as cultural information and Korana texts.

Other writers include the German linguists C.F. Wuras (1920) and C. Meinhof (1930), the ethnomusicologist Percival Kirby (1932), the traveller Hendrik Jacob Wikar (1935 [1779]), and other travellers and missionaries of the nineteenth century. More recently, historians have taken an interst in the Korana. These include Robert Ross (1975) and Teresa Strauss (1979), among others.

Origins and tribal divisions
It seems likely that the recent, historic location of the Korana people was both a dispersal point for the Khoekhoe nations in prehistoric times and an area of renewed settlement after Dutch colonization of the Cape (see Chapter 2). There can be little doubt that before colonization this area was inhabited by speakers of a dialect similar to that recorded in the early twentieth century by Engelbrecht and Maingard. The major disagreement among scholars is on whether the Korana can be said to be the aboriginal inhabitants of the northeastern Cape, or whether they are best seen as eighteenth-century refugees from the Cape Town area.

We know that the Korana were a cluster of some eight named Khoekhoe tribes who lived along the banks of the Orange, in the northeastern Cape, upstream of the Nama and the mysterious Einiqua. So little is known about their origin that the historian Robert Ross (1975) doubts their existence as a uniform ethnic group. In his view, the term 'Korana' was applied indiscriminately to various bands of raiders who moved about this part of the country. Nevertheless, individuals possessing a common language, ethnic identity, oral history, and memory culture lived in this area and called themselves 'Korana' in the twentieth century, and were the subject of ethnographic and linguistic studies by Engelbrecht (1936) and Maingard (1932; 1962; 1964). The extensive fieldwork by Engelbrecht and Maingard was largely completed by the early 1930s. Even then, much of the culture they described was preserved only in the memory of old men and women who were already classed as 'Coloureds' by the South African authorities.

Contrary to the often-cited story recorded by Wuras (1929: 290) that the Korana are the aboriginal inhabitants of their country, legend tells that the Korana were descended from a tribe of Cape Khoekhoe whose chief was named !Ora. This latter indigenous theory of origin was recorded by Stow (1905: 268–70) and Meinhof (1930: 13), among others. According to these accounts, the term 'Korana' (properly, !Orana or !Korana) is derived from the common gender plural form of the chief's name. Maingard (1932: 106–14) was sceptical. Not only was he critical of both Stow's sources and his use of them, but he even quoted Wuras against him. Some recent historians are not kindly disposed towards Stow's and Meinhof's version either. They emphasize instead the period of warfare in the northwestern Cape, around 1770 to 1820, and the new tribal configurations which emerged. One puts it rather boldly: 'The resulting tangle of social relationships, exacerbated in the frontier zone period, makes it well-nigh impossible to link Khoisan political groupings in the nineteenth century to any earlier Khoisan political history' (Legassick 1979: 251). So it seems that the Korana might or might not be descended from a Cape Peninsula clan. Any discernible differences between Cape Khoekhoe and Korana could be due either to historical changes or to ethnic differences.

My view is that Legassick and other recent writers go too far in their condemnation of earlier theories of migration. Maingard's (1932: 114) suggestion that groups may have 'trickled on to the Orange River in small sections' is an eminently reasonable compromise. As he points out, what we know of Cape Khoekhoe and Korana culture shows that these peoples were closer to each other than either was to Nama. Indeed Maingard (1964) later found linguistic evidence to support the view that the Orange River area boasted two groupings in historical times: tribes of the Lower Orange River, known as the *Einikwa* (Maingard's orthography) or 'Riverfolk', in the area east of modern Upington, and the tribes of the Upper Orange River, including the more intensively studied Korana groups. He found individuals in each of these areas who spoke different dialects. The western dialect (Einikwa or Einiqua) more closely resembled Nama than did the eastern, but was nevertheless essentially Korana. In Maingard's words: 'Thus Wikar's old division of the Einikwa and the Korakwa, which he based on social grounds, is fully vindicated on linguistic evidence' (1964: 66).

Ignoring the Einiqua, the tribal remnants identified in living populations by Maingard (1964: 57–60) included two main Korana groups: the *Kei !Korana* (his orthography) and the *≠ nu://'eis*. The latter were split into two subtribes: the *kx'am//'õãkwa* (Right Hands) and the *!geixa//'eis* (Sorcerers). In addition to these, there were remnants of other groups, including the *//kũbeku* (Springbokke or Springboks) and the */hõãn* (Katte, Katse, or Kats, i.e. 'cats'). The names for some of the divisions recorded by Maingard reflect the traditional segmentation of Khoekhoe groups into twos, seniority being indicated by terms such as 'great' (*kei*) or 'right hand', and juniority by the designation 'left hand'. The problem is that all these terms are relative, and historical accounts differ on the exact relationships between some of the groups. Stow (1905: 267–315), Maingard (1932: 106–33), and Engelbrecht (1936: 1–79) all give extensive, but at times confusing and conflicting, summaries of these relationships. For example, all refer to *!uri-ka-mã-khoena* (high-standing people), *hooge kraal* (high kraal), *hoogstaanders* (high-standing ones), *hoogmoedigevolk* (proud folk), etc., but these terms do not necessarily identify the same group. Sometimes 'high-standing' refers to a specific group who consistently called themselves 'the Hoogstanders' to the exclusion of all other names, and at other times merely to the chiefly family of some other group. Engelbrecht (1936: 27–8) also notes the indigenous distinction between the *boland* (up-country) and *onderveld* (down-country) groups. The former include the Great Korana, who call themselves the Taaibosch ('Tough-bush' people), and their offshoot, the Links ('Lefties'). The latter include groups who are believed to have remained behind at the time of early migrations, namely the Kats, Springboks, etc., and the 'high kraal', presumably the senior subdivision of the Links. The Links, sometimes seen as related to the !Gaixa-//'ēis or Towenaars (Maingard's 'Sorcerers'), are the group Maingard and

Engelbrecht knew best. The population Engelbrecht studied was a mixture of individuals, with diverse ancestral ties and oral histories to match. However, in a footnote Engelbrecht (1936: 25) does suggest – with an apology for the confusion his text will cause – a simplified explanation of the relationship: 'All this evidence points to the fact that there were two large divisions: (1) that of the Right Hand, or Great Korana, to which must therefore also be reckoned the Right Hand Tribe of Bethany; (11) the Left Hand division with the Links tribe.'

We still know relatively little about early Korana society, but we do know quite a bit about the memory culture preserved by certain individuals of Korana descent. The description which follows is therefore based on the later accounts of that memory culture. I make no apology for this. Recent historians like Elphick, Ross, and Legassick seem loath to present anything but almost isolated details about the Korana; they draw what general statements they do make from analogy with the Nama of the early twentieth century. Yet the memory culture as Maingard and Engelbrecht recorded it was rich in detail and intriguing in its implicit ideology, and occasionally in its revelation of indigenous anthropological understanding. Even if the Korana *mis*-remembered their culture, what they gave their ethnographers constitutes a valuable ideological statement much more interesting for our purposes than many a historical reconstruction.

Political organization

Camps were temporary, since before the present century the Korana were a nomadic people. They moved with their cattle on foot, by riding oxen, and even by raft, across the many rivers which run through their territories (see Engelbrecht 1936: 83–5).

However, land seems to have been 'owned' by the hereditary chief (the *gao-kx'aob* or ≠*nu:sab*), who held authority over the territory and its inhabitants and was the sole decision-maker in declarations of war (Engelbrecht 1936: 89). Each chief was the leader of a tribe or clan, often claiming patrilineal descent from a common ancestor. The chiefship was normally inherited by the chief's eldest son or, if he had no sons, by his brothers and their sons. Chiefs were sometimes elected by council, particularly if an heir proved incompetent to hold office. Under the chiefs were 'sub-chiefs' or 'field-cornets'. In Korana they were called literally 'the chief's right arm' or 'the chief's substitute', and they each held authority over a camp or 'kraal' (Engelbrecht 1936: 89–90).

The Korana camp

The indigenous designation for any social unit – a tribe, a tribal division, a clan, or a 'kraal' (in the sense of local kin group or homestead) – was //'ĕis (Engelbrecht's orthography), often suffixed to the name of the relevant unit. This term is found in a variety of forms in earlier accounts: //eis (feminine singular, in reference to the social unit), //eikwa or //aikwa (a syntactically masculine plural collective noun, but including females), //aina (the common gender plural form, synonymous with //aikwa), etc.

According to Engelbrecht (1936: 89–93), the Korana camp was formed in a great circle of huts (see Figure 9.2). Only members of the //'ĕis – the tribe or clan who owned the camp – occupied huts within this circle. The outsiders, in Engelbrecht's time called *bywoners* (an Afrikaans term which also means 'squatters'), lived outside the circle, along with a few clan leaders assigned the task of looking after them. These outsiders included unrelated Korana (those of other clans), Tswana, and Bushman servants.

The preferred campsite was always one with a large tree. The camp would be formed around this tree, although not necessarily with the tree in the exact centre. Among some Korana groups, the tree was known as the /haos (from /hao, 'to hang'), because meat was often hung in its branches to dry. Among other Korana groups, it was called the ≠nub heib ('sit tree', Engelbrecht's orthography), since it was the place where the council of men sat to discuss war, or other matters, and to try judicial cases. The tree also marked the place where men gathered to boil or roast meat, and no women were allowed to sit under it.

In the centre of the great kraal were a large common kraal for cattle, sometimes a smaller common kraal for calves, and others for goats and sheep. These kraals were made of bushes and branches. Sometimes milking cows were tied by their horns and roped to poles outside the kraals, and herdsmen were stationed nearby to watch over the stock. Also nearby and within the camp circle, stood the *doro* hut. This temporary building was erected immediately to the left of the cattle kraal (when seen from the headman or chief's hut), and it was used only for male initiation rites.

There does not seem to have been any necessity to align the camp according to compass bearings, but hierarchy was determined by relative directions, with reference to the hut of the chief or sub-chief. This hut occupied a position directly opposite the cattle kraal gate. To its immediate right (when facing the cattle kraal from the chief or sub-chief's hut) stood the hut of his eldest married son, then the huts of his other sons, in order of seniority, and then those of his brothers and their sons. In some tribes, the hut of the kraal head's youngest son occupied not the last position in the

168　*Khoisan ethnography*

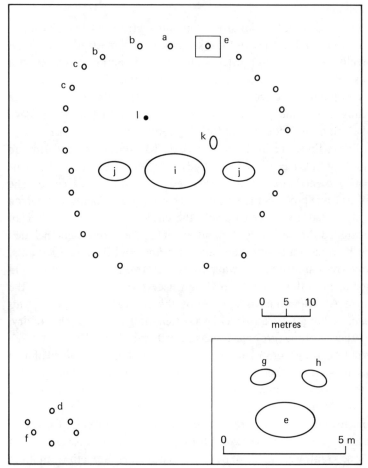

Figure 9.2 A Korana camp (from descriptions by Engelbrecht 1936: 89–93)
a chief or captain
b chief's married sons
c chief's brothers
d 'field-cornet'
e household of ordinary man
f servants
g unmarried girls
h unmarried boys and household servants
i cattle kraal
j sheep and goat kraals
k temporary male initiation hut
l camp tree (men's council and eating place)

line of huts to the right, but rather, the special position to the immediate left of that of the kraal head. The reason for this, according to Engelbrecht's informants, was that it was the youngest son's duty to look after the kraal head's wife (the lad's mother), in case of the old man's death (Engelbrecht 1936: 91). It is also conceiveable that a rather special relationship existed between this son and his mother, for the youngest child, irrespective of sex, was always the principal heir to his or her mother's estate (see Engelbrecht 1936: 191–2; cf. Carstens 1983a).

Subsistence and commensality

Like other Khoekhoe groups in historical times, the Korana were herders who also subsisted partly by hunting, gathering, and fishing, and partly by raiding their neighbours. Game was caught by a variety of means, including traps, bow and arrow, and knobkerrie. Their methods and even the taboos associated with hunting (e.g., not hunting while one's wife is menstruating, not killing more than the group can eat, etc.) resembled those of Bushman hunters (see Engelbrecht 1936: 86–9). As well as meat, gathered vegetables and fish were among the staples. Milk, fresh or sour (like yogurt), was the staple drink, and a kind of 'gravy' consisting of melted butter and cow-dung was considered a delicacy (1936: 112–13).

The Korana distinguished two types of meat, acccording to where it was eaten and who could eat it. One type was the 'men's meat', that cooked and eaten by men at the /haos, and the other was the meat cooked and eaten at the individual huts. Domesticated animals were butchered at the /haos and then cooked. Of cattle, most meat from the spine, backbone, and shoulder blades, as well as choice internal organs, were 'men's meat'; and specific parts of this meat, namely the kidneys and rectum, were reserved for the oldest man of the village. Of sheep and goats, only the heart, lungs, liver, paunch, and kidneys were reserved for men; the rest went to the huts. Game meat was not eaten at the /haos but went directly to the huts. However, the head, neck, and breast of any animal, domestic or hunted, was always reserved for its owner's mother's brother (Stow 1905: 272; Engelbrecht 1936: 123–25, 216–17).

Apart from the custom of men eating at the /haos, men and women could eat together elsewhere. As is customary in Khoekhoe society, wives held authority over household goods and over household food. A man would have to have permission from his wife in order to eat anything there. If she went out, she would leave instructions with her children as to what their father might or might not eat (Engelbrecht 1936: 96–7).

Some aspects of Korana kinship

The most obvious principle of Korana kinship, perhaps, is patrilineal descent, which is associated with primogeniture and a hierarchical relation between lineage-based local groups (see 'Political organization', above). Beyond this, Korana kinship is characterized by an unusual naming system common specifically to Khoekhoe-speaking peoples, by strict rules of conduct governed by joking and avoidance principles, and by an interesting variant of the Khoe relationship terminology structure. This entails both these joking and avoidance relationships and a system of marital exchange.

The naming system of the Korana included both patrilineal names (tribal and clan) and 'great names' (Engelbrecht 1936: 151–2). Great names (*kei khoe /'ona*) were transmitted from mother to son and from father to daughter. A group of brothers would all bear their mother's great name, while a group of sisters would bear the great name of their father. Therefore, given that their respective parents would have been named in the same way, a man shared his name with his maternal grandfather, and a woman shared hers with her paternal grandmother. This could be interpreted variously as 'cross-descent', in contrast to 'parallel' and reflecting the cross-sex transmission of names, or as 'alternating descent', reflecting the inter-generational links between same-sex namesakes. In addition to tribal, clan, and great names, Korana also bore names which referred to events occurring at the time of their birth (e.g., */Arob*, '[born beside the] Road'). These names were also applied to one's parents (e.g., */Arob is,* 'Road's mother'). Adults had nicknames (e.g., */Xa:-tama*, 'Hairy Chest'), which were in turn applied collectively, in either Korana or Afrikaans, to their children (e.g., the 'Hairy Chests'). In Engelbrecht's time, it was customary for a first-born son to bear his father's Christian name (with his mother's great name), and a first-born daughter to bear her mother's Christian name. In some Korana groups, it was customary for the second-born son to bear his maternal grandfather's Christian name.

The basic structure of the relationship terminology is illustrated in Figure 9.3. The terms presented are those recorded by Engelbrecht (1936: 152–4), with number-gender suffixes (-*b*, masc. sg. and -*s*, fem. sg.) removed. A full list of terms recorded by all ethnographers and linguists among the Korana is given in Table 16.2 (Chapter 16). The only inconsistency in the structure of indigenous-term usage suggested by any of them is that specific, named Korana individuals observed by Maingard (1932: 144) employed the stem *//nuri-* (Engelbrecht's *//nuli-*) for 'cousin by mother's sister' and 'uncle by marriage'. Engelbrecht's central concern was with Korana memory culture, and he did not record Dutch-derived terms. Maingard (1932: 144), though,

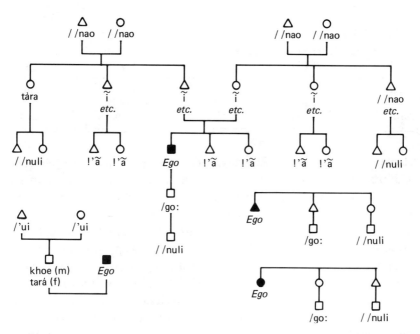

Figure 9.3 Korana relationship terminology: basic structure (suffixes -*b* [masc.] and -*s* [fem.] omitted)

noted the use of *moekis, oumas,* and *outab* (possibly the second and certainly the last being a Dutch–Korana compound) respectively for 'father's sister' or 'great aunt', and 'great uncle' or 'grandfather' (cf. Chapters 10 and 11).

The mother's brother stood in a peculiar relation to his sister's children; and to some extent, it seems that a maternal grandparent might stand in a similar relationship to his daughter's children (see Engelbrecht 1936: 154–7). By a custom known as ≠ *na*– ≠ *nab*, the mother's brother would take any defective goods from his sister's sons and daughter and replace them with better ones. It was also quite in order for a young man, at least, to take anything he liked which belonged to his mother's brother. After the mother's brother's death, his son would take his place in this relationship, which continued irrespective of the marital status of the parties involved. The opposite relationship was that between a father's sister (*tàras*) and her brothers' children, a relationship which connoted great respect and authority. This respect relationship also applied, to some extent, between brothers and sisters.

In fact, in relation to any given man, there were three classes of women: those prohibited as spouses, those permitted, and those who became

Table 9.1 *Korana relationship terms for women of male ego's generation*

FZD	FBD	Z	MZD	MBD
//nulis	—	—	—	//nulis
!'ãs (?)	!'ãs	!'ãs	!'ãs	—
tàras	tàras	tàras	tàras	tarás

eligible as mates only after a sacrifice was performed (Engelbrecht 1936:126–9). Any woman of the prohibited category was a *tàras* ('father's sister', etc.), or in some Korana groups, a *!'ãs* ('sister', etc.). The reciprocal term, which she would use for him, was *≠ xana-khoeb*. Individuals permitted as spouses were termed *//nuli-* ('cross-cousins', etc.). From the details given by Engelbrecht (cf. 1936: 127, 131, 153), it is possible to view the terminology of opposite-sex individuals within ego's generation as belonging to various overlapping categories, which I define (e.g., Barnard 1980a; 1987; cf. Chapter 16) as GRANDRELATIVES (including those termed *//nuli-*), SPOUSES (for females, *tará-*), AVOIDANCE SIBLINGS (*!'ã*), and RESPECT RELATIVES (*tàra-*). The classification of females of male ego's generation by these four terms is shown in Table 9.1. The overlap between the categories reflects two things: whether JOKING or AVOIDANCE categories are appropriate, and whether, within these larger categories, stronger or weaker terminology is to be employed. Regarding the first, there seems to have been some disagreement among Korana, specifically in the classification of FZD and MBS. Are they JOKING (reflecting the possibility of bilateral cross-cousin marriage), or AVOIDANCE (reflecting matrilateral cross-cousin marriage)? Regarding the second, the JOKING categories here are GRANDRELATIVE and SPOUSE, while the AVOIDANCE categories are AVOIDANCE SIBLING and RESPECT RELATIVE. Of these terms, SPOUSE is a 'stronger', more specific categorization than GRANDRELATIVE, and RESPECT RELATIVE is probably a more extreme avoidance classification than AVOIDANCE SIBLING.

An alliance theory view

The traditional understanding of Khoekhoe kinship stresses the hierarchical relations between patrilineal groups and customs like cattle-snatching on the part of a man's sister's sons. In my view, these interests reflect only part of this system, in the same way that studies of kinship generally, before Lévi-Strauss (1969 [1949]), failed to take adequate account of relations of marital alliance.

Never has an alliance theory view been more relevant to southern African ethnography than in the case of the Korana. Engelbrecht and his informants probably had no idea of the theoretical interest their statements held, but they left clear indications as to the importance of marriage in relations between groups (see also Barnard 1975). Consider this statement by Engelbrecht (1936: 55), citing one of his informants, Hendrick Flink (great name, *Alogob*): 'Flink states that the ancestors of all the divisions of the Bethany Hottentots took their wives from among the Towenaars. It has been vaguely suggested that the solution of this problem lies with the Taaibosch or the Links.' The 'Bethany Hottentots', it will be remembered, are the 'high-standing ones', in relation to the 'left-hand' Towenaars. Benjamin Kats (great name, *!Hamarib*), one of Engelbrecht's chief inform- ants, puts it more plainly: 'When the people of a kraal marry they have children. Their female children used to be married by the men of another kraal and the people of this (i.e. the latter) kraal were then the *little* of the other kraal (i.e. the one from which the women came) which was now the *great* one' (Engelbrecht 1936: 3; his emphasis).

Following Kats, we may take it that there existed an indigenous ideology of generalized exchange. How this ideology is played out in practice depends on the arrangements between 'kraals'. Certainly, Kats' statement suggests that the 'descent theory' view of Khoekhoe society, which lays emphasis on seniority among lineages for the 'great' and 'little' distinctions, may not be the answer. When coupled with the notion of marriage of a man to the category of the MBD (for a woman, the category of the FZS), his statement implies a much more 'alliance theory' model of Khoekhoe society than southern African ethnographers have generally imagined. Lévi-Strauss, presumably unfamiliar with Engelbrecht's ethnography, comments as follows on the Khoekhoe ethnography he did know:

Among the Hottentots, Hoernlé [1925] tells us, marriage between cross-cousins does not seem to have been the object of any positive obligation; it was only that marriage between parallel cousins was strictly prohibited. And yet, it is rare to find a kinship system so faultlessly built up about the dichotomy of cousins and the intermarriage of two classes as the Hottentot system. (Lévi-Strauss 1969 [1949]: 102)

Putting all this together with the fact that Khoekhoe 'great names' (as well as the patrilineal groups they cross-cut) form exogamous units, a compli- cated alliance structure can be generated. An idealized representation of such a system has been likened to Australian section systems in the categories and rules it might entail (Barnard 1975).

Marriage
Korana parents, in consultation with their own parents or elder same-sex siblings, often arranged marriages for their children (see Engelbrecht 1936: 130–6). Sometimes young men arranged their own marriages or sent

emissaries, but parental consent was still required. Bridewealth cattle might be driven to the prospective bride's home; and if they were kept, the marriage could go ahead. If they were driven back, the proposal was refused. Then a woman of the category *tàras* (FZ, FZD, etc.) would enter the picture. A man's *tàras* was responsible for ensuring that arrangements were successful. Her consent was required in order for him to marry. If fighting broke out between her ≠ *xana-khoeb*'s people and the intended in-laws, she had the power to stop it. She was treated with great respect, and in this she stood in clear opposition to the //*naob* or mother's brother. Both the groom's and the bride's mothers' brothers contributed cattle to the wedding feast. In fact, marriage involved a number of exchanges from both sides of the family, the most crucial being the *!u-* ≠ *'a:-gomas* (literally, 'hind-kaross slaughter cow') given by the groom for the feast, and the //*nanib* ('front-kaross [cow]') given by the groom to the bride's mother in recognition of her service in raising the bride from infancy.

Post-marital residence at the wife's paternal home was required until the birth of the first child, and yet another ceremonial payment of a cow, this time one which was pregnant or with a calf (Engelbrecht 1936: 135–6). Marriages could be dissolved in cases of incompatibility or barrenness, and a wide network of relatives could be involved in divorce negotiations, when they occurred (1936: 143–4). Illicit sex between unmarried people was said to be rare. Between married people (or between a married man and an unmarried woman), it was more common and to some extent even institutionalized. These relationships of *!xaus*, as they were called, had associated notions of pollution and rites of purification, such as the requirement that a man should visit a brother or a woman of the //*nuli* or *tarás* category (i.e., a classificatory 'wife'), to touch her or wash at her camp, before he came home to his actual wife (1936: 145–50).

Other rites and customs

Engelbrecht gives virtually no details at all of religious belief. He notes that some Korana had vague notions of an evil spirit called //*gaunab* or //*ganãb* and spooks or ghosts called *!'u:sana* (1936: 180), but this is the extent of his record. However, he does record details of rain and drought ceremonies, of magic and witchcraft beliefs (which he presumed to be borrowed from Bantu-speaking groups), burial practices, hunting magic, and male initiation ceremonies. The last two sets of customs were by far the most elaborate and intriguing (see Engelbrecht 1936: 157–61).

The male initiation ceremony, or *dorob*, involved a month of seclusion. The old men would inform the young man that he was about to be initiated, and immediately he would be taken to the cattle kraal and kept there until an initiation hut was built. The candidate was stripped and then dressed in a small girl's hind-kaross. Brass rings were put on his arms (as women wear them) rather than on his legs (which is the custom among men). Red ochre and fat were rubbed on his body. There was always plenty of meat to eat during the *dorob*, but the candidate was forced to eat his from the end of a sharp stick, rather than with his hands. On the last day, the candidate drank medicinal milk to 'purify' him from childish things and was again rubbed with ochre and fat. Finally, his mother's brother would take all the implements he had used during the month of seclusion and replace them with new ones.

The *dorob* ceremony, like so much in Khoekhoe custom, is reminiscent of those of the Bushmen, but more complex and enigmatic, and with a small, but I think ideologically significant, element of material reciprocity. Hunting magic was not involved in the *dorob* proper, but such a ceremony was said by one of Engelbrecht's informants to be 'but a continuation of the *dorob*' (1936: 162). This magic was quite different from that found among Bushmen. It was performed after the first kill following the young man's initiation. It involved the eating not of hunted but of herded meat (beef), the sharing of this meat between the young man and the oldest man, and the tying of a piece of sinew around the young man's waist. As always among the Korana, the mother's brother had a special role. He had to purify the lad by rubbing him with ochre and fat, and he received the meat and skin of the animal killed, in exchange for which he provided the ox for the hunter's feast.

10

The Nama and others

Introduction

The Nama, who today number about 90,000, are the best known of the Khoekhoe groups. As a distinct people, they probably originated in the northern Cape and later divided into their two large subdivisions, Great Nama and Little Nama (cf. Westphal 1963: 251). The Great Nama settled in the Great Namaqualand area of Namibia prior to European contact. Most of the Little Nama migrated to Namibia in tribal groups during the nineteenth century. Those who remained south of the Orange River have largely been absorbed into South Africa's 'Coloured' population, although Nama customs are still in evidence in the northeastern Cape. The bearers of these customs will be examined at the end of this chapter. They too are, in part, representatives of the Khoisan culture area.

Nama history, in the sense of chiefs, battles, and migrations, is well recorded, but our concern here is rather with 'traditional' Nama social organization, in so far as this can be extracted from historical accounts, early ethnography, and recent studies. Even the best of the early ethnography, that of South African anthropologist Winifred Hoernlé, is itself a construction from the memory of her informants. A letter from Hoernlé to the Secretary for South-West Africa, dated 14 April 1923, is most revealing. Part of it states:

The conditions of work among [the Nama] were not good. They were living an entirely artificial life, and had been doing so for many years, so that direct observation of the mode of life of a pastoral people was out of the question; and the whole structure of a town location made impossible for the people the grouping of relatives, and the observance of rules of behaviour, that obtain in their own natural surroundings. (Hoernlé 1987 [1923]: 175; full text of letter, pp. 174–83)

This short extract is intriguing in a number of ways. First, it points to Hoernlé's concern, made more explicit elsewhere in the letter, about the quality of life for the Nama. This had deteriorated considerably as a result of warfare and subjugation under oppressive colonial rule. The oppression was to remain through a further sixty-seven years of South African control over Namibia, and Hoernlé remained throughout her life (1885–1960) one of its chief opponents. Secondly, it shows the difficult conditions under which she worked, though the Nama themselves seem to have been most obliging. Thirdly, it illustrates Hoernlé's theoretical distinction between ideology and observed behaviour, a distinction which she helped to foster in the early days of functionalist anthropology. Fourthly, it intimates the value she, and others, have attached to discovering the ancient, pastoral culture of the Nama. This is an objective I share. However, it is equally interesting to consider the notion of the Nama's 'own natural surroundings' in light of recent comments on the search for 'true' or 'pure' hunter-gatherers (e.g., Barnard 1989a; Wilmsen and Denbow 1990). It is worth some reflection that Nama can *still* give accounts of their pastoral culture, perhaps as an ideology which never quite existed on the ground anyway, and that many of the customs Hoernlé describes do exist today in behavioural reality, in spite of more than a century of oppression. To me, this is one further argument for a view of culture which stresses its resilience and internal cohesion, rather than the fleeting nature of particular practices.

Figure 10.1 shows the place names mentioned in this chapter and the territories of the major Nama groups prior to the 1904 War. Although the tribes are now dispersed, some present-day chiefs still maintain chiefly control over their traditional locations. In this map, the northern ≠Aonin (Sesfontein Topnaars) are labelled !Gomen, in reference to their new identity after their separation from the main ≠Aonin group in the nineteenth century. The //Khau-/gôan (Swartbois) are shown at both their early location near Rehoboth, which they fled as a result of Herero incursions in the 1880s, and their subsequent home in the north.

Ethnographic studies of the Nama

Nearly all ethnographic work among the Nama has been carried out among the Namibian tribes. The earlier ethnographers were German missionaries, army officers, traders, and travellers. Notable among these were Theophilus Hahn (1867 [see also 1870]; 1878; 1881), Hugo von François (1896), Viktor Lebzelter (1934), Leonhard Schultze (or Schultze-Jena) (1907; see also 1914; 1928), and Heinrich Vedder (1928b; 1938 [1934]). Winifred Hoernlé conducted fieldwork among the Nama in 1912, 1913, and 1922–3 and published four important articles on their customs and social

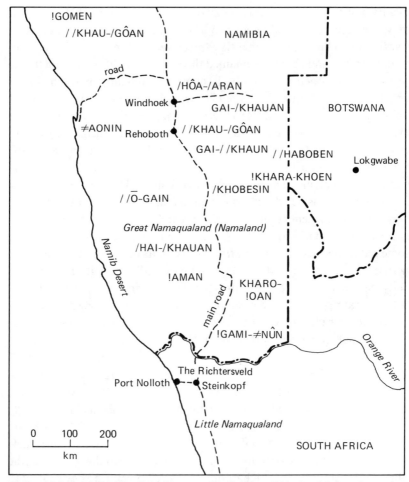

Figure 10.1 Southern Namibia (German South West Africa), with locations of
the Nama tribes prior to the War of 1904–7

organization (1918; 1923a; 1923b; 1925). A fifth paper of hers, apparently
the one used by Radcliffe-Brown in the preparation of his famous 'mother's
brother' lecture (Radcliffe-Brown 1924; or 1952: 15–31), was discovered in
1958 but remains unpublished (Carstens 1983a: 68). Most of Hoernlé's
papers on the Nama are included in a collection of her work edited by Peter
Carstens (Hoernlé 1985), and in general it is this version I shall cite here.
Most of her field notes were accidentally destroyed by fire in 1931, but her
diaries, which include a great deal of interesting material, survived. These
too, together with some letters from her fieldwork period, have recently
been published (Hoernlé 1987).

Several ethnographers are working among the Nama today. Most prominent of these are K.F.R. Budack, who has written widely on tribal history (e.g., 1969; 1972a; 1972b; 1986), and Sigrid Schmidt, who has written mainly on folklore and religion (e.g., 1975–6; 1980). I have little personal knowledge of the Nama, but I have made a number of very brief travels with and among Nama-speakers in South Africa and Namibia (in 1973, 1979, and 1982) and encountered others during my fieldwork in Botswana (in 1974 to 1975).

The Nama tribes
The Nama lived a nomadic way of life. Their main protective concern was not over land; it was over their cattle and women. Cattle theft and abduction were the causes of a great many recorded instances of fighting. Partly for this reason and partly because of extensive warfare in the late nineteenth century, the Khoekhoe have sometimes been described as a belligerent people. Yet, in contrast to the Nama of later times, the Cape Khoekhoe of the early historic period had no standing armies, and no military leaders except their hereditary chiefs. They valued not bravery in battle, but hunting prowess and wealth in the form of cattle (Elphick 1985: 53–7). This was probably once true of the Nama as well. With the incursion of other peoples, including various Bantu-speaking groups, the Dutch, and the Germans, a military organization gradually developed. The ultimate result was the almost total destruction of Nama tribal organization after the German colonization of South West Africa in the 1890s. By the time competent ethnographers arrived on the scene, 'traditional' Nama social structure was largely a memory cult, preserved in the minds of the elderly, but nowhere existent 'on the ground'.

When Hoernlé arrived among the Great Nama, earlier forms of local organization had been devastated by nearly a century of warfare and by the attempts of the German authorities to break up the tribes. Germany controlled South West Africa, now Namibia, from about 1890 (the exact date depends on one's definition of 'control') until 1915. Severe drought in the late nineteenth century, the rinderpest epidemic of 1897, and the 'Nama Revolt' of 1904–7, during which the great Nama chief Hendrik Witbooi met his death, also took their toll (see, e.g., Bley 1971 [1968]: 113–16, 124–6, 149–52). Nonetheless, Hoernlé's account (1985 [1925]: 39–56), based on both written sources and fieldwork, is among the best available, and was used extensively by Schapera (1930) as the model for Khoekhoe society as a whole.

In both historical and ethnographic literature the tribes are commonly

Table 10.1 *Nama tribal names and populations in 1876*

Modern orthography *Old orthography*	Afrikaans name (English name) *Dutch name*	1876 population
Gai-Naman (Great Nama)		
Gai-//khaun (//Khauben)	Rooi Nasie (Red Nation)	
Gei //Khauan	*Rooi Natie*	2,500
≠Aonin	!Kuiseb Topnaars	
≠Aunin (Mu//een)	*Topnaars*	750
!Gomen	Sesfontein Topnaars	
!Gumin		no data
!Gami-≠nûn	Bondelswarts, Bondels	
!Gami ≠ Nun	*Bondelswarts*	2,000
!Khara-khoen (!Khara-gai-khoen)	Kopers, Fransmanne	
!Khara Gei Khoin	*Simon Kooper Hottentotte*	800
//Haboben	Veldskoendraers	
//Haboben	*Veldschoendragers*	1,800
//Ō-gain	Groot Doden (Great Dead)	
//O Gein	*Groot Doode*	800
//Khau-/gôan	Swartboois	
//Khu /Gôan	*Swartboois*	1,000
Kharo-!oan (Tsain)	Keetmanshopers	
Karo-oas		300
[no modern equivalent]		
Khogeis		100
Gunungu (Lowlanders)		200
≠Kham-Naman (Little Nama or 'Oorlams')		
!Aman (!Amain)	Bethaniers	
!Aman	*Bethanie Hottentotte*	2,000
/Khobesin	Witboois, Witkams	
/Hobesen	*Witboois*	2,500
Gai-/khauan	Lamberts, Amraals	
Gei /Khauan	*Amraal Hottentotte*	600
/Hai-/khauan (≠Khari-/khauan)	Bersebaers	
/Hei /Khauan	*Berseba Hottentotte*	700
/Hôa-/aran (//Aixa-//ain, Toroxa-//ain)	Afrikaners	
//Aixa //Ain	*Afrikaners*	800

known by both their Nama and their Dutch or Afrikaans names. In the latter case, the name may be either a direct translation of the Nama name, the European name of the tribal capital, or the European surname of the chiefly lineage. The Nama themselves invariably use the Afrikaans forms today when speaking in the Afrikaans language. Writers in German and English have generally followed suit – using the Dutch or Afrikaans names in preference to English translations. While some English glosses are marginally acceptable, notably 'Red Nation' for the Gai-//Kauan or Rooi Nasie (also sometimes written Rooinasie), others are not. For example, 'Sandal Wearers' is not a usual English designation of the //Haboben or Veldskoendraers, though this is the literal meaning of their tribal name.

Table 10.1 shows the various tribal names of the Nama, together with their estimated populations in 1876. The population figures are from the report of Special Commissioner W. Coates Palgrave (1877: 94).

In Hoernlé's time, the 'indigenous tribes' or Great Nama were divided into seven tribes. These were believed to be descended from a group of five brothers. According to one legend, the ancestor of the Gai-//khaun, the senior tribe, was the eldest of these brothers. His younger brothers founded the !Gami-≠nûn, the //Haboben, the !Khara-khoen, and the //Khau-/gôan. Another legend says that the //Haboben, who are known to have recognized the authority of the !Gami-≠nûn chief during the early nineteenth century (Alexander 1967 [1838]: 187, 197), were an offshoot of the !Gami-≠nûn. The other two tribes, the //Ō-gain and the ≠Aonin, are thought to be offshoots of the Gai-//khaun (Hoernlé 1925: 4–5).

Hoernlé's 'incoming groups' are usually known collectively as the Oorlams or Orlams (an Afrikaans word of disputed etymology), but I prefer the literal translation of the Nama name, Little Nama. These include the /Hôa-/aran (known to Hoernlé as the //Aixa-//ain), the /Khobesin, the !Aman, the /Hai-/khauan, and the Gai-/khauan. These tribes came into Namibia from the south in the early nineteenth century. Their migrations were undertaken in search of better grazing land, but they led them into conflicts and bouts of mutual cattle-raiding with the Great Nama and Herero who were already there.

Budack (1972b) has written a useful account of the complex political history of the Nama in the late nineteenth century, and more recently (1986) a summary of relationships between the Nama tribes, as seen through the eyes of no less than ten writers from 1779 to 1975 (R.J. Gordon, Tindall, Olpp, Schinz, François, Schultze, Hoernlé, Vedder, Beach, and Hirschberg). Figure 10.2 illustrates the tribal alliances (cf. Budack 1986: 137). In some cases these represent claims of descent, but as with the Korana, ties of marital alliance seem to me to be implicit in the data (see 'Marriage' below). Virtually all the Great Nama tribes owed direct allegiance to the Gai-//khaun and paid tribute to the Gai-//khaun chief. Needless to say, this tribe suffered severely at the hands of the German forces. Most of their earlier clans had no representatives at all at the time of Hoernlé's fieldwork.

According to tradition, all the Great Nama are descended from a single line of ancestors. Each of the tribes (*!hauti*) was divided into up to fifteen exogamous, patrilineal clans or lineages (*!hau-!nati*, 'tribes-within'). Etymologically, these terms are related to a variety of words for general sociality and companionship, all with the stem *!hau-* (Kroenlein 1889: 156; cf. Budack 1972b: 247). The smaller units were hierarchically ranked, and

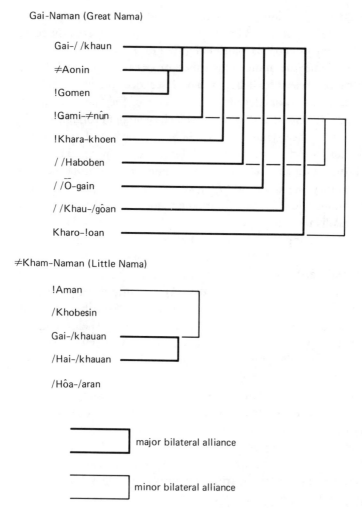

Figure 10.2 Traditional Nama tribal alliances (after Budack 1986)

within some tribes more than one order of segmentation was found. In other words, the term *!hau-!nas* (the singular form) could refer to any patrilineal unit smaller than the tribe. Indeed, the situation was yet more complex. The tribe Hoernlé knew best were the //Khau-/gôan. In 1923, when they numbered only about 200, they had ten such lineages, three of which bore the same name, /Gari. In fact, /Gari was not only the name of three patrilineages, but also a cross-descent 'great name' (see 'Naming', below). It had been the great name of a group of sisters whose husbands, unusually, had taken up permanent uxorilocal residence, and who had given birth to three sets of children who in turn established patrilineal domains in their name (Hoernlé 1985 [1925]: 44–7, 50–1 *passim*). Hoernlé reported such observations partly as evidence that before the present century Nama tribal organization was a dynamic segmentary force. I also prefer to see it in this way, in contrast to Schapera's (1930: 223) more pessimistic reading of Hoernlé's paper, a reading which emphasizes the destruction of tribal organization (cf. Carstens 1969: 96).

In many respects, it is all too easy to see Nama society in terms of a pre-1904 and post 1904 dichotomy. Their tribal organization was torn apart by the War of 1904–7, a conflict which grew from almost simultaneous revolts against German authority by the Nama and by their traditional enemies, the Herero. At the outbreak of the rebellion, in late 1904, there were only some 1,500 able-bodied fighting men on the Nama side, and less than half of them were equipped with up-to-date weapons. By January 1905, the German force in Namaland had been increased from 500 men to some 4,300 men and 2,800 horses (Bridgman 1981: 140). The result was inevitable. Many Nama were killed, their tribes scattered, and the authority of the chiefs reduced, though this was replaced to some extent by an increase in the authority of local leaders and a nominal allegiance to distant chiefs. Indeed, it could be argued that the powerful chiefs of the late nineteenth century were not typical representatives of the Khoekhoe chiefship. The earlier political organization was destroyed, but elements of the ideology which generated it did remain.

The Nama camp

Before the present century, Nama camps usually included between five and thirty huts. The huts were roughly circular or beehive-shaped, and their doors faced the centre of the encampment (see Hoernlé 1985 [1925]: 49–51; Schapera 1930: 228–9; Vedder 1938 [1934]: 52–6). As among the Korana, huts were hierarchically arranged; in the case of the Nama, the hut of the chief or highest-ranking camp member was placed in the west, facing east. Families and clans each occupied specific locations within the camp, according to their seniority. Within the clan, a further hierarchy was maintained, with elder brothers and their families and dependents to the right, and younger brothers and their families and dependents to the left. In spite of their nomadic way of life and segmentary inclinations when they were settled, each Nama tribe had its own territory which was claimed by the hereditary chief. At times, an entire tribe would camp in one great circle, but this was rare. Each clan normally had its own kraal elsewhere in the tribe's territory. As Hoernlé (1985 [1925]: 50) took extensive pains to stress, clan loyalty was 'always stronger than tribal loyalty', and the chief was 'little more than *primus inter pares*'. His authority depended on his maintaining links with his far-flung people.

A comparison with the Korana is interesting here (cf. Engelbrecht 1936: 89–93). Among the Korana, sub-chiefs resided at each kraal and period-ically met in councils which limited the powers of their tribal chiefs. Among the Nama, clan representatives lived at each tribal chief's kraal. The contrast is reminiscent of that between differing methods of political control among the Bantu-speaking peoples, where according to local custom royal wives could either be taken from the outlying districts, or 'placed' there as district heads (see Kuper 1982: 71–3, 103–7). In each case, the practice that was followed depended not on the whim of an individual chief, but on a culturally determined strategy of maintaining alliance links.

Khoekhoe in the past employed outsiders to act as servants and tend their stock. Among the Nama, these included Bushmen and Damara, while among the Korana, they included Bushmen, Bantu-speakers, and fellow Korana as well. In Korana country, such people camped outside the circular clan village. In the Nama case, the servants occupied low-status positions within the camp, and indeed within the family grouping, where they were placed to the left of the huts which they served. Among the Korana, the livestock were kept in the centre of the camp or village in separate kraals for cattle and sheep. Among the Nama, there were no separate enclosures for adult beasts apart from the perimeter fence of the entire camp. Cattle and sheep, at least in theory, were expected to lie in front of their owners' huts at night, while calves and lambs were placed in small enclosures in the middle of the camp.

Each hut was constructed of reed mats, made by the women, and these were placed on a carefully built frame made up of wooden spars and cross-bars bound together. The reeds expanded when wet, thus providing protection from the summer rains. The Nama could dismantle these huts within an hour's time and pack them on oxen for transport to a new camp. Thus the huts provided both permanent and fairly comfortable accommo-dation on the one hand, and mobility on the other (Vedder 1938 [1934]: 52; Haacke 1982). Inside the hut, each person had his or her own sleeping space. Domestic utensils were hung along the rafters. Bows, arrows, and spears were kept in the grass matting so that children could not reach them (Vedder 1938 [1934]: 52–3). Traditional huts in bark are rare today, but similar huts made of canvas are not uncommon, even in such settlements as Steinkopf in the northern Cape, where many residents own both a modern cement house and a 'real' house of the more or less traditional style (see 'The "Coloured" people of the northwestern Cape', below).

Men and women among the Nama

Among the Khoekhoe generally, men and boys have traditionally held the responsibility for herding cattle and hunting, while women have done the gathering. In spite of the practices of polygyny, of virilocal residence after initial uxorilocality and bride service, and of patrilineal and hierarchical tribal, clan, and lineage organization, women held considerable authority. In historical times, some women even became regents or temporary chiefs (see Vedder 1928b: 114–15). Nama women exerted considerable power within the household, which was and is their primary sphere of influence. They could own cattle and sheep, and they held control over the milk produced by the family herd. As Theophilus Hahn wrote:

In every Khoikhoi's house the woman, or *taras* [sic], is the *supreme ruler*; the husband has nothing at all to say. While in public the men take the prominent part, at home they have not so much power even as to take a mouthful of sour milk out of the tub, without the wife's permission. If a man ever should try to do it, his nearest female relations will put a fine on him, consisting in cows and sheep, which is added to the stock of the wife. (1881: 19; Hahn's emphasis)

Among the Nama, the senior brother has primary responsibility for bestowing his sisters in marriage, while among the Korana, the senior sister bestows her brothers (cf. Schapera 1930: 327; Engelbrecht 1936: 130–1). Kinship obligations were thus shared between the sexes in gender-specific contexts.

As among other Khoisan peoples, puberty ceremonies symbolically marked the division between males and females, though these have now largely disappeared. The Nama male puberty ceremony, like the ceremonies of the Cape Khoekhoe, the Korana, and some Bushman groups, involved a period of seclusion, scarification, and the observance of various taboos. Schapera (1930: 279–85) gives a detailed summary of boys' puberty ceremonies among the Khoekhoe generally. His comparisons suggest that different Nama groups at different times had different practices, some of which resembled Cape Khoekhoe ones (e.g., urinating on initiates, among Nama of Little Namaqualand), while others are unique. Unfortunately for us, Nama boys' ceremonies remain poorly recorded, as they disappeared before they could be studied by a competent ethnographer.

The female puberty ceremony is better described, and was quite elaborate in comparison to those of other Khoisan groups. Schapera (1930: 272–9) bases his account on Hoernlé's important paper on rites of transition (Hoernlé 1918: 70–4; or 1985: 62–7; see also Carstens 1982). The initiate was secluded, at her first period, in a special hut called the *kharu-oms*. She was attended by an elderly woman who had borne many children. This woman, the *aba tarás* or *kai tarás*, carried the girl so that her feet did not touch the ground. The girl stayed in seclusion for anything from two or three days to a month. All her near relatives took part in hunting on her behalf, and only female animals could be killed. The girl ate well and got plenty of milk to drink, but she was forbidden to touch cold water, the most ritually dangerous substance known to the Nama. Towards the end of her seclusion, she was 'cleaned' head to toe in wet cow dung. She was dressed in fine clothes, her face was painted, and she was loaded with presents by her friends and relatives. Then the boys, up to the age of sixteen or more, eagerly entered her hut. She dabbed the testicles of each one with buchu, in order to prevent the acquisition of sexual diseases or misfortune which might be caused by food prepared for the girl's feast, which then followed. Elements of this ceremony are still in practice today in some Nama areas (Hoff 1983: 10–12).

Nama kinship

One of the most common morphemes in the Nama language is *khoe* ('person'), which is used in constructions meaning 'friend', 'friendly', etc., and has a number of kinship meanings as well. Hahn (1882) noted *khoi-si-ga-gu* (his orthography) for 'to be married'; Kroenlein (1889: 209–10) recorded *khoixa* ('related'), *khoixagu* ('to be related to each other'), *khoixa-khoin* (meaning loosely either 'blood relatives' or 'friends'), etc. I have also found this last term in use for 'kinsfolk' (modern orthography, *khoexa khoen*, literally 'people with people'). Related terms in other Khoe languages generally carry the meaning 'spouse'. Nama do not seem to dwell on the idea of universal kinship classification in the way that Bushmen do, but instead emphasize patrilineal links, links through name lines, and close cognatic ties, all of which signify the *khoexa* relationship.

Relationship terminology

The Nama relationship terminology has a very similar structure to that of the Korana. The basic structure is shown in Figure 10.3. The terminology is complicated by the fact that there are often a number of terms for the same genealogical position. Such terms are distinguished by linguistic and social, rather than genealogical, context. More specifically, the choice of term is governed by the grammatical person of ego (whether ego is speaker, e.g., 'my mother', or referent, e.g., 'your mother' or 'his mother') and by the level of formality required. For reasons of space, only the most common terms are presented here, but a full list of indigenous terms is included in Table 16.2 (Chapter 16).

Senior cross-relatives are termed //*nao*-, while junior cross-relatives and

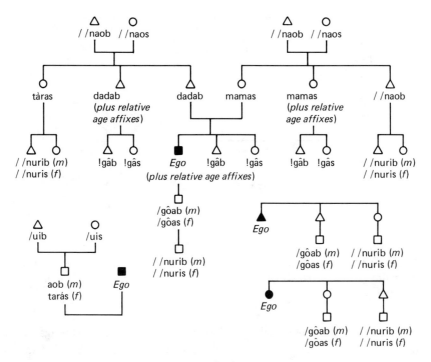

Figure 10.3 Nama kinship terminology: basic structure

those of the same genealogical level are //*nuri*-. Only those relatives in a //*nuri-gu* relationship (as they are designated reciprocally) are marriageable. From the available evidence it appears that in earlier times cross-cousins on either side were in this class, as they are today, although as with the Korana there are indications in the literature that matrilateral marriage was 'preferred' (see Barnard 1975: 11–16). The Nama mother's brother (//*naob*) was the object of intense joking behaviour, including obligatory cattle-snatching and the threat of wife-snatching on the part of a sister's son towards his mother's brother. Among the Nama, this relationship is known as //*nuri*//*as* or //*nuri*//*ab* (literally '//*nuri* exchange').

The opposite of the //*nao*- or //*nuri*- relationship was that designated by the morpheme *tàra*-, the RESPECT RELATIVE category. The primary genealogical referent was the father's sister, but, as with the Korana, this term may be used for any AVOIDANCE relative (a wider category than RESPECT RELATIVE; see Chapter 16). Since the decimation of the Nama clans, the father's sister has come to be called and treated more as an 'aunt' than as a 'female father', and the GRANDRELATIVE term //*naos* now replaces *tàras* for many Nama-speakers.

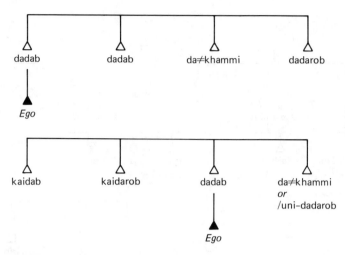

Figure 10.4 Nama kinship terminology: examples of relative age markers for first ascending generation consanguines (with elder brothers to the left and younger ones to the right)

Siblings are distinguished by relative age, and parents' siblings are distinguished by order of birth in relation to ego's parents. There is a fair degree of subtle variation in local usage, but the principles are simple. Relative seniority is paramount, and absolute seniority or juniority (who is first or last born) is generally indicated as well. Usually, the set of terms employed in any given family include the morphemes *kai* ('great'), ≠*khammi* ('little'), and *ro* (a diminutive). Two examples which I found in use among a group of brothers and their sons, in 1979, are illustrated in Figure 10.4. The term /*uni-dadarob* means 'last junior-father'; the other terms should be self-explanatory. Terms for mothers' sisters follow exactly the same pattern as that indicated here for fathers' brothers, though with the frequent use of the collateral term *migis* (from the Dutch for 'aunt'), as well as *ma*, *mama*, etc., with appropriate affixes. These terms, of course, reflect the placement of brothers in the traditional nineteenth-century camp, if not the modern village. In past times, a senior man would have his married sons to his right (the most senior furthest to the right, and the most junior immediately to the right), his daughters and their husbands in bride service to his left, and servants further to the left (Hoernlé 1985 [1925]: 51).

Naming

Traditionally, Nama children have borne the 'great name' (*kai khoe /ons*) of their opposite-sex parent (Hoernlé 1985 [1925]: 45–6, 50–1; Schapera 1930:

267–8). The system operates exactly as among the Korana. Men bear their mothers' names, and women bear their fathers'. Individuals are distinguished from their siblings by the use of epithets to indicate relative birth order: *kai-* (great one), *inagma-* (next one), ≠*nu-* ('dark' or third one), ≠*ari-* (little one), etc. Patrilineal clans are also distinguished according to relative seniority, as if 'brothers' with the same name, /Gari Kain, /Gari !Nagaman, etc. Few Nama today have great names, and they never employ them in dealings with outsiders. They use instead Christian names and patrilineal surnames. Nama also employ nicknames, which are independent of any system of inter-generational transmission.

There are other possibilities too. In fieldwork conducted in 1979, Trudeke Vuyk recorded an interesting variant of Nama naming customs among Nama of Lokgwabe, in the Kgalagadi District of Botswana (Vuyk n.d.: 14–15). There a first-born child receives the sex-specific name of its mother's father or father's mother. Later children are named after other grandparents, subsequently the parents' brothers and sisters, and finally the parents themselves. In the absence of direct evidence of diffusion, one might speculate that these naming practices are generated from within the Nama kinship structure itself, and this is hinted at in Vuyk's (n.d.: 18) discussion. It is also possible that there has been some earlier contact between the Nama who now live in Lokgwabe and Nharo from further north. Indeed, the existence of these practices among Nama casts a light shadow of doubt on my own longstanding premise (e.g., Barnard 1976a: 158–66) that Nharo naming practices are simply cultural borrowings from the !Kung (see also Chapter 16).

Marriage and exchange

I will not dwell here on the rules of marriage. It does seem likely that the general pattern in the past was for bilateral 'cross-cousin' marriage, or more precisely, marriage to one of the class designated //*nurib* or //*nuris*. By the 1920s, marriage with any first cousin was permitted, whereas in the past only cross-cousins were potential spouses (Hoernlé 1985 [1925]: 54). As among the Korana, there may have been an ideological preference for matrilateral marriage (cf. Barnard 1975), and in some tribes, specifically the Gai-//khaun, //Khau-/gôan, and //Haboben, 'marriage with the mother's brother's daughter is said to have been far more usual than marriage with the father's sister's daughter' (Hoernlé 1985 [1925]: 54).

In 1979, I had the good fortune to be able to interview a number of Nama elders of the Gai-//khaun and /Hai-/khauan tribes at Hoachanas and Berseba respectively. At Berseba, the chief told me that chiefs should marry the daughters of chiefs, preferably people who are already related (in his words, /aub ke me hōgu, '[such that] the blood must touch'). He added that sister-exchange was possible for chiefs, either to gain allies or to prevent intertribal wars. If chiefs were drawn into wars and subsequently discovered affinal connections with their enemies, they would stop fighting immediately. Chiefs had no influence over the marriages of their subjects, but allies regularly intermarried. The chief gave the example of the inhabitants of Berseba, Bethanie, and Gibeon, who have frequently intermarried in all directions since the last century. Families which intermarry were said to be of the same //gâus, a term which also designates the domestic unit, and which is distinct from the *omaris* or extended family.

Informants noted that upon marriage either the bridegroom or his family must give something to the bride's family. This gift, and indeed the process of its giving, is called the *sammās* (i.e., *sam-mās*, literally, 'breast-gift'). Ideally, the gift is a cow with a calf, presented by the groom to the bride's mother who 'raised her at the breast'. Before the gift can be made, however, bargaining is necessary; one of my informants claimed to have bargained for three days, another for an entire year. The procedure is fairly simple: the prospective bridegroom and his parents approach the bride's parents; the groom opens the discussion, and his parents argue on his behalf until the bride's parents give in. Once the marriage is agreed (whether three days or a year later), preparations can begin. At one time, it is said, the preparations could take up to six months, since it was necessary for the bride to make a large number of grass mats to cover the marital hut. The future husband, in the meanwhile, would concentrate on earning money to support his wife. Today, as in the past, goats and sheep, sometimes a cow, are slaughtered at the marriage ceremony.

The elders of Hoachanas noted two further categories of exchange, unrelated to marriage, but which are of special comparative interest. First, they noted the concept of //am, a verb meaning 'to give a present to make up for an insult to a person in the respect relationship'. The offence might be verbal or one of action, and the traditional payment was a goat or a cow. Even more interestingly, they described a non-kin relationship of mutual obligation, known as *sori-gu-s*, also reported by Schultze (1907: 318–19). *Sori*, as a verb, carries the literal meaning 'to drink part of a cup and give the rest to a friend', while -*gu-s* is simply the reciprocal suffix in its nominal form. Yet the relationship was described as non-reciprocal, in the sense that gifts were voluntary and not necessarily reciprocated. Nor were they to be requested, in contrast to the situation among some Bushman groups. In the old days, informants said, gifts included livestock and food, while today the relationship is 'only a matter of words'.

While restricted and generalized exchange of spouses may be things of the past, there is little doubt that reciprocity, marital and otherwise, remains an important component of Khoekhoe life. It is probably one which is closely tied to the politics of the family, and indeed the relations between the generations.

Inheritance and private property

Sections of the recently discovered field diaries of Winifred Hoernlé (analysed in Carstens 1983a), together with information contained in earlier published works (e.g., Schapera 1930: 325–6; Engelbrecht 1936: 191–2), provide a fascinating picture of the rules for the inheritance of private property among the Khoekhoe. Carstens' interpretation of Hoernlé's diaries emphasizes the relationship between inheritance and other aspects of Khoekhoe kinship, including patrilineal clan organization, cross-sex descent lines, uxori-virilocal residence, and the high status of women in their roles as wives and sisters.

A peculiarity of both Korana and Nama rules of inheritance is the notion of both primogeniture and ultimogeniture. Both sons and daughters inherited movable property, including livestock. The principal heir to a woman's estate was the youngest child, regardless of sex, while the eldest son (or, according to Hoernlé's notes, the eldest of either sex) was the principal heir to the father's estate (Carstens 1983a: 58–9). As among the Bushmen, land was communally owned; it was held in trust by the chief in council and could not be alienated. Carstens (1983a: 68) suggests that the high status of women actually prevented the accumulation of property in the hands of patrilineages. The house was owned by the senior female resident, who had the right to move it to a new locality after her husband's death.

There are a number of variations in the patterns reported, including what appear to be tribal peculiarities. Among the ≠Aonin, for example, the staple crop is the *!naras* melon, not found elsewhere. These sweet melons (rather like pumpkins) can be harvested through most of the year. They provide seeds and fruit which are cooked and made into cakes for storage. To this day, *!naras* patches are individually owned; they are inherited specifically by a man's youngest son, because he is responsible for looking after his parents as they grow old (Budack 1983: 5–6; see also Budack 1977; Köhler 1969).

Traditional Nama religion and ritual

The religion of the Nama today is Christian (mainly Calvinist and Lutheran). In former times, Nama religion, and particularly mythology, centred around the relations between two good beings: Tsûi-//goab, the deity, and Haiseb or Haitsi-aibib (old orthography, Heitsi-eibib), the folk hero; and two evil beings: //Gâuab, the devil-figure, and ≠ Gama- ≠ gorib, the wicked trickster. Their ontological status in the collective Nama mind has been the subject of much speculation (cf. Schapera 1930: 376–89; S. Schmidt 1975–6). Tsûi-//goab, //Gâuab and their respective protagonists, feature not only in Nama myths, but even – sometimes with their names changed – in Bushman ones (see, e.g., S. Schmidt 1989: 35–6, 87–91). One eminent commentator (Theal 1919: 110) regarded the mythology of Tsûi-//goab and //Gâuab simply as 'another version of Heitsi-eibib and ≠ Ga ≠ gorib [*sic*], cast in a more poetical mould'. There is certainly much truth in the similarity of the tales, though Theal himself was by his own admission 'entirely unacquainted with the Hottentot language' (1919: 91). He relied on Hahn (1881). Hahn is indeed the best primary source, but my reading of him suggests more a distinction between a sacred canon (Tsûi-//goab and //Gâuab) and a derivative secular or semi-sacred one (Haitsi-aibib versus ≠ Gama- ≠ gorib). The relation between all these characters will be dealt with in detail in Chapter 14.

The Nama are often said to be a superstitious people. A great many taboos are prevalent among them, even today (cf. Hoff 1983). Hoernlé (1918; 1922; 1923b; or 1985; 57–89) stresses especially the taboos and rites associated with water. Cold water, as well as raw meat and menstrual blood, is traditionally regarded as a source of great ritual danger, or *!nau*, which can cause misfortune and even death. Hoernlé (1923b; 1985: 57–74) examines four associated rites of transition which serve to overcome the dangers of *!nau*: female puberty rites, remarriage ceremonies which involve the mixing of human and animal blood, the treatment of certain diseases by the same method, and the ceremonies of purification after the death of a relative. These last ones, in Hoernlé's time, involved both blood and water. After a burial, mourners would dip their hands in cold water, boil up a mixture of blood and herbs, and deliberately sweat over the warm pots. Cold water was thrown on the grave, and blood or soot was used to mark the bellies of the immediate relatives of the deceased (but not a widow). A widow had to be secluded and kept from water and uncooked meat for a length of time which varied according to the individual. Finally, she was washed with moist cow dung, her hair was cut off, and she was ritually re-introduced to water. Moist cow dung was also similarly used in the female puberty ceremony.

In spite of Hoernlé's vivid description and a recent account by Trudeke Vuyk (n.d.: 17–18), which indicates that similar funeral practices are still found among Nama in Botswana, there is still some confusion over pre-Christian funeral rites and even over the orientation of the body in the grave. As among the Nharo, both east- and west-facing orientation is reported. In the 1920s, archaeologist F.W. Laidler excavated 36 early Khoekhoe graves in Namaqualand. He found a variety of orientations there, but a statistical tendency towards a north–south or northeast–southwest axis, with the face towards the east (Laidler 1929: 152). Engelbrecht (1936: 188), on the Korana, also reports that the dead faced east.

Vestiges of Khoekhoe culture among other peoples

It would be easy to ignore the Griqua, Basters, and Cape Coloured people. In South Africa they are often referred to as people of 'mixed race', but it might be more relevant to note that they are of 'mixed culture' (or more accurately, that their cultures contain elements of more obviously disparate origin than those of other peoples). Although they are in many ways different from the Khoekhoe proper, they nevertheless have some clearly identifiable Khoekhoe customs. This is particularly true of those of certain rural areas where stock-rearing forms a major part of the economic sphere of activity. Just as it has been said that there is a 'Bushman substratum' at the base of Khoekhoe culture (Murdock 1959: 57), it may be equally plausible, in at least some geographical locations, to talk of a 'Khoekhoe substratum' at the base of Griqua, Baster, or Coloured culture. Obviously it is not possible to present a full analysis of the question here. Instead, I will give a brief historical account of each group and suggest a few examples which may add support to this, as yet, tentative hypothesis.

The Griqua

According to early accounts (e.g., Lichtenstein 1928–30 [1811–12], ii- 303), the Griqua originated in the Cape Province as a result of the union of white employees of the Dutch East India Company, and Khoekhoe and Bushman women. Stow (1905: 316) notes that their tribal name is derived from that of a Khoekhoe group variously called Chariguriqua or Grigriqua, who in 1652 were said to be without any hereditary chief. In 1713, the Chariguriqua were reported to be living near St Helena Bay, north of Cape Town.

From an early settlement in the part of South Africa still known as Griqualand East, they migrated in small groups to what became known as Griqualand West (north of the Orange, between modern Kimberley and Upington). This country was at the time occupied by 'pure' Korana. By the early nineteenth century, at least two main Griqua groups had emerged there, one more Khoekhoe in descent and custom, and the other more

European. The former owed allegiance to Chief Adam Kok I (born about 1710), to his son Cornelis or Cornelius Kok I (born in 1746, succeeded to the chiefship in 1795), and to their descendants. Cornelis was literate and wealthy and had a reputation as a great herdmaster and hunter. Both these chiefs held their staffs of office by authority of the Dutch East India Company, as well as by their people, but their followers gradually acquired a reputation for nomadic plundering. The other main group, more European than Khoekhoe, owed allegiance to Barend Barends. This group became known as the Basters or Bastaards (see, e.g., Stow 1905: 339–61; Ross 1976: 12–21).

Around 1804, at the request of two ministers of the London Missionary Society, both groups ceased their wanderings and settled at Klaarwater (later called Griquatown) in the centre of Griqualand West. In 1813, again under pressure from missionaries, they stopped using 'Baster' and collectively adopted the name 'Griqua' (pronounced [xríkua], the -*qua* being a syntactically masculine plural suffix, but taken as semantically neutral for both gender and number). Here, their history becomes more complex. The missionaries chose a new leader, Andries Waterboer, to head the civil government, and the traditional leaders fled. Waterboer enlarged his sphere of influence and gained political control over ethnic Korana and Tswana who accepted him as a 'supreme chief'. A civil war followed. Eventually, the Cape governor advised Waterboer's enemy, Adam Kok III, to move to Nomansland (subsequently Griqualand East), across the Drakensberg between Basutoland (now Lesotho) and the coast. Kok and his people settled there in 1861 (see, e.g., Ross 1976: 104–23).

Griqua identity survives in the northern Cape, where individuals maintain their hereditary links with the chiefs and captains of the past. Their legal system was always a curious blend of Dutch and Mosaic law, and of monarchical and republican politics. The separation of powers were effected through the dual principle of a hereditary chiefship and an elected captaincy, along with an executive council and a parliament (Oberholster 1972: 358; cf. Carstens 1983b). Though derived from cultural mixing, all these social organizational attributes reflect the principle of checks and balances, which is as relevant to Khoekhoe social structure as to the United States constitution. They also reflect the tribal history of the Griqua, as a nomadic, pastoralist, and at times martial nation. As yet, no anthropologist has attempted an intensive study of their traditions, but it would be very surprising indeed if other elements of Khoekhoe social structure were not found to survive among this conservative people.

The Rehoboth Basters

An important secondary source on Baster society is the account by J.S. Marais (1939: 98–108), historian of the Cape Coloured people. Yet the classic study is that of Eugen Fischer (1913), then Professor of Anthropology at the University of Freiburg. Although Fischer was later disgraced by his involvement with the Nazis, his early work on the biology and culture of the Rehoboth Basters was much praised in liberal quarters, not least by Franz Boas, who maintained a sporadic but cordial correspondence with Fischer for over thirty years (Proctor 1988: 157).

The Rehoboth Basters, also known as the Rehobothers, number some 19,000 (Messina 1980: 35). Their language is customarily classified as a dialect of Afrikaans, but one whose closest European affinities appear to be with Plattdeutsch rather than Flemish or the Dutch of Holland (Franco Maria Messina, pers. comm.). The designation 'Baster', or, in the eighteenth century. 'Bastaard', was originally a term of abuse, but developed into a positive appellation. It is today the preferred term of the people themselves.

Among early writers, Schultze (1907: 116–20) stessed the Christian–communist foundation of Baster society. Fischer (1913: 229–31) argued that the Baster community was profoundly affected by missionary influence. Certainly, white missionaries were prominent in the struggles for political power in the early days of the community. In 1868, under the dual leadership of their missionary and their captain, some eighty or ninety Baster families trekked across the Orange River. They stopped at the site of present-day Warmbad, just north of the Orange, to draft a constitution. Their numbers decreased rapidly, but in 1870 some thirty families reached an unoccupied territory then claimed by the Gai-//khaun. At their missionary's suggestion, they named it Rehoboth (Hebrew for 'space'). These Basters, together with other, previously scattered families who were resettled there by the Germans around 1895, have remained ever since.

The 'pure' Rehobothers mix freely with the incoming 'Coloured' population, but they maintain a separate identity from other resettled groups. To this day, the Basters and others of mixed descent live on the east side of the main north–south road which runs through the Reserve, and Nama and Damara families, most of them very poor, live on the hill which lies on the west side. Within the last decade, some Basters seriously sought their own independent state, geographically encapsulated within Namibia. In relation to surrounding, undeniably Khoekhoe groups, the Basters seem to belong to some other ethnographic region, but their historical ties and existing economic relationships call into question the wisdom of fully excluding them from the category 'Khoisan'.

Culturally too, there are good grounds for considering them among the Khoisan peoples. Naming practices, for example, reflect both Afrikaans and Nama custom and display much of the complexity of the latter (Messina 1980). Descriptive Nama words and even mixtures of Nama and Afrikaans (e.g., ≠Nu-voet, literally 'black foot') are often used as nicknames. The method of giving Afrikaans Christian names bears a strong structural resemblance (though probably not a direct historical relationship) to !Kung naming practice. A first-born Baster son was traditionally named after his FF, the second, after his MF, the third, after his F, and the fourth, etc., after their FBs. Correspondingly, girls were named after the MM, then the FM, then the M, and the MZs.

The 'Coloured' people of the northwestern Cape

The long and rich history of the Cape Coloured people is the subject of the classic monograph by J.S. Marais (1939). Those of greatest significance to us are those 'Coloured' people (sometimes considered a branch of the Basters), who inhabit Little Namaqualand, in the northwestern Cape Province. They were studied in the early 1960s by Peter Carstens (1966), and have since become the object of renewed anthropological interest.

Little Namaqualand was originally claimed by Chief Kupido Witbooi of the /Khobesin. It was taken over for Baster settlement in the early nineteenth century. While most of the area was governed through councils (at first appointed, and later partly elected and partly appointed by the government and the churches), the Richtersveld retained Khoekhoe-style political structure. The local Khoekhoe throughout the area became integrated with the Basters, a fact noted by Hoernlé during her first field visit in 1912 (Hoernlé 1985 [1913]: 27). In recent times the higher social classes have become more 'European' (or 'Coloured'), but Nama is still spoken by many people. Martin West (1971), although primarily concerned with caste and class differences in his study of the coastal town of Port Nolloth, nevertheless also remarks that the historical origins of the groups which make up 'the Coloured caste' can be employed to emphasize 'ethnicity' (1971: 100–7). This is of even greater significance inland, with Namaqualand, where the Baster community maintains its historical identity, and where elements of Khoekhoe culture are more apparent.

The most visible sign of Nama culture is the architecture. Many people of this area still build round dwellings and (adjacent to them) open cooking huts in the traditional Khoekhoe manner. This practice is no longer maintained among the Nama in Namibia (cf. Haacke 1982). In Namaqualand today, the round 'mat house' (*matjieshuis*), where it is found, generally coexists with a square, European-style, 'wall house' (*muurhuis*) on the same plot of ground; but the mat house is considered the 'real' one. In Steinkopf, as late as the 1960s, some two-thirds of the population occupied these traditional Nama-style dwellings (Carstens 1966: 72–3), and they are still very common even among the higher strata of the community. There and in the Richtersveld, just as in ancient Nama times, the women build these huts, keep them in repair, and maintain proprietary interests in them, whereas European-style houses are built and maintained by the men (1966: 75).

Other aspects of Khoekhoe cultural retention in Steinkopf and nearby communities are in magic, folklore, and religious ideas, which coexist with strong Christian beliefs and practices. Perhaps most obvious among such beliefs is that in magic (Carstens 1966: 178–81). Inhabitants of Steinkopf included both *blikdraers* (Afrikaans for 'tin-carriers') and *bossiesdokters* ('bush doctors'). The former are mainly practitioners of evil magic. They carry in their tins strong-smelling medicines (a potion of jackal kidneys mixed with ashes is among the best) which cause misfortune to others. Sometimes this is done by putting such substances into another person's food or tea, but more often, it is done simply by thinking malicious thoughts. The 'bush doctors' counter this magic by potions of their own, sometimes tailored as antidotes to specific medicines of the sorcerers. A mixture of dried gecko (*Ptenopus garrulus*) and kidney fat, rubbed into incisions on the patient's arm and wrist, is said to be an especially good and safe medicine both to give 'strength' and for specific ailments, including snakebite. Unfortunately, this species of gecko would seem to be rather uniquely ferocious, for Carstens' informants told him that catching one is more dangerous than catching a snake! Therefore, this medicine is not often used.

Carstens (1966: 182–5) places special emphasis on the belief, prevalent in Steinkopf, that certain individuals can make direct contact with a mythical spirit called the /has or /nas. In Carstens' view, the term is probably derived from !'ôas (Nama for 'hare'). In any case, the /has has the form of a spring hare, with large red ears. It is recorded in a number of early sources on the Nama (cf. Schapera 1930: 369–70; Carstens 1975). In the past, only women 'had the /has', but by the time of Carstens' fieldwork some men had acquired it as well. It is said that in former times a woman who had the /has could transform herself into a lion, a jackal, or almost any other animal she might choose. This was done by rubbing her body with buchu from a tortoise shell. Informants told Carstens that the /has could only be seen at night, moving swiftly from place to place, flapping its ears and screaming like a jackal.

Carstens' general conclusions on supernatural belief express his view succinctly, a view which I am inclined to share:

The hypothesis offered here, therefore, is that the early inhabitants of Steinkopf merely transferred their conceptions of a supreme being and a spirit of evil to Christianity. Today the supernatural beliefs of the conservative people still reflect the early Christian–pagan pattern, while the 'new people' have transformed it by incorporating into their belief in God the functions of subordinate powers. (1966: 187)

I have only touched here on a fragment of Cape Coloured culture, that which reflects the culture of their Khoekhoe forebears. This fragment is not shared to such a degree anywhere outside Namaqualand. The rest of the Coloured heritage – Dutch, Indonesian, and African, Calvinist and Muslim, slave and free, rural and urban – is a worthy area for further research by folklorists as well as anthropologists, and is certainly an interesting subject with which to test the limits of regional comparison.

11

The Damara and Hai//om

Hunters or herders?

In this chapter, we shall examine the two major groups which transcend the hunter–herder boundary. The Damara, Hai//om, and various small groups of non-Kalahari foragers, all live in northern Namibia (see Figure 11.1). All these groups speak the language known as Nama, Nama-Damara, Damara-Nama, or Damara. They have engaged until recently in foraging activities, though in some groups livestock have long been kept as well. None of these groups is traditionally classified as 'Khoekhoe' (either by the Khoekhoe themselves or by outsiders), but they do have cultural attributes which align them as much with the Khoekhoe as with the Bushmen.

The Damara

The last powerful Damara chief was Cornelius Goraseb. He died in 1910 with this prophecy: 'I know that when I am no more, my peoples will be scattered like chaff in the wind' (First 1963: 37). The Germans granted Cornelius Goraseb the title *König* ('king'), and his grandson, the last to claim this title, died in 1976, in serious dispute with some of his fellow Damara leaders, and still without a kingdom. The Damara had already been scattered, and remaining Damara groups are found over an extensive area of northeastern, central, and southern Namibia. In the past, they were often attached as clients or servants to Nama or Herero clans. Not much is known about their way of life while under Nama and Herero domination in the nineteenth century and before. Even less is known, anthropologically, about the present way of life of Damara people.

However, with the comparative context of Khoisan society as our focal point, it is useful to try to draw together some of the most prominent features of the 'traditional' lifestyle, as these illustrate transformations of

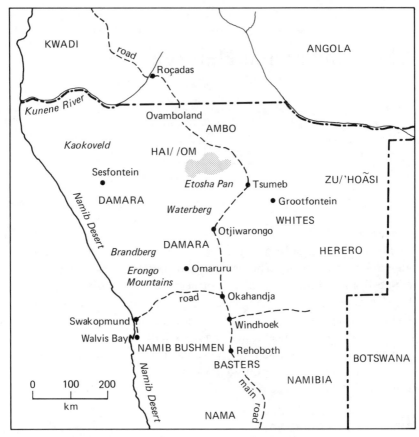

Figure 11.1 Northern Namibia (German South West Africa): the Damara, Hai//om, and other groups

the underlying features of Khoisan social structure and the historical processes which have given rise to them. This chapter will therefore concentrate on the Damara as they were during the golden age of Namibian ethnography (though certainly not the golden age of Namibia itself), the German colonial period before the wars of 1904–7 and 1914–17. Their history, as Vedder (1938 [1934]: 197) remarked, 'is entirely interwoven with that of the Namas and the Hereros during the years 1840 to 1880'. That was a period of great strife, particularly before the temporary peace agreement between the Nama and the Herero in 1870 (see e.g., Vedder 1938 [1934]: 196–403). While perhaps not a 'society' as anthropologists traditionally conceive of one, the Damara of that period, and since, do represent a 'culture'. It is the spirit of this culture which we must try to understand.

The leading ethnographer of the Damara was the Rhenish missionary and historian Heinrich Vedder (1923; 1928a; 1930). Other early ethnographers have included W.C. Palgrave (1877), Hugo von François (1896), and Viktor Lebzelter (1934). In the 1980s, Ben Fuller, a graduate student at Boston University, did extensive research with the Damara, and the publication of his work is keenly awaited.

Population and origins

Stow (1905: 257) estimated the Damara population in 1880 at around 30,000. In Vedder's time the Damara numbered about 25,000 (Vedder 1928a: 39). Today they number at least 90,000. Some used to call themselves ≠Nu Khoen (literally, 'Black People'), while their relatively low social status has in the past led unfortunately to the use of more derogatory terms by members of other groups. 'Damara' (technically the feminine dual form, but functioning as common plural) is the term the people themselves prefer.

Still, much confusion surrounds their designation. Early ethnographers called them 'Bergdama' or 'Berg Damara' ('Hill Damara' in German), apparently a loan translation of the indigenous *!Hom Daman*. Stow (1905: 261–4) refers to the Herero as 'the Ovaherero or Damara', while he calls the Damara 'the Berg-Damaras' (1905: 256–61). Be that as it may, they should not be confused with the Herero, who are Central-Bantu-speaking people sometimes referred to as the 'Cattle Damara' (from Nama *Gomaxa Daman*) in early ethnographies. Today, they are called 'Damara' by Bushmen and Tswana. Arguably, *Damara* is still the correct term for 'Herero' in the Tswana language. The similarity which has apparently caused this term to be applied to both the Herero and the Damara is their dark skins. Those cultural similarities they do share, notably in village layout, are no doubt due to borrowing, possibly from the time when many Damara acted as servants to Herero in the nineteenth century.

Although they share some genetic material with living Khoekhoe and Bushmen populations (see Chapter 2), the Damara are different in appearance and have long been regarded by themselves, by other inhabitants of their country, and by scholars, as distinct from these other groups too (cf. Nurse, Lane, and Jenkins 1976). Their relationship to the Khoekhoe and Bushmen was a subject of much speculation among nineteenth- and early twentieth-century ethnologists. The prevailing opinion in the nineteenth and early twentieth centuries was that the Damara, like the Bushmen, were for all practical purposes aborigines of southwestern Africa. Vedder (1928a: 41–2; 1938 [1934]: 107–19) argued against that view. In order to shed light on the problem he suggested a new and indeed simpler theory, namely that the Damara came down from North Africa as servants of the Nama. This theory is now thought highly unlikely, and Vedder himself was its only champion in his own time. His theory was based on somewhat spurious linguistic grounds, and apparently on the fact that Damara physically resemble neither the Nama nor other groups living in Namibia in his time. Indeed, Damara folklore claims that their original language was Zulu, which they lost because 'their forefathers stayed too long at the fire of the Khoekhoe' (S. Schmidt 1989, II: 61)!

There is no evidence, either linguistic or genetic, that the Damara are descended from North Africans, and no reason to suppose that their settlement in Namibia is recent. The arrival of the Damara in southwestern Africa certainly pre-dates that of the Nama and probably also that of the Central-Bantu-speaking Herero and Ambo peoples. Recent archaeological evidence suggests two phases of settlement in the Brandberg area: one characterized by microliths of the Wilton industry dating back about 5,000 years and the other, known as the Brandberg industry, dating from some 500 years ago. For the latter tradition, the data suggest a people who lived in huts with reinforced stone bases, who manufactured pottery, and who made metal tools. Very probably, these were the ancestors of the Damara (Jacobson 1981: 10–11).

Today, at about 7 per cent of the population, the Damara are one of the larger groups in Namibia. The largest group, the Ambo, accounts for some 49 per cent. The Damara inhabit mainly northwestern parts of the country, with pockets of settlement among the Nama to the south, on farms, and in the urban centres. They were once persecuted in the southern areas and, from before the turn of the century, have therefore tended to seek security in more inaccessible places, such as the Brandberg and the Kaokoveld (see, e.g., van Warmelo 1951). In recent decades, there has been a substantial urban population in Katutura, the western township of Windhoek. This now accounts for over 30 per cent of the total Damara population (van der Merwe 1983: 48).

Local organization
The Damara have always lacked the tribal community of the Nama, having no descent-defined tribal units or tribal chiefs. Vedder (1928a: 71) states that until German intervention in the 1890s, the Damara had no claim to land and no concept of land ownership. The Damara were perceived by outsiders as virtually lawless, apart from rules governing the inheritance of movable property, the transmission of names, and so on. This description, of course, needs to be taken with a grain of salt. What is likely is that in spite

of their close association with Nama and Herero, the Damara resembled the Bushmen in their regulation of group affairs, while, like the Nama of earlier times, they maintained a greater concern for movable property than land.

In Vedder's time, the Damara were divided into large, loose, locality-incorporative units. There were eleven of these. Their names and traditional locations (according to Vedder 1923, I: 9–10; 1928a: 42) are given below. I give their names first with Vedder's spellings and word divisions (traditional orthography) and secondly in modern orthography, where this differs. While in some cases these names reflect past and not present political divisions, Damara groups still recognize such groupings, often associated with modern district boundaries and local councils. The names of the groups are as follows: /Gowanin (east of Rehoboth, between Rehoboth and Hoachanas); Tsoa-xou-daman, today called Tsoaxauda-man or Tsoaxūdaman (in the valley of the Swakop River, near Swakop-mund); !Oe-gân, today called !Oe ≠ gân (in the Erongo Mountains); !Omen, today called !Ommen (at the Waterberg and along the Omaruru River); Aro-daman, today called Arodaman (at the Waterberg); Animin (reported by Vedder near Okahandja); Oumin (reported by Vedder east of the Waterberg); /Geiö-daman, today called /Gaiodaman (in the Outjo veld, north of Otjiwarongo); Aobe-//ain, today called Aube//aen (in the Omar-uru veld); Dâuna-daman or Dauredaman, today called Dâunâdaman or Dâuredaman (in the Brandberg); and Ao-guwun, today called Aoguwun (south of Sesfontein in the Kaokoveld).

Livelihood and subsistence

The customary, caste-like occupations of the Damara were servant and blacksmith. They served Nama and, to a lesser extent, Herero masters through the nineteenth century and possibly before. Vedder (1928a: 43–4) attributes their subsequent economic independence to the efforts of the Rhenish Mission in Rehoboth, which in 1860 obtained for them (from the local Herero chief) a grant of land near Omaruru. This grant, and a later one near Tsumeb, gained early recognition from the German authorities. Damara settlement has continued ever since. Further independence for many Damara came after the 1904 War, when they escaped both their Herero and Nama masters and the German forces.

As blacksmiths, the Damara provided iron heads for spears and arrows and iron axes. They also repaired guns and even grew tobacco for the Herero chiefs Tjamuaha and Maherero (Vedder 1928a: 43). The Daureda-man of the Brandberg also mined rock to make into smoking pipes, which found their way into the trade networks (Jacobson 1981: 11). Women as well as men cured skins and sewed them into clothing (Vedder 1928a: 49). The women, but apparently not the pre-pubescent girls, provided plant foods, and some 'collected' game. These included berries, roots and bulbs, and small animals, such as frogs, lizards and young birds and birds' eggs (Vedder 1928a: 50, 1938 [1934]: 62). An interesting method of food collection involves the harvester ant (*Messor barbarus capensis*), a small creature which amasses vast quantities of grass seed in its underground granaries. The Damara of the Brandberg today steal the seeds collected by these ants, especially in times of drought, and leave just enough behind to tide the ants over until the next harvest (Jacobson 1981: 9).

In historical times, the Damara considered themselves hunters. This activity even engaged the time and imagination of young boys (Vedder 1928a: 50). They would learn hunting skills with their contemporaries and bring home the fruits of these skills to roast on their mothers' fires. Like Bushmen, most Damara men hunted antelope and other game animals. Hunting was carried out either alone or in groups, preferably groups made up of co-initiates. The owner of the game was defined as the first to sink his arrow into the animal, and not necessarily the one who dealt the killing blow. When a large animal was killed, it was dragged back to the village and placed at the holy fire for distribution (see 'The encampment' and 'Religion and taboo', below).

As hunters, Damara burned off much of the grass in the winter months of August and September. This practice fostered the growth of seedlings which attracted game animals after the first rains. Yet it also caused much displeasure to the Herero, who depended on what meagre grazing land existed in those months for their cattle. For this reason, as well as their reputation as stock thieves, the Damara were mistrusted by other peoples of the country (Vedder 1928a: 42–3).

From aboriginal times, some Damara herded goats obtained in trade, or, more rarely, cattle. Yet according to common belief, their main preoccupation was raiding the great cattle herds of the Herero and the flocks of sheep owned by the Nama (Vedder 1938 [1934]: 62). This occupation was especially prevalent among those groups who had not been servants but had instead made their own living independently of the Nama tribes. The 'herders' among them are said to have left their animals to wander in the veld. Little care was taken to protect the flocks, though lambs were kept within a safe distance of the huts. Not all Damara took to herding, but those who did preferred goats to cattle, as the latter require much more work effort in order to maintain them (Vedder 1928a: 58–9). The Damara no doubt favoured the 'Zen' style of affluence which Sahlins (1974 [1977]: 1–39) attributes to the Bushmen. Purposeful underproduction in order to maximize time (rather than wealth) would seem to have characterized their style of life.

The encampment

The Damara word for 'encampment' was *!hais*, a term which evoked the notion of peace within the confines of the thorned enclosure (Vedder 1923, I: 16). Damara encampments were commonly occupied by a single extended family, and thus included only a few huts (see Vedder 1923: 16–17; 1928a: 48–9; 1938 [1934]: 61). Only rarely did they include more than ten such dwellings. Damara have long preferred to camp in sheltered locations, often in the mountains or behind groves of trees.

There were in the past two types of hut (Vedder 1923, I: 11–15; 1928a: 47–8; Lebzelter 1934: 114–15). The permanent hut was called the *oms*. Like the Khoekhoe one, the Damara *oms* was constructed from branches stuck in the ground and tied together at the top. However, instead of thick matting, loose grass and twigs were used to cover the frame, and such huts offered little protection from the environment. The *oms* was divided into sections, each used for a different purpose, and the door was covered with a skin. The huts were owned only by women, as a man would spend the day and the evening at the holy fire in the centre of the camp, and the night with one of his wives, in rotation. The temporary hut was called the *!nūs* (the Common Khoe term for 'hut') or */gaos*. This was more like a Bushman one, too small to stand up in, and was used only as a sleeping place. Even more than the hut, the family fire dominates the traditional social life of the Damara. As among the Bushmen, it is the hearth and not the house which is the focus of activity (see, e.g., Vedder 1928a: 44–5). When in the veld, a Damara would sometimes do without a house altogether or build a shelter just to cover his fire (1928a: 47–8).

The camp or village was generally centred on the holy fire (properly *sōxa /ais*, though this taboo term was avoided in conversation) and the camp tree (*!hai hais*) which stood near. It was at the holy fire (euphemistically */awa /ais*, the 'red fire'), that the male elders held council and ate meat. The Herero and the Hai//om also share the idea of a holy fire, though oddly those Damara groups most in contact with Herero lacked the notion. This led Vedder (1928a: 70) to question the otherwise obvious conclusion that the custom of lighting such a fire among these peoples has a common origin.

While the holy fire was located at the centre of each village, the location of the tree under which it was built determined the camp layout (see, e.g.,

Vedder 1923, I: 16–17). In the past, much the same seems to have been true of the Herero, for whom the tree, as well as the fire and the sacred cattle, was associated with their underworld deity or ancestral culture hero, Mukuru (see, e.g., Luttig 1933: 18–30). The Damara, like the Herero, would find a suitable, shady tree and place the fire immediately to the east. The tree was consecrated with the blood of a game animal, poured into a cut in the bark. After this, the holy fire could be lit. The doorways of all the huts faced the centre and the holy fire. Construction was primarily women's work, as the women were considered the owners of all the dwellings. Although the Damara never had a political hierarchy of the kind associated with the Nama, the Herero, or even the Hai//om, they did give pride of place to the 'owner' of the village, the first wife of the village elder. Her hut was distinguished from the others by a small porch in front.

It will be remembered that the Nama chief places his hut in the west of his village. The Damara orientation is the opposite. The 'owner' of the village has her hut in the east, and it faces west. This orientation is characteristic of Herero settlements, and is reported among the Hai//om as well. A comparison of the layouts of typical Damara, Hai//om, and Herero camps is shown in Figure 11.2. This illustration is a composite, derived from a variety of sources, including my own observations (cf. Vedder 1923, I: 16–17; 1928a: 48–9; Fourie 1926: 50–1; 1928: 84–7; Luttig 1933: 32–4; Lebzelter 1934: 84; Gibson 1956: 112–18; Urquhart 1963: 42–4). The absence of huts in the west, at least in the Herero case, reflects the preference of individuals to be located near the high-status east of their respective camps. In the traditional Herero camp, there is a further division between the southern half, where men establish their huts, and the northern, which is the women's place (see, e.g., Luttig 1933: 32–3), though this pattern is not found among the Hai//om or the Damara.

Kinship and marriage

Figure 11.3 shows the structure of a Damara kin terminology which I recorded in 1982. It is virtually identical to that of the Nama (Chapter 10), with only minor, non-structural differences, e.g., in the classification of parents' siblings. In this diagram, I have included not only suffixes and infixes (as for Nama) but also Dutch or Afrikaans-derived terms which I found in use. These terms seem to have been fully assimilated into the system and are used by the Damara when speaking their own language (cf. Barnard 1980d). The terminology structure presented here represents an idealized structure, recorded from knowledgeable informants, and not necessarily a structure which is found in practice among all Damara today. This structure is much more consistent with traditional Nama and Khoe

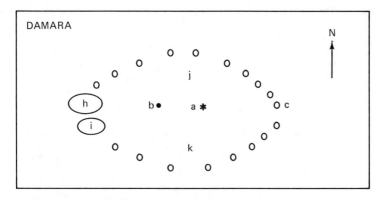

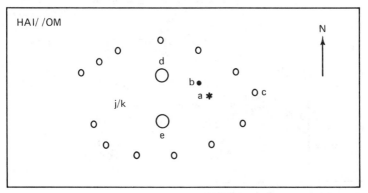

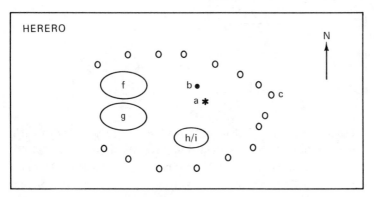

Figure 11.2 Traditional Damara, Hai//om, and Herero village layouts
a holy fire
b village tree
c hut of the senior resident
d young marriageable men's hut
e young women's hut
f oxen
g cows
h sheep or goats
i lambs
j dancing place (ritual)
k dancing place (common)

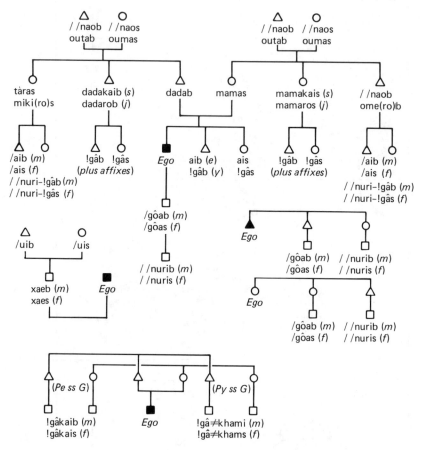

Figure 11.3 Damara kinship terminology: basic structure

Bushman usage than with what records we find in the writings of early ethnographers (notably Lebzelter 1934: 154–5; cf. Barnard 1976a: 241–2).

The marriage rules are not recorded in the early sources, but my Damara informants claimed that, although no longer found among the Nama, cross-cousin marriage is still practised preferentially among certain Damara groups. The Nama use the terms /*aib* and /*ais* to suggest illicit sexual relationships (themselves called /*ai-gun*). In the Damara dialect, /*aib* and /*ais* are the usual, perfectly acceptable terms for cross-cousins (cf. Nama //*nurib* and //*nuris*). In some Damara areas, cross-cousins are regarded as 'spouses' and termed as such. A man can tell anything he wishes to his female cross-cousin, even more than he would tell his real wife (Gordon 1971: 51). This is important, given that extensive, almost institutionalized, networks of gossip exist in Damara society. In contrast, strict avoidance is maintained between brothers and sisters, and between parents-in-law and children-in-law. Before Vedder's time, men arranged their children's marriages. Polygyny was common, and second marriages were accompanied by virtually no ceremony at all (Vedder 1923, ɪ: 52–5; 1928a: 55).

The Damara have much the same naming system as the Nama. Some Damara have as many as six names (Vedder 1923, ɪ: 46–50; 1928a: 54–5). Traditionally, one name was given by the child's father after some recent event. This naming was accompanied by great ceremony, including the father anointing his own body with oil, spitting on and rubbing the child, and presenting it with a charm containing medicinal powder. Great names (confusingly labelled *Familienname* by Vedder) pass from father to daughter and mother to son, and are the most important. According to my informants, their cross-descent great names, but not patrilineal surnames (possibly a recent introduction), identify exogamous units.

Social hierarchy

Vedder (1928a: 42) claimed that chieftainship was unknown in his time and that each large family functioned as an independent political unit. The eleven tribal divisions were more regional than kin based, and exercised no authority over their members. Nevertheless, Lebzelter collected genealogies which indicate a line of chiefs stretching back twenty-one generations. Vedder (1938 [1934]: 115) included this list in his history of South West Africa, but correctly warns against taking it at face value. Ironically though, the fact that the names of all these 'chiefs' were designated by Nama words, with Nama suffixes, adds a small bit of credence to Vedder's theory that the Damara originated long ago in North Africa and migrated south with the ancestors of the modern Nama.

Vedder (1928a: 42) also suggested that the Damara could be divided into two social classes. The upper class consisted of goat herders who lived mainly in the valleys. The lower class had few goats. They were essentially forager-plunderers and inhabited the southern plains. What goats they had were obtained either as booty or in barter with Tswana herdsmen. The lower class seem to have been made up of families who, as a result of warfare between different Nama tribes, had ended up with no masters.

Few precise vestiges of authority or prestige are found in the ethnographic record of the classic era. Vedder (1928a: 45) noted that one could tell a successful hunter by the number of leather rings on his wife's arms and legs. His implication is that some pride is attached to accomplishment in the hunt, but his description of this custom contrasts starkly with his comments on the slovenly manner of dress of the Damara of his time.

Rites of passage

A girl's first menstrual period was celebrated with a feast. Her father would slaughter a goat, if he had any, and the feast was open to all present in the village. As among Khoe-speaking Bushmen, the girl herself was confined in her hut, in silence, and tended by her mother and other female relatives. They would bedeck her in ornaments, teach her to prepare a powdered perfume to use in adult life, and instruct her in appropriate behaviour, especially in relation to her brothers. After puberty, a girl could not sit next to her brother, turn her back to him, or look him directly in the eye. Similar taboos also applied to her potential husband if one had been chosen for her (Vedder 1923, I: 52; 1928a: 50; Lebzelter 1934: 139).

Male initiation was a collective affair; only rarely would a boy or young man be granted a ceremony on his own. The father of each initiate provided a goat or a large game animal, but before these could be eaten elaborate preparations had to be made. A space was cleared, usually some distance from the village, and branches were placed around the cleared ground to form an enclosure. The head of the family who was organizing the feast would then gather roots and bitter herbs to soak in a wooden bucket. On the next day, the elders would lead the initiates in a hunt. Each initiate was equipped with a lance, a bow, and arrows. With senior men at the front and initiates at the back, a large group of men and boys would leave the camp. They marched in a straight line and shouted as they went. The game they killed was eaten only by the senior men. Meanwhile, one of the elders who had remained in camp would have cooked some of the goat over the holy fire. Before and after cooking, this meat was laid out in a highly ritualized fashion. The method of slaughter included the removal, by hand, of the beating hearts of the animals. After cooking, the men would blow up and tie off the intestines and gall bladder, for these had to be hung on the initiates when they returned to camp. The initiates could then drink from the bucket of bitter herbs prepared earlier, while the senior men ate their meal. After all of this, the initiates were instructed on proper conduct in married life, and the next day they returned to hunt again (Vedder 1928a: 50–2; Lebzelter 1934: 137–9).

The Damara did not, it seems, practise circumcision (which is generally foreign to Khoisan peoples), although Vedder (1928a: 52) explicitly likens this Damara ceremony to the circumcision rites of the Herero. The likeness was the intention, in each case, to bring close ties between men initiated at the same time. It was also believed that co-initiates would not die at the same time, and for this reason fathers did not allow two of their sons to be initiated together (1928a: 52).

There are other, obvious parallels, in the ceremonies of Bushman groups. The ceremony of the !Xõ (Heinz 1966: 125–34; 1978b) and of the western Nharo as described by Bleek (1928a: 23–5) are cases in point. As with the Nharo today, the Damara ceremony was not necessarily a once-and-only occasion. Damara men customarily went through three such initiations, or hunting rituals, each time advancing to a higher stage. Only after the third, which frequently took place in adulthood, were they granted the status of elder (Vedder 1928a: 52).

Religion and taboo

Astounding as it may seem, early Europeans in Namibia thought that the Damara had no religion at all. Then, in the early part of the twentieth century, investigations by Vedder revealed a rich cosmology. While practices relating to the holy fire are reminiscent of Herero customs, most aspects of cosmology fit into a pan-Khoisan constellation of religious ideas. Intriguingly, Damara cosmology was in some respects the antithesis of that of the Nama. This was particularly true of the isolated hill groups among whom Vedder conducted his important fieldwork.

The holy fire was not only the centre of village life but also an object of reverence (see Vedder 1923, I: 20–38; 1928a; 68–70; Lebzelter 1934: 115–16). For Vedder (1928a: 68), it was one of the three pillars of the Damara religion (the others being the deity //Gamab, and the evil spirits). A number of rules accompanied behaviour in its vicinity. The fire was said to be the source of good fortune in hunting and gathering, and any transgression of the rules of proper conduct could result in disaster. One had to be careful not to gulp one's food in front of the fire. Children were not allowed to play near the fire. If such things happened, the fire might have to be put out. A new holy fire could only be started after all other fires in the camp had been put out, and only a village headman and his assistant were allowed to be present in the camp when the new fire was lit. They made the fire by twirling a stick and reciting magical formulae. The holy fire was kept lit by the 'great wife', the first wife of the headman – also the custom among the Herero. She kept coals burning in her hut in order to replenish the holy fire when it died down. When they moved camp, she would have the honour of carrying the glowing coals at the head of the procession to the new site. The church (Lutheran or Catholic) has long since replaced the holy fire, and at least in some Damara areas, no vestige of the custom remains.

Like other Khoekhoe-speakers, the Damara called their supreme being //Gamab (Vedder 1923: I, 97–142; 1928a: 61–8). //Gamab was said to live in the sky, in a village laid out on the same plan as a Damara village. In the centre of his village is a large, shady fig tree, under which burns his holy fire. Around the fire, in a great circle, are the huts of all the Damara who have died, and in each hut lie the bones of its owner.

When a Damara dies, the soul leaves the body and takes the wide road which leads to //Gamab's village (Vedder 1928a: 61–2). At one point, a narrow road branches off, but the Damara do not know where it leads. At another point, there is a great cliff which overlooks a fire far below. If the deceased should fall off, his or her soul would be lost forever. There is no notion that wicked people fall over the edge and good people reach the sky. All Damara, provided they are careful, can get past the cliff. When the deceased nears //Gamab's village, other spirits come out to bid welcome. The new arrival is given a full bowl of liquid fat to drink, and then takes his or her place among the dead. Life in heaven is much like that on earth, only better. The reason why earth is so sparse in resources, say the Damara, is that heaven is so plentiful (Vedder 1928a: 63).

//Gamab was not the only mythical being among the Damara. The Nama folk hero, Haiseb or Haitsi-aibib, seems to have been the object of veneration among them at one time. Stow (1905: 261) reported that both Damara and Herero in his day bowed, in the Nama manner, to the stone heaps which mark the sites believed to be Haitsi-aibib's many graves (see Chapter 14). Damara and Hai//om folktales are sometimes told with 'Haiseb' as the name of the deity (e.g., S. Schmidt 1989, II: 62–3, 75–7).

Damara belief included a number of taboos, most importantly those which involved water (see, e.g., Vedder 1928a: 45–6). Water was thought to rob the hunter of his potential for success. Even the hunter's wife had to avoid water while he was hunting. Damara would wash with fat in order to avoid the consequences of water, and in the winter they covered themselves with ashes. These customs no doubt contributed to the European notion that the Damara were 'dirty', and possibly also helped to account for their relatively low status among other peoples.

Other taboos were related to female adolescence. Adolescent girls had to avoid eating spring hare, turtle, some birds, and even some berries, as well as certain parts of the flesh of slaughtered goats and game animals. Contravention of these taboos was believed to result in childlessness, illness, or death. Such maladies could be prevented, however, by the application of medicinal substances in incisions made under the breasts by older women. Afterwards, girls were free to enjoy the foods of adulthood

(Vedder 1928a: 49–50). Severe taboos were associated also with the birth of twins, which heralded great misfortune. In former times, the weaker of the two (or the boy if they were of opposite sex) would be buried alive (Vedder 1928a: 54).

Vedder (1928a: 46) remarks that the Damara showed little knowledge of medicinal substances or medical skills. Like other Khoisan peoples, they made tiny incisions in the skin at the site of injury or infection. In the case of more serious afflictions, they burned areas of skin with the blunt end of a root set on fire (1928a: 46–7).

The Damara today

Both Vedder (1923, I: 170–94; 1928a: 75–7) and Lebzelter (1934: 177–81) close their ethnographies with a discussion of the Damara in 'modern times'. Needless to say, these discussions are long since outdated. The modern Damara are changing with the rest of Namibia, though the changes they are undergoing are by no means uniform.

Robert Gordon (1971: 46–7) has described three categories of people he encountered twenty years before independence in the Okombahe Reserve (near the Erongo Mountains, 200 km northwest of Windhoek). In modern orthography, these are the /Oren (corresponding to the well-known 'Red' division of South African Xhosa society), the ≠ Am-khoen ('School people'), and an in-between group called the ≠ ao-//arasan. The ≠ Am-khoen stressed the value of education, and were critical of others for their drunkenness and sexual licence. The /Oren, in contrast, resented the imposition of white values. They thought of education as a waste of time, and they preferred to engage in traditional subsistence activities rather than wage labour.

Politically, the Nama are divided today between those who support the SWAPO government and those who support a political group known as the Damara Council. Geographically, they are divided between those who live in close contact only with other Damara and those who live in Nama or white-owned land, or in urban areas. All these divisions have wider cultural implications, and one would hope that future studies of the Damara, which will no doubt focus more on politics, economics, and demography, can also take these cultural implications into account.

The Hai//om

The Hai//om, once a famous Bushman people, have been neglected by recent generations of anthropologists. In the literature, their name is variously given as *Hai//om* (the glottal stop is present in speech but not indicated in the standard Nama orthography which the Hai//om use), *Hain//om* or *Hai//omn* (the *-n* being a plural suffix), or in early literature, *Hei//om* or *Heikum*. Their leading ethnographer was Louis Fourie (1926; 1928), medical officer to the South West Africa Administration in the 1920s. Other details were recorded by Lebzelter (1934: 80–8). K.F.R. Budack, as government anthropologist of the South West Africa Administration, conducted some research with the Hai//om in the 1970s and 1980s. Dagmar Wagner-Robertz (e.g., 1976) has done work on Hai//om shamanism, and Robert Gordon (e.g., 1989) has done archival research on recent Damara history. However, none of these researchers has yet produced a major account of Hai//om culture. In 1990 – the year of Namibian independence – Thomas Widlok, a postgraduate student at the London School of Economics, began intensive research on social change and economic relations among the Hai//om. His results are anticipated shortly, but in the meantime Fourie's work remains our most comprehensive source. In some areas, at least some of the customs recorded by Fourie survive. Accordingly, and in the absence of detailed recent data, I shall use the ethnographic present.

The Hai//om are one of the great ethnographic anomalies of the Khoisan culture area. They are significant in number. According to some recent estimates, they number perhaps as many as 11,000 (Thomas Widlok, pers. comm.). Their enigmatic name means 'tree-' or 'bush-sleepers'. As with the Damara, their origin has been the subject of speculation. They have long been thought of as !Kung who acquired the Nama-Damara language at some time in the not-too-distant past. Towards the end of the South African colonial period, the Hai//om were said to be maintaining vociferously their identity as non-!Kung, while officials insisted on classifying !Kung and Hai//om together as members of the same 'population group'.

Life in the Hai//om camp

There are many similarities between the Hai//om and the Damara (see, e.g., Fourie 1928: 87–8). Perhaps the most obvious examples are the holy fire, which is termed *hai /ais* (tree fire) in the Hai//om dialect, and its associated tree. The tree itself is called the *!hais*, a term which connotes peace and which the Damara use for the entire encampment. Unusually for a Khoisan people, special huts for unmarried men and pre-pubescent girls occupy the centre of the camp. Intriguingly, the placement of these mimics the positioning of Herero kraals for oxen and cows respectively (Figure 11.2). The Hai//om, like the Nama, call the encampment simply *//gâus* (village), and their village life seems to be a peculiar blend of the Damara (and Herero) notion of the centrality of the fire, a Nama-like idea of chiefly authority with gender hierarchy, and otherwise a Bushman lifestyle based on foraging for subsistence.

Each band has a *gaikhoeb* (literally 'great man') or 'chief' (Fourie's term). He selects each campsite and arranges the camp around an appropriate tree. He puts all his movable property on the place on which he will build his hut, while other members of the band pass on his left side to their places and drop their belongings. He then walks over to the tree and kindles the fire with his fire-sticks. He lights his pipe from the fire, and his wife takes coals from it to light a new fire, the *!ou /ais*, in front of the place where their hut is to be built. Others then take their fire freely from the same source, and afterwards the huts may be set up (Fourie 1928: 87–8). No fire is removed from the old camp, and only a chief may kindle the *hai /ais*. Normally, it is kept burning at all times, but if it should ever go out in the chief's absence, it will remain unlit until his return (Fourie 1928: 87).

The *gaikhoeb* and *gaikhoes* (his senior wife) truly deserve the appellation 'chief', as their authority and ritual power is more reminiscent of Nama or Herero chiefs than Bushman headmen. Indeed, not only are they important for their roles as fire-makers and fire-givers; they are also food-givers. During the rainy season (about February), the chief selects a day for the gathering of the first crop of the ≠*huin*, described by Fourie (1928: 98–9) simply as a tree-borne fruit. While the men remain in camp, the women go and gather the fruits from trees designated by the chief's wife. Upon their return to camp, the women deposit their bags of fruit in front of the chiefly couple's hut. The *gaikhoes* takes a handful from each bag and places these fruits under the central tree. The *gaikhoeb* then kindles the fire and applies medicinal substances 'to appease the fire for a plentiful harvest' (Fourie 1928: 99). He eats from the first fruits, and only then may the others consume their share.

Initiation ceremonies

Male initiation takes much the same form as that among other Bushman groups, but female initiation is rather different (see Fourie 1926: 57–9; 1928: 89–91). In some respects Hai//om female rites are more like those of the Khoekhoe than like those of other Bushmen.

Female initiation begins before puberty. Pre-pubescent girls are placed in a special 'young women's hut' (≠*kham-khoeti oms*) in the middle of the camp. They are attended by elderly women, who instruct them in domestic chores, such as how to prepare their husbands' food (men's and women's food are prepared separately). At the onset of menstruation, a new hut next to this one is made ready, and the menstruating girl is secluded there for four days. She is denied the use of fire, and older women cook for her and apply a mixture of red powder and fat to her hair. The women perform an elaborate dance, which men are not even permitted to watch. However, the young men are allowed to remain in camp on the last day of the ceremony, and on this day they pass in single file past the seclusion hut. As they pass, the initiate reaches out through the thatch and touches each boy's testicles with her thumb and forefinger. The Hai//om say that this will prevent any future infections the boys might otherwise have as a result of the young woman's menstrual danger. After the ceremony, the girl is free to marry.

Marriage and kinship

The form of the Hai//om marriage ceremony is recorded in some detail (Fourie 1928: 93). A young man eligible for marriage is called a *!gari-khoeb*. He asks his best friend to approach the parents of the girl of his choice, who will reply that they are too poor to give their daughter away. Next, the young man approaches the girl's parents himself, and receives the same reply. He argues his case, saying that he will bury the girl's parents when they die. If the girl's mother accepts the boy as a prospective son-in-law, she will take his arrows, left outside the parental hut, and place them in her daughter's hut. This seals the marriage. Meanwhile, the girl may run away, and the boy will go to live in the *!gari-khoes oms* (young men's hut) of his bride's camp. After some days, the boy, through his sister, will present gifts of beadwork to his new mother-in-law. She may then take her daughter to the *!gari-khoes oms*, where the marriage will be consummated. After consummation, the young man hunts to obtain both meat for the wedding feast and a skin for his new wife's skirt. In-law taboos are then strictly enforced. Most men, according to Fourie (1928: 92), have two wives, who may or may not be related. Each has a hut of her own, and the first wife holds a position of authority over the second.

Naming is a complex business (Fourie 1928: 94–5). Each child has at least three names. The first is given by the child's father's mother, and the second by the elderly woman who will have assisted during the mother's pre-natal confinement. The third name is a great name. A boy bears his mother's, and a girl is given her father's. Additionally, a boy may add his father's great name (with the suffix *-mab*, 'son of') to his own, and nicknames are common.

We know little of the system for classification of kin. Fourie's (1926; 1928) accounts, nevertheless, give interesting hints from which we can piece together some semblance of kinship structure. The Hai//om are said to live in exogamous, 'patrilineal' bands (1926: 59; 1928: 86). Post-marital residence is initially uxorilocal, but only for a few months. As among the Damara, 'cousins' are termed /aib and /ais. Marriage takes place 'between contiguous groups', and a man may not marry 'his cousins on either side or his brother's or sister's daughter' (1926: 59; 1928: 92). Although Schapera (1930: 104) interprets this as meaning that all cousin-marriage is forbidden, it is possible that Fourie did not fully appreciate the difference between parallel and cross-cousins, and equally likely that only first cousin marriage (and not marriage to other, more distant, /ain) is proscribed.

Hai//om descent has yet another peculiarity: inheritance of band chief-ship is matrilineal! When the chief or headman is near death, his eldest sister and her family are summoned. They leave their own band and settle among the woman's brother's people. After the chief's death and burial, this sister leads the band to a new campsite, where her eldest son becomes the new chief (1926: 61; 1928: 86). Finally, there is evidence that normal residence after puberty is not with one's parents but with one's grandparents. Dorothea Bleek records this Hai//om preference in one of her Nharo notebooks (m.s. [1920]), but gives no further details (cf. Barnard 1975: 16–17).

Little is yet recorded of other aspects of Hai//om culture. Information on religion is notably absent from all the early accounts. We know that certain dances are performed by men only and others by women only, and that some but not all have a religious significance (Fourie 1928: 95–6). In Fourie's time, dances were common in times of plenty, and differences were noted between different Hai//om groups in the Etosha region.

Relations with outsiders

Nomadic Hai//om have been reported in several locations in the Etosha region, but sources disagree as to the extent of their settlement. Three field researchers in the last fifteen years have all mapped the boundaries of their settlement quite differently (Thomas Widlok, pers. comm.). In the north of their territorial range, some work as herdsmen and gardeners for Ambo, with whom Hai//om individuals have intermarried at least since the 1920s (Lebzelter 1934: 83). Others live in the Etosha Game Reserve, and a great many inhabit the northern fringes of the farm districts of Grootfontein, Tsumeb, and Outjo, north of Otjiwarongo.

It would be wrong, however, to imagine that 'social change' is something which has occurred only since Fourie's accounts. As Gordon (1989) has shown, Hai//om individuals were heavily involved in the German–Herero War of 1904–7. Before that, Hai//om traded extensively in ivory, skins, ostrich feathers and eggshell beads, grain, tobacco, cannabis, honey, calabashes, iron, copper, and metal objects of various kinds. Early travellers' accounts (e.g., Galton 1853; Andersson 1856; 1861; Baines 1864; Chapman 1868; Palgrave 1877; Schinz 1891) are full of anecdotal records of inter-ethnic exchange between the peoples of the northwestern Kalahari, including trade between Hai//om, Damara, Zu/'hoãsi, and Ambo. It seems that the Hai//om were pivotal to these trade networks. This is hardly surprising, given their location between the populous areas of Ovamboland in the north and the lands of the Damara and others to the south, as well as the richness of their own country in both game and metal ores.

Other Nama-speaking hunter-gatherers

Several early writers recorded the existence of Nama-speaking Bushmen apart from the Hai//om. Among such writers, Viktor Lebzelter, Keeper of Natural History at the Vienna Museum, stands out as particularly worthy of mention. His accounts are based partly on his own experience of the country in 1926 to 1928 and partly on the work of others – army officers, other colonial officials, and missionaries.

Lebzelter (1934) reports on a number of such groups, often identified more by location than by ethnicity. In most cases, the evidence that they are Nama-speakers rests on his record of vocabulary, and especially kinship terms. The Nama-speaking Bushmen Lebzelter reported include the 'Dama Bushmen' (*Daman-Buschleute*) of Ukuambi (1934: 10–13), a separate group given as the 'Bushmen of Ukuambi' (1934: 13–14), and the 'Bushmen of Uukualuithi' (1934: 14–16), all in Ovamboland; the 'Bushmen of Naukluft' (1934: 90–101), in the Namib Desert; and some groups in southwestern Angola (1934: 7–9). The dialect of at least one of these groups, the Bushmen of Uukualuithi, seems to be virtually standard Nama, although differences between the other dialects does suggest a degree of linguistic as well as cultural separation.

Of all these groups, only one has achieved more than three pages' worth of recognition in any ethnography. This is the Namib Bushmen, the subject of German colonial reports by Trenk (1910) and Seydel (1910). They then numbered about 900 or 1,000. Trenk (1910: 166) describes them as speaking 'pure Nama', but hunting and gathering in good times and settling on the cattle camps of the Nama, the Basters, and the whites in bad times. In the past, they followed a seasonal pattern which has elements of those of both the G/wi and the !Kung. This involved band migrations across the dunes in the rainy season and early part of the dry season, when (especially in July) *!naras* melons are abundant. The Namib Bushmen then retreated to permanent waterholes, probably around August (Trenk 1910: 166, 168;

Schapera 1930: 91). Schapera describes the owners of these waterholes as 'bands', but these were probably quite small units, each more comparable to a G/wi extended family than to a G/wi band.

The Namib Bushmen hunted large game, including zebra and gemsbok. They used spears as well as bows and arrows, and whistled their hunting calls. According to Trenk (1910: 168–9), households were monogamous, with the man ruling over the wife. Marriage took place after puberty, adultery was punishable by death, and prostitution was unknown. A man's inheritance was divided equally between his widow and his natal family. Seydel (1910: 505–6) recorded the existence of formal legal procedures, with one or two judges empowered to call witnesses and decide the fate of the accused in criminal proceedings, a practice Schapera (1930: 154–5) attributes to Nama influence.

The precise relation of the Namib Bushmen to the Nama will probably never be known. It is not unlikely that they were once Nama themselves who had either fallen on hard times or simply settled in areas unsuitable for livestock. Vedder (1938 [1934]: 78) noted that the 'Saan' (a term he uses specifically for Nama-speaking Bushmen) 'stand in a close relationship to the Namas in religion, law, and custom, and [that] there are clear indications on the borders of their territories that there has been interbreeding'.

Conclusion

Today, Vedder's words have a much broader ring to them than he might have imagined. Not only is 'interbreeding' rightly taken for granted, but 'San', among scholars who use the term, now refers to all those Vedder would have called 'Bushmen'. One anthropologist has suggested (though not yet in print) that the term 'San-speakers' might properly include all Khoisan individuals. The 'San', in any sense of the word, do stand in a close cultural relation to the herders. In some spheres (e.g., religion, kinship, and political economy) a comparative analysis of Khoisan culture beyond the old hunter–herder divide is called for, while in others (e.g., settlement patterns) we can legitimately regard the hunters or the herders as relevant units of analysis. The remainder of this book is dedicated to understanding Khoisan ethnography in a regional context, or perhaps more accurately, in a variety of comparative contexts within the larger confines of Khoisan culture and society.

Part III

Comparisons and transformations

12

Settlement and territoriality among the desert-dwelling Bushmen

Introduction

Bushman settlement and territoriality have been subjects of much discussion over the years (see, e.g., Heinz 1972; 1979; Barnard 1979a; 1986a; 1991; Guenther 1981b; Cashdan 1983). Authors have approached the problem from a number of different perspectives. My early work on Kalahari Bushman settlement patterns (Barnard 1979a) was partly inspired by Hoernlé's 'South West Africa as a primitive culture area' (1923a), in which she argued that the distribution of water resources was an important determinant of Nama tribal and territorial organization. Here, I shall be re-examining Hoernlé's suggestion in relation to more recent work on the Kalahari Bushman peoples and some relevant theoretical ideas. The present chapter focuses not primarily on the actual ethnographic details of settlement and territoriality, which are summarized in earlier chapters, but on models derived from a comparative approach to the data.

The groups to be discussed include the four ethnic divisions of primary concern in earlier papers by Elizabeth Cashdan (1983) and me (Barnard 1979a; 1986a) – namely the Zu/'hoãsi, or Central !Kung; the G/wi and G//ana, treated together as the 'Central Kalahari Bushmen'; the Nharo; and the !Xõ. For some purposes (since Cashdan 1984a; 1984b) it is now useful to distinguish the two groups occupying the Central Kalahari Game Reserve as distinct peoples with different settlement patterns – specifically the G/wi, as studied by Silberbauer in the early 1960s, and the G//ana, as studied by Cashdan in the late 1970s. Thanks to H.P. Steyn's (1984) reconstruction of Southern Kalahari Bushman subsistence ecology, it is also possible to compare this population to the better known ones, from the standpoint of territoriality.

The seasonal cycle
The most obvious environmental variable in a dry climate is the availability of surface water. This, in turn, depends on seasonal changes in rainfall. Broadly, all southern Africa north of the southern Cape Province experiences rainy summers and dry winters (in the Cape, the pattern is the reverse, with dry summers and cold, stormy winters). The rainy period usually begins in October or November (sometimes known as the 'small rains'), and there is a heavier, second period of rain (the 'big rains') at the height of the summer, in January or February. All areas of the Kalahari experience sporadic summer rains and long winter dry periods.

Khoisan groups divide the year into seasons. Rainfall seems to be the single most important factor in the indigenous definition of seasonality, with temperature, vegetation, and subsistence activity also taken into account. Three Bushman groups for whom we have detailed information, though, are the !Kung (specifically the Zu/'hoãsi), the G/wi, and the Nharo. Their classifications of the seasons show similarities, but also some interesting differences.

Among the Zu/'hoãsi five seasons are distinguished: *!huma, bara, ≠obe, g!um,* and *g!a. !Huma* designates the time of the spring rains, October to November. The Zu/'hoãsi take advantage of rainwater which collects in the hollows of trees in order to establish temporary camps in mongongo groves. *Bara* is the time of the main summer rains, December to March. In this season, the summer plant foods appear. These include a great variety of melons, berries and other fruits, as well as leafy greens. The standing water which also occurs at this time makes it possible for Zu/'hoãsi and other !Kung to travel widely and pitch camp away from permanent waterholes. Therefore, communities are dispersed. *≠Obe* is the autumn, April to May. By this time the rains will have ended. Often, there will still be an abundance of food, including mongongo nuts, berries, and melons. *G!um* is the winter, from the end of May to late August. This season is marked by low nighttime temperatures, often below freezing, and mild days (24–27° C). At this time, the outlying water resources will have dried up, and the Zu/hoãsi will be forced to rely on the permanent waterholes, and bands gravitate towards them. It is also a time when other resources are relatively scarce. Although mongongos might still be available, other plant resources will be thinner than in preceding months. Finally, *g!a,* the spring dry season, marks the worst time of year. Resources are at their scarcest, and unappetizing root crops form the bulk of the diet (Lee 1972e; 339–40; 1984: 25–7).

The G/wi also divide the year into five seasons: *!hosa, n//aosa, badasa, g!uabasa,* and *saosa.* The G/wi notion of *!hosa* is roughly equivalent to the

!Kung *!huma*. *!Hosa* begins in August or September and lasts until late November or December. It is marked by high temperatures and the gradual flowering of the trees as a result of early rain. Nevertheless, it is essentially a dry season. The rainy season is *n//aosa*, described by Silberbauer's informants as 'the time when the grass is green and the antelope breed' (1981: 105). *N//aosa* lasts from the onset of the rains in late November or early December until late March or early April. *Badasa*, from March or April to May, is the season when tsama melons are present in abundance. It is also the season when the rains die out and the G/wi are forced to utilize the tsamas for water. The term *bada(-sa)* seems to be related to !Kung *bara*, although these words do not designate precisely the same time of year. *G!uabasa*, May to June, is when deciduous plants drop their leaves. Finally, *saosa*, from the middle or end of June until late August, is the time when food becomes scarce (Silberbauer 1981: 104–7).

The Nharo divide the year into three or four seasons. These bear some resemblance to the G/wi divisions, but perhaps not as much as one would expect from such a closely related language. The three-season calendar includes *n//aosa*, *saosa*, and *!ho*. *N//aosa*, from October or November until April, is the rainy season and seems to be recognized as the start of the year. *Saosa*, from about May until July, is the cold dry season. *!Ho*, from August to September, is the leanest time of year. The four-season calendar includes *n//aosa*, *!hú*, *saosa*, and *!ho*. In this case, the early rains (*n//aosa*) and late rains (*!hú*) are distinguished, with January or February marking the transition. The time of year is expressed linguistically through constructions like *n//ao-s-ka* (meaning 'during *n//ao-sa*'), but *!hú* and *!ho* do not take the usual feminine suffix *-sa* or infix *-s-* (Barnard 1985: 125–6). Nharo settlement patterns are less seasonally determined than those of the G/wi or the !Kung because water is more readily available in their territories.

The similarities between the classification of the seasons among these three groups no doubt partly reflect the similar natural cycle of rainfall, temperature change, and relative availability of vegetation. However, the differences are not directly related to either language or settlement pattern. The seasonal distinctions of the Khoe-speaking G/wi are closer to those of the Central !Kung (who speak a non-Khoe language) than to those of the Nharo (who speak a Khoe language). The G/wi and !Kung have opposite patterns of seasonal settlement and migration, with the Nharo today in-between; and the Nharo settlement pattern before the present century probably more closely resembled that of the !Kung. Obviously, more data on other groups are needed before definitive statements can be made for the Kalahari Bushmen generally, but the distinctions made by these three groups should be evidence enough that there is no simple relationship between the perception of seasonality and either linguistic affinity or social organization.

Group size and population movement

Kalahari Bushmen have a social organization based on etically definable groups: the domestic unit, the band, and (in the case of the Nharo and the !Xo) the band cluster. Aggregation of an entire band cluster is rare. The key unit for aggregation is the band.

The average size of the primary aggregating unit or 'band' varies considerably. The problem with making definitive statements is that great variation occurs even within populations. For example, the !Xõ surveyed have group sizes of eighteen to forty-eight individuals, territories of 1,000 to 2,200 square kilometres, and make zero to seven moves per annum (Hitchcock and Ebert 1989: 55). Two apparently independent surveys of the Dobe !Kung give figures of, respectively, nineteen to forty-two individuals occupying ranges of 675 to 1,370 square kilometres and making four to eighteen moves per annum, and fourteen to eighty-eight individuals occupying ranges of 87 to 400 square kilometres and making zero to four moves per annum (1989: 55). Reasons for such variation include: (1) differences in the interpretation of the data by writers, such as Hitchcock and Ebert, who have tried to summarize the work of others; (2) differences between ethnographers in their interpretation of observed behaviour among Bushman groups; (3) differential movement of populations on a random basis at the time they were studied; (4) the effects of specific conditions pertaining to the groups at the time they were studied; (5) variations in the annual cycle of the groups as a result of environmental factors; and (6) variations in the annual cycle of the groups as a result of social factors.

Obviously, measuring and accounting for population movement are complex problems. This is one reason why I tend to prefer structural analyses of these phenomena as a complement to the more quantitative approaches of most of my colleagues in Khoisan studies. Hitchcock and Ebert (1989) do present an analysis of Bushman settlement patterns which is both quantitative and structural. According to their model, the combination of high mobility and small group size is associated with the presence of surface water, and the combination of high mobility and large group size is associated with the absence of surface water. Low mobility, with small group size, occurs during the dry season among both populations who have access to surface water and ones which do not. Low mobility, with large group size, occurs during the wet season in areas with some surface water, while low mobility with *minimal* group size is found in areas which have no surface water. Hitchcock and Ebert offer few specific illustrations, but it is clear that high-mobility populations would include certain !Kung groups, while the Nharo would be counted among the low-mobility groups.

Not only must we distinguish the degree of mobility; it is frequently useful to distinguish the form of such mobility with reference to different types of territory. Tim Ingold (1986: 194–5) differentiates three kinds of population movement: nomadism, migration, and displacement. Nomadism is narrowly defined to include only movements which take place within ecological zones, while migration involves transhumance between zones, and displacement comprises shifts of sedentary settlements or of the ranges or orbits of nomadic and migratory populations. In the Bushman case, all three forms are found, though it is not always easy to differentiate ethnographically between the first two of these three ideal types.

The three components of population movement are well illustrated in the social organization of the G/wi and G//ana. Nomadism is particularly prevalent. The Central Kalahari Game Reserve has no permanent natural water resources, and bands move within their respective territories in order to exploit seasonal water and water-bearing melons. G/wi bands also disperse into family-sized units in the dry season (Silberbauer 1981: 191–8, 245–57). Silberbauer (1979: 117) has likened this time of year to the hibernation or dormant period in the lives of animals. It is a kind of 'social hibernation' when the G/wi escape the hardship and potential social tensions of the season by separating and exploiting dispersed resources, uncompetitively. A different form of nomadism – which Ingold terms 'fixed-point nomadism' – occurs among those G/wi and G//ana who live in the Ghanzi ranching area. There, individuals travel between boreholes. Fixed-point nomadism also occurs in the movements of families between the areas where abundant vegetable resources are located (Barnard 1980c; Guenther 1986a: 169–214 *passim*).

The migratory ideal is most prevalent in the east of G/wi–G//ana country. A variety of specific forms of territorial organization are found there, and G//ana groups migrate between river areas and desert areas, according to the season. The dry season is spent near permanent water resources, and the wet season is spent further afield where seasonal water, from rainfall, is available (Cashdan 1984b; 1986b).

Temporary displacement occurs in the occasional movement of G/wi and G//ana bands to neighbouring territories, and in the movements of these and several other Bushman groups to farms or ranches, river environments, and other outlying areas in times of drought (Cashdan 1984b). One form of territorial movement which is not found to any great extent among the living hunter-gatherers of the subcontinent, is permanent displacement. Yet where it has occurred, notably among the !Kung, as a result of South African military activities in the late 1980s, its effects have been decidedly harmful to the population (see, e.g., Marshall and Ritchie 1984). This case aside, among most Bushman groups there is a degree of flexibility in territorial ideology which permits the temporary occupation of territories by alien groups. This is prevalent especially within areas where Bushmen of the same or closely related ethnic groups are found, but it is also apparent across ethnic boundaries. Areas of the Ghanzi ranches support mixed populations of G/wi, G//ana, Nharo, and other Khoe-speaking Bushman peoples. Southern !Kung are found in that region as well, though they generally do not mix with the Khoe-speaking groups. Similarly, in eastern Botswana, members of a number of Khoe-speaking groups have shared the same resources and territories. This seems to have been especially true during the drought of the late 1970s and early 1980s (cf. Cashdan 1984b).

What these areas in western and eastern Botswana have in common is that they are also occupied by non-Bushman peoples. This may indeed account for the ability of one Bushman group to move into a territory which traditionally belonged to another Bushman group. In a sense, these territories may have been literally *alienated* by their occupation by non-Bushman ranchers and subsistence pastoralists. Nevertheless, such pastoralists and non-nomads exploit different ecological niches and often maintain separate boundaries from those of the hunter-gatherers. For example, Nharo band and band cluster territories frequently overlap those of the white ranchers. The fact that, in Botswana law, a particular ranch is owned by one cattle herder to the exclusion of all others, does not necessarily exclude hunter-gatherers from using it or from continuing to define their own territories, irrespective of legal title or wire fences.

'Territoriality', in the sense of defence of resources and spatial boundary maintenance, functions primarily in relation to like populations. When herders move into hunter-gatherer territories there is no necessary conflict, though there would be if other Bushmen were to move in and take over. Some Nharo have lived symbiotically with Afrikaner ranchers for nearly a century, as have !Kung with Tswana and Herero pastoralists (Guenther 1979a; Wilmsen 1986). In these cases, the incursion of non-hunter-gatherer populations has not led to explicit defence of territorial boundaries or to widespread displacement. In contrast, relations between Bushman bands in the northwestern Kalahari were, historically, tense, with trespass taken as a serious and even a capital crime (see, e.g., Schapera 1930: 155–9).

Structural interpretations
Seasonality and settlement
It is now well known that the Zu/'hoãsi and the G/wi of the early 1960s exhibited 'opposite' patterns of settlement. It is worth while examining more precisely the differences and similarities between these two groups, whose settlement patterns are illustrated schematically in Figure 12.1.

As I pointed out in Chapter 6, although !Kung and G/wi band territories are similar in size, the most important aggregating and dispersing units are not of the same order. !Kung aggregations involve two or more bands, who come together in the dry season to exploit permanent water at wells, which are owned and utilized by members of more than one band, and even by non-!Kung who live in the same areas. !Kung disperse as band-sized units in the wet season, when they can live on seasonal water. The G/wi, in contrast, disperse into family units in the dry season and aggregate as band-sized units in the wet season. At least in the 1960s, the total lack of surface water in the dry season prevented band aggregations at this time of year, while wet season aggregations and migrations in search of seasonal food and water supplies, including tsama melons, were advantageous.

Given two seasons (wet and dry) and two patterns of settlement (aggregation and dispersal), there are four logical possibilities. All of these are represented in Kalahari Bushman ethnography. The !Kung aggregate in the dry season and disperse in the wet season, while the Central Kalahari Bushmen do the opposite. !Xõ and Nharo settlement patterns show less seasonal variation but are nevertheless very different. In the present context, the !Xõ may loosely be described as 'permanently dispersed', and the Nharo, 'permanently aggregated'. Figure 12.2 (cf. Barnard 1986a: 50–1) represents this model in diagrammatic form.

Nucleation and territoriality
In 'Kalahari Bushman settlement patterns' (Barnard 1979a), I suggested that these four groups could be ranked according to their degree of nucleation, which I, perhaps erroneously, equated with territoriality. From most nucleated to least nucleated, the ranking was as follows; !Xõ, Central Kalahari Bushmen, !Kung, and Nharo. This, I noted, shows a direct correlation with the lack of availability of water resources (Barnard 1979a: 141). Figure 12.3 is a schematic representation of this composite continuum.

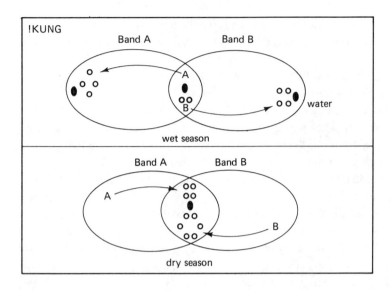

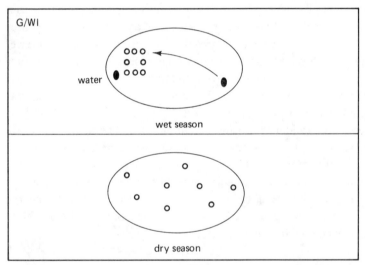

Figure 12.1 A schematic representation of !Kung (Zu/'hoã) and G/wi settlement patterns (black ovals represent water sources)

In fact, none of these models is sufficient to explain territoriality. It is necessary to consider some of the reasons why Bushmen choose one settlement pattern over another, and further, the implications such reasons may have for our use of terms like 'territoriality', 'group cohesion', 'nucleation', and so on. As often as not, arguments about these matters are frustrated by conceptual confusion. For example, on the !Kung, Lee writes:

	dry season aggregation	dry season dispersal
wet season aggregation	NHARO	G/WI
wet season dispersal	!KUNG	!XÕ

Figure 12.2 A comparative model of Kalahari Bushman settlement: aggregation and dispersal (after Barnard 1968a)

least water, most nucleated			most water, least nucleated
!XÕ	G/WI	!KUNG	NHARO

Figure 12.3 A comparative model of Kalahari Bushman settlement: nucleation and the availability of surface water (after Barnard 1979a)

'Although conflict over resources is rare, the threat of conflict in general serves as an adaptive spacing mechanism that keeps groups well distributed on the land *without recourse to any kind of territorial exclusivity*' (1979b: 399; my emphasis). Commenting on Lee's statement, Wilmsen remarks: 'This is territorial defense in anybody's language' (1983: 14)! Virtually no one to date has seen fit to define precisely what they mean by 'territoriality' in the Bushman context.

It seems to me that what is implied by usages such as those of Wilmsen here, and perhaps of Heinz on the !Xõ is that 'territoriality' involves some sort of congruence between social and geographical boundaries. Yet in Heinz's view, this notion can be applied to animals as well as humans: 'Territoriality in its simplest form is intolerance confined to space, as it is exhibited by an animal towards another of the same species' (1972: 406). This is not the same thing as 'nucleation', a term which is generally employed in a purely etic sense, as in Yellen and Harpending's 'Hunter-gatherer populations and archaeological inference' (1972; cf. Barnard 1983). Wilmsen's dialectical notion of 'territoriality' coupled with tenure, on the other hand, expresses both objective and ideological principles at the same time. My present view is that we might do better to distinguish these principles, if at all possible, and employ the term 'nucleation' in a strictly etic sense, and 'territoriality' at least primarily in an emic sense. The problem is that 'territoriality' is almost inevitably very much a product of an observer's interpretation and thus never as emic as one might like it to be.

Locality and group membership

One way around this issue might be through David Turner's approach to 'ideology and elementary structures'. In an article by that title (1978), Turner argues that kinship and locality function as mediating principles between production and ideology. On the basis of this configuration, he classifies societies as either kinship confederational or locality incorporative. Kinship-confederational societies are those in which kinship ties are more important than ties of residence, while locality-incorporative societies are those in which residence overrides kinship in determining group membership. In the latter, a person becomes a member of the group among whom he is living, in spite of his kinship ties to other groups. In my view, kinship confederation and locality incorporation are best seen as alternative principles which operate, to a greater or lesser extent, in the same society, and not as societal types in themselves. Thus what we are concerned with is the dominant such principle in any given case (see Barnard and Good 1984: 146–8).

Characterizing Kalahari Bushman societies in this way, the !Xo can be seen as utilizing a kinship-confederational principle relatively more than the other groups. Ties to one's natal band cluster are the determining factors for one's affiliation. The !Xõ's proverbial distrust of strangers may not be so much an expression of his territoriality, but rather an expression of the corporateness of his kinship groupings. In contrast, the !Kung and Nharo exemplify a preference for the locality-incorporative principle in at least one important respect: their personal naming system allows any person whom they wish to accept as a band member to be so accepted and treated as kin. In order to incorporate even non-!Kung or non-Nharo into society, all that is needed is to give the person a !Kung or Nhyaro name. The Central Kalahari Bushmen are more difficult to assess in these terms: the G/wi and G//ana, and perhaps other Bushmen too, may well operate in terms of both these principles (kinship-confederational and locality-incorporative), seasonally, and with differences according to their degree of acculturation or resettlement.

It is therefore useful to distinguish at least three separate concepts here: (1) group membership, (2) territoriality, and (3) nucleation. Group membership in the Bushman context consists of the ideological premise of belonging to a given band, band cluster or other social unit. This of course often implies a territorial identity or notion of 'citizenship', in that such groups may be associated with particular localities. Group membership should further be distinguished both from 'visiting' (which implies no right of domicile) and from 'potential group membership' (which implies an unclaimed right of domicile).

Territoriality is a more difficult notion largely because different authors use the term in many different ways. Some anthropologists use it as a purely observational construct, rather as in animal ethology; others as a purely subjective, ideological construct; and still others as a more complicated construct which relates the Bushman's subjective notions to the anthropologist's observations. Cashdan (1983: 49–51, 62–3) distinguishes 'perimeter defence' from 'social boundary defence', but argues for the inclusion of both in her definition of 'territoriality'. Guenther's (1981b: 115–17) treatment of the subject, more than any other to date, illustrates even further the multivariant nature of the problem. He isolates seven dimensions of 'territoriality', including: relations with neighbouring groups, ecological and demographic pressures, spatial parameters of the territory in question, social parameters of such a territory, the 'cultural sphere' with which territoriality is associated (e.g. economics, ritual), the explicitness of the spatial boundaries, and the association between territoriality and aggression.

Finally, nucleation consists of the observed tendency of individuals to remain within a definable territory over a period of time. Some Bushman societies can be described as relatively nucleated, and others relatively anucleate (Yellen and Harpending 1972: 247–8). This is not quite the same thing as aggregation, but both aggregation and nucleation may be similarly problematic, in that the levels of aggregation and of nucleation (e.g. band, band cluster, etc.) will differ from society to society. Furthermore, even such concepts as 'band' and 'band cluster' are but heuristic devices whose substantive definitions will depend as much on indigenous notions of group membership as on observed behaviour.

Territoriality as a maximization strategy

As I have pointed out above, Bushman groups with ample resources, such as the Nharo and the !Kung, are less territorial than those with fewer resources, such as the !Xõ. The !Xõ seem to defend territorial boundaries to a greater extent than other groups, as if to preserve special access to the limited resources of their environment. However, as Cashdan (1983: 47–8) pointed out, animal populations tend to have the reverse mechanism operating in their systems of territorial defence. Various species of

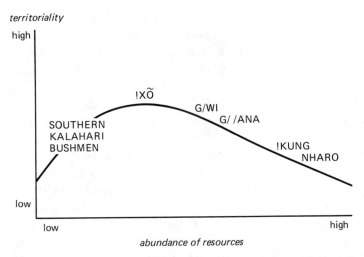

Figure 12.4 A comparative model of Kalahari Bushman settlement: territoriality and the abundance of resources (after Barnard 1991)

monkeys, birds, hyenas, and so on, exhibit increased territorial behaviour when they have more resources to defend. Why should this be so?

It is possible to preserve an essentially maximization-oriented view of these cases, but only if we recognize the possibility of a threshold of abundance, beyond which it is not necessary for groups to defend their territories (Barnard 1991; cf. Richardson 1986 [1982]). According to this theory – illustrated in Figure 12.4 – people (or indeed animals) who live in areas of very scarce resources will have nothing worth defending and exhibit a relative lack of territoriality. There are probably no living Bushmen in this category, though in historical times the Bushmen of the Kalahari Gemsbok National Park, the driest part of the Kalahari, may have approximated this pattern (Steyn 1984). Those (like the !Xõ) who live in areas of somewhat greater abundance and with a need to defend what they have, will engage in territorial defence to a high degree. Yet those (like the Nharo and the !Kung) who live in areas of the greatest abundance will be less territorial. Each !Kung or Nharo group will have access to ample resources in its own territories.

It may well be an adaptive strategy for the !Xõ to maintain a highly territorial organization, but their notions of social and spatial boundaries are, of course, culturally as well as environmentally determined. These notions relate just as much to their wish to preserve group cohesion, and exclude others from encroaching on their lands and utilizing their limited resources, as they do to maintaining perimeter defence (Barnard 1986a: 47–

8). Much of their apparent territoriality is attributable to their ethnicity, not only as !Xõ but as members of particular !Xõ band clusters. There is little contact between !Xõ band clusters, apparently because the !Xõ wish to maintain these boundaries. They also possess a more nucleated form of social interaction than other Bushman groups, and this entails limitations on movement across spatial boundaries. This is not, perhaps a necessary result of the scarcity of resources, but neither is it inconsistent with enabling the !Xõ optimal use of the relatively evenly distributed resources of their territories. Band cluster units, each including several bands, occasionally occupy territories as large as 5,000 square kilometres, in very sparsely populated conditions (estimated from map, Heinz 1979: 467).

In contrast, the !Kung occupy more variable resource bases, in smaller territories, and with a greater population density. In the Dobe-!Kangwa region, band territories range in size from 300 to 1,000 square kilometres (estimated from map, Yellen 1977: 39) – about average for Bushman groups. There is effectively no larger unit than the band. Nevertheless, bands share resources, particularly dry season waterholes. Their territories are clearly defined, but they overlap where waterholes and other shared resources are found, and permission is freely given for individuals of different bands to hunt, gather and take water (see, e.g., Lee 1976 [1972]; 1979b: 333–69; Yellen 1976; Wilmsen 1989b). Overlapping boundaries have been reported elsewhere as well, most notably among the G//ana of the eastern C.K.G.R. (Cashdan 1984a: 447–9). The G//ana in this area lack permanent waterholes, but share rights of access to patches of water-bearing melons. These rights are held by individuals rather than bands, and in this sense G//ana ideology differs significantly from what seems to be the !Kung notion of joint ownership, by bands, of territories which lie between their boundaries.

Putting all this together, we need to distinguish not only group member-ship, territoriality, and nucleation, but also the units of territorial occupa-tion and the degree of exclusivity which given units exercise over their territories. A summary of the relation between territoriality and the units, or levels, of social organization is shown in Table 12.1.

Conclusions
Commenting on attempts by archaeologists to reconstruct prehistoric seasonal mobility, A.J.B. Humphreys (1987: 34) has suggested that 'current models . . . represent idealized abstractions that in all probability do not reflect what actually happened in the past'. Rather: 'The whole thing can be compared to a game of chess – we may be able to work out some of the

Table 12.1 *Territoriality and levels of social organization*

	family	band	band cluster
!KUNG	*non-territorial*	*overlapping territories*	—
G/WI	*temporarily associated with territory*	*exclusive territories*	—
G//ANA	*temporarily associated with territory*	*overlapping territories*	—
!XÕ	*territorial*	*territorial*	*exclusive territories*
NHARO	*non-territorial*	*territorial*	*exclusive territories*

rules but we can never reconstruct the actual moves' (1987: 38). Though there are noteworthy exceptions, to me the ethnographic literature often reads like a summary of the moves. Sometimes there is an indication of the strategy, but rarely much in the way of rules. In this chapter, I have tried to map out at least the basic rules and some of the principles behind the game, as played differently by different Kalahari Bushman groups.

Settlement and territoriality are complex and closely related problems. Each has at its core a set of environmental and a set of ideological factors. Claims to resources may be exclusive or non-exclusive. Spatial boundaries may be sharply demarcated or overlap. The reasons for such differences depend both on historical and cultural specifics, and on the micro-environmental factors which determine seasonal and other movements. Movements may be of groups or of individuals, and may occur within or between territorial domains. If there is a hallmark of Bushman social structure, it is flexibility, not territoriality (cf. Guenther 1986c). Yet it is flexibility within certain environmental and logical constraints. The *patterns* of settlement and territoriality, in the literal sense of that word, can be seen only through a comparative perspective on the problems outlined above.

13

Politics and exchange in Khoisan society

Introduction

Politics and exchange are broad issues which touch a great variety of concerns within Khoisan ethnography. The purpose of this chapter is not to cover the vast literature on the subject. Most of the topics discussed in this literature are touched on in Part II of this monograph; and detailed, if sometimes conflicting, studies of political and economic relations are readily available (e.g., Lee 1979b; Wilmsen 1989a). The politics of gender relations is also well covered, especially for the !Kung (e.g., Lee 1974; 1979b: 250–80; 1981 [1978]; Draper 1975a; 1975b; see also Chapter 3). The specifics of politics among the Khoekhoe are dealt with in the historical literature (e.g., Bley 1971 [1968]; Bridgman 1981), and need not concern us here (see also Chapter 10).

Rather, my purpose here is to raise a few questions of topical interest and some questions of relevance to regional comparative concerns. Oddly, comparative interests do not figure strongly in the literature on politics and economics. No one since Schapera (1930) has made any serious attempt to understand Khoekhoe exchange relations in terms of wider Khoisan interests, and no one among current writers on Bushman society seems to have taken any comparative interest at all in the politico-economic systems of the Khoekhoe or Damara.

Problems in politics and ethnicity
Confusion in representations of the Bushmen

The present debate in Bushman studies, focused as it is on contact history, fails to address the question of Khoisan culture. The recent polemics in the pages of *Current Anthropology* (Solway and Lee 1990; Wilmsen and Denbow 1990) have left aside many issues of great importance for the understanding of Khoisan society. This is not to suggest that the debate is not worth while. On the contrary, it has helped specialists to clarify their understanding of historical processes which have operated within Bushman societies over the past several centuries. It has also spelled out for non-specialists the fact that Bushmen are not the wild creatures of the veld that people who know better often portray them as. Yet it has temporarily obscured what it means to be a 'Bushman', a 'San', or a 'Mosarwa'.

Edwin N. Wilmsen (1989a; 1989b), in particular, seems to see Bushmen mainly as a propertyless class subjugated by outsiders. While there is much truth in his description, it is quite untrue that *Bushman* is merely a category of class relations and not a cultural entity. What is true is that 'Bushmen' only came to be defined by that collective term (or by 'San' or 'Basarwa') in relation to outsiders; but precisely because of this, the term has ethnic as well as class connotations (Barnard 1988c: 9, 22–4). The category is polythetic, and its nature can perhaps best be conceived in the abstract as what a Khoekhoe might call *Sāxasis* (*sā-xa-si-s*). The nearest English equivalent would be the rather less elegant *Bushmanliness* or (to use the Nama root) *Sanliness* – the representation of what it is to be 'San' or 'Bushman'.

In fact, we need to distinguish at least three quite distinct aspects of the representation of Bushman identity. These refer to:

(1) 'Bushman' as a representative of an underclass, in Wilmsen's sense. This is probably the original sense in which the Nama term *sāb* or *sās* (common gender plural, *sān*) was used, but it is not the sense in which the term and its equivalents are used either by Bushmen themselves or by most scholars.

(2) 'Bushman' (or an equivalent term) as a self-designation. Nharo, for example, recognize themselves as belonging to a category known by the Tswana term *Masarwa* (not *Basarwa*). This category includes Nharo, G/wi, ≠Au//eisi, etc., but excludes Kgalagari, dispossessed Nama, and others who might form part of Wilmsen's underclass category.

(3) 'Bushman' as a cultural category defined by analysts according to scientific criteria, or indeed by lay observers (explorers, ranchers, etc.) according to folk notions which approximate those of scientific or scholarly discourse.

The first aspect is the primary concern of nation-states. In order to avoid the assumption that this is identical to the second, the Botswana government has, since the late 1970s, used the designation 'RADS' rather than

'Basarwa', 'San', or 'Bushmen'. RADS or 'Remote Area Dwellers' are the rural poor, including mainly ethnic Bakgalagari and Basarwa. The fact that 'Remote Area Dwellers' are often so designated, in capital letters, seems to imply a kind of 'ethnicity' too. Yet it is precisely because of the non-ethnic nature of the label that it is possible for the government to give special attention to individuals who are called by it. The Remote Area Development Workshop of May–June 1978 (for Minutes, see Ministry of Local Government and Lands 1978) marked a turning point in policy towards Basarwa and other disadvantaged groups, not only because a set of national policy objectives were formulated (pp. 126–8 of the Minutes), but also because officials now had a way of speaking about remote groups without emphasizing their cultural or racial differences from the majority population (see also Wily 1982a; 1982b; Hitchcock and Holm 1985; Hitchcock 1988b).

The second sort of 'San' or 'Bushman' is quite evidently an 'ethnic' kind, by anyone's definition. The indigenous idea of being a 'Bushman', a 'Mosarwa', or a *n/ua khoe* (Nharo for 'red person'), is growing in importance, as individuals have more opportunity and more need to define their culture in multi-cultural contexts. It is real to the people who make such definitions, but of course this does not necessarily imply that it is appropriate in all contexts. People who did not in the past relish the idea of being called 'vagabonds' (in Nama, *sān*) may today take pride in this label. More commonly, though, they choose to be identified as members of more specific, linguistic groups – Nharo, G/wi, !Xõ, or whatever.

The third representation of 'Bushman' is plainly artificial, but at its best it is objective and remains the most important subcategory for historians, anthropologists, and linguists. This is the primary category for cultural-comparative purposes and the one with which most of this book deals. What is interesting is that it does not necessarily coincide with either of the other two subcategories. This is no cause for alarm, any more than are the diverse usages of the word 'European' in English. In South Africa a 'European' is any white person, even one who has never been to Europe. In Britain, the term 'European' may either include the British (whose island lies within most of the world's idea of 'Europe') or specifically exclude them ('European' being short for 'Continental European'). The word 'Bushman' and its historical synonyms 'Sonqua', 'San', etc. are similar, though it must be recognized that at present such words are employed chiefly by outsiders. Bushman identity is increasing in response to outside pressures, but precisely in order to explain such changes, anthropologists still need to consider cultural phenomena independently of these developments. The hallmark of Bushman society has always been *adaptation*, whether to the natural environment or to changing social conditions (cf. Barnard 1988c). Adaptation, as a product of the foraging ethos, is a key to understanding both the Bushman consciousness and the culture and social organization which characterize these 'hunting' groups and distinguish them from their 'herding' neighbours.

State intervention and rights in land

Khoisan peoples have suffered a similar fate to other peoples under state control. The colonial era brought savage attempts by authorities, particularly in German South West Africa, to subjugate tribal chiefs. In general, the herding peoples were the first to suffer the fate of state intervention. Bushmen were more often left alone, except when, as individuals, they were involved in stock theft or raiding.

In more recent times, states (first colonial and later national ones) have exerted pressure through redefining the areas in which Bushmen may live and what activities they may engage in. There have been anomalies in Botswana. The most obvious is the Central Kalahari Game Reserve. This was established in 1958 for the protection of Bushmen; but in the 1980s its designation as a 'game reserve', as opposed to a tribal territory, led to pressure from European wildlife organizations, as well as the authorities in Botswana, to empty the area of its human inhabitants (see Hitchcock 1985). In 1990, the Botswana government abandoned its plans to resettle C.K.G.R. inhabitants in the Kweneng district, to the south, and in both the Reserve and the Kweneng, hunting and gathering activities are now on the increase (Susan Kent, pers. comm.)

One effect of state domination throughout southern Africa has been the extension of the 'doctrine of supreme chief'. This doctrine is well known worldwide and is indeed implicitly recognized in international law. Yet in southern Africa it has had particularly unfortunate consequences, especially after European colonialism was replaced by South African domination. The application of the doctrine in the reign of Queen Victoria, or Kaiser Wilhelm, was far less problematic for many inhabitants than that by the Administrator-General of South West Africa in more recent times. One could hardly imagine Victoria or even Wilhelm dispossessing aboriginal inhabitants without taking into consideration their rights of occupation. Indeed, in 1895 Major Leutwein, governor of South West Africa, concluded a treaty with the Captain Aribib, chief of the Hai//om. On behalf of the imperial government, Leutwein granted the Hai//om protection of the authorities and the rights to occupy and utilize their traditional lands, in exchange for the formal cession of those lands (in the feudal sense) to the state (Gordon 1989: 144–6). It is a fine legal point whether this treaty is still in effect; similar treaties between the British crown and the aboriginal inhabitants of the present United States of America and Canada have been the subject of unsuccessful claims in those countries.

The problem with recent notions of land rights in southern Africa is that the technicalities of feudal land tenure, and with them the doctrine of aboriginal possession in natural law (as interpreted by Roman–Dutch theorists), have generally been discounted, in favour of a notion of the state as supreme authority. Like the State President of South Africa, the Administrator and subsequently the Administrator-General of South West Africa exercised his role as 'supreme chief' in a dictatorial manner. The authority of the 'state' (in the person of its chief administrator) to define all tribal boundaries and even to 'divide existing tribes' and 'constitute a new tribe as necessary' was enshrined in South African law in 1927, and in South West African law in 1928. It was by this authority that the dispossession of !Kung lands was effected (Gordon 1989: 151–2). The new Namibian administration has inherited not only the existing socio-economic problems of its people, but also a plethora of legal issues to take account of in defining their future (cf. Guenther 1986d; Lee 1988a).

Equality and inequality

It is commonplace to regard hunter-gatherers as having distinctive political, and especially economic, forms of organization. Yet, while some of these typically hunter-gatherer features of society (e.g., egalitarianism) are much more applicable to Khoisan foragers than to Khoisan herders, there are nevertheless similarities which have until now escaped notice. In the economic domain of Khoekhoe and Damara society, institutionalized gift-giving is as important as it is in some Bushman societies. Likewise, marital exchanges involving the transfer of goods, often cited as a typical feature of pastoralist societies, are found among Kalahari hunter-gatherers. The existence of these customs should cause us to rethink our notions of what constitutes a typical 'hunting' or 'herding' society and to consider the notion of a pan-Khoisan constellation of economic institutions. Similar arguments are relevant to other social spheres as well, as we shall see in Chapter 14 (with reference to religious ideas) and Chapters 15 and 16 (with reference to kinship).

Real property among hunters and herders

Hunter-gatherer territories are not 'property' in quite the same sense as property is defined in Western legal systems, but such territories do possess some of the same characteristics of 'property' as the term is conventionally employed in anthropological monographs on non-hunting-and-gathering peoples. Bushmen retain, through birth, marriage, and residence, rights of special access to particular territories. The right which they lack – crucial to 'ownership' and 'property' as more narrowly defined – is the right of alienation. Bushmen cannot dispose of areas which they occupy or have special access to: they cannot sell them or give them away. They can only utilize their resources, permit others to utilize them, and, in some cases only, deny or discourage access.

David Riches (1982: 114–17) has written that the concept of territorial 'ownership' is inapplicable to the Bushmen because permission to use the resources of one's territory is virtually always granted. In his view, only the right to refuse permission implies ownership. Similar problems in the definition of this concept have been reported in other parts of the world too. However, I would argue that the term is applicable in that 'ownership' is the best translation available for the concept expressed in many Bushman languages by the word *kau* or *k'au*, meaning roughly 'to own' (as a verb) or 'owner' (as a noun). The term is the same one employed to describe other kinds of 'ownership': for example, ownership of movable property such as tools and clothing, and in some cases ownership of rights over people.

Among the Bushmen, nomadism is practised within defined territories; and when one group utilizes resources belonging to another, permission must be sought from the owners of these resources. There are different degrees of 'ownership' (see, e.g., Marshall 1965: 251). Game animals are owned by no one, as they migrate between band territories and across the boundaries of ethnic groups. On the other hand, water-filled pans and wells are under the jurisdiction of local groups. Although water is always given freely, the headman or other members of the core kin groups of a band must nevertheless grant travellers or visitors permission to take it. Rights to vegetable resources are generally more exclusively controlled and belong to one band cluster, band, or even family, according to the customs of the particular Bushman society concerned. The degree to which rights to such resources are defended depends again on local custom (see Cashdan 1983).

Among Khoisan pastoralists, rights to real property are more difficult to define. There are two reasons for this. In the first instance, these groups have changed much more rapidly and in ways which were extraordinarily detrimental both to the people themselves and to the chance for good ethnographic descriptions of concepts of ownership of real property. In the second instance, property is a more nebulous concept for herders than for hunter-gatherers. The herders in general have a tradition of permanent migration, rather than transhumance. Nevertheless, descriptions and commentaries available to Schapera (1930: 319) suggested that they had a system of communal ownership over land. Schapera (1930: 319, 321) rejected the idea that either this system or the widespread systems of sharing and exchange, of food, livestock, and material culture, indicated any form of 'communism'. Earlier writers (e.g., von François 1896: 222) had suggested it did.

Universal kinship and 'primitive communism' among the hunters

Bushman groups invariably possess systems of universal kin categorization (Barnard 1978a; 1981; see Chapter 15). This practice does not seem to be as prevalent, or at least is not as definitively recorded, among the Khoekhoe or Damara. The limits of kin categorization among these peoples would seem to be based primarily on notions of social interaction and presumed common descent, rather than on an ideology which requires everyone to be treated as kin. In other words, most Bushman societies recognize a notion that people can and must identify everyone as belonging to one category or another, while Khoekhoe do not.

Universal kin classification affords many hunting and gathering societies the mechanism for distributing both movable property and rights over natural resources. Other forms of social classification, either kinship based or non-kinship based, define the social limits of particular arenas of distribution. Clearly, without such subsidiary forms of social classification these societies would exist in a state of 'primitive communism'. Yet since universal kin classification is never the sole means of determining an individual's sphere of social action, complete primitive communism is impossible.

Richard Lee (1988b) takes a slightly different view. In his definition of primitive communism, he recognizes a relative egalitarianism and an emphasis on the communal ownership of land, rather than specifically the lack of hierarchical institutions. For Lee (1988b: 254–5), even chiefly societies qualify as retaining primitive communist principles in a 'semi-communal' social structure. His examples of this semi-communal form are all from other parts of the world; but if the Bushmen are among the last primitive communists, then the Khoekhoe and Damara could well lay claim to being paradigm cases of semi-communalism too.

To what extent are the Bushmen communistic? This dilemma lies at the root of the quarrel, in the mid-1970s, between Elizabeth Wily and H.J. Heinz (see Chapter 4). The Basarwa Development Officer, Liz Wily (e.g., 1982a), argued that Bushman social organization exemplified principles of collective ownership and communal will, while the ethnographer, H.J.

Heinz (1973), argued instead that it exhibited the characteristics of the incipient 'capitalist' principles of private ownership and free enterprise. Both had interpreted their respective experiences at the !Xõ settlement at Bere, where Wily had served as teacher and Heinz as benefactor and development planner, as evidence for the equation of Bushman ideology with their own. Neither was correct, of course. The combined institutions of political action by consensus, universal kinship with social equality, individual and collective ownership of different types of property, formal rules for use of real property, and the wide distribution of movable property, imply a poltico-economic framework which is typical of small-scale non-pastoralist societies and no others.

While the Bushmen are as distant from Rousseau's (1971 [1755]: 176–202) notion of 'natural man' as members of almost any other society, they nevertheless possess the attribute of social equality he sought to explain. This state of equality is not pre-social, as Rousseau supposed, but it is, arguably, pre-agricultural and pre-pastoral (cf. Testart 1981: 1982; Flanagan 1989; Gulbrandsen 1991). Similarly, Bushmen do resemble Sahlins' (1974 [1968]: 1–39) prototypical 'original affluent society', not because their needs or wants are few, but because they have in many cases chosen one form of 'affluence' over another. Specifically, those who have had the opportunity have often chosen to maximize time rather than wealth. Others, of course, have not had the choice. Bushmen in general do not have the capital, in the form of livestock or water resources, to achieve the level of wealth which they desire. I accept Sahlins' characterization, but only with qualifications. Many Bushman groups have until quite recently lived in a state of relative equality and 'original affluence', but the decline of this state began the moment economic interaction with the non-foraging world first took place. This was, in some cases, perhaps two millennia ago, not, as some have assumed, in the nineteenth or twentieth centuries. For many hundreds or thousands of years, Bushmen have been existing in an intermediate state, with transitions in both directions (cf. Marks 1972; Schrire 1980; Motzafi 1986).

In Chapter 8, I noted the tendency towards buying and selling meat, rather than exchanging it, among the Nharo at Hanahai. It is significant, however, that despite such new buying and selling arrangements between social groups previously defined spatially as a band clusters, these Nharo give meat freely, in the traditional manner, within the bands that make up a given band cluster. There is a temptation to regard buying/selling relationships as indicative of social change, simply because they have not occurred before. Yet it could well be that they define age-old divisions between social and territorial units – units which would not previously have had any contact at all with each other. In this respect, it is not surprising that they buy and sell meat. It would perhaps be more surprising if they did give meat freely across band cluster boundaries, for to give it away across such boundaries might well imply a closer relationship than people wish to have, or have ever had before. If Bushmen are communists, then their communism is confined to the 'commune', which itself is defined at band or band cluster level, and not any collective unit beyond these levels.

Hierarchy and exchange among the herders

What happens among the herders is somewhat different, though not as different as some might think. It should not be forgotten that Khoekhoe and Khoe Bushman social organization share a common origin and common structures, in spite of differences in subsistence pursuits. Selections of the field diaries of Winifred Hoernlé provide a vivid picture of the complicated set of rules for the inheritance of private property among the Nama, rules seemingly very alien to Bushman society. Yet Carstens' (1983a) interpretation of the Hoernlé diaries correctly emphasizes the relationship between inheritance and other aspects of Khoekhoe kinship and is consistent with the notion that Khoekhoe ideas on property are related to Bushman ones. Among both Bushmen and Khoekhoe, land is held communally and movable property is owned individually. By adopting cross-descent name lines, Khoekhoe society has developed a mechanism for regulating marriage and exending relationships of inheritance, perhaps not quite universally, but according to structural principles essentially similar to those of the Western Khoe Bushmen. Certainly, a vestige of universal kin classification may be present in a man's distinction between women he calls *tarás* (wife, cross-cousin, etc.) and those he calls *tàras* (sister, parallel cousin, father's sister, etc.).

Lineages stand in relation to others according to rules of seniority and alliance. Senior lineages were those whose ancestors were first-born in a group of brothers; junior lineages were descended from later-born sons. In terms of alliance, there is evidence of an hypogamous ideology, seniority being attributed to wife-givers and juniority to wife-takers (cf. Engelbrecht 1936: 3). Other areas of hierarchical classification included a distinction between members and non-members of the residential group, and a distinction between the Khoekhoe themselves and their servants. Such hierarchical distinctions could be disruptive to the full recognition of an ideology of universal kin categorization. In so far as kin categorization was extended to individuals of different places in the social hierarchy, this extension seems to have been for specific purposes, such as marriage regulation and possibly in distinguishing joking from avoidance partners. In addition, Khoekhoe close relatives and especially siblings were involved in hierarchical relations, in that great emphasis was placed on order of birth in both same-sex and opposite-sex sibling interaction.

An apparent difference between the Bushmen and the Khoekhoe is that Bushmen regulate the distribution of property by means other than the kinship structures, most notably through formal gift-giving arrangements which cross-cut the kinship domain. Among the Nama and Damara, formalized gift-giving has other primary functions which seem today to be mainly symbolic. Nevertheless, there are more similarities between the exchange systems of the Bushman and non-Bushman Khoisan peoples than have commonly been recognized.

The !Kung notion of *hxaro* (Wiessner 1977; 1982) is extremely well known to anthropologists today and is seen as virtually a paradigm case of a *hunter-gatherer* exchange mechanism. However, formalized exchange of this type is not recorded among the G/wi, for example, who are probably the second-best known Bushman group today. A recent study of sedentary G/wi by Kazuyoshi Sugawara (1988b) reveals that gift-giving is much more important than barter or purchase in the acquisition of goods, especially clothing, but the gifts he recorded include mainly 'hand me downs'.

A similar system to the !Kung and Nharo ones is found among the Nama. *Sori-gu-s* (also known as *mā-gu-s*, 'giving to each other') is a ceremonial form of gift-giving with, according to Schapera (1930: 321), 'mutual obligation and assistance in all aspects of life'. Indeed the relationship as Schapera described it implied the right to take any property from a *sori* partner, thus making it a more powerful relationship than *hxaro* among the !Kung, the mutual //aĩ relationship among the Nharo, or any other known form of exchange among southern African hunter-gatherers. My own record of the *sorigu* relationship, described in Chapter 10, suggests that gifts were voluntary and not necessarily reciprocated. It operates very much as in the !Kung and Nharo cases, and whether perceived as primarily symbolic or as functional, does serve to redistribute goods through social networks.

The obligatory cattle-snatching relationship between a mother's brother and his sister's children (Nama //nuri//as or //nuri//ab; Korana ╪na- ╪nab) is a similar, although more specialized, kind of exchange. It is similar not only in that it expresses a non-parental dependent relationship, with mutual sharing, but also in that it spreads wealth from those who have it to those who do not. Like other forms of egalitarian or symbolic, reciprocal exchange, it too acts as an equalizing mechanism.

Two 'board games' and the ethos of exchange

An informant's statement, recorded by Engelbrecht as a Korana text, well illustrates the economic ethos of Khoekhoe culture, and more specifically, the Khoekhoe attitude towards their livestock. The text portrays the rules of a game played on the ground, but in much the same manner as board games such as backgammon, in the West.

They took ten small stones and put them on the ground and put a man at some distance from them . . . Another man sat where the stones were and then the man standing away was made to count backwards. He must speak as follows: 'From ten lying there take one stone away; from nine lying there take one stone away; from eight . . .' Take away the single stone lying there. That is the end. If he miscounted, he had to pay a goat. He must count very fast. (Engelbrecht 1936: 225–6)

Such stone-counting games are common today among other Khoisan peoples. The notion of being fined for miscounting, and the idea of transfer of livestock for seemingly trivial reasons, show both the significance and the inherent transience of livestock in the eyes of the Khoekhoe (cf. Marks 1972). To me, the Korana game is a metaphor for the regular rounds of stock theft and recovery which characterized Khoekhoe economic activity for many centuries. If you count your goats carelessly, they disappear.

The Khoekhoe are not the only southern African peoples who play such games. A similar game is played among the Nharo. Interestingly, though they have no cattle themselves, the Nharo players refer to the stone counters as 'cattle'. In contrast to Khoekhoe and Herero, who play the same game, they do not gamble. Nharo play either individually or in two teams of two, and sometimes players help their opponents to make the best moves. When it looks as though they are about to lose, Nharo players will simply give up; they do not like playing to the finish. The two sides then start again on an equal footing, and stop when they get bored.

While it would be wise not to read too much into these descriptions, the differences between the apparent attitudes of the Korana and the Nharo towards their games is interesting. It could well be indicative of a greater distinction between Khoekhoe and Bushman social relations. The herders play for cattle, which are won and lost with the drop of a stone in the sand. The Nharo play, seemingly, to accumulate useless stone counters, but when they do accumulate them, they give them away and start the game again.

Hunters and herders: problems of typology and comparison

Roughly speaking, there are two forms of social organization among Khoisan groups who subsist only partly by hunting and gathering. One form is represented by the integrated economy of subsistence herding, raiding, plant-gathering, hunting, and trade, which characterized Khoek-hoe and Damara society prior to the present century. The other is represented by the modern part-time foragers who practise subsistence herding and wage labour in association with neighbouring peoples. Although, within both categories, such a typological distinction of purely economic activity is blurred by historical changes in subsistence strategy, nevertheless each does seem to represent a different form of socio-economic system with regard to aspects of social relations.

In earlier days of Khoisan ethnography, there was an emphasis on patrilineal descent and virilocal residence. This was accurate enough for the Khoekhoe, but quite inaccurate as a general characterization of local organization among the hunter-gatherers. The prominence of the Hai//om data at the time (e.g., Fourie 1928) and misleading reports from the !Kung (e.g., Kaufmann 1910; Brownlee 1943) were probably the main cause. Julian Steward's (1955 [1936]: 122–50) classic division of hunter-gatherers into 'patrilineal' and 'composite' types was the result. Elman Service (1962: 61–83) renamed the patrilineal type 'patrilocal', but the fallacy remained. According to Steward and Service, small-scale hunter-gatherer societies (e.g., Bushmen, Australian Aborigines, and various central African groups) were made up of bands formed on the basis of virilocal residence and consequent patrilineal descent, whereas hunter-gatherer societies (e.g., the Andaman Islanders, and northern North American Indian groups) which occupied larger territories and enjoyed larger aggregating units emphasized bilateral kinship ties. Composite-band societies distinguished different levels of band organization, such as 'local bands' and 'regional bands'. The irony is that Bushman bands tend to be formed on the basis of bilateral kinship as well. Comparing the consangineous kinship ties of adults within a number of !Kung, Nharo, and !Xõ bands, H.P. Steyn (1980) shows that *de facto* parent–daughter links (34.7 per cent) are nearly twice as common as parent–son ones (19.4 per cent), and brother–sister links (24.5 per cent) are over twice as common as either brother–brother (10.2 per cent) or sister–sister ones (11.2 per cent). Not only that, but Bushman bands too are frequently grouped into 'regional' units (band clusters), though these units tend to be ideological units of land occupation rather than units of aggregation.

One broad division to be made within the category 'hunting and gathering societies' is between those which store and those which do not store resources to any great extent. This distinction, emphasized particu-larly by Alain Testart (e.g., 1981), places desert-dwelling Bushmen, in contrast to the hunter-gatherer-fishermen of the Okavango or the Khoekhoe herders of Namibia, on the non-storing end of the spectrum. A similar contrast is James Woodburn's (e.g., 1980; 1982a), between immediate-return and delayed-return economic systems. According to this opposition, the !Kung and most other Bushmen are regarded as immediate-return (i.e., obtaining subsistence without work input requiring a return on investment at a later date). Fishermen, herders, and part-time hunter-gatherers, who do invest in the future, have delayed-return economies. These distinctions are highly useful, not so much typologically, but for their aid in elucidating the mechanisms of reciprocity in small-scale societies. Woodburn and Testart alike are trying to subdivide the category 'hunter-gatherer', and implicitly each liken some hunter-gatherer societies to non-hunter-gatherers, both in their possession of the capacity for storing food and planning ahead (e.g., in making nets, herding livestock to be consumed at a future date), and in the distinctions of social hierarchy which are related to the pursuit of particular strategies of production.

A related topic is the degree to which we can understand the categories 'hunting and gathering societies', and 'pastoral societies', as constituting forms of social organization whose similarities cross-cut ethnographic regions. While some aspects of social organization are directly related to subsistence activities, others are only indirectly related. There is, nevertheless, an argument for examining the degree to which different hunting and gathering societies, for example, resemble each other in politics, kinship, or religion. There are also good grounds for examining units larger than the ethnographic region or culture area as conceived here. For example, Marco Bicchieri (1969) once compared three African hunting and gathering societies with reference to a number of ecological and social factors. In spite of obvious differences in environment and exploitation technique (his examples included undifferentiated desert Bushmen, scrub-forest Hadza, and tropical forest, net-hunting Mbuti), he noted similarities in group structure, decision-making procedures, education, and other aspects of social life. James Woodburn (1982b) has compared social aspects of death in four African hunting and gathering societies, and found a number of similarities between them. Nicolas Peterson (1979) compared the !Kung with desert-dwelling Australian Aborigines, with reference to territoriality. He concluded that past comparisons were misleading in that authors compared the ideology of the Aborigines with the behaviour of the !Kung (see also Yengoyan 1968). Similarly, I have recently looked at the relation between kinship and cosmology in Australian and southern African hunter-gatherers (Barnard 1989b). Like Peterson, I argue that the similarities between the two are greater than others have suggested.

Both such comparisons and comparisons between societies of the same ethnographic region are necessary in order to determine the relations between production and other aspects of social organization. It is precisely because the Khoisan culture area consists of both hunting and herding societies that comparisons within this culture area can be so fruitful (see also Barnard 1988a; Chapter 16).

14

Aspects of Khoisan religious ideology

Introduction

A clue to the way to approach Khoisan religious ideology comes in a classic account of North American Indian blood sacrifice. In his paper on the origin of the Skidi Pawnee sacrifice, Ralph Linton (1926: 455–60) looked not merely to individual Skidi ideas and ritual practices, some of which were known to be of non-Pawnee origin, but to what he called the 'underlying concepts' of the ceremony. Commenting on the similarity between Skidi and Aztec blood sacrifices, he noted: 'The traits themselves probably had the same origin in both cases, but their combination was, in each instance, an independent local development' (1926: 465).

Another clue is found closer to home. Depicted on the cover of four volumes of the 'Bushman and Hottentot Linguistic Studies' series (e.g., Traill 1975) is a rock painting, said to be from a site called Swallewkranz. The painting shows three running figures. Two are quite ordinary male figures, but the third is peculiar. It has one body and two arms, but ten heads, and eight legs. Jeffrey Gruber (1975: 48) offers an explanation. The 'ungrammatical' figure might well represent an ungrammatical sentence, which in English might come out something like: 'The people runs [*sic*]'. While it is doubtful if the Swallewkranz figure was actually intended as part of a grammar lesson, it is intriguing to reflect on the ways in which the 'grammar' of Bushman thought can be manipulated, whether through language, rock art, ritual, mythology, or theology.

My aim in this chapter is to explore the grammar of Khoisan religion, with an eye to exposing the underlying concepts which cross-cut the ethnic boundaries. My emphasis will be on ideology rather than ritual, although the latter could no doubt be analysed in a similar vein (cf. W. Schmidt 1929; Schapera 1930: 395–99; Lewis-Williams and Biesele 1978; S. Schmidt 1979; 1986a; Lewis-Williams and Dowson 1989).

Some common features of Khoisan religion
In contrast to other African peoples, the Khoisan do not worship their ancestors. On the contrary, among some groups discussion of dead individuals is held to be in very bad taste. The ancestors may be mentioned collectively, but not as individuals. An exception is Haitsi-aibib, the mythical ancestor figure of the Nama. He is a secular folk hero who is reputed to have died and been reborn many times.

Quite apart from ancestor worship, Khoisan peoples do involve the spirits of the dead in curing rituals. Bushman, Khoekhoe, and Damara medicine men use these spirits in various ways, the best-known example being the Bushman medicine dance. Almost all Bushman groups hold medicine dances at which one or more men enter a trance state. While in trance, the medicine man is believed to remove illnesses from the bodies of those in attendance. These illnesses are transmitted to a spirit, who takes them away. In this case, the spirits are used to good ends; yet the people believe that the essential nature of the spirits is evil. The common core of Khoisan ritual includes male and female initiation rites too. Generally, the Khoe-speaking peoples (whether hunters or herders) have the most elaborate male ceremonies. Nearly all such beliefs and rituals are quite different from those of the Bantu-speaking peoples.

In many of the languages spoken by Khoisan peoples, the word for 'spirit of the dead' is g//ãũa. This word is also used to mean 'God' in some languages (or by some individuals), and 'Devil' in others. All Khoisan peoples claim belief in a high god. Some peoples attribute to him both good and evil characteristics, and others separate these characteristics, and attribute them to two beings. Some, notably the pre-Christian Damara, the !Kung, and the Khoe Bushmen of the central Kalahari, say that he lives in the sky and that the souls of the dead travel to his village after death and burial. Among other features of Khoisan religion, belief in the moon as a supernatural being, the belief that spirits and sometimes humans can transform themselves into animals, and the mythology (described in Chapter 5) which underlies such beliefs, are widespread – even across the hunter–herder divide.

God and Moon
The most geographically isolated of all Khoisan groups are the //Xegwi or Batwa of the eastern Transvaal. They were described by their ethnographer as follows: 'The living Batwa believe in the existence of a supreme being, /a'an. Their ideas about this being are very vague . . .' (Potgieter 1955: 29). E.F. Potgieter went on to describe /A'an as the creator, as a being to whom

the spirits of the dead go, and as one who is not prayed to but occasionally addressed with raised voice, as if speaking to a human. A lesser deity, described as */a'an 'e la tleni* (/A'an the small) assists /A'an. Potgieter (1955: 29–30) also mentioned evidence which, he claimed, 'seems to point to a former more systematic worshipping of the moon': that the Moon is the giver of rain, and through rain, food; and that good fortune is described by the //Xegwi with the expression 'the moon is full', while suffering leads them to say 'the moon is small' (or 'dark').

This is about all Potgieter says on traditional //Xegwi religious belief. It is hardly much of an account of a religious system. Nevertheless, his short, little-read monograph on this isolated people does confirm that the same elements of Khoisan religion – a high god, a lesser deity, the transmigration of the souls of the dead, and the importance of the Moon – are found far and wide across southern Africa. In this context, it is well to bear in mind that the Khoisan peoples are linguistically as diverse as nearly any on the African continent: the //Xegwi language is genetically more distant from Nama than Yoruba is from Zulu, or English is from Hindi.

Of particular interest is Potgieter's attribution of moon-worship to the //Xegwi. Schapera (1930: 395) claimed that both Bushmen and Khoekhoe 'worship the Moon'. The Cape Khoekhoe in the seventeenth century were said to be moon-worshippers, apparently only because new moon and full moon were the times when they danced their prayers (see, e.g., Schapera 1930: 374–6). There is no doubt that the Moon is important in Khoekhoe and Bushman symbolism, or that the lunar cycle marks propitious times for dancing. Even today in the Kalahari, dances are most often held at full moon. Yet, moon-worship is largely a fantasy of European ethnographers.

Peter Kolb, perhaps the most perceptive of early Khoisan ethnographers, gives a slightly different version from others of his day. Particularly revealing is Theophilus Hahn's (1881: 41) free translation from the original German edition of Kolb's account. This differs in some respects from Kolb's English text on the subject (1968 [1731]: 90–111), but at least accurately reflects Hahn's own deep personal knowledge of Khoekhoe (in his case, Nama) religion:

It is obvious that all Hottentots believe in a God. They know him and confess it; to him they ascribe the work of creation, and they maintain that he still rules over everything and that he gives life to everything. On the whole he is possessed of such high qualities that they could well describe him . . . Because the station of a chief is the highest charge, therefore they call the Lord *Gounia*, and they call the moon so, as their visible God. But if they mean the Invisible, and intend to give him his true name, they call him *Gounia Tiquaa*, i.e., the God of all gods. (Peter Kolb, quoted in Hahn 1881: 41; cf. Kolb 1968 [1731]: 93–4, 96)

Thus, the Moon is not the Khoekhoe God himself; nor in this case does he seem to be regarded as a separate deity. He is the visible manifestation of God. On the other hand, Guido Medley's English translation of Kolb suggests that the Moon *is* a separate being, 'the Subject and Representative of the High and Invisible' (Kolb 1968 [1731]: 96). This may have been what Kolb intended, and indeed it may be what the Cape Khoekhoe actually believed. Yet to me it seems less convincing than Hahn's version as an expression of typical Khoisan theology.

The failure of many Khoisan ethnographers to define the status of the Moon (or even point out the Moon's inherent existential ambiguity) probably stems from their failure either to see the structural position of the Moon in relation to other entities, or to explore the cosmo-semantic or syntactic context of indigenous statements about the Moon. Much the same goes for statements about God, the minor deity, or deities generally, and is true of recent as well as older works.

Khoisan concepts of 'God'

The concept 'God' is usually expressed in Nharo as *n!adiba* (which otherwise means 'sky'). Sometimes N!adiba is called Hieseba, which is his unique, divine name, and sometimes by the term *!xuba*, which, like its Nama cognate *!khūb*, means 'lord' or 'master' in a secular as well as a religious sense. Nharo *n!adi-* has several related meanings and can be taken in the masculine singular or (more rarely) other grammatical forms.

A Nharo medicine man once told me that there are three classes of being: N!adiba or Hieseba (God), *g//āũne* (the evil spirits or the spirits of the dead), and *khuene* (people). He then went on to talk about each in turn, beginning not with just a single male God, but with the male God and his wife N!adisa. The word *n!adisa* is, in fact, '*God*' in the feminine singular, a form which would be grammatically incorrect if it were used in reference to 'the sky' in a secular sense. When the old man came to mention the fact that God the Sky is father of the Moon and the Sun, he began to use the word *n!adisara* (fem. dual) in place of *n!adisa* (fem. sg.). God the Sky now had two wives, and one was Mother of the Moon, and the other, Mother of the Sun. The male Moon and female Sun are husband and wife. They mate beneath the earth, and their children are the moon and sun the next day. The Moon also begets, this time apparently without sexual intercourse, a male child, who is the moon at first crescent. Sometimes the moon at first crescent is described as the old moon reborn. Snails are also said to be 'children of the moon', and in Nharo the word for snail is *n//ueba* (which means 'moon'), just as in Nama the word is *//khâxaes* (which means, literally, 'moon-copulate'). The fact that these stems, *n//ue* and *//khâ*, are etymologically unrelated but in each language carry both of the two meanings, testifies to the near certainty that we are not dealing here merely with homonyms, although recent diffusion of the concept itself is quite possible. An association of the Moon either with the High God (*!khwa*, 'the Rain', keeper of menstrual taboos) or with the Mantis (*/kaggen*, the trickster figure) has long been argued for the /Xam on both etymological and mythological grounds (see, e.g., Schapera 1930: 172–3; S. Schmidt 1973; Hewitt 1986: 40–1, 137–8; cf. Bleek and Lloyd 1911). The relationship expressed in the Khoe examples (Nama and Nharo), however, is more subtle: snails, like the Moon, are said to have perpetual life, or to have the capability of death and rebirth.

The point made by the Nharo medicine man is not that heavenly bodies have many offspring, or that he does not know how many gods there are; his point is that the components of the universe stand in systematic, and indeed 'kin' relation to each other (see Barnard 1989b: 209–11). In Nharo, it is not possible to specify grammatical gender without also specifying grammatical number. In these examples, the fluidity of discursive meaning which would be apparent to any Nharo-speaker, results partly from the linguistic necessity to employ grammatical number. Grammatical number, of course, also expresses meaning, and the medicine man was able to use grammatical number to convey some of his ideas on the nature of the universe. Such meaning is subtle, and comparable to the meaning sometimes conveyed by grammatical gender in Nharo and other Khoe languages. For example, *tsane* (common gender plural, here denoting fluidity) means 'water', *tsasa* (fem. sg.) means 'pool' or 'pond', and *tsaba* (masc. sg.) means 'borehole' (see Barnard 1985: 13–15, 82; Vossen 1986).

Grammatical number and gender are utilized according to conscious and logical rules, which tell us perhaps the Whorfian way in which a Nharo-speaker thinks, but not necessarily what he believes. To invert the argument of Needham's *Belief, language, and experience* (1972), belief is an inner state, to some extent independent of language. Implied in this definition is a notion of the intrinsic untranslatability, into either English *or Nharo*, of the experience of the Nharo universe which lies behind the structures, whether these structures be linguistic, mental, or, for that matter, metaphysical. Needham's provocative treatment of the polythetic nature of 'belief' in English highlights the complex relation between thought and language. Nevertheless, it leaves aside much that is implicit in the world view of the Nharo medicine man, or the Nuer for whom God is not 'believed in' (in the modern, Western sense), because they take his existence for granted

(Evans-Pritchard 1956: 9, cf. Needham 1972: 22–5). Nharo thought is simultaneously both enabled and constrained by the grammatical categor- ies utilized by a Nharo-speaker, but religious experience lies yet deeper in the Nharo consciousness.

Khoe languages, such as Nharo and Nama, are very different from Northern and Southern Bushman languages. They have an in-built mor- phological facility for abstract expression. For example, in Nama one can say: *khoe* (person), *khoekhoe* (person of people, in other words 'Nama'), *khoesi* (friendly or human), *khoesis* (humanity, kindness, friendliness, or friendship), *khoexa* (kind), *khoexasis* (kindliness [more abstract than 'kindness']), *khoesigagus* (friendship, intimacy, or marriage), *khoexakhoeb di* (my intimate friend), and so on (Hahn 1881: 17; Kroenlein 1889: 209–10). In !Kung, as far as I know, one cannot. Yet in !Kung and other isolating Khoisan languages, the choice of a word may mean to the outsider more than is intended by the speaker. According to Lorna Marshall (1962: 223–5) the !Kung great god has eight names, and seven of these, including notably //Gauwa (G//aua), are also the names of the lesser god, his 'grandchild'. E.N. Wilmsen (pers. comm.) suggests that, rather as in Islam, these 'names' signify attributes of God, intelligible to us partly through scientific, linguistic analysis, and partly through folk etymology. The former (lingusitic analysis) may be of greater historical and therefore regional-comparative interest, but the latter (folk etymology) could be more revealing in the ways of thought of the !Kung today.

Gods, heroes, and spirits

In general, Bushman religion emphasizes the relation between deity and humanity, whereas Khoekhoe religion emphasizes the relation between deity and deity. For all Khoisan peoples, though, God has one or more adversaries. These are almost always called by one of the related terms *g//ãũa-* or *g//ama-* (with appropriate grammatical suffixes), no matter what the language. God and spirits either act independently, or are merged as a single being or set of beings associated with the spirits of the dead. These, in turn, may be conceptually distinguished from the ancestors (the spirits being evil, and the ancestors, good). Usually, the High God is the Creator. Although for some peoples he is remote and not directly active in the world, he nevertheless is believed to have a presence in the world as well as in the sky. His goodness, or his moral ambiguity, varies with the degree to which the high-god concept assumes identity with other, more evil, elements of the spirit world.

For the !Kung, among whom God merges into evil spirit, he commits incest and cannibalism (Marshall 1962: 229; cf. Lee 1984: 106–7). For the G/wi, among whom his form is quite separate from that of the evil being, God is a vegetarian (Silberbauer 1981: 52). The G/wi god N!adima, although remote, seems particularly to be responsible for the regulation of order in the universe, including the environment. N!adima and his wife N!adisa are, by definition, 'the sky'. They live above the earth, in a place with much water and vegetation; and they are the 'parents' of all human-kind and of the animals, or at least the mammals, who live under their parental gaze (Silberbauer 1981: 51–6). In slight contrast, the !Xõ creator-god Gu/e is said by some to have a wife and children, and by others, to be unmarried (Heinz 1975a: 22). He is complemented by a second, 'younger brother' force, /Oa, who lives 'somewhere beyond the sky though lower than Gu/e' (1975a: 22). As in other Khoisan religions, these !Xõ concepts are associated respectively with 'good' and 'evil', though the distinction between them 'is not always apparent or clear' (1975a: 22). In terms of a hierarchy of theological differentiation, it does seem as though the !Kung and to some extent the !Xõ do not distinguish sharply between good and evil beings, whereas the G/wi and other Khoe-speaking peoples generally do.

Among the Khoekhoe, there is a more highly structured system of beliefs about the deities and the interrelation between them, though even here the deities merge into one another too. Indeed, it is sometimes difficult to tell, historically or across dialect boundaries, whether we are speaking of the same or different beings. Among the pre-Christian Nama we can clearly identify four beings, or at least four terms for beings, which stand in a clear, structural relation to each other: Tsûi-//goab and //Gâuab, and Haitsi-aibib (Haiseb) and ≠Gama-≠gorib. Their relations and spheres of influence are illustrated in Table 14.1.

Tsûi-//goab is the Nama creator, good and omnipresent, but not omnipotent. //Gâuab is his rival. The etymology of the term 'Tsûi-//goab' has been a matter of debate for over a century, and many theories have been put forward, especially by early Khoisan specialists (see, e.g., Schapera 1930: 376–7). One of particular interest was the most prevalent theory at the turn of the century: that *Tsûi-//goab* originally meant 'sore knee' (Hahn 1881: 61–2). For almost every philological theory there was a Nama myth, and in the myth to support this derivation, Tsûi-//goab had fought repeatedly with //Gâuab and repeatedly lost, yet nevertheless grew stronger with each bout. In the final battle, Tsûi-//goab destroyed //Gâuab with a

258 Comparisons and transformations

Table 14.1 *Structural relations among Nama beings*

	sacred sphere	*secular sphere*
good	Tsûi-//goab celestial collective worship avoidance relative (father)	Haitsi-aibib terrestrial individual intercession joking relative (grandfather or mother's brother)
evil	//Gâuab celestial collective ill fortune	≠Gama-≠gorib terrestrial individual bad luck

blow behind the ear. Just before expiring, //Gâuab gave Tsûi-//goab a blow to the knee. The myth is also said to explain why Tsûi-//goab walks with a limp.

The relation between Tsûi-//goab and //Gâuab is commensurate with the relation between the ancestor-hero Haitsi-aibib and his adversary ≠Gama-≠gorib. Haitsi-aibib, like Tsûi-//goab (and seemingly //Gâuab, who is said to be still among us), died many times and was reborn (Hahn 1881: 65–7; see also Hahn 1878). As with Tsûi-//goab, Haitsi-aibib quickly disposed of his rival in combat. In mythical time, ≠Gama-≠gorib would dig a hole, then tell any passer-by to throw a stone at his forehead. Yet ≠Gama-≠gorib had a hard head and the stone would bounce back and kill whoever threw it. The stone-thrower would then fall backwards into the hole. When Haitsi-aibib heard about the wicked ≠Gama-≠gorib, he went to see him but declined the inevitable invitation to cast his stone. Instead, he distracted ≠Gama-≠gorib and hit him behind the ear. ≠Gama-≠gorib died and fell into his own hole.

Haitsi-aibib's death and rebirth is recounted in another story. In this story, he ate poisonous berries and fell ill. He then told his son that, should he die, he wished to be buried with soft stones over his grave. Haitsi-aibib soon died and was duly buried; he then came to life again, and continued wandering the countryside. Piles of stones throughout Namibia and South Africa are said to be his graves, and Nama and Damara travellers place stones and sacrifices at his many 'graves' so that he will let them pass safely on their journeys. Haitsi-aibib is also credited with the ability to change himself into the form of many species of animal, and in Nama and Damara mythology this character sometimes replaces the Jackal, the Hare, and so on, who figure prominently as tricksters within /Xam, !Kung, Nharo, and other Bushman mythology – indeed they do in Nama mythology. Yet

Haitsi-aibib always uses his powers to do good. Like Tsûi-//goab and //Khâb (the Moon), Haitsi-aibib comes from the east, the sacred direction; and like the Moon, he grows big and then small again. According to some, Haitsi-aibib's mother and wife is the Sun, who is also said to be mother and wife to the Moon.

In fact, Tsûi-//goab, Haitsi-aibib, and perhaps the Moon too, are pretty much interchangeable in Khoekhoe mythology, as are //Gâuab and ≠Gama-≠gorib (cf. Hahn 1881: 130–7; S. Schmidt 1986b). The difference, as Peter Carstens (1975) has argued, is that the celestial god Tsûi-//goab operates only in a collective sphere of influence. The Nama would pray, addressing him as *ao* (father), and priests of the various Nama tribes would sacrifice animals to him in collective worship at specific times of year, hoping, but never being sure, that he would favour his people. By contrast, the terrestrial ancestor figure Haitsi-aibib operates in an individual sphere. Individual Nama who pile stones on his graves pray to him as their //*naub* (grandfather or mother's brother). Thus, these two beings may be regarded as essentially distinct in Nama belief and practice, even if interchangeable in Nama myth. In contrast, they appear to be merged in Nharo belief, where *Hieseba* is said to be the 'name of God' (*N!adi-ba-m di m /ui*). This term is simply the Western Khoe Bushman form of *Haiseb*. To my knowledge it has no cognate in any Central, Eastern, or Northern Khoe Bushman dialects, though it is found among the Hai//om as *Haiseb* (cf. S. Schmidt 1989, II: 75–7).

So what of //Gâuab? *G//ãũa*, or with gender suffixes, //*gâuab*, *g//ãũaba*, *g//amama*, etc., is almost universally a term for the evil god, the evil aspect of the good god, the evil spirits, or the spirits of the dead. Individual Nharo use the term for all these things, while apparently recognizing complete equivalence only between the last two: for most Nharo, evil spirits *are* the spirits of the dead. Nharo, unlike some Khoe-speaking Bushmen (cf. Silberbauer 1981: 112–14), recognize no other category of evil spirit. Some Nharo have no notion of a supreme *g//ãũaba*, whereas others, like the G/wi to the east and the Nama to the west, have a quite definite concept of him as a unique being (cf. Guenter 1986b: 215–49). The !Kung seem to recognize G//ãũa either as the unique Evil Spirit or as part of, or equivalent to, the High God. To them, the wind is also said to be *g//ãũa*, perhaps as a metaphor for misfortune, or possibly a vehicle on which the great Lesser Spirit travels. //*Gâuab* is also the Christian Nama word for 'Satan'. As Schapera (1930: 396) remarks: 'The beliefs regarding //Gaua . . . are not crystallized into clear-cut conceptions, but are vague, inconsistent, and ambiguous.'

The Damara, however, seem to have had a different version of the spirit world (see Vedder 1923, I: 97–142; 1928a: 61–8). Before their conversion to Christianity, they absorbed elements of both Khoekhoe and Herero religion. Yet Vedder (1928a: 61) claimed to have discovered isolated clans in the northwest of Namibia who still retained their early traditions. Curiously, these groups made no distinction between the good and the evil god, having only one term, //*Gamab* or //*Gâuab*, the term the Nama traditionally use for their evil deity. It would be easy to say, as the Nama and the missionaries probably did, that the Damara had a //Gâuab cult or worshipped the Devil, or that the two Nama gods are, among the Damara, merged into one. Yet any such statement, though in some sense true, would certainly be an oversimplification. To the Damara //Gamab is not the creator, for Vedder's Damara had no notion of creation. This //Gamab, unlike the Nama gods Tsûi-//goab and //Gâuab, frequently interceded in individual human affairs, usually by causing death with his invisible arrows. But like these beings, and unlike Bushman *g//ãũasi* or *g//ãũane* (the !Kung and Nharo plural forms respectively), the Damara //Gamab did not roam the earth. He would shoot his arrows from his village in the sky. He is not malicious, for he has no 'moral personality' (Vedder 1928a: 62). //Gamab's village is laid out like a Damara one, with a shady tree and a holy fire in the middle. The elders there prize human flesh as a great delicacy; and sometimes, when //Gamab would not help them obtain it, they would send scorpions, snakes, thorns, and knives, to attack the living. On earth, sorcerers also try to enlist //Gamab's support, in this case to stop the elders of heaven from succeeding; for their power too is a gift of //Gamab.

The Damara conception of //Gamab, then, has elements in common with the //Xegwi god /A'an, and with the Nharo, G/wi, and !Kung 'spirits' (*g//ãũa-*). It also has much in common with the G/wi conception of G//amama, who casts down from the sky evil and invisible wooden arrows. These lodge in women, from whom their evil diffuses through the bands, especially at times of seasonal aggregation (Silberbauer 1981: 54). Among the Nharo, evil spirits and alleged sorcerers shoot invisible grass arrows and perform other magic for ill or good. More obviously, the Damara //Gamab has parallels with the Nama deities, Tsûi-//goab and //Gâuab, and perhaps with the mythological character, ≠Gama-≠gorib. The Damara concept of //Gamab suggests inversions and transformations of interrelated aspects of these belief systems, which no doubt could be explicable either synchronically within a structuralist framework of equivalences and oppositions, or diachronically within a socio-economic determinist framework like the one Carstens (1975) has proposed specifically for the last hundred years or so of Nama history.

Mythology, scripture, and conversion

As with Khoisan belief, a characteristic feature of Khoisan mythology is the tendency of ideas, in this case myths or stories, to travel across linguistic, cultural, and environmental boundaries. One Nharo 'myth' or 'story' (*hua*) may illustrate the point. Briefly, the story tells of a band of people who set out to build a hut so tall it would reach the sky. The sky watched with interest as the hut grew taller and taller, but he eventually knocked it down, saying, 'You mustn't build a hut so high; you can't reach me'. I wrote that story down in 1974, early in my fieldwork. A year later I recorded the same story among a different group of Nharo some 100 kilometres away. The second version came during an evening of story-telling, about the Trickster Jackal, the Hare, the Moon, the Mantis, and so on; but this time, the site of the great hut was revealed as Cape Town. Only then did I recognize that the story referred to the Tower of Babel! Upon my questioning, the story-teller admitted that he had learned it from an itinerant white preacher – a fact that seemingly had been quite irrelevant in the story-teller's decision to include it in the evening's performance (cf. Guenther 1989: 71).

Mythology undoubtedly does reveal systems of belief and explanation. However, a given myth may become just as much a part of one belief system as part of another. While I would not claim that the intended Judaeo-Christian meaning of this myth was lost on the story-teller when he first heard it, I would nevertheless argue that the social and mythological context in which I heard the Bushman version was truly a Bushman one. It is characteristic of Bushman mythology, and of Bushman culture generally, that ideas can pass from one group to another, from one system to another, without any indigenous acknowledgement of the potential for transformation of such a system. Ideas, and stories, are easily assimilated without threat to the belief system as a whole.

For similar reasons, the notion of radical conversion through religious experience would seem to be largely inapplicable in Bushman society. This, however, is less true in Khoekhoe society, where religion, like social structure, is less flexible and perhaps less adaptive, and where the events of the last three centuries have forced on individuals new, more rigid, forms both of social structure and of religious doctrine. It is difficult to isolate the reasons for these, but it seems to me that there were differences both between Bushmen and Khoekhoe social structure and, to a lesser extent, between the style and political context of missionization among the two groups, which account for the greater fluidity of Bushman religious ideas (see, e.g., Vedder 1938 [1934]: 220–2, 467–9). Missionization among most Bushman groups has been altogether more low-key. Only a small fraction of Bushmen have in any sense been converted to Christianity, and I doubt whether many of these, except perhaps at one or two permanent mission settlements in northeastern Namibia, have displayed even the pretence of giving up their traditional beliefs. Bushman belief, as studies by Silberbauer (1981) and Biesele (1978) have shown, hinges on a kind of eco-socio-theology in which the natural, the social, and the spiritual are manifest in a single indigenously defined 'ecosystem'. Flexibility in group structure and social relations are coupled with equal flexibility on the plane of belief and explanation.

A more extreme view of flexibility as the cornerstone of Bushman religion comes from Mathias Guenther. In his masterly article 'Bushmen religion and the (non)sense of anthropological theory of religion', Guenther (1979b) dismisses functionalist and structuralist approaches in favour of what he terms 'religion as anti-structure'. He argues that Bushman religion in particular, and religion in general, is characterized by disorderliness, idiosyncrasy, and a lack of functionality. I find much of Guenther's argument highly convincing. However, I think he underestimates the structural uniformity of Khoisan religions when taken collectively and not one by one. It is not that fluidity denies structure, as Guenther contends. Rather, fluidity in religious belief functions as an indigenous creative and explanatory device and as a product of linguistic and social circumstances, both within and beyond broadly defined structural frameworks. Like the fluidity in patterns of settlement and seasonal migration, fluidity in belief supplements such frameworks and allows them to persist.

Theophilus Hahn once commented on what he regarded as the excessive dogmatism of missionaries among the Nama. His argument for the use of Khoekhoe rather than Hebrew or Greek terms in Bible translation occurs in his book, *Tsuni-//goam: the supreme being of the Khoi-khoi* (1881: 150–1), amidst a proto-structuralist defence of F. Max Müller's theory of the 'psychical identity of mankind'. At the time, Calvinists and Lutherans were competing with each other to gain converts, by appeal to theological arguments which were unintelligible within the Nama system of belief. Hahn was always a man of controversy; he was also the son of a missionary and grew up with Nama, as well as German, virtually as a mother tongue. Of his many battles with the establishment, one centred on his objection to the translation of the Judaeo-Christian concept 'God' as *Elob* (from the Hebrew *Eloah* or *Elohim*), rather than *Tsûi-//goab*, which, he argued, was the Nama equivalent. To this day, the Bible is known in Nama as *Elob Mîs* (or *Elobmîs*) – 'The Word of God'. In *Elob Mîs* (1966), the borrowed term *Elob* alternates with the indigenous term *!Khūb* (Lord). The Judaeo-Christian God is no longer referred to as Tsûi-//goab, even though this was the name given in the translation of the Gospels by J.H. Schmelen (1831), probably the first missionary to preach in the Nama language. Kroenlein's Nama dictionary (1889: 65) lists no fewer than eight derivative expressions from *Elob* (excluding purely grammatical variants), for example, *elosi* (divine), *elo-!ao-!gâxa* (God-fearing), and *eloxoresa* (ungodliness, sin). In contrast, concepts such as 'Almighty' (*Hoa/gaixab*), 'Comforter' (*//Khae-≠gao-oab*), 'Redeemer' (*Ore-aob*), and 'Holy Spirit' (*!Anu Gagab*) are all rendered today by loan-translations with fully indigenous Nama morphemes.

The interaction between Khoisan and Western religious ideas is a fascinating area for historical research and an area which might in itself yield much insight into pre-Christian Khoisan religion (cf. Kuper 1987: 150–66). Early white settlers in the northern Cape, pious but geographically ignorant, believed that the graves of Haitsi-aibib were monuments left by the Children of Israel on their way to Canaan (Hahn 1881: 47). Educated ethnographers have alluded metaphorically at least, to modern Khoekhoe as descendants of the 'lost tribes' (Maingard 1931); and indeed the 'Hamitic theory' of the origin of the Khoekhoe language was the subject of the Ph.D. thesis of the foremost Khoisanist of the nineteenth century, W.H.I. Bleek (1851). Others have simply drawn upon the obvious parallels between Old Testament and Khoisan beliefs in their interpretations of the latter. Even New Testament parallels are not unkown. As one missionary claimed, 'John the Baptist was a Bushman' (Philip 1828, I: 13). Equally, parallels between Haitsi-aibib and Christ do not go unnoticed by Khoekhoe Christians, though these two persons are not, to my knowledge, regarded as aspects of the same being. Nor, apparently, is Haitsi-aibib explicitly equated with Tsûi-//goab in the sense of the *Homoousion* of Christian theology (i.e., as having 'the same substance'), though the potential is obvious.

Conclusion

On the surface, Khoisan religions are as diverse as any aspects of Khoisan culture. Yet some of their religious ideas, including concepts of God, the spirits, and the dead, as well as myths and ritual practices, are held in common, even between hunters and herders. Such religions are characterized: (1) by structures which may be held constant, transformed, or inverted, through time or across ethnic boundaries, and (2) by a fluidity of religious belief and religious discourse which is sometimes difficult to define in purely structural terms.

In Khoisan society, especially in the case of the Bushmen, assimilation of new ideas is non-problematic, and religious notions have a fluid character which has led historically to cross-cultural uniformity and, at the same time, to intra-cultural diversity. In the case of the Khoekhoe and Damara, the greater rigidity of form has given rise to a greater tendency towards structural transformation, rather than fluidity of discourse, although both elements are present in these religions too.

Ironically, the greater structural consistency of Khoekhoe and Damara religions seems to have made these peoples more, rather than less, receptive to Christian conversion (Barnard 1988b: 230–2). Variation in beliefs and belief structures are prevalent (1) within the culture area as a whole, (2) within given Khoisan societies both through time and in the present, and (3) within the idiosyncratic belief systems of individual people. Such variations, whether the product of structural transformation or of moral or cognitive ambiguity, are best understood within a regional approach which includes both structural and interpretive methods.

15

Bushman kinship: correspondences and differences

Introduction

In an earlier paper (Barnard 1981), I compared the kinship systems of four well-known Bushman groups. I shall re-examine these same systems here, with a view towards uncovering the underlying structures which are implicit in the data. In the final section, I shall look again at the relationship terminology structure of the Eastern ≠ Hoã, in the light of the comparisons drawn between the other Khoisan systems. My method of comparison is deliberately both intuitive and formal, and as such may put off radicals on both sides – zealous formalists and passionate interpretivists, alike. Its advantage is that it does help to elucidate structures which are otherwise only partly known.

In Chapter 12, I compared the settlement patterns of the !Kung, Nharo, G/wi, and !Xõ and noted the considerable differences between them. The kinship systems of these four groups also exemplify a diversity of forms. Nevertheless, they have two important common attributes – universal kin categorization and a universally extended distinction between joking partners and avoidance partners. Implicit in these attributes is a common set of relationship categories whose labels differ according to both language and the classification of specific genealogical positions. The more significant differences all stem from transformations in the defining principles of these categories. These include the means by which the joking/avoidance distinction is extended, the relationship between the joking/avoidance distinction and the rules of marriage, and the presence or absence of an explicit ideology (in addition to a practice) of universal kin-category extension.

The concept of universal kin classification

Universal kin classification is a form of social classification which encompasses the whole of society and which is based on notions of kinship and affinity. I distinguish two types of universal kinship – empirical and ideological (Barnard 1978a). An empirically universal system is one in which a person associates only with 'kin'. An ideologically universal system is one in which, however imprecise the means of kin category extension, a person must classify as members of some kin category all those with whom he or she associates. In an ideologically universal system, there is no such category as 'non-kin'. Of the five peoples discussed in this chapter, the !Kung, Nharo, and G/wi have ideologically universal systems, the !Xõ have an empirically universal system, and the Eastern ≠ Hoã have a system of unknown universality.

The underlying categories of Khoisan relationship terminologies
Theoretical considerations
In *Research practices in the study of kinship*, Anthony Good and I attacked the excessive formalism of much traditional work in componential and transformational analysis (Barnard and Good 1984: 52, 53–5). The point of such analysis should be *not* to account for all and only the genealogical referents covered by a particular term. Nor should it be to test the 'psychological validity' of anything. Rather, a good formal analysis is one which records the basic structure of a terminology clearly and simply, and which can then be used to aid in understanding the non-terminological aspects of a kinship system. In my experience, regional comparative analysis has proved to be vastly more revealing in both these aspects than either the 'all-and-only' method or any attempt to 'test' for cognition. The all-and-only method emphasizes precision at the expense of understanding, and tests of cognition, as often as not, give spurious results. Neither method is consistent with the goals of modern linguistics (see Chomsky 1965: 28–33), or for that matter, modern social anthropology (cf. Borland 1979: 334–7; Keen 1985).

My method to some extent follows the long tradition in Australian kinship studies (e.g., Radcliffe-Brown 1913; 1930–1; Scheffler 1978) of trying to explain particular systems through a wider pattern. The problem is that the Khoisan systems do not form patterns of dividing and unfolding structures in the same way that Australian ones do (cf. Barnard 1989b). The answer is to be more flexible in structural comparison, and to allow intuition to take over where the more rigid methods of formal analysis reach a dead end. This is the method I developed originally in my study of Nharo kinship (Barnard 1976a). Through this method, I have tried to come up with a description of both the general underlying structure of Khoe kinship (Barnard 1980a; 1987) and a conjectural history of its development in relation to the systems of some of the other Khoisan peoples (1988a).

However, not until now have I tried to describe the kinship systems of the non-Khoe-speaking Bushmen in terms of the categories of the Khoe-speaking peoples. This is what I intend to do here.

The underlying categories of Khoisan kinship are much the same as those defined in these earlier papers, though with one qualification. Specifically, it is not possible to state very precisely the genealogical makeup of some of the categories for the Khoisan as a whole. At first glance, the assumption of such categories might strike one as sleight of hand, but the situation for Khoisan terminologies in general is not qualitatively different from that of the terminologies of the Khoe-speaking peoples. All we have to abandon is the notion that the lineal/collateral and cross/parallel distinctions are somehow logically prior to the joking/avoidance dichotomy. Some terminologies, such as the !Kung one, distinguish lineals (ancestors and descendants of ego) from collaterals (siblings of lineals and their descendants). Others, including the !Xo one and all those of the Khoe-speaking peoples, distinguish instead parallel relatives (lineals and same-sex siblings of lineals, and their descendants) and cross-relatives (opposite-sex siblings of lineals, and their descendants). Yet all the known Khoisan terminologies do appear to make a distinction between joking partners and avoidance partners. Therefore I shall assume that the joking/avoidance distinction is 'deeper'.

The categories

The two basic categories of the underlying structure of Bushman kinship are JOKING and AVOIDANCE. The capital letters in these words indicate the status of these as deep categories which both cross-cut linguistic boundaries and identify more than one term within the relationship terminologies of specific peoples.

Within each of these higher-level categories are a maximum of four lower-level categories. JOKING contains: GRANDRELATIVE, JOKING SIBLING, SPOUSE, and JOKING IN-LAW. GRANDRELATIVE nearly always includes grandparents and grandchildren, and commonly also some uncles and aunts, and nephews and nieces. JOKING SIBLING comprises those siblings and classificatory 'siblings' (e.g., parallel cousins) who are in the JOKING category. SPOUSE includes real and classificatory spouses. These three categories are found in every known Khoisan system. The last JOKING category, JOKING IN-LAW, does not always occur. In many systems, JOKING affines are incorporated into the GRANDRELATIVE category. I reserve the term JOKING IN-LAW specifically for the category which includes relatives emically defined as 'in-laws'. Thus it is always a 'named' category.

AVOIDANCE contains a different set of potential lower-level categories:

PARENT/CHILD, AVOIDANCE SIBLING, COMPEER, and AVOIDANCE IN-LAW. A fifth potential category, RESPECT RELATIVE, is relevant only to the systems of the herding peoples and will be discussed in the next chapter. The PARENT/ CHILD category is found in every Khoisan system and includes the reciprocal relationship between parents and children. It also includes classificatory 'parents' and 'children'. AVOIDANCE SIBLING comprises those siblings and classificatory 'siblings' who are in the AVOIDANCE category. The indigenous terms for AVOIDANCE SIBLINGS are normally the same as those for JOKING SIBLINGS. Proof that this really is a separate category is four-fold: (1) structurally, in all systems the categorization of other relatives is altered by the relative sex of the linking sibling; (2) terminologically, the JOKING and AVOIDANCE categories themselves may be distinguished even if there is no unique term for JOKING SIBLING or AVOIDANCE SIBLING; (3) jurally, appropriate 'joking' and 'avoidance' conduct is defined culturally; and (4) behaviourally, it is observable. The third AVOIDANCE category is COMPEER. The term itself is borrowed from Gruber's (1973) analysis of the Eastern ≠ Hoã system, but I use it in a different, and indeed more literal, sense. It means 'co-parent' (cf. Spanish *compadre*, 'godfather'). In my usage, it refers to relatives (usually uncles and aunts) who occupy a parent-like social status but who are called by a different indigenous term from that used for parents. Reciprocally, it refers to nephews, nieces, and others who occupy a child-like category. Finally, AVOIDANCE IN-LAW is a named, affinal category of avoidance. It is found in all systems for which we have data on affinal usage, and it is generally designated by the same term as that in use for JOKING IN-LAWS. Its existence as a separate category can be justified by the same reasoning as applied above with reference to JOKING and AVOIDANCE SIBLINGS.

The !Kung system

The following brief summary of !Kung kinship comprises a more formal representation of the system than the ethnographic description given in Chapter 3. The orthography and details of genealogical usage are based on Wilmsen's (1989a: 171–80) account.

The !Kung have what Lowie (1928) would describe as a 'lineal' structure for classifying relatives of the first ascending generation, and what Murdock (1949) would describe as an 'Eskimo' cousin terminology. In other words, direct or lineal relatives are distinguished from collaterals. In terms of JOKING and AVOIDANCE categorization, the basic system can be represented as in Figure 15.1. Here a plus sign represents a JOKING relative and a minus sign, an AVOIDANCE relative.

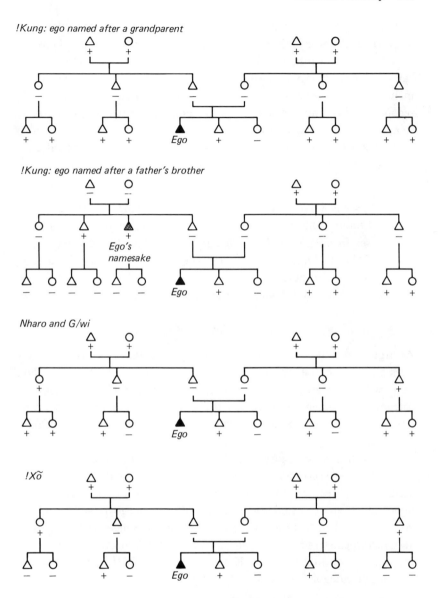

!Kung: ego named after a grandparent

!Kung: ego named after a father's brother

Nharo and G/wi

!Xõ

Figure 15.1 !Kung, Nharo, G/wi, and !Xõ JOKING and AVOIDANCE categorization

The !Kung JOKING category includes GRANDRELATIVE, JOKING SIBLING, and SPOUSE. Because of the existence of name relationships, it is not possible to state, etically, genealogical specifications of the categories. However, we can say that if ego is named after a grandparent, then GRANDRELATIVES will include namesakes, grandparents and grandchildren, first cousins and second cousins, and various affines (including potential spouses). JOKING SIBLINGS include same-sex siblings and some distant affines. Very unusually for a Bushman system, the category SPOUSE includes real spouses only. The kinship terms may be mapped onto the JOKING categories as indicated below.

> GRANDRELATIVE: *!un!ã'a* (senior or equal, same sex as ego), *!uma* (junior, same sex as ego), *txũma* (senior, equal or junior, opposite sex from ego), *!unba* (male co-parent-in-law, literally 'namesake-father'), and *!untae* (female co-parent-in-law, literally 'namesake-mother');
>
> JOKING SIBLING: *!o* (elder 'brother'), *!ui* (elder 'sister'), and *tsĩ* (younger 'sibling');
>
> SPOUSE: *!hõa* (husband) and *dshau* (wife).

An argument could be made for considering *!unba* and *!untae* as representatives of a JOKING IN-LAW category, but I prefer to consider them as affinal terms within a larger GRANDRELATIVE category. Indeed this GRANDRELATIVE category is a 'named' one in that all the terms in the category except *txũma* have the stem *!u* or *!un*, a term which has the primary kinship meaning 'namesake'.

The AVOIDANCE category includes PARENT/CHILD, AVOIDANCE SIBLING, COMPEER, and AVOIDANCE IN-LAW. The PARENT/CHILD category appears to include only real parents and children. AVOIDANCE SIBLINGS include opposite-sex siblings and some distant affines. If ego is named after a grandparent, then COMPEERS will include parents' siblings and their spouses, and reciprocally, siblings' children. AVOIDANCE IN-LAWS include ego's spouse's AVOIDANCE relatives. Kinship terms are distributed within the AVOIDANCE category as follows.

> PARENT/CHILD: *ba* or *mba* (father), *tae* (mother), *!'hã* (son), and ≠ *xae* (daughter);
>
> AVOIDANCE SIBLING; *!o* (elder 'brother'), *!ui* (elder 'sister'), and *tsĩ* (younger 'sibling');
>
> COMPEER: *tsu* (males) and *g//a* (females);
>
> AVOIDANCE AFFINE: ≠ *xũm* (males) and */'utsu* (females).

If ego is named after an uncle or an aunt, then the relationship terms are applied differently, because the GRANDRELATIVE and COMPEER categories are reversed on the side of the family from which ego gets his or her name. Take for example the case presented in Chapter 3, where male ego is named after one of his father's brothers. He calls this FB *!un!ã'a* ('namesake/ grandfather/cousin/grandson'). He calls the FB's siblings (excluding ego's father) *!o*, *!ui* or, if younger than ego, *tsĩ* ('siblings'). He calls the FB's parents, children and siblings' children *tsu* ('uncle/nephew') and *g//a* ('aunt/niece'). Thus on the FB's side of the family, members of the FB's generation are given terms which would normally be applied to grandparents and cousins; grandparents and cousins, in turn, are given terms which would otherwise be applied to uncles and aunts. The JOKING and AVOIDANCE categories as applied in this example are shown in the second chart of Figure 15.1.

On the opposite side of the family from which ego receives his name, the normal sequence of generation terms is the same as it would be if ego were named after a grandparent. On this side of the family, and indeed for distant and non-consanguineally related people, ego's namesake is always *!un!ã'a*; and ego's father's and mother's namesakes are *tsu* (in the case of males) and *g//a* (in the case of females), i.e., classificatory 'uncles' and 'aunts'. When two strangers meet, the elder classifies the younger according to the place of the younger's name in the elder's genealogy (see, e.g., Lee 1972e: 357).

People termed *!un!na*, *txũma*, *!unba*, *!untae*, *!o* (m.s.), *!ui* (w.s.), *tsĩ* (same sex), and *!hõa* or *dshau* are joking partners, who may tease, insult, and make sexual jokes with each other (with certain exceptions); and an especially close joking relationship exists between a child and the person he or she is named after. People termed *ba*, *tae*, *!'hã*, *≠xae*, *!o* (w.s.), *!ui* (m.s.), *tsĩ* (opposite sex), *≠xũm* and */'utsu* are avoidance partners, who must be respected. Avoidance partners keep their distance, both socially and physically. Some of Marshall's (1976: 249–50) informants even demonstrated for her the proper distances which should be maintained between avoidance partners sitting together.

The Nharo system

I have presented the structure of Nharo kinship terminology usage in some detail in Chapter 8. Here, I shall confine my comments to the essential features of the terminology and to some comparisons between Nharo and other systems.

The Nharo have long been in contact with the !Kung and share with them their system of naming and namesake-equivalence. However, their relationship-terminology structure and marriage rules are very different. In this respect, the Nharo resemble their linguistic relatives, the other Khoe-speaking peoples. The Nharo relationship terminology exhibits the classic features of 'bifurcate merging' and 'Iroquois' types; that is, it distinguishes parallel relatives from cross-relatives, rather than lineals from collaterals. It also distinguishes structurally between consanguines and affines, although some terms cross-cut this distinction. There is a small set of reciprocal, sex-aspecific relationship terms, which can be used to classify anyone in Nharo society. More specific terms are employed to distinguish 'fathers', 'mothers', and 'children', but these need not concern us here (cf. Barnard 1978b; Chapter 16).

In Nharo, JOKING relatives are called *g//ai*, and AVOIDANCE relatives are called *!au*. The JOKING categories are GRANDRELATIVE, JOKING SIBLING, and SPOUSE, while the AVOIDANCE categories are PARENT/CHILD, AVOIDANCE SIBLING, and AVOIDANCE IN-LAW. The JOKING categories, and the terms and genealogical specifications which define them, are given below.

> GRANDRELATIVE: *tsxõ* or *mama* (namesake, grandparent, grandchild, cross-uncle or aunt, cross-cousin, cross-nephew or niece, JOKING affine);
>
> JOKING SIBLING: *ki* (elder same-sex sibling or parallel cousin), *!uĩ* (younger same-sex sibling or parallel cousin);
>
> SPOUSE: *khue* (spouse, spouse's same-sex sibling, same-sex sibling's spouse).

The AVOIDANCE categories are as follows.

> PARENT/CHILD: *g//o* (parent, parallel uncle or aunt, child [especially adult son or daughter], parallel nephew or niece), */ua* (child);
>
> AVOIDANCE SIBLING: *ki* (elder opposite-sex sibling or parallel cousin), *!uĩ* (younger opposite-sex sibling or parallel cousin);
>
> AVOIDANCE IN-LAW: */ui* (AVOIDANCE affine).

Joking affines are defined as spouse's *g//ai* and their reciprocals, and avoidance affines are defined as spouse's *!au* and their reciprocals. Like other Khoisan peoples, the Nharo use their system of categorization to determine categories of incest and marriage. Only joking partners of the GRANDRELATIVE or *tsxõ* category are marriageable. While the system may loosely be described as one of 'cross-cousin marriage', marriage between actual cross-cousins is rare. Often, as in the case cited above, real cross-cousins are classified as 'brother' and 'sister', and not as 'cross-cousins' at all, since they and their respective siblings receive their names from the same set of grandparents.

The G/wi system

Like all Khoe-speaking peoples, the G/wi make cross/parallel and not lineal/collateral distinctions in their classification of relatives. They do not possess rules to extend kin categorization through namesake equivalence, since their personal names are unique. Their circle of kin relations is relatively shallow.

JOKING categories include GRANDRELATIVE, JOKING SIBLING, SPOUSE, and JOKING IN-LAW, and AVOIDANCE categories include PARENT/CHILD, AVOIDANCE SIBLING, and AVOIDANCE IN-LAW. The JOKING terms are distributed as follows.

> GRANDRELATIVE: *baba* (grandfather, MB, FZH), *mama* (grandmother, FZ, MBH), *n//odi* (cross-cousin, cross-nephew or niece);

> JOKING SIBLING: *gjibaxu* (elder same-sex sibling or parallel cousin), *gijaxu* (younger same-sex sibling or parallel cousin);

> SPOUSE: *k'ao* (H, HB [ws], ZH [ws]), *g//eis* (W, WZ [ms], BW [ms]);

> JOKING IN-LAW: */ui* (JOKING affine).

AVOIDANCE relatives are classified as follows.

> PARENT/CHILD: *ba* (F, FB, MZH), *gje* (M, MZ, FBW), */ua* (child, parallel nephew or niece);

> AVOIDANCE SIBLING: *gjibaxu* (elder opposite-sex sibling or parallel cousin), *gijaxu* (younger opposite-sex sibling or parallel cousin);

> AVOIDANCE-IN-LAW: */ui* (AVOIDANCE affine).

Baba, mama, and *n//odi* are equivalent to Nharo *tsxõ* (G/wi reciprocal, *n//odi-ku*; Nharo, *tsxõ-ku*). *Ba, gje,* and */ua* are equivalent to Nharo *ki* and *!ui*. *K'ao* and *g//eis* are equivalent to Nharo *khue*. The G/wi use the term */ui* both for joking affines (who for the Nharo are *tsxõ*) and avoidance affines (Nharo, */ui*), hence the category JOKING IN-LAW. As in Nharo, avoidance relatives are called *!au* or *!ao* (literally, 'to be afraid [of]'), but there is no specific term for joking relatives apart from *!ao-kjima,* 'non-avoidance' or 'not feared'. In short, there are only two basic differences between the Nharo and G/wi systems – one being the wider meaning of the term */ui* in G/wi, and the other being the G/wi division of the Nharo category *tsxõ*

(GRANDRELATIVE) into senior male (*baba*), senior female (*mama*), and equal or junior (*n//odi*). Both differences are primarily linguistic or formal-structural and not sociological. The latter seems to reflect the usage of the !Kung naming system by the Nharo.

The !Xõ system

The terminology structure of !Xõ distinguishes three JOKING categories, namely GRANDRELATIVE, JOKING SIBLING, and SPOUSE, plus three AVOIDANCE categories, PARENT/CHILD, AVOIDANCE SIBLING, and AVOIDANCE IN-LAW. At this level of abstraction, the !Xõ system is identical to Nharo, though in other respects the !Xõ system is quite unique.

The JOKING terms are distributed in the following manner.

> GRANDRELATIVE: $\neq e$ (grandfather, grandchild [either sex], MB, FZH, ZC [ms], probably BC [ws] and HB, WZ [same sex or younger than ego]), //*am* (grandmother, FZ, MBW, WZ [older than ego]);

> JOKING SIBLING: $\odot xa$ (same-sex elder sibling or senior parallel cousin), $\neq xan$ (same-sex younger sibling or junior parallel cousin);

> SPOUSE: η/η (spouse), !*oa* (deceased spouse's same-sex sibling).

The AVOIDANCE categories, with their terms and genealogical specifications, are distributed as follows.

> PARENT/CHILD: $\tilde{a}$ (F, FB*, MZH*), *kai* (M, MZ*, FBW*), $\odot a$ (child, BC [ms]*, probably ZC [ws]*, and cross-cousin*);

> AVOIDANCE SIBLING: $\odot xa$ (opposite-sex elder sibling or senior parallel cousin), $\neq xan$ (opposite-sex younger sibling or junior parallel cousin);

> AVOIDANCE IN-LAW: /*a hã* (F-in-law, WB), $\odot a$ η/η (M-in-law, child-in-law, HZ).

Heinz does not record the terms used by a female ego. Therefore, certain genealogical specifications given above, namely BC (ws), HB, and ZC (ws) are my hypothetical additions, based on the internal logic of the system. The genealogical points of reference marked with an asterisk require the suffix -!*au*, 'extended kin', to be added to the relationship term stem. For example, one would say *na ã* for 'my father', but *na ã !au* 'for my stepfather', 'my FB', 'my MZH', etc. The unusual term !*oa*, implies the actual or potential practice of levirate or sororate; before the death of one's first spouse, a HB or WZ would be classified as $\neq e$ or //*am*.

The !Xõ system, like that of the !Kung, alternates generational terms. At least for lineals, ≠ *e* (senior male joking partners, and junior joking partners of either sex) and //*am* (senior female joking partners) alternate with *ã* (senior male avoidance partners), *kai* (senior female avoidance partners) and ⊙*a* (junior avoidance partners of either sex). ≠ *e*, //*am*, same-sex ⊙*xa* and ≠ *xan*, *n*/*n* and !*oa* are joking partners, and *ã*, *kai*, ⊙*a*, opposite-sex ⊙*xa* and ≠ *xan*, /*a hã* and ⊙*ŋ*/*ŋ* are avoidance partners.

Like the Khoe-speaking peoples (Nharo, G/wi, etc.), the !Xõ distinguish parallel relatives from cross, but there are differences. The Khoe-speaking peoples usually apply senior and junior terms according to the real relative ages of, e.g., parallel cousins, whereas the !Xõ distinguish senior and junior according to the relative ages of the parents' siblings in respect of ego's parents. For example, a !Xõ FeBs is ⊙*xa* (and not ≠ *xan*)) regardless of whether ego is older or younger than he is. The Nharo and G/wi practice is particularly consistent with an ideology of universal kin categorization, and the !Xõ practice may reflect the fact that the !Xõ do not extend relationship terms to as many genealogical points of reference, or to as many individuals.

Unlike the Nharo, G/wi, and other Bushman groups who distinguish parallel from cross-relatives, the !Xõ classify cross-cousins as AVOIDANCE (see Figure 15.1). The principle behind this seeming peculiarity is the same as that which permits the classification of distant kin among the G/wi: a joking partner's joking partner is a joking partner, etc. The difference is that the !Xõ apply such rules not only to distant, but also to close kin. For the !Xõ, joking partners' joking partners and avoidance partners' avoidance partners are always joking; and joking partner's avoidance partners and avoidance partners' joking partners are always avoidance. Cross-cousins being joking partners' (parents' opposite-sex siblings') avoidance partners (children) are thus avoidance. More specifically, as the children of close relatives of the JOKING category, they are termed 'classificatory children', ⊙*a* !*au*. A case could be made for a separate category of COMPEER here, but I prefer the interpretation which considers such relatives as part of a loosely defined PARENT/CHILD category. ⊙*a* literally means 'child', and ⊙*a* !*au* is, in fact, also the term employed for both step-children and same-sex siblings' children. Since they are mutual 'classificatory children', cross-cousins are AVOIDANCE relatives and not marriageable. In contrast, the closest JOKING relationship is between mutual ≠ *e*; and ≠ *e* (along with !*oa*) is the marriageable category. Apart from the exclusion of cross-cousins, this category is the !Xõ equivalent of Nharo *tsxõ* and G/wi *n*//*odi*.

Table 15.1 *Gruber's interpretation of the Eastern ≠ Hoã terminology*

Term	genealogical referents and Gruber's gloss
Primary terms	
kyxana	FF, MF, FeB, MB; (COMPEER) EXTENDED MALE PARENT
kyxoõ	FM, MM, MeZ, FZ, yGC, CC, GCC, yBCC, MyZCC; (COMPEER) EXTENDED KIN
ši-m'zale	FZC, MBC; (COMPEER) SELF
ki-si	eG, FeBC, MeZC; (COMPEER) OLDER EXTENDED SELF
//kam	yG, FyBC, MyZC; (COMPEER) YOUNGER EXTENDED SELF
ču	F; (COMPEER) MALE PARENT
ču-≠gao	FyB; (COMPEER) YOUNGER EXTENDED MALE PARENT I
gye	M; (COMPEER) FEMALE PARENT
gye-≠gao	MyZ; (COMPEER) YOUNGER EXTENDED FEMALE PARENT J
//qo'oe	C, FZCC, MBCC; (COMPEER) OFFSPRING
//qo'oe-≠gao	eGC, FeBCC, MeZCC; (COMPEER) OLDER EXTENDED OFFSPRING
Composite terms	
ču ki-si	FeB
ču //kam	FyB
gye ki-si	MeZ
gye //kam	MyZ
ki-si //qo'oe	eGC, FeBCC, MeZCC
//kam //qo'oe	yGC, FyBCC, MyZCC

The Eastern ≠ Hoã terminology: a puzzle
Gruber's analysis

In 1973, linguist Jeffrey Gruber published a formal analysis of the Eastern ≠ Hoã relationship terminology. Table 15.1 illustrates the essential elements of his analysis. For this table I have kept Gruber's analytical terms, but for ease of comparison I have placed them in the same order as in my own analysis, below (Table 15.2).

Gruber's paper makes explicit what he calls the 'underlying categorical specifications' of the terminology (1973: 446–8). His method uses a generative model which is derived explicitly from Chomsky's (1965) 'standard theory'. Instead of reducing distant genealogical specifications to primary denotata, Gruber seeks the base structures signified by the terms. These structures appear through what he terms 'categories', perhaps more accurately described as significata (cf. Goodenough 1956). Gruber's 'categories' are ordered by sets of rules, which in turn generate *relationship categories* in the more conventional sense of that term. For example, the term *kyxoõ* is defined as '(COMPEER) EXTENDED KIN, where KIN may be either PARENT or OFFSPRING' (1973: 435). 'EXTENDED', 'COMPEER', and even the

Table 15.2 *Barnard's interpretation of the Eastern ≠ Hoã terminology*

CATEGORY and *term*	my gloss
GRANDRELATIVE	
kyxana	senior male GRANDRELATIVE
kyxoõ	senior female GRANDRELATIVE, equal GRANDRELATIVE, junior GRANDRELATIVE
ši-m'zale	equal GRANDRELATIVE (cross-cousin)
SIBLING	
ki-si	senior SIBLING
//kam	junior SIBLING
PARENT/CHILD	
ču	genealogical father
ču-≠gao	classificatory FATHER
gye	genealogical mother
gye-≠gao	classificatory MOTHER
//qo'oe	CHILD (genealogical or classificatory)
//qo'oe-≠gao	senior classificatory CHILD
PARENT/CHILD or COMPEER (designated by descriptive terms)	
ču ki-si	father's elder same-sex SIBLING
ču //kam	father's younger same-sex SIBLING
gye ki-si	mother's elder same-sex SIBLING
gye //kam	mother's younger same-sex SIBLING
ki-si //qo'oe	elder SIBLING's CHILD
//kam //qo'oe	younger SIBLING's CHILD

brackets around the word, are all precisely defined. Gruber's notion of COMPEER is defined differently from my category by that name. His COMPEER is defined as 'kin on the same age level (as a given kin)' (1973: 433). Parentheses around the word 'COMPEER' in his categorical descriptions indicate the optional application of his COMPEER rule, which is in essence identical to the 'merging rule' of classic transformational analysis (e.g., Lounsbury 1964; Scheffler and Lounsbury 1969). It equates same-sex siblings. Gruber's notion of EXTENDED is more complicated. It refers to 'any sufficiently close kin (of some other direct kin) who is specifically either of the same line of descent as (cf. English *grand, great,* or *once-removed*) or of the same generation as (cf. English *second, third,* etc.) [*sic*]' (1973: 434).

From an ethnographic point of view, the terminology represents a structure not quite like any other Khoisan one, but with features similar enough to those of the other systems to make comparison worth while. The problem here, obviously, is the lack of observational data or associated jural rules, such as what category one may (or must) marry. Nor is it known how precisely, if at all, joking and avoidance relatives are distinguished.

The following re-analysis of his data may shed some light on the deeper meaning of ≠ Hoã kinship.

An alternative interpretation

My interpretation of the ≠ Hoã system is given in Table 15.2. I think it is clearer and simpler than Gruber's, and it is more intelligible within the larger system of Khoisan kinship as a whole. All that we know of the social-semantic (as opposed to formal-semantic) definitions of these categories is what can be deduced from the terminology structure itself, and what can be inferred from comparisons with the relationship terminologies of other Khoisan peoples. Without venturing into undue speculation, we need only assume that ≠ Hoã kinship is not inconsistent with those patterns of social organization which are held in common among the Zu/'hoã !Kung, the Nharo, the G/wi, and the !Xõ.

Most of the terminology is plain enough. Probably only the glosses 'father' and 'mother', for *ču* and *gye* respectively, carry their normal English meaning. The others all carry a wider categorical specification, and therefore I present them in capital letters. Indeed, it seems not unlikely that most ≠ Hoã relationship terms are used also for more distant relatives than those specified in Gruber's (1973: 430) denotational chart.

However, there is one problem which seems to cause confusion in the specification of categories. The striking feature of the ≠ Hoã system, in comparison to those of the Khoe-speaking peoples, is the seeming ambiguity of the categorization of the FeB (*ču ki-si*) and MeZ (*ču //kam*), and semi-reciprocally, that of the yGC, FyBCC and MyZCC (all //*kam* //*quo'oe*). This 'ambiguity' is two-fold, but is not as problematic as it may seem.

In the first instance, relative sex in relation to linking siblings is only significant in ≠ Hoã when ego is tracing to a senior relative. Thus 'the law of uniform reciprocals' (Scheffler 1977) does not hold. Of course, such a transgression of 'legal' principles is not unique to the Eastern ≠ Hoã (cf. Barnes 1978; Good 1978); nor is the formal symmetry of the terminology violated in the process. It is possible that the Eastern ≠ Hoã composite terms do not reflect a change in category at all, but merely serve to identify genealogical positions. If this is true, they could be considered 'descriptive' terms. The form *ču ki-si*, for example, might be considered equivalent to the English possessive construction, *father's brother*, rather than the kinship term *uncle*. Two other ≠ Hoã terms, *ki-si //qo'oe* and //*kam //qo'oe*, may be used in an extended-descriptive sense, specifically when *ki-si* and //*qo'oe* are taken as classificatory rather than real siblings.

The second instance of 'ambiguity' here is of a different kind. It is represented by the dual categorization of FeB, MeZ, yGC, FyBCC, and MyZCC. These genealogical specifications are labelled as *kyxana* or *kyxoõ* (in Khoe terms, GRANDRELATIVE), and at the same time *ču ki-si* or *gye ki-si* (senior PARENT/CHILD), or *//kam //qo'oe* (classificatory junior SIBLING). In fact, this is not unlike the option afforded by some Khoe systems, in their dual categorization of joking affines as both GRANDRELATIVES and JOKING IN-LAWS, or in the dual categorization of certain AVOIDANCE relatives as either both RESPECT RELATIVES and AVOIDANCE IN-LAWS or both RESPECT RELATIVES and PARENT/CHILD (Barnard 1987: 203, 205; cf. Chapter 16). The difference is that dual categorization among the Khoe-speaking peoples functions only within each respective higher level category, JOKING and AVOIDANCE. The ≠Hoã practice could reflect the fact that there exists no universal polar dichotomy between JOKING and AVOIDANCE categories, in that in their terminology the dual categorization of FeB, MeZ, yGC, FyBCC and MyZCC places these relatives in *both* categories. If this interpretation is correct, then relative age is what matters most for the ≠Hoã, and not the joking/avoidance distinction. The choice between a usage indicating category GRANDRELATIVE and one indicating PARENT/CHILD probably depends on the social context.

Another, more formal, reading of the structure is possible. Such a reading would distinguish parents' elder same-sex siblings as joking partners (*kyxoõ*) and classify parents' younger same-sex siblings as avoidance partners, or more precisely classificatory 'parents' (*ču-≠gao* and *gye-≠gao*). Reciprocally, one's younger same-sex siblings' children would be joking partners, (*kyxoõ*), and one's older same-sex siblings' children would be avoidance partners (*//qo'oe-≠gao*). Although very unusual, such a practice would not be inconsistent with the hierarchical classification of same-sex siblings. In Koekhoe society, siblings and parents' siblings are classified according to rules of hierarchy *within* the relevant categories, whereas here it would seem that the categories themselves are altered. The altering of categories here might even reflect a non-hierarchical family structure in which the grandparent/grandchild relationship (always a joking one among the Khoisan) is valued. Either way, the distance between same-sex siblings is treated as 'generational', and a junior same-sex sibling's child becomes a classificatory 'grandchild'. A conjectural model of joking/avoidance relationships among Eastern ≠Hoã close kin, expressed in terms of a distinction between hypothetical JOKING and AVOIDANCE categories, is shown in Figure 15.2. I present it not so much as a hypothesis to be tested by the next reader to visit the ≠Hoã, but the logical outcome of

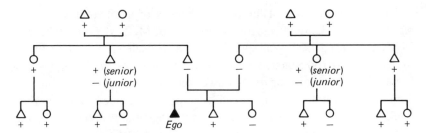

Figure 15.2 Eastern ≠ Hoã JOKING and AVOIDANCE categorization: a conjectural model

≠ Hoã classification when seen from a Common Bushman point of view.

Another interesting feature of this terminology is the definition of the GRANDRELATIVE term *kyxoõ*. Gruber's definition is conveyed through a complicated justification of his own methodology and an attempt at a monothetic interpretation. Yet the term is not so problematic if its polythetic character is recognized. In my representation of the system (Table 15.2), it has two meanings: 'senior female GRANDRELATIVE' and 'junior GRANDRELATIVE [regardless of sex]'. The !Xõ term ≠e is in fact comparable. Each of these terms, Eastern ≠ Hoã *kyxoõ* and !Xõ ≠e, designates more than one class or subcategory of kin.

Yet another curious feature of this system is the term *ši-m'zale*, which is a loan word from Kgalagari. According to Gruber (1973: 437) the term means 'cross-cousin', but I would be very surprised if it did not refer to more distant relatives as well. Why this term should be borrowed and no others is a mystery. However, there are precedents elsewhere among Khoisan peoples, such as the use of *mzala* among the //Xegwi and the use of *ndzira* among the Tshwa. Indeed, the use of the French term *cousin* in Germanic languages, since the thirteenth century in the case of English, may be comparable too.

Conclusion

The kinship systems of the five peoples described here are in some ways very different. Yet the two basic similarities between the four for which we have sufficient data – (1) a clear distinction between joking partners and avoidance partners, and (2) universal kin classification – are striking. The first similarity may be peculiar to the Bushmen, or the Khoisan peoples, while the second similarity is common among hunter-gatherers worldwide.

The unique property of the Eastern ≠ Hoã system, from a comparative

Bushman point of view, is that a number of genealogical positions stand in two rather than one of the cross-culturally defined categories. This could mean that the JOKING and AVOIDANCE categories do not exist among the Eastern ≠ Hoã, or (as I would prefer to see it) that they lie deeply submerged in the structure.

16

Khoe kinship: underlying structures and transformations

Introduction

If, as Lee and DeVore (1968: 3) claim, 'the hunting way of life has been the most successful and persistent adaptation man has ever achieved', there is no reason to suppose that the transition between hunting and herding is always in one direction. In historical times, Khoisan herders have been known to return to the earlier form of subsistence activity, particularly in times of hardship and drought (e.g., Marks 1972). Nineteenth-century Damara left their Nama and Herero masters to live by gathering, hunting, and raiding (Vedder 1928a: 42–3). Modern Bushmen in Botswana who have acquired and then lost livestock have also been able to return to their previous lifestyle (Vierich 1977). The Early Khoe Bushmen may also be an example of a people who became herders, or clients of herders, then returned to hunting again.

Some elements of kinship and social structure are more directly linked in ecological constraints and influences than others. Those which are more easily affected by changes in the subsistence pattern are, in a relative sense, part of the surface structure, and those which are not so easily affected are part of the deep structure of any given kinship system (Barnard 1987; 1988a). The distinction is not entirely new. Steward (1955: 78–97) was wrestling with the same problem when he spoke of a 'cultural core' as a device to identify the significant features of a 'culture area type' or a 'cross-cultural type'. For Steward, the 'uniformities' of a culture area, resulting from common origins or introduced by diffusion, were to be distinguished from the 'regularities' of ecological adaptation found in common between historically unrelated cultures. The 'cultural core' consisted essentially of the latter. In the context of a culture area, it consisted of those aspects of culture which were determined by the methods of environmental exploitation.

In the Khoisan case, there are unusual complications. This culture area includes both hunters and herders and therefore has no 'cultural core' in Steward's sense. However, in my understanding, the truly core elements of a culture or culture area are those which are *not* so susceptible to change. These elements, which form the underlying structure of a group of related cultures, are those which are held constant through history.

The uniformity of Khoe kinship structure
The structure of Khoe kinship is remarkably uniform. Khoe relationship terms identify only a small number of kinship categories which, with certain accountable differences, are defined similarly in terms of both genealogical position and socially approved behaviour for all Khoe-speaking groups. Another common feature of the systems is the practice of designating category membership by reciprocal in addition to egocentric relationship terms (see Barnard 1987: 197–9). For example, there will be a term meaning 'brothers to each other' (e.g., Nharo *!uĩ-ku*), as well as one for 'my older brother' and one for 'my younger brother'. Most Khoe kinship systems also allow for the extension of kin category membership beyond known consanguineous or affinal links, and most Khoe-speaking peoples recognize a jural rule of marriage to members of one specific relationship category. This will be either that of bilateral or that of matrilateral cross-cousins.

Kin categories
Each of the two higher level categories, JOKING and AVOIDANCE, may be divided into up to four lower level categories. JOKING includes GRANDRELA-TIVE, JOKING SIBLING, SPOUSE, and JOKING IN-LAW. AVOIDANCE includes PARENT/CHILD, AVOIDANCE SIBLING, RESPECT RELATIVE and AVOIDANCE IN-LAW. The distribution of kin within these categories is shown for the Khoe-speakers generally in Table 16.1. The category COMPEER, which I defined in Chapter 15 in reference to the !Kung system, is inapplicable here. Khoe systems merge those relatives who would fall under this label into the category PARENT/CHILD.

Egocentric relationship terms
Egocentric usages in various Khoe languages are illustrated in Table 16.2 and summarized in Table 16.3. In some terminologies I have indicated the grammatical necessity of person-number-gender possessive prefixes by placing hyphens before the appropriate terms. In all Khoe languages number-gender suffixes (in Nama, number-gender-case suffixes) are

Table 16.1 *Genealogical referents of Khoe kin categories*

JOKING
GRANDRELATIVE: grandparent, MB and MBW, FZ and FZH (Khoe Bushman only), cross-cousin (except posssibly Korana FZD [ms] and MBS [ws], who are sometimes regarded as RESPECT RELATIVES), spouse's JOKING relative (Western Khoe Bushman and Khoekhoe only), same-sex namesake; and the reciprocals of all of these. Only GRANDRELATIVES are marriageable.

JOKING SIBLING: same-sex sibling, same-sex parallel cousin.

SPOUSE: spouse, spouse's same-sex sibling, same-sex sibling's spouse.

JOKING IN-LAW: spouse's JOKING RELATIVE and JOKING relative's spouse. (As a category exclusive of GRANDRELATIVE, Central and Northern Khoe Bushman only.)

AVOIDANCE
PARENT/CHILD: parent, parent's same-sex sibling, child, same-sex sibling's child, opposite-sex namesake (only Khoekhoe-speakers have opposite-sex namesakes).

AVOIDANCE SIBLING: opposite-sex sibling, opposite-sex parallel cousin.

RESPECT RELATIVE: FZ and FZH and their reciprocals, close AVOIDANCE relatives (Khoekhoe only).

AVOIDANCE IN-LAW: spouse's AVOIDANCE relative and AVOIDANCE relative's spouse.

Table 16.2 *Khoe egocentric relationship terms*

Khoekhoe
Nama (sources: Hoernlé 1925: 18–23; Schultze 1907: 299–303; my fieldnotes; standard orthography with phonetic transcription in square brackets)

JOKING (no general term)
(1) *//nao* [n//ao] (senior, and sometimes MBC), *//nuri* [n//uri] (equal or junior), *//nuri-!gâ* [n//uri-!ã] (cross cousin), */ai* [/'ai] (marriageable; archaic or taboo)
(2) *!gâ kai* [!ã kai] (senior), *!gâ ≠khammi* [!ã ≠khami] or *!gâ-sa* [!ã-sa] (junior)
(3) *xae* [xae] (archaic or taboo), *ao* [ao] (m.), *tará* [tará] (f.)
(4) — (or) */ui* [/'ui]

AVOIDANCE *tara* [tara] (or) *!oa* [!'oa]
(1) *//gu* [//u] (elder, someone else's; very formal), *sao* [sao] (elder, someone else's), *ai* [ai] or *î* [ī:] (elder, respect), *abo* [apo] (m., elder, one's own; archaic), *dada* [tata] (m., elder; often with relative age suffix), *mama* [mama] (f., elder, familiar; often with relative age suffix), */gôa* [/õa] or *ôa* [õa] (younger)
(2) *!gâ kai* [!ã kai] (senior), *!gâ ≠khammi* [!ã ≠khami] or *!gâ-sa* [!ã-sa] (junior)
(3) *tàra* [tàra] (f., especially senior), *dada* [tata] (m., senior or elder), *ai kai* [ai kai] (f., senior; archaic), *tàra ôa* [tàra õa] (junior or younger)

Table 16.2 (*contd.*)

<hr>

(4) /*ui* [/'ui], *!na* [n!a] (formal)

Korana (sources: Engelbrecht 1936: 127, 130–1, 152–4, except where otherwise noted; orthography after Engelbrecht; cf. Maingard 1932: 143–5)

JOKING (no general term recorded)
(1) //*nao* (senior), //*nuli* or //*nuli-sa* (equal or junior)
(2) !'*ã* (often with relative-age prefix or suffix)
(3) *khoe* (m.), *xai* (m.), *tará* (f.)
(4) — or /'*ui*

AVOIDANCE *tàra* (opposite-sex, man speaking) (?), ≠ *xana-khoe* (opposite-sex, woman-speaking) (?)
(1) //'*ũ* (Beach 1938:231: ɔ̃*up*, 'father'), *aitjo* (Wuras 1920:89: 'mother'), *sau* (Meinhof 1930:134: 'mother'), *tata* (or) *ta:* (m., elder; vocative ?; often with relative-age prefix or suffix), *mama* (or) *ma:* (f., elder; vocative ?; often with relative-age prefix or suffix), *ĩ* (elder, referential), /*go:* (younger), *õa* (younger), (Maingard 1932:144)
(2) !'*ã* (often with relative-age prefix or suffix)
(3) *tàra* (f.), *tata* or *ta:* (m.) (?), ≠ *xana-khoe* (non-marriageable man; possibly synonymous with male AVOIDANCE SIBLING)
(4) /'*ui* (sometimes with a suffix)

Central and Northern Khoe Bushman

G/wi
(sources: Silberbauer 1972:309–13; 1973:70–6; 1981:142–9); my fieldnotes)

G//ana
(source: my fieldnotes; cf. Tanaka 1969:15; 1978a: 132–3; 1980:103–7)

JOKING -*!ao-kjima*
(1) -*baba* (m., senior), -*mama* (f., senior), -*n//odi* (generally, equal or junior)
(2) -*gjibaxu* (elder), -*gijaxu* (younger)
(3) -*k'ao* (m.), -*g//eis* (f.)
(4) -/*ui*

-*!ao-tama*
(1) -*baba* (m., senior), -*mama* (f., senior), -*n//odi* (generally, equal or junior)
(2) -*ki* (elder), -*dabahã* (m, younger), -*!uĩ* (f., younger)
(3) -*k'ao* (m.), -*g//eis* (f.)
(4) -/*ui*

AVOIDANCE -*!ao* or -=*!ao*
(1) -*ba* (m., senior) -*gje* (f., senior) -/*ua* (junior)
(2) -*gjibaxu* (elder), -*gijaxu* (younger)
(3) —
(4) -/ui

-*!ao*
(1) -*ba-g//o* (m., senior) -*ma-g//o* (f., senior) -/*ua* (junior)
(2) -*ki* (elder), -*dabahã* (m., younger), -*!uĩ* (f., younger)
(3) —
(4) -ui

Table 16.2 (*contd.*)

Buga (Bukakhoe) (source: H.J. Heinz, unpublished relationship term charts	*Kxoe* (sources: terms from Köhler 1966a:164–5; hypothetical categorization from Barnard 1980a: 116–17)
JOKING (no general term recorded) (1) *dada* (m., senior), *mama* (f., senior), (equal/junior terms not recorded) (2) *dasi* (elder), *damase* (younger) (3) (no male term recorded), *//e-kwe* (f.) (4) */ui*	(no general term recorded) (1) (no specifically senior terms recorded), *n//ori* (junior) (2) *taçi* (elder), *damaçi* (younger) (3) (no terms recorded) (4) */'ui* (?)
AVOIDANCE (no general term recorded) (1) *ba* (m., senior), *ma* (f., senior), */oa* (junior) (2) *dasi* (elder), *damase* (younger) (3) — (4) */ui*	(no general term recorded) (1) *//ui* (senior) *çiri* (m., senior, 'your'), *çao* (f., senior, 'your'), *nde* (m., senior, one's own), *mba* (f., senior, one's own), */oã* (junior) (2) *taçi* (elder), *damaçi* (younger) (3) — (4) */'ui*

Western Khoe Bushman

Nharo and *Ts'aokhoe* (source: my fieldnotes)	*≠Haba* (source: my fieldnotes)
JOKING -*g//ai* or -*!au-tama* (1) -*tsxõ* or *mama* (2) -*ki* (elder), -*luĩ* (younger) (3) -*khue* or -*g//ai*, -*k'au* (m.), -*g//ais* (f.) (4) —	-*!au-tama* (1) -*tsxõ* or *mama* (2) -*gabaxu* (3) -*k'au* (m.) -*g//ais* (f.) (4) —
AVOIDANCE -*!au* or *papa* (1) -*g//o* or *papa*, *au* (m., elder, one's own), *ai* (f., elder, one's own), *sau* (elder, someone else's), -*/ua* (younger) (2) -*ki* (elder), -*!uĩ* (younger) (3) — (4) -*/ui*	-*!au* (1) -*g//o* or *papa*, *bam* (m., elder, one's own), *je* (f., elder, one's own), *som* (m., elder, someone else's), *sidi* (f., elder, someone else's), -*/ua* (younger) (2) -*gabaxu* (3) — (4) -*/ui*

Table 16.3 *Summary of Khoe egocentric relationship term usage within lower level categories*

JOKING

(1) GRANDRELATIVE. *Khoekhoe*: in normal usage, senior and junior terms are distinguished. *Central and Northern Khoe Bushmen*: in normal usage, senior and junior terms are distinguished, and senior terms are futher distinguished only by real sex. *Western Khoe Bushmen*: one basic term and synonym.

(2) JOKING SIBLING. *Khoekhoe*: one basic term (relative age distinguished by suffixes). *Central and Northern Khoe Bushmen*: terms are distinguished only by real sex and/or relative age or seniority. *Western Khoe Bushmen*: one term, or terms distinguished only by relative age.

(3) SPOUSE. *Khoekhoe*, and *Central and Northern Khoe Bushmen*: terms are distinguished only by real sex. *Western Khoe Bushmen*: one basic term.

(4) JOKING IN-LAW. *Khoekhoe*: category generally assimilated with GRANDRELATIVE; alternatively, one term. *Central and Northern Khoe Bushmen*: one term. *Western Khoe Bushmen*: category assimilated with GRANDRELATIVE.

AVOIDANCE

(1) PARENT/CHILD. *Khoekhoe*: one basic term, plus specific terms to distinguish relative age. *Central and Northern Khoe Bushmen*: generally, specific terms only. *Western Khoe Bushmen*: one basic term (and synonym), plus specific terms to distinguish relative age.

(2) AVOIDANCE SIBLING. *Khoekhoe*: one basic term (relative age distinguished by suffixes). *Central and Northern Khoe Bushmen*: terms are distinguished only by real sex and/or relative age or seniority. *Western Khoe Bushmen*: one term, or terms distinguished only by relative age.

(3) RESPECT RELATIVE. *Khoekhoe*: one basic term. *Khoe Bushmen*: no specific RESPECT RELATIVE category.

(4) AVOIDANCE IN-LAW. *Khoekhoe*: one basic term. *Khoe Bushmen*: one term.

---

normally used with egocentric relationship terms. For simplicity, however, these suffixes have been omitted in Table 16.2. Also omitted are non-indigenous terms, specifically those derived from Dutch or Afrikaans, which are found in Khoekhoe dialects (Barnard 1980d). My Nama-language example is based on usage consistent with Hoernlé's (1925) account; Damara and probably Hai//om usage is slightly different (see Chapter 11).

As the tables show, there is a remarkable similarity among the systems. There are a great many cognate terms, and, with few exceptions, these occur in the same categories. The exceptions are *ao* or *au* (primary meanings: 'man', 'husband' in Khoekhoe; 'my father' in Western Khoe Bushman); *ba*, *baba* or *papa* (variously either a senior male GRANDRELATIVE term or a PARENT/CHILD term); and *ma* or *mama* (either a GRANDRELATIVE term or a senior female PARENT/CHILD term). Within the categories, terms almost invariably have the same meaning with reference to generation, relative age, and sex.

There is a general rule that same-sex sibling, spouse, and same-sex namesake links retain higher level category, and that parent/child, opposite-sex sibling, and opposite-sex namesake links change higher level category. For example, if a man is my AVOIDANCE relative, then his wife is also my AVOIDANCE relative, and his parents are my JOKING relatives. This rule holds true for most relationships – the most notable exceptions being in the classification of cross-cousins, and in the Khoekhoe case, FZ and BC(ws).

Some differences among the systems

Three differences between the egocentric terminologies are apparent. Two of these distinguish Central (and probably Northern) from Western Khoe Bushman systems: first, there is the categorical distinction in the Central Khoe Bushman systems between JOKING consanguines and JOKING affines; and secondly, there are the separate junior and senior relationship terms within the Central Khoe Bushman categories GRANDRELATIVE and PARENT/CHILD, and separate male and female terms within the senior GRANDRELATIVE category. These differences do not affect JOKING and AVOIDANCE categorization. The third difference does. This is the existence of the special category RESPECT RELATIVE in the Khoekhoe systems.

The first difference stems from the Central Khoe Bushman custom of referring to all in-laws, whether JOKING or AVOIDANCE, as /*ui* or /*wi*. This is of purely linguistic but not of sociological significance (Barnard 1987: 202–3).

The second difference is a more complicated matter. Relative age and generation are sociologically significant among the Khoe-speakers, even among those peoples whose relationship terminologies do not distinguish between senior and junior referents. For example, a man does not behave in the same way towards his elderly grandmother as he does towards his marriageable cross-cousin, though both may be called by the same term. GRANDRELATIVE terminology is summarized schematically in Table 16.4. Senior relatives are defined as those in generations above ego's (e.g., grandparents, cross-uncles or cross-aunts), equal relatives are those in ego's own generation (e.g., cross-cousins), and junior relatives are those in generations below ego's (e.g., grandchildren, cross-nephews or cross-nieces).

The Western Khoe Bushmen use one term for all individuals in the GRANDRELATIVE category, the Central Khoe Bushmen use three, and the

Table 16.4 *Khoe egocentric GRANDRELATIVE terminologies*

	Khoekhoe	Central and Northern Khoe Bushman	Western Khoe Bushman
senior	//nao	baba (m.), mama (f.)	tsxõ
equal	//nuri	n//odi	tsxõ
junior	//nuri	n//odi	tsxõ

Khoekhoe use two. Terms may be said to be 'structurally identical' when relationships traced through one are always the same as relationships traced through the other; they may be said to be 'structurally significant' when this is not the case. Central Khoe Bushman *baba* and *mama* are structurally identical since the difference between them is only one of real sex, which is not structurally significant. Relationships traced through a *baba* are equivalent to relationships traced through a *mama*. Thus the real distinction here is between two, and not three, structural types: the Western Khoe Bushman type, with one structurally significant term, and the Khoekhoe and non-Western Khoe Bushman type, with two structurally significant terms (see Barnard 1987: 203–4).

The third difference is the presence of a specific RESPECT RELATIVE category among the Khoekhoe. This category is peculiar because its primary genealogical referent, FZ, is placed in the 'wrong' higher level category. In other systems she is a GRANDRELATIVE and therefore a JOKING partner. The general rule that an opposite-sex sibling link changes higher level category is superseded by a special rule which is dependent upon the patrilineal descent system of the Khoekhoe. The former is an element of the underlying structure of all Khoe systems, and the latter is a surface-structural feature attributable to the role of the FZ in Khoekhoe society. Ego's FZ, rather than being distinguished from ego's F because of her AVOIDANCE relationship to him, is herself classified as AVOIDANCE because of her role as ego's senior female agnate. She is like a 'female father'. In fact, *tàra-(s)* may sometimes be glossed, man speaking, 'any female AVOIDANCE partner of my patrilineal localized group' (see Engelbrecht 1936: 127, 130–1). Among the Central Khoe Bushmen, the Western Khoe Bushmen, and the many modern Nama groups who today lack patrilineal kin groups, there is no equivalent of this term or the lower level category it designates. The FZ's special categorization is dependent upon her role within ego's patrilineal kin group, and where such kin groups do not exist, her role is transformed to that of a sort of 'female mother's brother' and her category to that of GRANDRELATIVE.

A man's *tàras*, his Z or FBD, is responsible for keeping discipline in the household, among her brothers and ultimately her brothers' sons:

A sister was a *tàras*, that is, a person to be respected, not to be spoken to or of lightly. In the old days an oath by a sister was one of the greatest oaths a man could take, and a sister could generally be relied on to stop any fight in which her brother was taking part . . . The eldest sister of a man is his *Gei Tàras*, his great respected one. (Hoernlé 1925: 22)

The term *tàra* always implies respect and very often implies authority. In some Korana tribes, a man's *tàras* was responsible for bestowing him in marriage (Engelbrecht 1936: 130–1). Among the Nama the term *tàras* was traditionally applied, at least by men, to their FZs, their Zs, and presumably also their parallel cousins, who were all classificatory 'sisters' (see Hoernlé 1925: 21–2). The FZs and 'sisters' alike reciprocated with the same term but with the diminutive suffix *-oa* ('child') added. Hoernlé (1925: 19) lists the term for FZH as '*Tatab*' (modern orthography: *dadab*), which is also a word for 'father'. She also lists an archaic term for FZ, namely '*Éis Geis*' (modern orthography: *ais kais*), literally 'great mother' (1925: 19). In its most general sense, *tàra* seems to mean 'AVOIDANCE partner', a sense which in fact it retains today with the dissolution of the Nama clans and the resulting transformation of relationships of the RESPECT RELATIVE category earlier this century. In Hoenlé's two examples, it overlaps categories AVOIDANCE SIBLING and PARENT/CHILD.

A short, conjectural history of Khoe kinship

The following account traces the likely history of the kinship systems of the Khoe-speaking peoples, as implied in the terminological usages described above. A much fuller treatment of the topic is found in my paper 'Kinship, language and production' (Barnard 1988a: 39–44).

From Early Khoe Bushman to Khoekhoe

No matter what the precise historical transformation from Early Khoe to Khoe Bushman and Khoekhoe, we can posit a structural transformation from Khoekhoe to Central Khoe Bushman, or from Central Khoe Bushman to Khoekhoe. For reasons which will shortly become apparent, the Central Khoe Bushman system will be taken as the model for Early Khoe Bushman kinship. Just as a herding economy is statistically associated, cross-culturally, with patrilineality, an economy dependent upon scarce resources is associated with bilaterality and very small localized groups. With the migration of Early Khoe Bushmen to the eastern or central

Kalahari (see Chapter 2), environmental conditions necessitated small, bilateral band organization.

It is reasonable to imagine that in a cognatic Khoe society the role of the FZ would be in jeopardy. The other members of the RESPECT RELATIVE (*tàra*) category are members of additional AVOIDANCE categories as well. Only the FZ and BC(ws) are categorized uniquely as RESPECT RELATIVES. The answer to the dilemma of a 'female father' in a formerly patrilineal society, turned bilateral, is obvious. She no longer controls her brother's and her brother's son's affairs and she becomes a 'female mother's brother'. The general rule of higher level categorization, that an AVOIDANCE partner's AVOIDANCE partner is JOKING, would dictate that she become her BC's JOKING partner. In any Khoe system there is only one JOKING category to which a consanguine of a generation other than one's own can belong, and that is category GRANDRELATIVE. Just as a Khoekhoe MB is a 'grandfather' (*//naob*), so a Khoe Bushman FZ should become a 'grandmother' or 'female mother's brother' (*//naos*). FZ should be transformed from the category of extreme respect to that of familiarity.

The RESPECT RELATIVE to GRANDRELATIVE transformation has occurred in exactly the expected manner among several Nama groups who no longer live in patrilineal clan villages. The terms I have found among Gai /Khauan and /Hai /Khauan are as follows: F and FB are termed *//gub, saob*, etc. (depending on sociolinguistic factors), while MB is termed *//naob*; similarly, M and MZ are termed *//gus, saos*, etc., while FZ is termed *//naos*. Many Nama also speak Afrikaans today, and their Afrikaans terms parallel the Nama ones, i.e., F and FB are termed *pa*, while MB is *oom*; M and MZ are termed *ma*, while FZ is *tannie*. What is interesting about this system is that it is structurally identical to that of the Central Khoe Bushmen. The G//ana terms, for example, are: *ki-ba-g//o-ma* (F and FB), *ki-bab-ma* (MB), *ki-ma-g//o-sa* (M and MZ), and *ki-mama-sa* (FZ). The transformation which has taken place in the modern Nama system is illustrative of the same process which may have taken place among the Early Khoe Bushmen. Alternatively, it represents the inverse of the historical transformation which created those elements of Khoekhoe categorization which are not found in the Khoe Bushman systems.

Accompanying these changes among the Early Khoe Bushmen, there would also have been a modification of the role of the MB. The Khoekhoe institution known as ≠*na-*≠*nab*, *//nuri//as*, or *//nuri//ab* (joking exchange) is particularly asymmetrical. It involves not only obligatory cattle snatching on the part of the ZS, but also exchange of the MB's good beasts, or indeed other possessions, for the ZS's poor ones. The practice has been well documented by Hoernlé (1925: 22–3) for the Nama, and by Engelbrecht (1936: 127–8, 154–7) for the Korana. In his lecture, ' The mother's brother in South Africa', Radcliffe-Brown (1924) noted that this form of behaviour seemed to accompany both its antithesis, the extreme avoidance FZ/MB role, and the institution of patrilineal descent. The Khoe material upholds his hypothesis rather better than the more famous Tsonga (BaThonga) case, to which Radcliffe-Brown gave more attention.

From Early Khoe Bushman to Western Khoe Bushman

We may assume that the Early Khoe system was probably like that of Central Khoe Bushmen rather than the Western Khoe Bushmen, where these differ, because of the likely diffusion of name relationships from the !Kung to the Western Khoe Bushmen. This naming system, in turn, has allowed the transformation of Khoe egocentric terminology to its logical extreme, nearly complete reciprocity in the use of egocentric kinship terms. Senior, equal, and junior GRANDRELATIVES, for example, may all be called by the same term (*tsxõ* or *mama*).

The evidence that the Western Khoe Bushmen borrowed the !Kung naming system may best be expressed through several independent lines of reasoning. First, the system occurs throughout !Kung territory; yet, of all the Khoe Bushman peoples, only those few whose land borders on !Kung territory use the system. These latter constitute the Western Khoe Bushmen.

Secondly, various !Kung-speaking peoples use different sets of names. Names common in one area may be unknown in other areas (E.N. Wilmsen, pers. comm.). Among the Western Khoe Bushmen, the inventory of names appears to be much the same from one area to another. There is a much greater correlation between the sets of names used by the ≠Au//eisi and the Nharo (29.9 per cent), than between the sets of names used by the ≠Au//eisi and their next-nearest fellow !Kung, the Zu/'hoãsi of CaeCae (17.0 per cent) (Barnard 1976a: 160).

Thirdly, although the meaning of most names is not known either among the ≠Au//eisi or among the Nharo, it is my impression that names can be identified as ≠Au//ei words more often than they can be identified as Nharo words. The fact that few names can be glossed in either language would seem to testify to the antiquity of the system, or to the possibility that the system may have come from some third and unknown language. Since the naming system occurs among all the !Kung but not among all Khoe Bushmen, its occurrence in the Early Khoe Bushman system would seem highly unlikely.

Fourthly, there is both biological and linguistic evidence to suggest a long period of contact between !Kung and Nharo. The Nharo show greater genotypic similarity to the four !Kung groups tested by Harpending and Jenkins (1973: 195, 197) than to the Nama. The Nharo are, with respect to some factors, not genetically distinguishable from the !Kung groups. The evidence of linguistic contact is the high percentage of vocabulary shared between the Zu/'hoã and Nharo languages, 11.5 per cent in a lexicostatistical comparison by Lee (1965: 24; cf. Westphal 1971: 387–8). A superficial comparison between Snyman's *Žu/'hõasi woordeboek* (1975) and my *Nharo wordlist* (Barnard 1985) leads me to belive it could even be much higher in some lexical fields, though it is possible that much of this vocabulary is common Khoisan and therefore not necessarily the result of borrowing.

Lastly, I suspect that the Western Khoe Bushman relationship term stems *tsxõ* and *mama* are not of Khoe origin, but borrowed from !Kung. In Central Khoe Bushman dialects, as in Khoekhoe, the stem *n//odi* (Nama *//nuri*) names category GRANDRELATIVE in reciprocal usage. *Tsxõ*, presumably from either !Kung *tsu* (an AVOIDANCE term) or the !Kung stem *txũ* (a JOKING term), is not used in any Khoe dialects other than the Western ones, and *mama* carries this meaning only in Western Khoe Bushman dialects. This category, of course, is the one through which Western Khoe Bushman personal names are transmitted. In !Kung, *tsu* may also be affixed to relationship terms to express step-kin relationship (Marshall 1957a: 15) or genealogical distance (E.N. Wilmsen, pers. comm.). Dorothea Bleek (1924: 64) recorded *tsu*, *txuŋ*, and *txũ*, sometimes in compound forms, among the words for FF, MF, FB, MB, ZS, SS, DS, and even FM. Bleek (1924: 64) recorded *mama* as the !Kung vocative term for 'grandparent'; and in Nharo too, the term is most commonly employed in the vocative (*mama-e*). According to Marshall,

Mama is a word, heard often, which is not strictly a kinship term. It is applied m.s. and w.s. to any male or female when people wish to express pleasure, gratitude, or affection and it includes an element of respect. It is applied so frequently to grandparents that it becomes almost an alternative to the terms. (Marshall 1957a: 15).

Summary

The differences in kin categorization which exist among the Khoe kinship systems probably result directly from changes in descent and naming rules which occurred after the dispersal of the Khoe-speaking peoples. Probably at least some branches of the Early Khoe, like the Khoekhoe, were patrilineal, herding groups. With the dissolution of patrilineal organization, the RESPECT RELATIVE category is abandoned as well, and the role of the FZ changes to that of a 'female mother's brother'. Centuries ago, the Western Khoe Bushmen came into contact with the !Kung and acquired from them their system of naming people after their grandparents or other joking relatives and extending kin categorization universally throughout society by means of namesake equivalence. The acquisition of the naming system also made possible, and even likely, the use of reciprocal relationship term stems in egocentric terms for both senior and junior members of each of the Khoe kin categories. Western Khoe Bushman relationship terms, except those for siblings, thus came to be self-reciprocal.

17

Conclusions

Overview

Throughout this book I have tried to convey some idea of the historical and structural linkages between Khoisan cultures. I have also tried to cover a wide range of ethnographic and related literature on the Khoisan peoples. Still, much has been left aside, in particular much material dealing with rural development, plant and animal ecology, nutrition, and so on. These topics have direct relevance to the lives of Khoisan individuals today, if not so much to the comparative study of Khoisan culture.

There was a time when 'social organization' meant mainly kinship, with a dash of politics and economics, and a word or two about religion. In spite of appearances, this is not my own view of that concept in the abstract. Nevertheless, my interest in kinship has in some respects given special prominence to this aspect of society in the present work. Beyond that, the comparison of kinship systems gives a clearer picture of cultural structures than does any other area of anthropological enquiry. The mechanisms for clarifying relatives reflect both the linguistic origins and the social environments of the peoples who possess them. They highlight both the historical connections between cultures and the common structures which underlie them.

The preceding five chapters are, in a sense, themselves 'conclusions' to the ethnographic summaries which make up Chapters 3 to 11. The remainder of this concluding chapter will therefore concern some of the methodological and theoretical issues which have emerged, sometimes implicitly, in earlier discussions. These are grouped into three broad areas. The first section below deals with the disparate character of Khoisan ethnography. The second section concerns the apparent tension between historical and structural approaches. The third concerns the nature of structural comparison.

Ethnography and ethnographers

The number of researchers who have done work on Khoisan peoples is enormous. Research has grown phenomenally in recent decades, especially on the Bushmen, or Basarwa, of Botswana (Hitchcock 1986: 388–95). The Marshall Expeditions (Peabody–Harvard Smithsonian Kalahari Expeditions), including associated personnel involved with recent projects, comprise no fewer than 23 research workers. The Harvard Kalahari Research Project includes 14 (see also Lee 1979a). The Smithsonian Institution–George Washington University Archaeological and Ethnoarchaeological Research Project includes 11. The Kalahari Research Committee of the University of the Witwatersrand has incorporated 20 members of staff from that institution and elsewhere. The University of New Mexico Kalahari Project has had 23 affiliated personnel. The Botswana Government Remote Area Development Programme has employed no fewer than 53 consultants, advisers, and officials with a direct knowledge of Basarwa affairs; and many more fieldworkers have been involved in related studies, either as individuals or through other agencies. A great number of others from Tokyo, Kyoto, Austin, Toronto, London, Munich, Bonn, Bayreuth, and elsewhere have made their mark too.

There is a real sense in which specific Bushman groups have been 'colonized' by the major universities of the world. This has implications both for the development of Bushmanist schools of thought in academic circles and for the further absorption of Bushman peoples into world culture. Yet none of this is new. A reflection on the writings of the turn of the century shows a similar picture. The problems I have had in sifting through the data of recent writers are probably not much different from those which bedevilled I. Schapera more than sixty years ago, when he compiled the first comparative ethnography of the Khoisan peoples (Schapera 1930). In many respects, the earlier material is easier to handle today than the new, because it has a timeless character. I do not mean that it represents a true point in time when the 'traditional' culture really existed, but rather that it has come to us as a finite source. The ethnography of today is rapidly changing our pictures of Khoisan society, but Khoisan society itself was affected as much by the 1904 War as by the recent colonial and civil wars in Angola and Namibia. In our attempts to understand social and ecological change we should not overlook that cultural continuity which implicitly defines change itself.

I do not set that much store by the argument that says that ethnographers inflict their individual personalities upon the data, still less by that which says that the people inflict their culture on the ethnographer's psyche in some mystical way. However, the diversity of ethnographic material deserves comment. Lorna Marshall (1976), Richard Lee (1979b), and Edwin N. Wilmsen (1989a) all have different views of !Kung society, not in points of detail, but in their fundamental understandings of what the !Kung think and do, and how they relate to the outside world. These different views are largely independent of the changes in !Kung society, and reflect varied conceptions of the very idea of culture.

We can isolate a number of factors which divide Khoisan ethnographers. These include: *occupational background* (e.g., army officer, missionary, farmer, student), *occupational level* (postgraduate student, senior academic), *academic discipline* (anthropology, zoology, linguistics), *school of anthropology* (*Kulturkreislehre*, British social anthropology, ecological anthropology), *theoretical premises* (functionalist, structuralist, Marxist), *broad theoretical interests* (human evolution, cultural ecology, social organization, belief systems), and *specific interests* (nutrition, settlement patterns, family life, folklore). That would be my basic list, though any social scientist can no doubt think of more factors, and many more examples within each of these. The fact that so many different kinds of writers have commented on the Khoisan peoples has enriched the ethnographic record, and made its understanding more complex, and more interesting, than if this had not been the case. The richness of Khoisan ethnography owes almost as much to the diversity of ethnographers as to that of the Khoisan peoples whom they have studied.

History, structure, and agency

In his recent book, Edwin N. Wilmsen (1989a) examines the historical and continuing contact between the Zu/'hoãsi and outsiders. He challenges the classic view of Bushman society which places the emphasis on the Bushmen's abstract 'antiquity' at the expense of their history (cf. Guenther 1980; Barnard 1989a). The historical school of Wilmsen and others (cf. Schrire 1980; 1984; Gordon 1984; 1989; Denbow 1984) portrays a more accurate description of the place of Bushman groups in the southern African economic system as a whole. Yet it does this by focusing on those aspects of culture which are most susceptible to outside influences – those related to production and trade. These are among the least 'structural' of cultural elements. Although they are of great importance, they lie at the opposite end of the spectrum from those which give Bushmen, and other Khoisan peoples, their cultural identities. Wilmsen's approach grants the Bushmen history, but it minimizes the uniqueness and resilience of their cultures. All sides in the on-going 'Bushman debate' (see also Solway and Lee 1990; Wilmsen and Denbow 1990) are addressing relations between Khoisan groups and outsiders, not the understanding of Khoisan, or even Bushman, culture as a real entity.

I am interested not only in relations between people, but also in relations between cultural elements as objects in themselves. These objects may collectively provide a framework for Khoisan society as a whole. They may constrain, but they also permit action. They are manipulated by actors, but they also define the limits of behaviour and thought. As a 'structuralist' in the broadest sense, I see culture as a configuration whose interrelationships are as important as its elements. The object of my interest here, then, is the way in which culture unfolds, or more mundanely, is moulded by social action – both internal and external. The purpose of action to the actor may or may not be identical with the resultant form. Culture is not so much *sui generis*, in the sense of Lowie (1966 [1917]) or Kroeber (1952), as self-regulating. This does not mean that it is not affected by nature or by cultures outside. On the contrary, it means that through outside pressures, as well as through internal historical change, it changes and develops within a larger system. This larger system can just as easily be ideological as economic. Seen in this way, changes in Nama kinship, for example, involve transformations of Khoisan kinship structures rather than their replacement by European ones (Barnard 1980d).

It is my contention that Khoisan culture, and culture in general, is a resilient, hierarchical structure of structures, which can and should be analysed in its own right. The emphasis in much recent work has been on production and trade. Carstens (1983) has shown that changes in production have resulted in diverse emphases in ideology. In his example, the significance of Haitsi-aibib among the Nama increased as a result of culture contact. Yet what is fundamental is the relationship between Haitsi-aibib and Tsûi-//goab in the first place. To explain change, we need to understand the basic structure of belief. My view of social and cosmological structure reverses the Marxist and Stewardian (e.g., Steward 1955: 37, 88–9, 93–4; Friedman 1974) emphases on 'base' (Steward's 'culture core') over 'superstructure' and gives primacy to the latter. I prefer to see 'superstructure' as a *deep* cultural structure. Production and exchange relations do not create the deep structure. Rather, this structure is played upon and altered by historical changes in the modes of production of specific population groups.

The problem of comparison

Ethnographic comparison and the biographical fallacy

The 'comparative method' is still a living force in anthropology, though perhaps not in the same sense as envisaged twenty or thirty years ago (cf. Holy 1987). As a methodological tool, regional comparison has been on the increase in the last few decades, and a variety of specific perspectives can be accommodated within this approach (see, e.g., Damas 1968; 1975; Davis 1977; Scheffler 1978; Kuper 1980). Yet there are other schools of thought which challenge regional comparison as a theoretical perspective, largely in implicit ways.

One work which offers a provocative challenge to the theoretical viewpoint expressed here is Alan Campbell's *To square with Genesis* (1989). One chapter is of special interest. With his own Wayãpí of Brazil watching from the sidelines, Campbell (1989: 142–63) there provides a technical discussion of the distinctions between the kinship systems of the Cuiva of Colombia and the Kariera of Western Australia. His comparisons are lucid and imaginative, though confusingly he labels both these systems 'Dravidian' in reference to their common, yet unspecified, 'bundle of relational principles'. As in Lévi-Strauss' (1969 [1949]) classification of kinship systems, the distinction between the 'Cuiva' and 'Kariera' subtypes seems to be made on logical rather than strictly ethnographic grounds. Indeed Campbell suggests that the Cuiva structure (which reverses the well-known alternate-generation equivalences of the Kariera one) should have been predictable as a possibility, even before it was discovered by an ethnographer (cf. Arcand 1977: 33; Allen 1982; 1986). I agree with him, but he is right for the wrong reasons.

The fact that the Cuiva beat 'us' to the discovery of 'their' system suggests to me that there might really be underlying principles, out there, to be discovered by disinterested scientists. The fact that the far-away theorist's idea of a 'two-line prescription' is inapplicable to some South American systems is no reason to abandon the idea for those systems to which it does apply. For that matter, one could well argue that the Cuiva *do* have 'two-line prescription', if we allow that their lines are not patrilines, but cross-descent lines like the exogamous great names of the Khoekhoe, Damara, and Hai//om. The failure here is that the theorists simply have not had a wide enough range of imaginary building blocks with which to construct their systems.

Equally, one could argue, as Radcliffe-Brown (e.g., 1913; 1930–1) and Lévi-Strauss (e.g., 1969 [1949]: 146–220) did, that there really *are* underlying matrimoieties embedded in Kariera kinship structure. The Kariera themselves did not recognize them at the time they were studied in the early twentieth century, because they no longer needed to. They had already acquired the four named sections which took their place. As comparisons to other Australian systems suggest, sections were most likely generated long ago by cross-cutting unilineal divisions like those inadvertently illustrated in the classic anthropological diagrams (Testart 1978). Conjectural history aside, one might still distinguish layers of structural relationship, some of which are perceived by the actors and others of which are not. Taking this view, Aram Yengoyan (1978: 147–51) argues for a system which entails three sets of categories: *conscious categories*, *actual categories* (including conscious categories and unconscious, cultural categories as well), and *potential categories* (including actual categories and others not culturally realized). Yengoyan's approach is in essence similar to the one I advocate here, though more formalized. Such an approach is made possible, even essential, through a theoretical stance based on controlled comparison.

Yet the greater fallacy of Alan Campbell's approach (see especially Campbell 1989: 164–5) is his implicit assumption that ethnography is but collective biography. Ironically, his own comparative treatment of formal aspects of the Kariera and Cuiva terminologies is itself evidence against this biographical fallacy. Here he is not alone. Many anthropologists on both sides of the Atlantic seem to have overlooked the classic conception of culture as the superorganic (cf. Kroeber (1952 [1917]: 22–51). It is, of course, nonsense to suggest that we can literally compare one 'people' to another, though this phrase is a convenient one and as such is often heard. We may say we are comparing peoples, but what we really mean is that we are comparing cultures. The confusion arises from an ambiguity of language.

Contradiction, analogy, and the comparative method

Evans-Pritchard is reputed to have said that the comparative method is 'the only method in social anthropology', and further, that it is 'impossible' (see Evans-Pritchard 1965). While perhaps it is not really the only method, certainly it is not impossible. It may be more accurate to say that comparison leads to contradiction. As is well known, in 1931 Kurt Gödel published a proof than any mathematical system sophisticated enough to use arithmetic will either be incomplete or possess contradictions (Gödel 1962 [1931]). By analogy, though one cannot 'prove' it in the same sense, it might be fair to say that any anthropological analysis sophisticated enough to make use of comparison will have contradictions in points of detail and interpretation. Yet that is the least of our worries.

Evans-Pritchard's reputed remark probably intimated his concern with the difficulty over cultural 'translation', the ultimate contradiction of anthropology – that of putting the idiom of one culture into that of another. At a crude level, it is indeed impossible to come up with an exact translation of one culture in terms that another can precisely accommodate. Nor is translation really quite distinguishable from comparison. Translation here is, of course, a metaphor. Though it was not Evans-Pritchard's intention, one could argue that translation is no more than a metaphor for comparison itself. In his work and that of many more recent writers, translation is usually conceived as a point of mediation between 'our' culture and 'theirs'. Implicitly, if we translate, or compare, compare *only* 'them' and 'us', we are bound to see 'them' as but refractions of ourselves. In contrast, broader but controlled comparisons illuminate constellations of cultures and foster understanding by increasing the breadth of vision.

If we conceive of culture not so much as 'speech' or as a 'text' but as a *grammar*, then appropriate correspondences can be found. These correspondences are analogous to the correspondences which make up comparative studies in linguistics, both historical and structural. Nor does it matter what linguists are really up to these days. There is a tendency among some anthropologists who borrow models from linguistics to assume that the model must be up-to-date, or it loses its potency. Roger Keesing's (1972: 299–300, 326; 1979: 14–15) statements about learning from new trends in linguistics are clear examples, though Keesing certainly cannot be accused of any technical failing in employing the models he draws on. This keeping-up-with-the-Joneses fallacy stems from either a failure to recognize that all models are intrinsically heuristic, or, in Keesing's case, an assumption that language and culture are part of the same system. In my view, a model borrowed from linguistics ceases to be a linguistic model and becomes an anthropological one when it is applied to anthropological problems. Its explanatory value for anthropology is not affected by subsequent changes in its status within linguistics. Even Chomsky's well-known criticism of attempts at 'extending concepts of linguistic structure to other cognitive systems' (1968: 66) is similarly misplaced.

The key, for anthropology as much as for linguistics, is to see the system and not merely its elements, and indeed precedents for this lie firmly embedded within anthropology itself. Here, I appeal less to Durkheimian sociology or Lévi-Straussian structuralism, and more to the common-sense views of American anthropology in its golden era. 'Every kinship system is also a little system of classificatory thought, and unconscious peoples sometimes are as ingenious in their logical productions as ethnologists in their analyses' (Kroeber 1936: 339). More succinctly, 'Every culture is a structure . . .' (Kluckhohn 1943: 426).

A cultural system can be posited at almost any level from the universal, as conceived by Lévi-Strauss, to the idiosyncratic, as held by a hermit. Most commonly it is taken to be that of an 'ethnic group' or a 'nation', as these are indigenously defined. Yet my preference, as should be obvious by now, is for a larger unit, beyond the ones understood by most of one's informants. For me, the region, or the culture area, is the cultural system. To change metaphor slightly, that cultural system itself represents a metaphorical 'language' whose 'dialects' are often both mutually intelligible and best understood as products of a common set of rules and a common 'vocabulary' of related customs and institutions. Khoisan culture is such a 'language', and the various Khoisan cultures are its 'dialects'.

References

Alexander, Sir James E. 1967 [1838]. *An exploration of discovery into the interior of Africa.* Cape Town: Struik.

Allen, N.J. 1982. A dance of relatives. *Journal of the Anthropological Society of Oxford* 12(2): 139–46.

    1986. Tetradic theory: an approach to kinship. *Journal of the Anthropological Society of Oxford* 17(2): 97–109.

Almeida, António de. 1965. *Bushmen and other non-Bantu peoples of Angola: three lectures.* Johannesburg: Witwatersrand University Press for the Institute for the Study of Man in Africa.

Andersson, Charles John. 1856. *Lake Ngami; or explorations and discoveries during four years' wanderings in the wilds of south western Africa.* London: Hurst and Blackett.

    1861. *The Okavango river: a narrative of travel, exploration, and adventure.* London: Hurst and Blackett.

Arcand, Bernard. 1977. The logic of kinship, an example from the Cuiva. *Actes du XLIIe congrès international des Américanistes*, vol. 2, pp. 19–34.

Baines, Thomas. 1864. *Explorations in south-west Africa.* London: Longman, Green, Longman, Roberts, and Green.

Barnard, Alan. 1975. Australian models in the South West African highlands. *African Studies* 34: 9–18.

    1976a. Nharo Bushman kinship and the transformation of Khoi kin categories. Ph.D. thesis, University of London.

    1976b. Khoisan classification. *I.A.I. Bulletin* 46(4): 12.

    1978a. Universal systems of kin categorization. *African studies* 37: 69–81

    1978b. The kin terminology system of the Nharo Bushmen. *Cahiers d'études africaines*, Vol. 18(4), No. 72: 607–29, 652.

    1979a. Kalahari Bushman settlement patterns. In Philip Burnham and Roy F. Ellen (eds.), *Social and ecological systems.* London: Academic Press (A.S.A. Monographs 18), pp. 131–44.

    1979b. Nharo Bushman medicine and medicine men. *Africa* 49: 68–80.

    1980a. Kin terminology systems of the Khoe-speaking peoples. In J.W. Snyman (ed.), *Bushman and Hottentot linguistic studies, 1979.* Pretoria: University of South Africa, pp. 107–33.

1980b. Sex roles among the Nharo Bushmen of Botswana. *Africa* 50: 115–24.

1980c. Basarwa settlement patterns in the Ghanzi ranching area. *Botswana Notes and Records* 12: 137–48.

1980d. Convergent structures in Nama and Dutch–Afrikaans kinship terminologies. *V.O.C.* 1(1): 25–34.

1980e. Kinship and social organization in Nharo cosmology. *Deuxième congrès international sur les sociétés de chasseurs-collecteurs/Second International Conference on Hunting and Gathering Societies.* Quebec: Dépt. d'anthropologie, Université Laval, pp. 31–54.

1981. Universal kin categorization in four Bushman societies. *L'Uomo* 5: 219–37.

1983. Contemporary hunter-gatherers: current theoretical issues in ecology and social organization. *Annual Review of Anthropology* 12: 193–214.

1984. *The perception and utilization of morama and other food plants by the Nharo of western Botswana.* Edinburgh: Centre of African Studies, University of Edinburgh (Occasional Paper No. 4).

1985. *A Nharo wordlist, with notes on grammar.* Durban: Department of African Studies, University of Natal (Occasional Publications No. 2).

1986a. Rethinking Bushman settlement patterns and territoriality. *Sprache und Geschichte in Afrika* 7(1): 41–60.

1986b. Some aspects of Nharo ethnobotany. In Rainer Vossen and Klaus Keuthmann (eds.), *Contemporary studies on Khoisan 1.* Hamburg: Helmut Buske Verlag (Quellen zur Khoisan-Forschung 5.1), pp. 55–81.

1987. Khoisan kinship: regional comparison and underlying structures. In Ladislav Holy (ed.), *Comparative anthropology.* Oxford: Blackwell, pp. 189–209.

1988a. Kinship, language and production: a conjectural history of Khoisan social structure. *Africa* 58: 29–50.

1988b. Structure and fluidity in Khoisan religious ideas. *Journal of Religion in Africa* 18: 216–36.

1988c. Cultural identity, ethnicity and marginalization among the Bushmen of southern Africa. In Rainer Vossen (ed.), *New perspectives on Khoisan.* Hamburg: Helmut Buske Verlag (Quellen zur Khoisan-Forschung 7), pp. 9–27.

1989a. The lost world of Laurens van der Post? *Current Anthropology* 30: 104–14.

1989b. Nharo kinship in social and cosmological perspective: comparisons between southern African and Australian hunter-gatherers. *Mankind* 19: 198–214.

1991. Social and spatial boundary maintenance among southern African hunter-gatherers. In Michael J. Casimir and Aparna Rao (eds.), *Mobility and territoriality: social and spatial boundaries among foragers, fishers, pastoralists and peripatetics.* New York: Berg Publishers, pp. 137–51.

Barnard, Alan and Anthony Good. 1984. *Research practices in the study of kinship.* London: Academic Press (A.S.A. Research Methods 2).

Barnes, R.H. 1978. The principle of reciprocal sets. *Man* (n.s.) 13: 475–6.

Baucom, Kenneth L. 1974. Proto-Central Khoisan. In Erhard Voeltz (ed.), *Third Annual Conference on African Linguistics, 7–8 April 1972.* Bloomington: Indiana University (African Series, Vol. 7), pp. 3–37.

Beach, D.M. 1938. *The phonetics of the Hottentot language.* Cambridge: W. Heffer and Sons.

Bicchieri, M.G. 1969. A cultural ecological comparative study of three African foraging societies. In David Damas (ed.), *Contributions to anthropology: band societies*. Ottawa: National Museums of Canada (Bulletin No. 228), pp. 172–96 and chart.

Biesele, Megan. 1971. Hunting in semi-arid areas – the Kalahari Bushmen today. In *Proceedings of the Conference on Sustained Production from Semi-Arid Areas* (Botswana Notes and Records Special Edition No. 1). Gaborone: Botswana Society, pp. 62–7.

    1975. Folklore and ritual of !Kung hunter-gatherers. Ph.D. dissertation, Harvard University.

    1976. Aspects of !Kung folklore. In Richard B. Lee and Irven DeVore (eds.), *Kalahari hunter-gatherers: studies of the !Kung San and their neighbors*. Cambridge, MA: Harvard University Press, pp. 303–24, 402.

    1978. Sapience and scarce resources: communication systems of the !Kung and other foragers. *Informations sur les sciences sociales/Social Science Information* 17(6): 921–47.

Biesele, Megan, with Robert Gordon and Richard Lee (eds.). 1986. *The past and future of !Kung ethnography: critical reflections and symbolic perspectives, essays in honour of Lorna Marshall*. Hamburg: Helmut Buske Verlag (Quellen zur Khoisan-Forschung 4).

Biesele, M. and R.E. Murry, Jr. 1983. *Alternative food plants for arid regions: final project report*. Report to the U.S. National Science Foundation (BNS-8023941).

Bleek, D.F. 1923. *The Mantis and his friends: Bushman folklore*. Cape Town: Maskew Miller.

    1924. Bushman terms of relationship. *Bantu Studies* 2: 57–70.

    1928a. *The Naron: a bushman tribe of the central Kalahari*. Cambridge: Cambridge University Press.

    1928b. Bushmen of Central Angola. *Bantu Studies* 3: 105–25.

    1929a. *Comparative vocabularies of Bushman languages*. Cambridge: Cambridge University Press.

    1929b. Bushman folklore. *Africa* 2: 302–13.

    (ed.). 1931–6. Customs and beliefs of the /Xam Bushmen (from material collected by Dr W.H.I. Bleek and Miss L.C. Lloyd between 1870 and 1880). *Bantu Studies* 5: 167–79 (Part I); 6: 47–63 (Part II); 6: 233–49 (Part III); 6: 323–42 (Part IV); 7: 297–312 (Part V); 7: 375–92 (Part VI); 9: 1–47 (Part VII); 10: 131–62 (Part VIII). (Part I is incorrectly printed as '. . . !Xam Bushmen', and Part VI is entitled 'Beliefs and customs . . .'.)

    (ed.). 1936. Special speech of animals and moon used by the /Xam Bushmen (from material collected by Dr W.H.I. Bleek and Miss L.C. Lloyd between 1870 and 1880). *Bantu Studies* 10: 163–99.

    1937a. Grammatical notes and texts in the /auni language. *Bantu Studies* 11: 253–8.

    1937b. /auni vocabulary. *Bantu Studies* 11: 259–78.

    1942. [Introduction.] In A.M. Duggan-Cronin, *The Bushman tribes of Southern Africa*. Kimberley: The Alexander McGregor Memorial Museum, pp. 1–14.

    1956. *A Bushman dictionary*. New Haven: American Oriental Society (American Oriental Series Vol. 41).

M.S. *I !kuṅ + Naron 1–53*. Unpublished field notebook dated 1920. Located in the Bleek Collection, Archives of the J.W. Jagger Library, University of Cape Town.

Bleek, Guilelmus [W.H.I. Bleek]. 1851. *De nominum generibus linguarum Africae Australis, Copticae, Semiticarum aliarumque sexualium*. Bonn: A. Marcus.

Bleek, W.H.I. 1858. *The library of His Excellency Sir George Grey, KCB. Philology Vol. I. South Africa*. London/Leipzig: Trübner and Co.

   1864. *Reynard the Fox in South Africa, or Hottentot fables and tales*. London: Trübner and Co.

   1869. *A comparative grammar of South African languages, Part II*. London: Trübner.

   1872. The concord, the origin of pronouns and the formation of classes or genders of nouns. *Journal of the Anthropological Institute* 1: lxiv-xc.

   1875. *A brief account of Bushman folklore and other texts*. London: Trübner and Brockhaus.

Bleek, W.H.I. and L.C. Lloyd. 1911. *Specimens of Bushman folklore*. London: George Allen and Co.

Bley, Helmut. 1971 [1968]. *South-West Africa under German rule, 1894–1914* (trans. by Hugh Ridley). London: Heinemann.

Blurton Jones, Nicolas Konner and Melvin J. Konner. 1976. !Kung knowledge of animal behavior (or: The proper study of mankind is animals). In Richard B. Lee and Irven DeVore (eds.), *Kalahari hunter-gatherers: studies of the !Kung San and their neighbors*. Cambridge, MA: Harvard University Press, pp. 325–48, 402.

Boëseken, A.J. 1972–4. The meaning, origin and use of the terms Khoikhoi, San and Khoisan. *Cabo* 1(1) (Aug. 1972): 5–10; 2(2) (Jan. 1974): 8–10.

   1975. On changing terminology in history [reply to Elphick 1974–5]. *Cabo* 2(3) (Nov. 1975): 16–18.

Borland, C.H. 1979. Kinship term grammar: a review. *Anthropos* 74: 326–52.

Brearley, John. 1984. A musical tour of Botswana, 1982. *Botswana Notes and Records* 16: 45–57.

   1988. Music and musicians of the Kalahari. *Botswana Notes and Records* 20: 77–90.

Breuil, (Abbé) Henri. 1955. *The White Lady of the Brandberg*. London: The Trianon Press for the Abbé Breuil Trust.

Bridgman, Jon M. 1981 *The revolt of the Hereros*. Berkeley: University of California Press.

Brownlee, Frank. 1943. The social organization of the !Kung (!Un)) Bushmen of the North-western Kalahari. *Africa* 14: 124–9.

Budack, K.F.R. 1969. Inter-Ethnische Namen in Südwestafrika. In Ethnological Section, Department of Bantu Administration and Development (eds.), *Ethnological and linguistic studies in honour of N.J. van Warmelo*. Pretoria: Government Printer, pp. 211–31.

   1972a. Die traditionelle politische Struktur der Khoekhoen in Südwestafrika (Stamm und Stammersregierung, auf historischer Grundlage). D.Phil thesis, University of Pretoria.

   1972b. Stam en stamkaptein by die Khoe-Khoen in Suidwes-Afrika. In J.F. Eloff and R.D. Coertze (eds.), *Ethnografiese studies in Suidelike Afrika*. Pretoria: J.L. van Schaik, pp. 246–90.

1977. The ≠Aonin or Topnaar of the lower !Kuiseb valley and the sea. In A. Traill (ed.), *Khoisan linguistic studies 3*. Johannesburg: African Studies Institute, University of the Witwatersrand, pp. 1–42.

1983. A harvesting people on the South Atlantic coast. *Ethnologie/Ethnology* (South African journal of ethnology) 6(2): 1–7.

1986. Die Klassifikation der Khwe-khwen (Naman) in Südwestafrika. In Rainer Vossen and Klaus Keuthmann (eds.), *Contemporary studies on Khoisan 1*. Hamburg: Helmut Buske Verlag (Quellen zur Khoisan-Forschung 5.1), pp. 107–43.

Burrow, John. 1801–4. *Travels in the interior of southern Africa in the years 1797 and 1798* (2 vols.). London: Cadell and Davies.

Campbell, A.C. 1976. Traditional utilisation of the Okavango Delta. In *Proceedings of the Symposium on the Okavango Delta and its Future Utilisation*. Gaborone: Botswana Society, pp. 163–73.

Campbell, Alan Tormaid. 1989. *To square with Genesis: causal statements and shamanic ideas in Wayapi*. Edinburgh: Edinburgh University Press.

Campbell, John, 1815. *Travels in South Africa, undertaken at the request of the [London] Missionary Society*. London: Black and Parry.

1822. *Travels in South Africa, undertaken at the request of the London Missionary Society, being a narrative of a second journey in the interior of that country* (2 vols.). London: Westley.

Carstens, W. Peter. 1966. *The social structure of a Cape Coloured reserve*. Cape Town: Oxford University Press.

1969. Some aspects of Khoikhoi (Hottentot) settlement patterns in historical perspective. In David Damas (ed.), *Contributions to anthropology: ecological essays*. Ottawa: National Museums of Canada (Bulletin No. 230), pp. 95–101.

1975. Some implications of change in Khoikhoi supernatural beliefs. In Michael G. Whisson and Martin West (eds.), *Religion and social change in Southern Africa: Anthropological essays in honour of Monica Wilson*. Cape Town: David Phillips, pp. 78–98.

1982. The socio-economic context of initiation ceremonies among two Southern African peoples. *Revue canadienne des études africanes/Canadian Journal of African Studies* 16: 505–22.

1983a. The inheritance of private property among the Nama of southern Africa reconsidered. *Africa* 53: 58–70.

1983b. Opting out of colonial rule: the brown voortrekkers of South Africa and their constitutions. *African Studies* 42: 135–52.

Cashdan, Elizabeth A. 1977. Subsistence, mobility, and territorial organization among the //Ganakwe of the northeastern Central Kalahari Game Reserve, Botswana. Unpublished report to the Botswana government.

1979. Trade and reciprocity among the River Bushmen of northern Botswana. Ph.D. dissertation, University of New Mexico.

1980a. Property and social insurance among the //Gana. *Deuxième congrès international sur les sociétés chasseurs-cuelliers/Second International*

Conference on Hunting and Gathering Societies. Quebec: Dépt. d'anthropologie, Université Laval, pp. 717–34.

1980b. Egalitarianism among hunters and gatherers. *American Anthropologist* 82: 116–20.

1983. Territoriality among human foragers: ecological models and an application to four Bushman groups. *Current Anthropology* 24: 47–66.

1984a. G//ana territorial organization. *Human Ecology* 12: 443–63.

1984b. The effects of food production on mobility in the central Kalahari. In J. Desmond Clark and Stephen A. Brandt (eds.), *From hunters to farmers: the causes and consequences of food production in Africa*. Berkeley: University of California Press, pp. 311–27.

1985. Coping with risk: reciprocity among the Basarwa of Northern Botswana. *Man* (n.s.) 20: 454–74.

1986a. Hunter-gatherers of the northern Kalahari. In Rainer Vossen and Klaus Keuthmann (eds.), *Contemporary studies on Khoisan 1*. Hamburg: Helmut Buske Verlag (Quellen zur Khoisan-Forschung, 5.1), pp. 145–80.

1986b. Competition between foragers and food producers on the Botletli River, Botswana. *Africa* 56: 299–318.

1987. Trade and its origins on the Botletli River, Botswana. *Journal of Anthropological Research* 43: 121–38.

Cashdan, Elizabeth A. and William J. Chasko, Jr. 1976. *Report on the Bakgalagadi settlements of Molapo and /o ≠ we in the Central Reserve*. Gaborone: Ministry of Local Government and Lands.

1977. People of the middle and upper Nata River area: origins, population, economics and health. Unpublished report to the Botswana government.

Chapman, James. 1968. *Travels in the interior of South Africa* (2 vols). London: Bell and Daldy.

Chasko, W.J., Jr., G.T. Nurse, H.C. Harpending, and T. Jenkins. 1979. Serogenetic studies on the 'Masarwa' of northeastern Botswana. *Botswana Notes and Records* 11: 15–23.

Childers, Gary W. 1976. *Report on the survey/investigation of the Ghanzi farm Basarwa situation*. Gaborone: Government Printer.

Chomsky, Noam. 1965. *Aspects of a theory of syntax*. Cambridge, MA: M.I.T. Press.

1968. *Language and mind*. New York: Harcourt, Brace and World.

Clark, J.D. 1959. *The prehistory of Southern Africa*. Harmondsworth: Penguin.

Cooke, C.K. 1965. Evidence of human migrations from rock art of Southern Rhodesia. *Africa* 35: 236–85.

Correia, J.A. 1925. Une étude de l'ethnographie d'Angola. *Anthropos* 10: 321–31.

Cowley, Clive. 1968. *Fabled tribe: a journey to discover the River Bushmen of the Okavango swamps*. London: Longmans (Longman, Green, and Co.).

Damas, David, 1968. The diversity of Eskimo societies. In Richard B. Lee and Irven DeVore (eds.), *Man the hunter*. Chicago: Aldine, pp. 111–16.

1975. Three kinship systems from the central Arctic. *Arctic Anthropology* 12(1): 10–30.

Dapper, Olfert. 1933 [1668]. Kaffrarie, of lant der Hottentots (Kaffraria, or land of the Hottentots), with translation by I. Schapera. In I. Schapera (ed.), *The early*

Cape Hottentots. Cape Town: The Van Riebeeck Society (Vol. 14), pp. 6–77.

Dart, Raymond A. 1937a. The hut distribution, genealogy and homogeneity of the /*?auni*-≠*khomani* Bushmen. *Bantu Studies* 11: 159–74.

1937b, The physical characters of the /*?auni*-≠*khomani* Bushmen. *Bantu Studies* 11: 175–246.

Davis, J. 1977. *People of the Mediterranean: an essay in comparative social anthropology.* London: Routledge and Kegan Paul.

Deacon, H.J. 1976. *Where hunters gathered: a study of Holocene Stone Age people in the eastern Cape.* Claremont: South African Archaeological Society (Monograph Series 1).

Deacon, Janette. 1982. *The Later Stone Age of southernmost Africa.* Oxford: British Archaeological Reports (International Series 213).

Denbow, James R. 1984. Prehistoric herders and foragers of the Kalahari: the evidence of 1500 years of interaction. In Carmel Schrire (ed.), *Past and present in hunter-gatherer studies.* Orlando: Academic Press, pp. 175–93.

Denbow, James and Alec Campbell. 1986. The early stages of food production in southern Africa and some potential linguistic correlations. *Sprache und Geschichte in Afrika* 7.1: 83–103.

Denbow, James R. and Edwin N. Wilmsen. 1983. Iron Age pastoralist settlements in Botswana. *South African Journal of Science* 79: 405–8.

Dickens, Patrick. 1977. Source and goal in !xõ. In J.W. Snyman (ed.), *Bushman and Hottentot linguistic studies, 1975.* Pretoria: University of South Africa, pp. 74–81.

Dickens, Patrick and A. Traill. 1977. Collective and distributive in !Xõo. In A. Traill (ed.), *Khoisan linguistic studies 3.* Johannesburg: African Studies Institute, pp. 132–44.

Doke, C.M. 1936. Games, plays and dances of the ≠*khomani* Bushmen. *Bantu Studies* 10: 461–71.

Dornan, S.S. 1917. The Tati Bushmen (Masarwas) and their language. *Journal of the Royal Anthropological Institute* 47: 37–112.

1925. *Pygmies and Bushmen of the Kalahari.* London: Seeley, Service and Co.

Dowson, Thomas A. 1988. Revelations of religious reality: the individual in San rock art. *World Archaeology* 20: 116–28.

Draper, Patricia. 1972. *See* Harpending, Patricia Draper.

1975a. !Kung women: contrasts in sexual egalitarianism in foraging and sedentary contexts. In Rayna P. Reiter (ed.), *Toward an anthropology of women.* New York: Monthly Review Press, pp. 77–109.

1975b. Cultural pressure on sex differences. *American Ethnologist* 2: 602–16.

1978. The learning environment for aggression and antisocial behavior among the !Kung. In Ashley Montagu (ed.), *Learning non-aggression: the experience of non-literate societies.* Oxford: Oxford University Press, pp. 31–53.

Draper, Patricia and Elizabeth Cashdan. 1988. Technological change and child behaviour among the !Kung. *Ethnology* 27: 339–65.

Eggan, Fred. 1950. *Social organization of the western Pueblos.* Chicago: University of Chicago Press.

1954. Social anthropology and the method of controlled comparison. *American Anthropologist* 56: 743–60.

(ed.). 1955 [1937]. *Social anthropology of North American tribes* (enlarged edition). Chicago: University of Chicago Press.

Ehret, Christopher. 1967. Cattle-keeping and milking in eastern and southern African history: the linguistic evidence. *Journal of African History* 8: 1–17.

1982. The first spread of food production to Southern Africa. In Christopher Ehret and Merrick Posnansky (eds.), *The archaeological and linguistic reconstruction of African history*. Berkeley: University of California Press, pp. 158–81.

Eibl-Eibesfeldt, Irenäus. 1972. *Die !Ko-Buschmanngesellschaft: Aggressionskontrolle und Gruppenbindung*. Munich: Piper.

1974a. The myth of the aggression-free hunter and gatherer society. In Ralph L. Holloway (ed.), *Primate aggression, territoriality and xenophobia*. New York: Academic Press, pp. 435–57.

1974b. !Ko-Buschleute (Kalahari) – Trancetanz. *Homo* 24: 245–52.

1975. Aggression in !Ko-Bushmen. In R.T. Williams (ed.), *Psychological anthropology*. The Hague: Mouton, pp. 317–31.

1980. G/wi Buschleute (Kalahari) – Krankenheilung und Trance. *Homo* 31: 67–78.

Ellenberger, Victor. 1953. *La Fin tragique des Bushmen, les derniers hommes vivants de l'âge de la pierre*. Paris: Amiot Dumont.

Elob Mîs [The Word of God]. 1966. Cape Town: The Bible Society of South Africa.

Elphick, Richard. 1974–5. The meaning, origin and use of the terms Khoikhoi, San and Khoisan [reply to Boeseken 1972–4]. *Cabo* 2 (2) (Jan. 1974): 3–7; 2(3) (Nov. 1975): 12–15.

1977. *Kraal and castle: Khoikhoi and the founding of White South Africa*. New Haven and London: Yale University Press.

1979. The Khoisan to *c*. 1770. In Richard Elphick and Hermann Giliomee (eds.), *The shaping of South African society, 1652–1820*. Cape Town and London: Longman, pp. 3–40.

1985. *Khoikhoi and the founding of White South Africa* (revised edition of Elphick 1977). Johannesburg: Ravan Press.

Ember, Melvin and Carol R. Ember. 1983. *Marriage, family, and kinship: Comparative studies of social organization*. New Haven: HRAF Press.

Engelbrecht, J.A. 1936. *The Korana: an account of their customs and their history, with texts*. Cape Town: Maskew Miller.

England, Nicholas M. 1968. Music among the zũ'/'wã-si of South West Africa and Botswana. Ph.D. dissertation, Harvard University.

Epstein, H. (revised in collaboration with I.L. Mason). 1971. *The origin of the domesticated animals of Africa* (2 vols.). New York: Africana Publishing Corp.

Estermann, Carlos, 1946–9. Quelques observations sur les Bochimans !kung de l'Angola méridionale. *Anthropos* 41–4(4–6): 711–22.

1956. *Etnográfia do sudoeste de Angola, Volume I: Os povos Não-Bantos e o grupo étnico dos Ambós*. Oporto: Junta de Investigações do Ultramare (Vol. IV).

1976 [1956]. *The ethnography of southwestern Angola, Volume I: The non-Bantu peoples; the Ambo ethnic group* (edited by Gordon D. Gibson). New York: Africana Publishing Company.

Evans-Pritchard, E.E. 1956. *Nuer religion*. Oxford: Clarendon Press.

1965. The comparative method in social anthropology. In *The position of women in primitive societies and other essays in social anthropology*. London: Faber and Faber, pp. 13–36.

Fabian, Johannes. 1965. !Kung Bushman kinship: componential analysis and alternative interpretations. *Anthropos* 60: 663–718.

First, Ruth. 1963. *South West Africa*. Harmondsworth: Penguin Books.

Fisher, Eugen, 1913. *Die Rehobother Bastards und des Barstardierungsproblem beim Menschen*. Jena: Gustav Fischer.

Flanagan, James G. 1989. Hierarchy in simple 'egalitarian' societies. *Annual Review of Anthropology* 18: 245–66.

Fourie, Louis. 1926. Preliminary notes on certain customs of the *Hei//om* Bushmen. *Journal of the S.W.A. Scientific Society* 1: 49–63.

1928. The Bushmen of South West Africa. In C.H.L. Hahn, H. Vedder, and L. Fourie, *The native tribes of South West Africa*. Cape Town: Cape Times, pp. 79–105.

François, Hugo von. 1896. *Nama und Damara. Deutsch Süd-West-Afrika*. Magedeburg: Baensch.

Frazer, J.G. 1911–15 [1890]. *The golden bough* (third edition). London: Macmillan.

Friedman, Jonathan. 1974. Marxism, structuralism and vulgar materialism. *Man* (n.s.) 9: 444–69.

Galton, Francis. 1853. *The narrative of an explorer in tropical South Africa*. London: John Murray.

Gibson, Gordon D. 1956. Double descent and its correlates among the Herero of Ngamiland. *American Anthropologist* 58: 109–39.

Gillett, Simon. 1969. Notes on the settlement in the Ghanzi district. *Botswana Notes and Records* 2: 52–5.

Gödel, Kurt. 1962 [1931]. *On formally undecidable propositions*. New York: Basic Books.

Goldblatt, I. 1971. *History of South West Africa from the beginning of the nineteenth century*. Cape Town: Juta and Company.

Good, Anthony. 1978. The principle of reciprocal sets. *Man* (n.s.) 13: 128–30.

Goodenough, Ward. 1956. Componential analysis and the study of meaning. *Language* 32: 195–216.

Goody, J.R. 1959. The mother's brother and the sister's son in West Africa. *Journal of the Royal Anthropological Institute* 89: 59–88.

1976. *Production and reproduction: a comparative study of the domestic domain*. Cambridge University Press.

Gordon, Robert. 1971. Towards an ethnography of Bergdama gossib. *Namib und Meer* 2: 45–57.

1984. The !Kung in the Kalahari exchange: an ethnohistorical perspective. In Carmel Schrire (ed.), *Past and present in hunter-gatherer studies*. Orlando, FL: Academic Press, pp. 195–224.

1985. Primitive accumulation and Bushman policy in South West Africa. In Carmel Schrire and Robert Gordon (eds.), *The future of former foragers: Australian and Southern Africa*. Cambridge, MA; Cultural Survival (Occasional Papers 18), pp. 25–36.

1986a. Once again: How many Bushmen are there? In Megan Biesele, with

Robert Gordon and Richard Lee (eds.), *The past and future of !Kung ethnography: critical reflections and symbolic perspectives, essays in honour of Lorna Marshall.* Hamburg: Helmut Buske Verlag (Quellen zur Khoisan-Forschung 4), pp. 53–68.

1986b. Bushman banditry in twentieth-century Namibia. In Donald Crummey (ed.), *Banditry, rebellion and social protest in Africa.* London: James Currey/ Portsmouth, NH: Heinemann, pp. 173–89.

1989. Can Namibian San stop dispossession of their land? In Edwin N. Wilmsen (ed.). *We are here: politics of aboriginal land tenure.* Berkeley: University of California Press, pp. 138–54.

Greenberg, Joseph H. 1950. Studies in African linguistic classification: IV. The click languages. *Southwestern Journal of Anthropology* 6: 223–37.

1955. *Studies in African linguistic classification.* New Haven: Compass Publishing Company.

1963. *The languages of Africa.* Bloomington: Indiana University Research Center in Anthropology, Folklore and Linguistics (Publications No. 25).

Grevenbroek, Johannes Gulielmus [Jan Willem de Graevenbroek]. 1933 [1695]. Gentis Hottentotten nuncupatae descriptio (An account of the Hottentots), with translation by B. Farrington. In I. Schapera (ed.), *The early Cape Hottentots.* Cape Town: The Van Riebeeck Society (Vol. 14), pp. 161–299.

Gruber, Jeffrey S. 1973. ≠Hõã kinship terminology. *Linguistic Inquiry* 4: 427–49.

1975. Plural predicates in ≠Hõã. In A. Traill (ed.), *Bushman and Hottentot linguistic studies.* Johannesburg: African Studies Institute (Communications No. 2), pp. 1–50.

Guenther, Mathias G. 1973. Farm Bushmen and mission bushmen: socio-cultural change in a setting of conflict and pluralism of the San of the Ghanzi District, Republic of Botswana. Ph.D. thesis, University of Toronto.

1974. Farm Bushmen: socio-cultural change and incorporation of the San of the Ghanzi district, Republic of Botswana. Unpublished report to the Botswana government.

1975a. San acculturation and incorporation in the ranching areas of the Ghanzi district: some urgent anthropological issues. *Botswana Notes and Records* 7: 167–70.

1975b. The trance dancer as an agent of social change among the farm Bushmen of the Ghanzi district. *Botswana Notes and Records* 7: 161–6.

1976. From hunters to squatters: social and cultural change among the Ghanzi farm Bushmen. In Richard B. Lee and Irven DeVore (eds.), *Kalahari hunter-gatherers: Studies of the !Kung San and their neighbors.* Cambridge, MA: Harvard University Press, pp. 120–33.

1977. Bushman hunters as farm labourers. *Revue canadienne des études africaines/ Canadian Journal of African Studies* 11: 195–203.

1979a. *The farm Bushmen of the Ghanzi District, Botswana.* Stuttgart: Hochschul Verlag.

1979b. Bushman religion and the (non)sense of anthropological theory of religion. *Sociologus* 29: 102–32.

1980. From 'brutal savages' to 'harmless people': notes on the changing Western image of the Bushmen. *Paideuma* 26: 123–40.

1981a. Men and women in Nharo belief and ritual. *Namibiana* 3(2): 17–24.

1981b. Bushman and hunter-gatherer territoriality. *Zeitschrift für Ethnologie* 106: 109–20.

1983. Buschmänner (Nharo). In Klaus E. Müller (ed.), *Menschenbilder früher Gesellschaften: ethnologische Studien zum Verhältnis von Mensch und Natur*. Frankfurt and New York: Campus Verlag, pp. 75–107.

1986a. 'San' or 'Bushmen'? In Megan Biesele, with Robert Gordon and Richard Lee (eds.), *The past and future of !Kung ethnography: critical reflections and symbolic perspectives, essays in honour of Lorna Marshall*. Hamburg: Helmut Buske Verlag (Quellen zur Khoisan-Forschung 4), pp. 27–51.

1986b. *The Nharo Bushmen of Botswana: tradition and change*. Hamburg: Helmut Buske Verlag (Quellen zur Khoisan-Forschung 3).

1986c. From foragers to miners and bands to bandits: on the flexibility and adaptability of Bushman band societies. *Sprache und Geschichte in Afrika* 7(1): 133–59.

1986d. Acculturation and assimilation of the Bushmen of Botswana and Namibia. In Rainer Vossen and Klaus Keuthmann (eds.), *Contemporary studies on Khoisan 1*. Hamburg: Helmut Buske Verlag (Quellen zur Khoisan-Forschung 5.1), pp. 346–73.

1988. Animals in Bushman thought, myth and art. In Tim Ingold, David Riches, and James Woodburn (eds.), *Hunters and gatherers II: Property, power and ideology*. Oxford: Berg, pp. 192–202.

1989. *Bushman folktales: oral traditions of the Nharo of Botswana and the /Xam of the Cape*. Stuttgart: Franz Steiner Verlag Wiesbaden.

1990. Convergent and divergent themes in Bushman myth and art. In Karl-Heinz Kohl, Heinzarnold Muszinski, and Ivo Strecker (eds.), *Die Vielfalt der Kultur: ethnologische Aspekte von Verwandtschaft, Kunst und Weltauffassung*. Berlin: Dietrich Reimer Verlag, pp. 237–54.

Gulbrandsen, Ørnulf. 1991. On the problem of egalitarianism: the Kalahari San in transition. In Reidar Grønhaug, Georg Henricksen, and Gùnnar Haaland (eds.), *Ecology of choice and symbol: essays in the honour of Fredrik Barth*. Bergen: Alma Mater.

Gusinde, Martin. 1966. *Von gelben und schwarzen Buschmännern*. Graz: Akademische Druck- und Verlagsanstalt.

Haacke, Wilfrid H.G. 1982. Traditional hut-building technique of the Nama (with some related terminology). *Cimbebasia* (Series B) 3: 77–98.

Hahn, Theophilus. 1867. Die Nama-Hottentotten: ein Beitrag zur südafrikanischen Ethnographie. *Globus* 12: 238–42, 275–9, 304–7, 332–6.

1870. Die Buschmänner. Ein Beitrag zur südafrikanischen Völkerkunde. *Globus* 18: 65–8, 81–5, 102–5, 120–3, 140–3, 153–5.

1878. The graves of Heitsi-eibeb. A chapter on the pre-historic Hottentot race. *Cape Monthly Magazine* 16 (May): 257–65.

1881. *Tsuni-//goam: the supreme being of the Khoi-khoi*. London: Trübner and Co.

1882. *On the science of language and its study, with special regard to South Africa*. Cape Town: Herrmann Michaelis.

Hall, Martin. 1987. Preface. In John Parkington and Martin Hall (eds.), *Papers in the prehistory of the Western Cape, South Africa.* Oxford: British Archaeological Reports (International Series 332), Vol. 1, pp. 1–3.

Hall, Martin and Andrew B. Smith (eds.). 1986. *Prehistoric pastoralism in southern Africa.* Vlaeberg: South African Archaeological Society (Goodwin Series Vol. 5).

Hall, S.L. 1986. Pastoral adaptations and forager reactions in the eastern Cape. *South African Archaeological Society Goodwin Series* 5: 42–9.

Harpending, Henry. 1976. Regional variation in !Kung populations. In Richard B. Lee and Irven DeVore (eds.), *Kalahari hunter-gatherers: studies of the !Kung San and their neighbors.* Cambridge, MA: Harvard University Press, pp. 152–65, 398.

Harpending, Henry and Trefor Jenkins. 1973. Genetic distance among Southern African populations. In M.H. Crawford and P.L. Workman (eds.), *Methods and theories of anthropological genetics.* Albuquerque: University of New Mexico Press, pp. 177–99.

Harpending, Patricia Draper [Patricia Draper]. 1972. !Kung Bushman Childhood. Ph.D. dissertation, Harvard University.

Hart, T. 1987. Porterville survey. In John Parkington and Martin Hall (eds.), *Papers in the prehistory of the Western Cape, South Africa.* Oxford: British Archaeological Reports (International Series 332), Vol. 2, pp. 403–23.

Heinz, H.J. 1966. The social organization of the !kõ Bushmen. M.A. thesis, University of South Africa.

1968. An investigation on the social structure of Bushmen on a Ghanzi farm. Unpublished report to the District Commissioner, Ghanzi.

1970. *Experiences gained in a Bushman pilot settlement scheme (interim report).* Johannesburg: Dept. of Pathology, University of the Witwatersrand (Occasional Paper No. 1).

1972. Territoriality among the Bushmen in general and the !ko in particular. *Anthropos* 67: 405–16.

1973. *Bere: a balance sheet.* Johannesburg: Dept. of Pathology, University of the Witwatersrand (Occasional Paper No. 4).

1975a. Elements of !ko Bushmen religious beliefs. *Anthropos* 70: 17–41.

1975b. Acculturation problems arising in a Bushman development scheme. *South African Journal of Science* 71: 78–85.

1978a. The Bushmen in a changing world. In Phillip V. Tobias (ed.), *The Bushmen: San hunters and herders of Southern Africa.* Cape Town: Human and Rousseau, pp. 173–8.

1978b. The male initiation of the !Ko Bushmen and its acculturative changes. Paper presented at the International Conference on Hunting and Gathering Societies, Paris, June 1978.

1979. The nexus complex among the !xõ Bushmen of Botswana. *Anthropos* 74: 465–80.

1986. A !Xõ Bushmen burial. In Rainer Vossen and Klaus Keuthmann (eds.), *Contemporary studies on Khoisan 2.* Hamburg: Helmut Buske Verlag (Quellen zur Khoisan-Forschung 5.2), pp. 23–36.

n.d. [*c.* 1970–3]. The people of the Okavango delta. Unpublished series of six manuscripts comprising: I   The /xokwe Bugakwe; II   The end of a people

(the swamp //anekwe); III   The river //anekwe; IV   The /andakwe Bugakwe;
V   The Tzexa; VI   Tales and fables of the //anekwe, Yei, and Bugakwe.
Heinz, Hans-Joachim and Marshall Lee. 1978. *Namkwa: life among the Bushmen.*
London: Jonathan Cape.
Heinz, H.J. and B. Maguire, n.d. [1974]. *The ethno-biology of the !kõ Bushmen: their
ethno-botanical knowledge and plant lore.* Gaborone: Botswana Society (Occa-
sional Paper No. 1).
Heinz, H.J. and O. Martini. 1980. The ethno-biology of the !xõ Bushmen: the
ornithological knowledge. *Ethnomedizin* 6(1/4): 31–59.
Hewitt, Roger L. 1986. *Structure, meaning and ritual in the narratives of the Southern
San.* Hamburg: Helmut Buske Verlag (Quellen zur Khoisan-Forschung 2).
Hitchcock, Robert K. 1978a. *Kalahari cattle posts: a regional study of hunter-
gatherers, pastoralists, and agriculturalists in the western sandveld region,
Central District, Botswana* (2 vols.). Gaborone: Ministry of Local Government
and Lands.
  1978b. A history of research among Basarwa in Botswana. Unpublished paper
  deposited in the Botswana National Archives.
  1980. Tradition, social justice and land reform in central Botswana. *Journal of
  African Law* 24: 1–34.
  1985. Foragers on the move: San survival strategies in Botswana parks and
  reserves. *Cultural Survival Quarterly* 9(1): 31–6.
  1986. Ethnographic research and socioeconomic development among Kalahari
  San: some tables. In Megan Biesele, with Robert Gordon and Richard Lee
  (eds.), *The past and future of !Kung ethnography: critical reflections and
  symbolic perspectives, essays in honour of Lorna Marshall.* Hamburg: Helmut
  Buske Verlag (Quellen zur Khoisan-Forschung 4), pp. 375–423.
  1987. Socioeconomic change among the Basarwa in Botswana: an ethnohistorical analysis. *Ethnohistory* 34: 220–55.
  1988a. Settlement, seasonality, and subsistence stress among the Tyua of
  northern Botswana. In Rebecca Huss-Ashmore, with John J. Curry and
  Robert K. Hitchcock (eds.), *Coping with seasonal constraints.* Philadelphia:
  The University Museum, University of Pennsylvania (MASCA Research
  Papers in Science and Archaeology, Vol. 5), pp. 65–85.
  1988b. Decentralization and development among the Ju/Wasi, Namibia. *Cultural Survival Quarterly* 12(3): 31–3.
Hitchcock, Robert K. and James I. Ebert. 1984. Foraging and food production
among Kalahari hunter/gatherers. In J. Desmond Clack and Steven A. Brandt
(eds.), *From hunters to farmers: the causes and consequences of food production
in Africa.* Berkeley: University of California Press, pp. 328–48.
  1989. Modeling Kalahari hunter-gatherer subsistence and settlement systems.
  Implications for development policy and land use planning in Botswana.
  Anthropos 84: 47–62.
Hitchcock, Robert K. and John D. Holm. 1985. Political development among the
Basarwa of Botswana. *Cultural Survival Quarterly* 9(3): 7–11.
Hoernlé, A. Winifred. 1913. Richterveld, the land and its people. Johannesburg:
Council of Education, Witwatersrand.

1918. Certain rites of transition and the conception of *!nau* among the Hottentots. *Harvard African Studies* 2: 65–82.

1922. A Hottentot rain ceremony. *Bantu Studies* 1: 3–4.

1923a. South-West Africa as a primitive culture area. *South African Geographical Journal.* 6: 14–28.

1923b. The expression of the social values of water among the Nama of South West Africa. *South Africa Journal of Science* 20: 514–26.

1925. The social organization of the Nama Hottentots of Southwest Africa. *American Anthropologist* 27: 1–24.

1985. *The social organization of the Nama and other essays* (edited by Peter Carstens). Johannesburg: Witwatersrand University Press.

1987. *Trails in the thirstland: the anthropological field diaries of Winifred Hoernlé* (edited by Peter Carstens, Gerald Klinghardt, and Martin West). Cape Town: Centre for African Studies, University of Cape Town (Communications No. 14).

Hoff, Ansie. 1983. Die konsep geluk by die Nama. *Ethnologie/Ethnology* (South African journal of ethnology) 6(2): 9–15.

Holy, Ladislav. 1987. Introduction. Description, generalization and comparison: two paradigms. In Ladislav Holy (ed.), *Comparative anthropology*. Oxford: Blackwell, pp. 1–21.

Honken, H. 1977. Submerged features and Proto-Khoisan. In A. Traill (ed.), *Khoisan linguistic studies 3*. Johannesburg: African Studies Institute, pp. 145–69.

How, Marion Walsham. 1962. *The Mountain Bushmen of Basutoland*. Pretoria: J.L. van Schaik.

Howell, Nancy. 1979. *Demography of the Dobe !Kung*. New York: Academic Press.

Humphreys, A.J.B. 1987. Prehistoric seasonal mobility: What are we really achieving? *The South African Archaeological Bulletin* 42: 34–8.

Ingold, Tim. 1986. *The appropriation of nature: essays on human ecology and social relations*. Manchester: Manchester University Press.

Inskeep, R.R. 1969. The archaeological background. In Monica Wilson and Leonard Thompson (eds.), *The Oxford history of South Africa*, Vol. I. Oxford: Clarendon Press, pp. 1–39.

Jacobson, Leon. 1981. The Brandberg. *Rossing* (the magazine of Rossing Uranium Ltd.), December 1981, pp. 8–11.

Jeffreys, M.D.W. 1968. *Some semitic influences in Hottentot culture* (Fourth Raymond Dart Lecture, 1967). Johannesburg: Witwatersrand University Press for the Institute for the Study of Man in Africa.

Jenkins, Trefor. 1968. Genetic studies on the Khoisan peoples of southern Africa. *Proceedings of the Third Congress of the South African Genetics Society, Pretoria 1966*, pp. 1–6.

1972. Genetic polymorphisms of man in Southern Africa. M.D. thesis, University of London.

Jenkins, Trefor, A.B. Lane, G.T. Nurse, and J. Tanaka. 1975. Sero-genetic studies on the G/wi and G//ana of Botswana. *Human Heredity* 25: 318–28.

Jenkins, Trefor and Phillip V. Tobias. 1977. Nomenclature of population groups in southern Africa. *African Studies* 36: 49–55.

Jenkins, Trefor, A. Zoutendyk, and A.G. Steinberg. 1971. Red-cell enzyme polymorphisms in the Khoisan peoples of southern Africa. *American Journal of Human Genetics* 23: 513–32.

Josselin de Jong, J.J.B. de. 1977 [1935]. The Malay Archipelago as a field of ethnological study. In P.E. de Josselin de Jong (ed.), *Structural anthropology in the Netherlands*. The Hague: Marinus Nijhoff, pp. 166–82.

Joyce, J.W. 1938. Report on the Masarwa in the Bamangwato Reserve, Bechuanaland Protectorate. *League of Nations Publications*, C112, M98, VI.B., 'Slavery', Annex 6, pp. 57–76.

Katz, Richard. 1976. Education for transcendence: !Kia healing with the Kalahari !Kung. In Richard B. Lee and Irven DeVore (eds.), *Kalahari hunter-gatherers: studies of the !Kung San and their neighbors*. Cambridge, MA: Harvard University Press, pp. 281–301, 400–1.

1982. *Boiling energy: community healing among the Kalahari Kung*. Cambridge, MA; Harvard University Press.

Kaufmann, Hans. 1910. Die ≠Auin. Ein Beitrag zur Buschmannforschung. *Mitteilungen aus den deutschen Schutzgebeiten* 23: 135–60.

Keen, Ian. 1985. Definitions of kin. *Journal of Anthropological Research* 41: 62–90.

Keenan, Jeremy. 1977. The concept of the mode of production in hunter-gatherer societies. *African Studies* 36: 57–69.

Keesing, Roger M. 1972. Paradigms lost: the new anthropology and the new linguistics. *Southwestern Journal of Anthropology* 28: 299–322.

1979. Linguistic knowledge and cultural knowledge: some doubts and speculations. *American Anthropologist* 81: 14–36.

Kent, Susan. 1988. Changing mobility patterns and diversity among former nomadic foragers of the Kalahari, Botswana. Paper presented at the Fifth International Conference on Hunting and Gathering Societies, Darwin, N.T., Australia, August–September 1988.

1989a. And justice for all: the development of political centralization among newly sedentary foragers. *American Anthropologist* 91: 703–12.

1989b. Cross-cultural perceptions of farmers as hunters and the value of meat. In Susan Kent (ed.), *Farmers as hunters – the implications of sendentism*. Cambridge: Cambridge University Press, pp. 1–17.

Kent, Susan and Helga Vierich. 1989. The myth of ecological determinism – anticipated mobility and site spatial organization. In Susan Kent (ed.), *Farmers as hunters – the implications of sedentism*. Cambridge: Cambridge University Press, pp. 96–130.

Kirby, Percival R. 1932. The music and musical instruments of the Korana. *Bantu Studies* 6: 183–204.

1936a. A study of Bushman music. *Bantu Studies* 10: 205–52.

1936b. The musical practices of the /'auni and ≠khomani Bushmen. *Bantu Studies* 10: 373–431.

Klein, Richard G. 1986. The prehistory of Stone Age herders in the Cape Province of South Africa. In Martin Hall and Andrew B. Smith (eds.), *Prehistoric pastoralism in southern Africa*. Vlaeberg: South African Archaeological Society (Goodwin Series, Vol. 5), pp. 5–12.

Kluckhohn, Clyde. 1943. Covert culture and administrative problems. *American Anthropologist* 45: 213–27.

Köhler, Oswin. 1960. Sprachkrititsche Aspekt zur Hamitentheorie über die Herkunft der Hottentotten. *Sociologus* 10: 69–77.

1962. Studien zum Genussystem und Verbalbau der zentralen Khoisan-Sprachen. *Anthropos* 57: 529–46.

1963. Observations on the Central Khoisan Language Group. *Journal of African Languages* 2: 227–34.

1966a. Die Wortbeziehungen zwischen der Sprache Kxoé-Buschmanner und dem Hottentottischen als geschichtliches Problem. In Johannes Lukas (ed.), *Neue Afrikanistische Studien*. Hamburg: Deutsches Institut für Afrika-Forschung, pp. 144–65.

1966b. Tradition und Wandel bei den Kxoe-Buschmannern von Mutsiku. *Sociologus* 16: 122–40.

1969. Die Topnaar-Hottentotten am unteren Kuiseb. In Ethnological Section (eds.), *Ethnological and linguistic studies in honour of N.J. van Warmelo*. Pretoria: Ethnological Section, Department of Bantu Administration and Development (Ethnological Publications No. 52), pp. 99–122.

1971a. Die 'Krankheit' im Denken der Kxoe-Buschmanner. In Veronika Six, Norbert Cyffer, Ludwig Gerhardt, and Ekkehard Wolff (eds.), *Afrikanische Sprachen und Kulturen – ein Querschnitt (Festschrift Johannes Lukas)*. Hamburg: Deutsches Institut für Afrika-Forschung (Hamburg Beitrage zur Afrika-Kunde 14), pp. 317–25.

1971b. Die Khoe-sprachigen Buschmanner der Kalahari. Ihre Verbreitung und Gliederung. In *Kölner geographische Arbeitennen (Festschrift Karl Kayser)*. Wiesbaden: Franz Steiner, pp. 373–411.

1973. Die rituelle Jagd bei den Kxoé-Buschmännern. *Kölner ethnologische Mitteilungen* 5: 215–57.

1975. Geschichte und Probleme der Gliederung der Spachen Afrikas. In Herman Baumann (ed.), *Die Völker Afrikas und ihre traditionellen Kulturen*. Wiesbaden: Steiner, Vol. I, pp. 135–373.

1976. Zum Begriff der 'Freiheit' bei den Khoe-Bushmännern. In Balthasar Straehelin, Silvio Jenny, and Stephanos Geroulanos (eds.), *Engadiner Kollegium 'Freiheit'. Aktulle und Beiträge aus verschiedenen Gebieten zum Problem der Freiheit*. Zurich: Editio Academica, pp. 63–79.

1977. New Khoisan linguistic studies. *African Studies* 36: 255–78.

1978. Tierzauber und Krankheit bei den Kxoe-Buschmännern. *Afrika und Uberesse* 61: 35–58.

1978–9. Mythus Glaube und Magie bei den Kxoe-Buschmännern. Bericht aus den Studienergebnissen 1959–1974. *Journal of the South African Scientific Society* 33: 9–49.

1981. Les langues khoisan. In Jean Perrot (ed.), *Les Langues dans le monde ancien et moderne*. Paris: Éditions du Centre National de la Recherche Scientifique, pp. 455–615.

1984. Der Kxoé-Buschmann Ndó erzhalt aus seinem Leben. *Namibiana* 5(1): 171–94.

1986. Allgemeine und sprachliche Bemerkungen zum Feldbau nach Oraltexten der Kxoé-Buschleute. *Sprache und Geschichte in Afrika* 7(1): 205–72.

1989. *Die Welt de Kxoé-Buschleute im sudlichen Afrika, Band I: Die Kxoe-Buschleute und ihre ethnische Umbgebung.* Berlin: Dietrich Reimer Verlag.

Kolb, Peter [Peter Kolbe, Peter Kolben]. 1968 [1731]. *The present state of the Cape of Good Hope*, Vol. I (trans. Guido Medley). New York and London: Johnson Reprint Company.

Konner, M. 1977. Infancy among the Kalahari Desert San. In P. Herbert Leiderman, Stephen R. Tulkin, and Anne Rosenfeld (eds.), *Culture and infancy: variations in human experience.* New York: Academic Press, pp. 287–328.

Kroeber, A.L. 1936. Kinship and history. *American Anthropologist* 37: 338–41. (Reprinted in Kroeber 1952, pp. 202–5.)

1952. *The nature of culture.* Chicago: University of Chicago Press.

Kroenlein, J.G. 1889. *Wortschatz der Khoi-khoin (Namaqua-Hottentotten).* Berlin: Deutsche Kolonialgesellschaft.

Kuper, Adam 1970. *Kalahari village politics: an African democracy.* Cambridge: Cambridge University Press.

1975. The social structure of the Sotho-speaking peoples of southern Africa. *Africa* 45: 67–81, 139–49.

1979. Regional comparison in African anthropology. *African Affairs* 78: 103–13.

1980. Symbolic dimensions of the Southern Bantu homestead. *Africa* 50: 8–23.

1982. *Wives for cattle: bridewealth and marriage in Southern Africa.* London: Routledge and Kegan Paul.

1987. *South Africa and the anthropologist.* London: Routledge and Kegan Paul.

Kuper, Adam and Simon Gillett. 1970. Aspects of administration in western Botswana. *African Studies* 29: 169–82.

Laidler, F.W. 1929. Burials and burial methods of the Namaqualand Hottentots. *Man* 29: 151–3.

Lebzelter, Viktor. 1928. Die religiösen Vorstellen der //Khun-Buschmänner, der Buschmänner der Etoshapfanne und des Ovambo-Landes, und der Ovambo-Bantu. In *Festschrift P.W. Schmidt.* Vienna, pp. 407–15.

1928–9. Bei den !Kuṅ-Buschleuten am oberen Omuramba und Ovambo (Südwestafrika). *Mitteilungen der Anthropologische Gesellschaft Wien* 59: 12–16.

1934. *Eingeborenenkulturen in Südwest- und Südafrika.* Leipzig: Karl W. Hiersemann.

Lee, Richard B. 1965. Subsistence ecology of !Kung Bushmen. Ph.D. dissertation, University of California at Berkeley.

1968a. What hunters do for a living, or, how to make out on scarce resources. In Richard B. Lee and Irven DeVore (eds.), *Man the hunter.* Chicago: Aldine, pp. 30–48.

1968b. The sociology of !Kung Bushman trance performances. In Raymond Prince (ed.), *Trance and possession states.* Montreal: R.M. Bucke Memorial Society, pp. 35–54.

1969a. !Kung Bushman subsistence: an input–output analysis. In David Dama (ed.), *Contributions to anthropology: ecological essays.* Ottawa: National Museums of Canada (Bulletin No. 230), pp. 73–94. (Reprinted in Vayda 1969, pp. 47–79.)

1969b. Eating Christmas in the Kalahari. *Natural History* December 1969: 14–22, 60–3. (Reprinted in Lee 1984, pp. 151–7.)

1972a. Population growth and the beginnings of sedentary life among the !Kung Bushmen. In Brian Spooner (ed.), *Population growth: anthropological implications*. Cambridge, MA: M.I.T. Press, pp. 329–42.

1972b. The intensification of social life among the !Kung Bushmen. In Brian Spooner (ed.), *Population growth: anthropological implications*. Cambridge, MA: M.I.T. Press, pp. 343–50.

1972c. Work effort, group structure and land use in contemporary hunter-gatherers. In P.J. Ucko, R. Tringham, and D.W. Dimbleby (eds.), *Man, settlement and urbanism*. London: Duckworth, pp. 177–85.

1972d. !Kung spatial organization: an ecological and historical perspective. *Human Ecology* 1(2): 125–47. (Reprinted in Lee and DeVore 1976, pp. 73–97.)

1972e. The !Kung Bushmen of Botswana. In M.G. Bicchieri (ed.), *Hunters and gatherers today*. New York: Holt, Rinehart and Winston, pp. 327–68.

1973. Mongongo: the ethnography of a major wild food resource. *Ecology of Food and Nutrition* 2: 307–21.

1974. Male–female arrangements and political power in human hunter-gatherers. *Archives of Sexual Behavior* 3(2): 167–73.

1976 [1972]. !Kung spatial organization: an ecological and historical perspective. In Richard B. Lee and Irven DeVore (eds.), *Kalahari hunter-gatherers: studies of the !Kung San and their neighbors*. Cambridge, MA; Harvard University Press, pp. 73–97.

1979a. Hunter-gatherers in process: The Kalahari Research project, 1963–1976. In George M. Foster, Thayer Scudder, Elizabeth Colson, and Robert V. Kemper (eds.), *Long-term field research in social anthropology*. New York: Academic Press, pp. 303–21.

1979b. *The !Kung San: men, women, and work in a foraging society*. Cambridge: Cambridge University Press.

1981 [1978]. Politics, sexual and nonsexual, in an egalitarian society: the !Kung San. In Gerald D. Berreman (ed.), *Social inequality: comparative and developmental approaches*. New York: Academic Press, pp. 83–102.

1984. *The Dobe !Kung*. New York: Holt, Rinehart and Winston.

1986. !Kung kin terms, the name relationship and the process of discovery. In Megan Biesele, with Robert Gordon and Richard Lee (eds.), *The past and future of !Kung ethnography: critical reflections and symbolic perspectives, essays in honour of Lorna Marshall*. Hamburg: Helmut Buske Verlag (Quellen zur Khoisan-Forschung 4), pp. 77–102.

1988a. The gods must be crazy, but the state has a plan: government policies towards the San in Namibia and Botswana. In Brian Wood (ed.), *Namibia 1884–1984: readings on Namibia's history and society*. London: Namibia Support Committee, pp. 539–46.

1988b. Reflections on primitive communism. In Tim Ingold, David Riches, and James Woodburn (eds.), *Hunters and gatherers I: History, evolution and social change*. Oxford: Berg, pp. 252–68.

Lee, Richard B. and Irven DeVore. 1968. Problems in the study of hunters and gatherers. In Richard B. Lee and Irven DeVore (eds.), *Man the hunter*. Chicago: Aldine, pp. 3–12.

(eds). 1976. *Kalahari hunter-gatherers: studies of the !Kung San and their neighbors*. Cambridge, MA: Harvard University Press.

Lee, Richard and Susan Hurlich. 1982. From foragers to fighters: South Africa's militarization of the Namibian San. In Eleanor Leacock and Richard Lee (eds.), *Politics and history in band societies*. Cambridge: Cambridge University Press/Paris: Éditions de la Maison des Sciences de l'Homme, pp. 327–45.

Legassick, Martin. 1979. The Northern Frontier to 1820: the emergence of the Griqua people. In Richard Elphick and Hermann Giliomee (eds.), *The shaping of South African society, 1652–1820*. Cape Town: Longman, pp. 243–90.

Lenssen-Erz, Tilman. 1989. Catalogue [including 'The conceptual framework for the analysis of the Brandberg rock paintings', pp. 361–70]. In Harald Pager, *The rock paintings of the upper Brandberg, Part I: Amis Gorge*. Cologne: Heinrich-Barth-Institut, pp. 342–73.

Lepsius, C.R. 1863 [First edition: 1854]. *Standard alphabet for reducing unwritten languages and foreign graphic systems to a uniform orthography in European letters*, 2nd edition. London: Williams and Noregate; Berlin: W. Hertz.

Lévi-Strauss, Claude. 1969 [First edition: 1949]. *The elementary structures of kinship*, 2nd edition (trans. James Harle Bell, John Richard von Sturmer, and Rodney Needham, ed.). Boston: Beacon Press.

Lewis-Williams, J.D. 1980. Ethnography and iconography: aspects of southern San thought and art. *Man* (n.s.) 15: 467–82.

1981a. *Believing and seeing: symbolic meanings in southern San rock paintings*. London: Academic Press.

1981b. The thin red line: southern San notions and rock paintings of supernatural potency. *South African Archaeological Bulletin* 36: 5–13.

1982. The economic and social context of southern San rock art. *Current Anthropology* 23: 429–49.

1983a. *The rock art of southern Africa*. Cambridge: Cambridge University Press.

(ed.). 1983b. *New approaches to southern African rock art*. Cape Town: South African Archaeological Society (Goodwin Series 4).

1983c. An ethnographic interpretation of a rock painting from Barkly East. *Humanitas, RSA* 9: 245–9.

1984. Ideological continuities in prehistoric southern Africa: the evidence of rock art. In Carmel Schrire (ed.), *Past and present in hunter-gatherer Studies*. Orlando, FL: Academic Press, pp. 225–52.

1986. Paintings of power: ethnography and rock art in southern Africa. In Megan Biesele, with Robert Gordon and Richard Lee (eds.), *The past and future of !Kung ethnography: critical reflections and symbolic perspectives, essays in honour of Lorna Marshall*. Hamburg: Helmut Buske Verlag (Quellen zur Khoisan-Forschung 4), pp. 231–73.

1988. *Reality and non-reality in San rock art* (Twenty-fifth Raymond Dart Lecture, 1987). Johannesburg: Witwatersrand University Press for the Institute for the Study of Man in Africa.

Lewis-Williams, J.D. and Megan Biesele. 1978. Eland hunting rituals among the northern and southern San groups: striking similarities. *Africa* 48: 117–34.

Lewis-Williams, J.D. and Thomas A. Dowson. 1989. *Images of power: understanding Bushman rock art*. Johannesburg: Southern Book Publishers.

Lewis-Williams, J.D. and J.H.N. Loubser. 1986. Deceptive appearances: a critique of southern African rock art studies. *Advances in World Archaeology* 5: 253–89.

Lichtenstein, M.H.C. [Hinrich]. 1811–12. *Reisen im südlichen Afrika in dem Jahren 1803, 1804, 1805 und 1806* (2 vols.). Berlin: C. Salfeld.

1928–30. *Travels in Southern Africa in the years 1803, 1804, 1805 and 1806* (trans. Anne Plumtre). Cape Town: The Van Riebeeck Society (Vols. 10, 11).

Linton, Ralph. 1926. The origin of the Skidi Pawnee sacrifice to the Morning Star. *American Anthropologist* 28: 457–66.

London Missionary Society. 1935. *The Masarwa (Bushmen): report of an inquiry by the South African District Committee of the London Missionary Society*. Alice: Lovedale Press.

Lounsbury, Floyd G. 1964. A formal account of the Crow- and Omaha-type kinship terminology. In Ward Goodenough (ed.), *Explorations in cultural anthropology*. New York: McGraw Hill, pp. 351–93.

Louw, J.A. 1979. A preliminary survey of Khoi and San influence in Zulu. In A. Traill (ed.), *Khoisan linguistic studies 5*. Johannesburg: Department of Linguistics, pp. 8–21.

1986. Some linguistic influence of Khoi and San in the prehistory of the Nuni. In Rainer Vossen and Klaus Keuthmann (eds.), *Contemporary studies on Khoisan 2*. Hamburg: Helmut Buske Verlag (Quellen zur Khoisan-Forschung 5.2), pp. 141–68.

Lowie, Robert H. 1928. A note on relationship terminologies. *American Anthropologist* 30: 263–8.

1947 [First edition: 1920]. *Primitive society*, 2nd edition. New York: Liveright Publishing Corporation.

1966 [1917]. *Culture and ethnology*. New York: Basic Books.

Luttig, Hendrik Gerhardus. 1933. *The religious system and social organization of the Herero: a study in Bantu culture*. Utrecht: Kemink en Zoon N.V.

McCall, D.F. 1970. *Wolf courts girl: the equivalence of hunting and mating in Bushman thought*. Ohio University Occasional Papers in International Studies, Africa Series No. 7.

Maggs, T.M.O'C. 1967. A quantitative analysis of the rock art from a sample area in the western Cape. *South African Journal of Science* 63: 100–4.

Maingard, L.F. 1931. The lost tribes of the Cape. *South African Journal of Science* 28: 487–504.

1932. Studies in Korana history, customs and language. *Bantu Studies* 6: 103–62.

1934. The linguistic approach to South African prehistory and ethnology. *South African Journal of Science* 31: 117–43.

1957. Three Bushman languages. *African Studies* 16: 37–71.

1958. Three Bushman languages; Part II: The third Bushman language. *African Studies* 17: 100–15.

1961. The central group of click languages of the Kalahari. *African Studies* 20: 114–22.

1962. *Korana folktales: grammar and texts*. Johannesburg: Witwatersrand University Press.

1963. A comparative study of Naron, Hietshware and Korana. *African Studies* 22: 97–108.

1964. The Korana dialects. *African Studies* 23: 57–66.

Malherbe, V.C. 1981. The Khoi captains in the third frontier war. In Susan Newton-King and V.C. Malherbe, *The Khoikhoi rebellion in the Eastern Cape (1799–1803)*. Centre for African Studies, University of Cape Town (Communications No. 5), pp. 66–137.

Manhire, Anthony. 1987. *Later Stone Age settlement patterns in the sandveld of the south-western Cape Province, South Africa.* Oxford: British Archaeological Reports (International Series 351/Cambridge Monographs in African Archaeology 21).

Marais, J.S. 1939. *The Cape Coloured people, 1652–1937.* London: Longmans, Green and Co. Ltd.

Marks, Shula. 1972. Khoisan resistance to the Dutch in the seventeenth and eighteenth centuries. *Journal of African History* 13: 55–80.

Marshall, John and Claire Ritchie. 1984. *Where are the Ju/wasi of Nyae Nyae? Changes in a Bushman society: 1958–1981.* Cape Town: Centre for African Studies, University of Cape Town (Communications No. 9).

Marshall, Lorna. 1957a. The kin terminology system of the !Kung Bushmen. *Africa* 27: 1–25. (Reprinted in Marshall 1976, pp. 201–42.)

1957b. N!ow. *Africa* 27: 232–40.

1959. Marriage among !Kung Bushmen. *Africa* 29: 335–65. (Reprinted in Marshall 1976, pp. 252–86.)

1960. !Kung Bushman bands. *Africa* 30: 325–55. (Reprinted in Marshall 1976, pp. 156–200.)

1961. Sharing, talking, and giving: relief of social tensions among !Kung Bushmen. *Africa* 31: 231–49. (Reprinted in Marshall 1976, pp. 287–312; and in Lee and DeVore 1976, pp. 349–71, 402.)

1962. !Kung Bushman religious beliefs. *Africa* 32: 221–52.

1965. The !Kung Bushmen of the Kalahari Desert. In James L. Gibbs, Jr (ed.), *Peoples of Africa.* New York: Holt, Rinehart and Winston, pp. 241–78.

1969. The medicine dance of the !Kung Bushmen. *Africa* 39: 347–81.

1976. *The !Kung of Nyae Nyae.* Cambridge, MA: Harvard University Press.

Mauny, Raymond. 1967. L'Afrique et les origines de la domestication. In Walter W. Bishop and J. Desmond Clark (eds.), *Background to evolution in Africa.* Chicago and London: University of Chicago Press, pp. 583–99.

Mazel, Aron D. 1989. Changing social relations in the Thukela Basin, Natal 7000–2000 BP. In Janette Deacon (ed.), *Goodwin's legacy.* Vlaeberg: The South African Archaeological Society (Goodwin Series 6), pp. 33–41.

Meinhof, Carl. 1909. *Lehrbuch der Nama-Sprache.* Berlin: George Reimer.

1930. *Der Koranadialekt des Hottentotischen.* Berlin: Dietrich Reimer.

Messina, Franco Maria. 1980. Naming pattern and reference system of the Basters. *V.O.C.* 1: 35–50.

Ministry of Local Government and Lands. 1978. *Minutes of Remote Area Development Workshop held at B.T.C. Gaborone, 29 May–2 June 1978.* Gaborone: Ministry of Local Government and Lands.

Mossop, E.E. 1935. A table of tribal names mentioned in Wikar's journal with their

324   *References*

probable equivalents. In E.E. Mossop (ed.), *The journals of Wikar, Coetsé and van Reenen*. Cape Town: The Van Riebeeck Society (Vol. 15), pp. 13–19.

Motzafi, Pnina. 1986. Whither the 'true Bushmen': the dynamics of perpetual marginality. *Sprache und Geschichte in Afrika* 7.1: 295–328.

Murdock, George Peter. 1949. *Social structure*. New York: Macmillan.

  1959. *Africa: its peoples and their culture history*. New York: McGraw-Hill Book Company.

Murray, M.L. 1976. *Present wildlife utilization in the Central Kalahari Game Reserve, Botswana: a report on the C.K.G.R. Reconnaissance Survey*. Gaborone: Department of Wildlife, National Parks and Tourism.

Nadel, S.F. 1952. Witchcraft in four African societies: an essay in comparison. *American Anthropologist* 54: 18–29.

Nama/Damara: Spelreels No. 2/Nama/Damara: Orthography No. 2. 1977. Windhoek: Department of Bantu Education.

Needham, Rodney. 1972. *Belief, language, and experience*. Oxford: Blackwell.

  1973. Prescription. *Oceania* 42: 166–81.

Newton-King, Susan. 1981. The rebellion of the Khoi in Graaff-Reinet: 1799 to 1803. In Susan Newton-King and V.C. Malherbe, *The Khoikhoi rebellion in the Eastern Cape (1799–1803)*. Centre for African Studies, University of Cape Town (Communications No. 5), pp. 12–65.

Newton-King, Susan and V.C. Malherbe. 1981. Introduction. In Susan Newton-King and V.C. Malherbe, *The Khoikhoi rebellion in the Eastern Cape (1799–1803)*. Centre for African Studies, University of Cape Town (Communications No. 5), pp. 1–11.

Nienaber, G.S. 1956. Die vroegste verslae aangaande Hottentots. *African Studies* 15: 29–35.

  1960. 'n ou ongepubliseerde lys Hottentot- en Xhosaworde. *African Studies* 19: 157–69.

  1963a. The origin of the name 'Hottentot'. *African Studies* 22: 65–90.

  1963b. *Hottentots*. Pretoria: J.L. van Schaik.

Nurse, G.T. 1972. Musical instrumentation among the San (Bushmen) of the central Kalahari. *African Music* 5(2): 23–7, 49.

  1977. The survival of the Khoisan race. *Bulletin of the International Committee for Urgent Anthropological and Ethnological Research* 19: 39–46.

Nurse, G.T. and T. Jenkins. 1977. *Health and the hunter-gatherer: biomedical studies on the hunting and gathering populations of southern Africa*. Basel: S. Karger.

Nurse, G.T., A.B. Lane, and T. Jenkins. 1976. Sero-genetic studies on the Dama of South West Africa. *Annals of Human Biology* 3: 33–50.

Nurse, G.T., J.S. Weiner, and Trefor Jenkins. 1985. *The peoples of southern Africa and their affinities*. Oxford: Clarendon Press (Research Monographs on Human Population Biology No. 3).

Oberholster, J.J. 1972. Griquas. In D.J. Potgieter (editor-in-chief), *Standard encyclopaedia of southern Africa*. Cape Town: Nasou, Vol. 5, pp. 353–8.

Obermaier, Hugo and Herrbert Kühn. 1930. *Bushman art: rock paintings of South-West Africa*. London: Humphrey Milford/Oxford University Press.

Oliveira Santos, Carlos A.M. de. 1958. *Os Vassekele do Cuando – contribuição para o seu estudo*. Lisbon: Instituto Superior de Estudes Ultramarinos.

Orpen, Joseph Millerd. 1964 (1908). *Reminiscences of life in South Africa from 1846 to the present day*. Cape Town: C. Struik.

Osaki, Masakazu. 1984. The social influence of change in hunting technique among the Central Kalahari San. *African Study Monographs* 5: 49–62.

Owens, Mark and Delia Owens. 1985. *Cry of the Kalahari*. Boston: Houghton Mifflin Company.

Pager, Harald. 1971. *Ndedema, a documentation of the rock paintings of Ndedema Gorge*. Graz (Austria): Akademische Druck Verlagsansalt.

1989. *The rock paintings of the upper Brandberg, Part I: Amis Gorge*. Cologne: Heinrich-Barth-Institut.

Palgrave, W. Coates. 1877. *Report of W. Coates Palgrave, Esq., Special Commissioner to the tribes north of the Orange River, of his mission to Damaraland and Great Namaqualand in 1870*. Cape Town: Cape of Good Hope, Ministerial Department of Native Affairs.

Parkin, David. 1987. Comparison as the search for continuity. In Ladislav Holy (ed.), *Comparative anthropology*. Oxford: Blackwell, pp. 53–69.

Parkington, John E. 1984a. Soaqua and Bushmen: hunters and robbers. In Carmel Schrire (ed.), *Past and present in hunter-gatherer studies*. Orlando, FL; Academic Press, pp. 151–74.

1984b. Changing views of the Later Stone Age of South Africa. *Advances in World Archaeology* 3: 89–142.

1987. Changing views of prehistoric settlement in the Western Cape. In John Parkington and Martin Hall (eds.), *Papers in the prehistory of the Western Cape, South Africa*. Oxford: British Archaeological Reports (International Series 332), Vol. 1, pp. 4–23.

Passarge, S. 1905. Das Okawangosumpfland und seine Bewohner. *Zeitschrift für Ethnologie* 37: 649–716.

1907. *Die Buschmänner der Kalahari*. Berlin: Dietrich Reimer.

Peterson, Nicolas. 1979. Territorial adaptation among desert hunter-gatherers: the !Kung and Australians compared. In Philip Burnham and Roy F. Ellen (eds.), *Social and ecological systems*. London: Academic Press (A.S.A. Monographs 18), pp. 111–29.

Philip, John. 1828. *Researches in South Africa, illustrating the civil, moral and religious condition of the native tribes* (2 vols.). London: Duncan.

Potgieter, E.F. 1955. *The disappearing Bushmen of Lake Chrissie: a preliminary survey*. Pretoria: J.L. van Schaik.

Proctor, Robert. 1988. From *Anthropologie* to *Rassenkunde* in the German anthropological tradition. In George W. Stocking, Jr. (ed.), *Bones, bodies, and behavior: essays on biological anthropology*. Madison, WI: University of Wisconsin Press, pp. 138–79.

Pullum, Geoffrey K. and William A. Ladusaw. 1986. *Phonetic symbol guide*. Chicago/London: University of Chicago Press.

[Radcliffe-] Brown, A.R. 1913. Three tribes of Western Australia. *Journal of the Royal Anthropological Institute* 43: 143–70.

1924. The mother's brother in South Africa. *South African Journal of Science* 21: 542–55. (Reprinted in Radcliffe-Brown 1952, pp. 15–31).

1930–1. The social organization of Australian tribes. *Oceania* 1: 34–63, 206–46, 322–41, 426–56.

1952. *Structure and function in primitive society.* London: Cohen and West.

Ramsay, Jeff. 1988. Some notes on the Colonial era history of the Central Kalahari Game Reserve region. *Botswana Notes and Records* 20: 91–4.

Redinha, José. 1962. *Distribuição etnica de Angola.* Luanda: Centre de Informação e Tourismo.

Richardson, Allan. 1986 [1982]. The control of productive resources on the Northwest Coast of North America. In Nancy M. Williams and Eugene S. Hunn (eds.), *Resource managers: North American and Australian hunter-gatherers.* Canberra: Australian Institute of Aboriginal Studies, pp. 93–112.

Riches, David. 1982. *Northern nomadic hunter-gatherers: a humanistic approach.* London: Academic Press.

Ritchie, Claire. 1987. The political economy of resource tenure in the Kalahari: San survival in Namibia and Botswana. M.A. thesis, Boston University.

Roos, Tielman. 1931. Burial customs of the !kau Bushmen. *Bantu Studies* 5: 81–3.

Ross, Robert. 1975. The !Kora Wars on the Orange river, 1830–1880. *Journal of African History* 16: 561–76.

1976. *Adam Kok's Griquas: a study in the development of stratification in South Africa.* Cambridge: Cambridge University Press.

Rousseau, Jean-Jacques. 1971 [1755]. Discours sur l'origine et les fondements de l'inégalité parmi les hommes. In *Discours sur les sciences et les arts* and *Discours sur l'origine de l'inégalité.* Paris: G.F. Flammarion, pp. 139–235.

Rudner, Jalmar and Ione Rudner. 1978. Bushman art. In Phillip V. Tobias (ed.), *The Bushmen: San hunters and herders of Southern Africa.* Cape Town: Human and Rousseau, pp. 57–75.

Russell, Margo and Martin Russell. 1979. *Afrikaners of the Kalahari: white minority in a black state.* Cambridge: Cambridge University Press.

Rycroft, D.K. 1978. Comments on Bushman and Hottentot music recorded by E.O.J. Westphal. *Review of Ethnology* 5(2/3): 16–23.

Sahlins, Marshall. 1974 [1972]. *Stone age economics.* London: Tavistock Publications.

Sampson, C. Garth. 1974. *The Stone Age archaeology of Southern Africa.* New York and London: Academic Press.

Śaraṇa, Gopala. 1975. *The methodology of anthropological comparisons: an analysis of comparative methods in social and cultural anthropology.* Tuscon: University of Arizona Press (Viking Fund Publications in Anthropology 53).

Sbrzesny, Heidi. 1976. *Die Spiele der !ko-Buschleute unter besonderer Berücksichtigung ihrer sozialisierenden und gruppenbindenden Funktionen.* Munich: Max-Planck-Gesellschaft (Monographien zur Humanethologie 2).

Schapera, I. 1926. A preliminary consideration of the relationship between the Hottentots and the Bushmen. *South African Journal of Science* 23: 833–66.

1927. The tribal divisions of the Bushmen. *Man* 27: 68–73.

1929. The tribal system in South Africa: a study of the Bushmen and the Hottentots (2 vols.). Ph.D. thesis, University of London.

1930. *The Khoisan peoples of South Africa: Bushmen and Hottentots.* London: George Routledge and Sons.

(ed.). 1933. *The early Cape Hottentots*. Cape Town: The Van Riebeeck Society (Vol. 14).

1939. A survey of the Bushman question. *Race relations* 6 (2): 68–83.

1952. *The ethnic composition of Tswana tribes*. London: London School of Economics (L.S.E. Monographs on Social Anthropology No 11).

1953. Some comments on comparative method in social anthropology. *American Anthropologist* 55: 353–62.

Scheffler, Harold W. 1977. On the 'rule of uniform reciprocals' in systems of kin classification. *Anthropological Linguistics* 19: 245–59.

1978. *Australian kin classification*. Cambridge: Cambridge University Press.

Scheffler, Harold W. and Floyd G. Lounsbury. 1969. *A study on structural semantics: the Siriono kinship system*. Engelwood Cliffs, NJ: Prentice-Hall.

Schinz, Hans. 1891. *Deutsch Südwest Afrika*. Oldenburg and Leipzig: Schulz.

Schmelen, J.H. (trans.). 1831. *Annoe kayn hoeaati Nama-kowapna gowayhiihati* [Holy Good News Written in the Nama Language]. Cape Town: Bridekirk.

Schmidt, Sigrid. 1973. Die Mantis religiosa in den Glaubensvorstellungen der Khoesan-Völker. *Zeitschrift für Ethnologie* 98: 102–27.

1975–6. Alte Götter der khoisan-sprechenden Völker im südlichen Afrika. *Journal of the South West African Scientific Society* 30: 59–74.

1979. The Rain Bull of the South African Bushmen. *African Studies* 38: 201–24.

1980. *Märchen aus Namibia: Volkserzählungen der Nama un Dama*. Dusseldorf/Cologne: Eugen Diederichs Verlag.

1986a. Tales and beliefs about Eyes-on-His-Feet: the interrelatedness of Khoisan folklore. In Megan Biesele, with Robert Gordon and Richard Lee (eds.), *The past and future of !Kung ethnography: critical reflections and symbolic perspectives, essays in honour of Lorna Marshall*. Hamburg: Helmut Buske Verlag (Quellen zur Khoisan-Forschung 4), pp. 169–94.

1986b. Heiseb – Trickster und Gott der Nama und Damara in Südwestafrika/Namibia. In Rainer Vossen and Klauss Keuthmann (eds.), *Contemporary Studies on Khoisan 2*. Hamburg: Helmut Buske Verlag (Quellen zur Khoisan-Forschung 5.2), pp. 205–56.

1989. *Katalog zur Khoisan-Volkserzählungen des südlichen Afrikas* (2 vols.). Hamburg: Helmut Buske Verlag (Quellen zur Khoisan-Forschung 6.1 and 6.2).

Schmidt, Wilhelm. 1929. Zur Erforschung der alten Buschmann-Religion. *Africa* 2: 291–301.

Schneider, David M. 1984. *A critique of the study of kinship*. Ann Arbor: University of Michigan Press.

Schott, Rüdiger. 1964. Die sozialen Beziehungen zwischen ethnischen Gruppen in Südafrika. Habilitation thesis, University of Bonn.

Schrire, Carmel. 1980. An inquiry into the evolutionary status and apparent identity of San hunter-gatherers. *Human Ecology* 8: 9–32.

1984. Wild surmises on savage thoughts. In Carmel Schrire (ed.), *Past and present in hunter-gatherer studies*. Orlando, FL: Academic Press, pp. 1–25.

Schultze, L. [L. Schultze-Jena]. 1907. *Aus Namaland und Kalahari*. Jena: Gustav Fischer.

1914. *Das deutsche Kolonialreich, Volume 2, Part 2: Südwestafrika*. Leipzig and Vienna: Bibliographischen Instituts, pp. 131–295.

1928. Zur Kenntnis des Körpers der Hottentotten und Buschmänner. *Zoologische und anthropologische Ergebnisse einer Forschungsreise im westlichen und zentralen Südafrika*, Vol. 5, Part 3, pp. 147–227.

Schwarz, E.H.L. 1928. *The Kalahari and its native races*. London: H.F. and G. Witherby.

Seiner, Franz. 1909. Ergebnisse einer Bereisung des Gebiets zwischen Okawango und Sambesi (Caprivi-Zipfel) in den Jahren 1905 und 1906. *Mitteilungen aus den deutschen Schutzgebieten* 22: 1–111.

1910. Die Bushmänner des Okawango- und Sambesigebietes der Nordkalahari. *Globus* 97 (22): 341–5, and 97 (23): 357–60.

Service, Elman R. 1962. *Primitive social organization: an evolutionary perspective*. New York: Random House.

Seydel, E. 1910. Aus der Namib. *Deutsches Kolonialblatt* 31: 501–6.

Sheller, Paul. 1977. The people of the Central Kalahari Game Reserve: a report on the reconnaissance of the Reserve, July–September 1976. Gaborone. Unpublished report.

Shostak, Marjorie. 1983 [1981]. *Nisa: The life and works of a !Kung woman*. Harmondsworth: Penguin.

Shrubsall, F. 1898. The crania of African bush races. *Journal of the Anthropological Institute* 27: 263–90.

Silberbauer, George B. 1961. Aspects of the kinship system of the G/wi Bushmen of the central Kalahari. *South African Journal of Science* 57: 353–9.

1963. Marriage and the girl's puberty ceremony of the G/wi Bushmen. *Africa* 33: 12–24.

1965. *Report to the Government of Bechuanaland on the Bushman Survey*. Gaberones [Gaborone]: Bechuanaland Government.

1972. The G/wi Bushmen. In M.G. Bicchieri (ed.), *Hunters and gatherers today*. New York: Holt, Rinehart and Winston, pp. 271–326.

1973. Socio-ecology of the G/wi Bushmen. Ph.D. thesis, Monash University.

1974. Social change among the Bushmen of the eastern Ghanzi ridge. Unpublished paper deposited in the Botswana National Archives.

1979. Social hibernation: the response of the G/wi band to seasonal drought. In Madalon T. Hinchey (ed.), *Symposium on drought in Botswana*. Gaborone: The Botswana Society, in collaboration with Clarck University Press, pp. 112–20.

1981. *Hunter and habitat in the central Kalahari desert*. Cambridge: Cambridge University Press.

1982. Political process in G/wi bands. In Eleanor Leacock and Richard Lee (eds.), *Politics and history in band societies*. Cambridge: Cambridge University Press/ Paris: Éditions de la Maison des Sciences de l'Homme, pp. 23–35.

Silberbauer, G.B. and A.J. Kuper. 1966. Kgalagari masters and Bushman serfs: some observations. *African Studies* 25: 171–9.

Singer, R. and J.S. Weiner. 1963. Biological aspects of some indigenous African peoples. *Southwestern Journal of Anthropology* 19: 168–76.

Smith, Andrew B. 1984. Adaptive strategies of prehistoric pastoralism in the southwestern Cape. In M.J. Hall, G. Avery, D.M. Avery, M.L. Wilson, and A.J.B.

Humphreys (eds.), *Frontiers: Southern African archaeology today*. Oxford: British Archaeological Reports (International Series 207), pp. 131–42.

1986. Competition, conflict and clientship: Khoi and San relationships in the western Cape. *South African Archaeological Society Goodwin Series* 5: 36–41.

1987. Seasonal exploitation of resources on the Vredenburg Peninsula after 2000 B.P. In John Parkington and Martin Hall (eds.), *Papers in the prehistory of the Western Cape, South Africa*. Oxford: British Archaeological Reports (International Series 332), Vol. 2, pp. 393–402.

Snyman, J.W. 1970. *An introduction to the !Xũ language*. Cape Town: A.A. Balkema.

1975. *Žu/'hõasi fonologie en woordeboek*. Cape Town: A.A. Balkema.

Solway, Jacqueline S. and Richard B. Lee. 1990. Foragers, genuine or spurious? Situating the Kalahari San in history. *Current Anthropology* 31: 109–46.

Spohr, Otto H. 1962. *Wilhelm Heinrich Immanuel Bleek: a bio-bibliographical sketch*. Cape Town: University of Cape Town Libraries (Varia Series No. 6).

Spuhler, James N. 1973. Anthropological genetics: an overview. In M.H. Crawford and P.L. Workman (eds.), *Methods and theories of anthropological genetics*. Albuquerque: University of New Mexico Press, pp. 423–51.

Steward, Julian. 1955. *Theory of culture change*. Urbana: University of Illinois Press.

Steyn, H.P. 1971a. Die socio-ekonomiese lewe van die Nharo. M.A. thesis, Universiteit van Stellenbosch.

1971b. Aspects of the economic life of some nomadic Nharo Bushman groups. *Annals of the South African Museum* 56: 275–322.

1980. Die San versus die patrilineêre bende. *Ethnologie/Ethnology* (South African journal of ethnology) 3: 9–17.

1981a. Nharo plant utilization: an overview. *Khoisis* 1 (Stellenbosch).

1981b. *The Kalahari Bushmen*. Cape Town: Hollandisch Afrikaans Uitgevers Maatschappij).

1984. Southern Kalahari San subsistence ecology: a reconstruction. *The South African Archaeological Bulletin* 39: 117–24.

1985. *The Bushmen of the Kalahari*. Hove, England: Wayland (Original Peoples series).

Story, Robert. 1958. Some plants used by the Bushmen in obtaining food and water. *Botanical Survey of South Africa*, Memoir No. 30 (Pretoria).

Stow, George W. 1905. *The native races of South Africa: a history of the intrusion of the Hottentots and Bantu into the hunting grounds of the Bushmen, the aborigines of the country*. London: Swan Sonnenschein.

1930. *Rock paintings in South Africa, from parts of the Eastern Province and Orange Free State* (with introduction and descriptive notes by Dorothea F. Bleek). London: Methuen and Co.

Strauss, Teresa. 1979. *War along the Orange: the Korana and the border wars of 1868–9 and 1878–9*. Centre for African Studies, University of Cape Town (Communications No. 1).

Sugawara, Kazuyoshi. 1984. Spatial proximity and bodily contact among the Central Kalahari San. *African Study Monographs*, Supplementary Issue No. 3, pp. 1–43.

1988a. Visiting relations and social interactions between residential groups of the Central Kalahari San: hunter-gatherer camp as a micro-territory. *African Study Monographs* 8: 173–211.

1988b. The economics of social life among the Central Kalahari San (G//anakhwe and G/wikhwe) in the sedentary community at !Koi!kom. Paper presented at the Fifth International Conference on Hunting and Gathering Societies, Darwin.

Summers, Roger. 1967. Iron Age industries of Southern Africa, with notes on their chronology, terminology, and economic status. In Walter W. Bishop and J. Desmond Clark (eds.), *Background to evolution in Africa.* Chicago and London: University of Chicago Press, pp. 687–700.

Szalay, Miklós. 1983. *Ethnologie und Geschichte: zur Grundlegung einer ethnologischen Geschichtssahreibung; mit Beispielen aus der Geschichte der Khoi-San in Südafrika.* Berlin: Dietrich Reimer Verlag.

Tagart, E.S.B. 1933. *Report on the conditions existing among the Masarwa in the Bamangwato Reserve of the Bechuanaland Protectorate and certain other matters appertaining to the Natives living therein.* Pretoria: Government Printer.

Tanaka, Jiro. 1969. The ecology and social structure of Central Kalahari Bushmen: a preliminary report. *Kyoto University African Studies* 3: 1–26.

1971. *Busshuman: Seitai jinruigakuteki kenkyu.* Tokyo: Shisaku-sha.

1976. Subsistence ecology of the Central Kalahari San. In Richard B. Lee and Irven DeVore (eds.), *Kalahari hunter-gatherers: studies of the !Kung San and their neighbors.* Cambridge, MA: Harvard University Press, pp. 98–119.

1978a. *A San vocabulary of the central Kalahari: G//ana and G/wi dialects.* Tokyo: Institute for the Study of Languages and Cultures of Asia and Africa.

1978b. A study of the comparative ecology of African gatherer-hunters with special reference to San (Bushman-speaking people) and Pygmies. *Senri Ethnological Studies* 1: 189–212.

1980. *The San, hunter-gatherers of the Kalahari: a study in ecological anthropology* (revised English edition of Tanaka 1971, trans. by David W. Hughes). Tokyo: University of Tokyo Press.

1982. Adaptation to arid environment: a comparative study of hunter-gatherers and pastoralists in Africa. *African Study Monographs,* Supplementary Issue 1, pp. 1–12.

1987. The recent changes in the life and society of the Central Kalahari San. *African Study Monographs* 7: 37–51.

1989. Social integration of the San society from the viewpoint of sexual relationships. *African Study Monographs* 9: 153–65.

Tanaka, Jiro, Kazuyoshi Sugawara, and Masakazu Osaki. 1984. Report of the San (Basarwa) investigation carried out during 1982–3. Unpublished report to the Botswana government.

Ten Rhyne, W. 1933 [1686]. Gentis Hottentotten nuncupatae descripto (An account of the Hottentots), with translation by B. Farrington. In I. Schapera (ed.), *The early Cape Hottentots.* Cape Town: The Van Riebeeck Society (Vol. 14), pp. 84–157.

Testart, Alain. 1978. *Des classifications dualistes en Australie: essai sur l'évolution de l'organisation sociale.* Paris: Editions de la Maison des Sciences de l'Homme.

1981. Pour une typologie des chasseurs-cueilleurs. *Anthropologie et sociétés* 5(2): 177–221.

1982. *Les Chasseurs-cueilleurs ou l'origine des inégalités.* Paris: Société d'ethnographie.

Theal, George McCall. 1902. *The beginning of South African history.* London: T. Fischer Unwin.

1907. *History and ethnography of Africa south of the Zambesi,* Vol. 1. London: Swan Sonnenschein.

1919. *Ethnography and condition of South Africa before 1505* (second edition). London: George Allen and Unwin.

Thomas, Elizabeth Marshall. 1959. *The harmless people.* London: Secker and Warburg.

Thornton, R.J. 1983. 'This dying out race': W.H.I. Bleek's approach to the languages of Southern Africa. *Social Dynamics* 9(2): 1–10.

Tobias, P.V. 1955. Physical anthropology and somatic origins of the Hottentots. *African Studies* 14: 1–15.

1956a. The evolution of the Bushmen. *American Journal of Physical Anthropology* (n.s.) 14: 384.

1956b. On the survival of the Bushmen. *Africa* 26: 174–86.

1964. Bushman hunter-gatherers: a study in human ecology. In D.H.S. Davies (ed.), *Ecological studies in southern Africa.* The Hague: Junk, pp. 67–86.

Tordoff, William. 1973. Local administration in Botswana, Part I. *Journal of Administration Overseas* 12(4): 172–83.

Traill, A. 1973. 'N4 or S7': another Bushman language. *African Studies* 32: 25–32.

1974. *The compleat guide to the Koon.* Johannesburg: African Studies Institute (Communication No. 1).

(ed.). 1975. *Bushman and Hottentot linguistic studies.* Johannesburg: African Studies Institute (Communication No. 2).

1977a. The tonal structure of !xõ. In J.W. Snyman (ed.), *Bushman and Hottentot linguistic studies, 1975.* Pretoria: University of South Africa, pp. 11–47.

1977b. The phonological status of !Xõo clicks. In A. Traill (ed.), *Khoisan linguistic studies 3.* Johannesburg African Studies Institute, pp. 107–31.

1978a. Research on non-Bantu languages. In L.W. Lanham and K.P. Prinsloo (eds.), *Language and communication studies in South Africa.* Cape Town: Oxford University Press, pp. 117–37.

1978b. The languages of the Bushmen. In Phillip V. Tobias (ed.), *The Bushmen: San hunters and herders of southern Africa.* Cape Town and Pretoria: Human and Rousseau, pp. 137–47.

1979a. The !Xóõ strength hierarchy. In J.W. Snyman (ed.), *Bushman and Hottentot linguistic studies, 1977.* Pretoria: University of South Africa, pp. 1–38.

1979b. Another click accompaniment in !Xóõ. In A. Traill (ed.), *Khoisan linguistic studies 5.* Johannesburg: African Studies Institute, pp. 22–9.

1980. Phonetic diversity in the Khoisan languages. In J.W. Snyman (ed.), *Bushman and Hottentot linguistic studies, 1979.* Pretoria: University of South Africa, pp. 167–89.

1985. *Phonetic and phonological studies of !Xóõ Bushman*. Hamburg: Helmut Buske Verlag (Quellen zur Khoisan-Forschung 1).

1986. Do the Khoi have a place in the San? New data on Khoisan linguistic relationships. *Sprache und Geschichte in Afrika* 7(1): 407–30.

1988. A first linguistic monograph on Nharo: a review of Alan Barnard's *Worldlist*. In Rainer Vossen (ed.), *New Perspectives on the study of Khoisan*. Hamburg: Helmut Buske Verlag (Quellen zur Khoisan-Forschung 7), pp. 155–8.

Trenk, P. 1910. Die Buschleute der Namib, ihre Rechts- und Familienverhältnisse. *Mitteilungen aus den deutschen Schutzgebieten* 23: 166–70.

Turner, David H. 1978. Ideology and elementary structures. *Anthropologica* (n.s.) 20: 223–47.

Urquhart, Alvin W. 1963. *Patterns of settlement and subsistence in southwestern Angola*. Washington, DC: National Academy of Sciences – National Research Council (Publication No. 1096).

Valiente Noailles, Carlos. 1988. *El circulo y el fuego: sociedad y derecho de los kúa*. Buenos Aires: Ediar.

Van der Merwe, J.H. (ed.). 1983. *National atlas of South West Africa (Namibia)/ Nationale atlas van Suidwes-Afrika (Namibia)*. Windhoek: Directorate of Development Co-ordination.

Van der Post, Laurens. 1958. *The lost world of the Kalahari*. London: Hogarth Press.

1961. *The heart of the hunter*. London: Hogarth Press.

Van der Post, Laurens and Jane Taylor. 1984. *Testament to the Bushmen*. Harmondsworth: Penguin.

Van Warmelo, N.J. 1951. *Notes on the Kaokoveld (South West Africa) and its people*. Pretoria: Government Printer.

Vayda, Andrew P. (ed.) 1969. *Environment and cultural behavior*. New York: Natural History Press.

Vedder, Heinrich. 1923. *Die Bergdama* (2 vols.). Hamburg: L. Friedrichsen and Co.

1928a. The Berg Dama. In C.H.L. Hahn, H. Vedder, and L. Fourie, *The native tribes of South West Africa*. Cape Town: Cape Times, pp. 37–78.

1928b. The Nama. In C.H.L. Hahn, H. Vedder, and L. Fourie, *The native tribes of South West Africa*. Cape Town: Cape Times, pp. 107–52.

1930. Die Bergdama in Südwest-Afrika. *Africa* 3: 178–90.

1938 [1934]. *South West Africa in early times*, trans. and ed. by Cyril G. Hall. London: Oxford University Press.

Viegas Guerreiro, Manuel. 1968. *Bochimanes !khũ de Angola: estudo etnográfico*. Lisbon: Instituto de Investigação Científica de Angola, Junta de Investigações do Ultramar.

[Vierich, Helga]. Helga Vierich-Esche. 1977. *Interim report on Basarwa and related poor Bakgalagadi in Kweneng District*. Gaborone: Ministry of Local Government and Lands.

Vierich, Helga. 1982a. The Kūa of the southern Kalahari: a study of the socio-ecology of dependency. Ph.D. dissertation, University of Toronto.

1982b. Adaptive flexibility in a multi-ethnic setting: the Basarwa of the southern Kalahari. In Eleanor Leacock and Richard Lee (eds.), *Politics and history in band societies*. Cambridge: Cambridge University Press/Paris: Editions de la Maison des Sciences de l'Homme, pp. 213–22.

Vinnicombe, Patricia. 1967. Rock painting analysis. *South African Archaeological Bulletin* 22: 129–41.

1972. Myth, motive, and selection in southern African rock art. *Africa* 42: 192–204.

1976. *People of the eland: rock paintings of the Drakensberg Bushmen as a reflection of their life and thought*. Pietermaritzburg: University of Natal Press.

1986. Rock art, territory and land rights. In Megan Biesele, with Robert Gordon and Richard Lee (eds.), *The past and future of !Kung ethnography: critical reflections and symbolic perspectives, essays in honour of Lorna Marshall*. Hamburg: Helmut Buske Verlag (Quellen zur Khoisan-Forschung 4), pp. 275–309.

Vossen, Rainer. 1984. Studying the linguistic and ethno-history of the Khoe-speaking (central Khoisan) peoples of Botswana, research in progress. *Botswana Notes and Records* 16: 19–35.

1986. Some observations on nominal gender in Naró. In Franz Rottland (ed.), *Festschrift zum 60. Geburtstag von Carl F. Hoffmann*. Hamburg: Helmut Buske Verlag (Bayreuther Beitrage zur Sprachwissenschaft), pp. 373–90.

1988a. Khoe linguistic relationships reconsidered: the data. In Rainer Vossen (ed.), *New Perspectives on the study of Khoisan*. Hamburg: Helmut Buske Verlag (Quellen zur Khoisan-Forschung 7), pp. 67–108.

1988b. Khoe linguistic relationships reconsidered. *Botswana Notes and Records* 20: 61–70.

1990. Die Khoe-Sprachen. Ein Beitrag zur Erforschung der Sprachgeschichte Afrikas. Habilitation thesis, University of Bayreuth.

Vuyk, Trudeke. n.d. [1979]. Men and women: cattle and agriculture in a Kalahari village. Unpublished paper.

Wadley, Lyn. 1987. *Later Stone Age hunters and gatherers of the southern Transvaal: Social and ecological interpretations*. Oxford: British Archaeological Reports (International Series 380/Cambridge Monographs in African Archaeology 25).

1989. Legacies from the Later Stone Age. In Janette Deacon (ed.), *Goodwin's legacy*. Vlaeberg: The South African Archaeological Society (Goodwin Series 6), pp. 42–53.

Wagner, Roy. 1986. *Symbols that stand for themselves*. Chicago/London: University of Chicago Press.

Wagner-Robertz, Dagmar. 1976. Schamanismus bei den Hain//om in Südwestafrika. *Anthropos* 71: 533–54.

Wellington, John H. 1967. *South West Africa and its human issues*. Oxford: Clarendon Press.

Werner, H. 1906. Anthropologische, ethnologische und ethnographische Beobachtungen über die Heikum und Kungbuschleute. *Zeitschrift für Ethnologie* 38: 241–68.

West, Martin. 1971. *Divided community: a study of social groups and racial attitudes in a South African town*. Cape Town: A.A. Balkema.

Westphal, E.O.J. 1956. The non-Bantu languages of southern Africa. Supplement to A.N. Tucker and M.A. Bryan, *The non-Bantu languages of north-eastern Africa*. London: Oxford University Press for the International African Institute, pp. 158–73.

    1962a. On classifying Bushman and Hottentot languages. *African Language Studies* 3: 30–48.

    1962b. A reclassification of southern African non-Bantu languages. *Journal of African Languages* 1: 1–8.

    1963. The linguistic prehistory of southern Africa: Bush, Kwadi, Hottentot, and Bantu linguistic relationships. *Africa* 33: 237–65.

    1971. The click languages of southern and eastern Africa. In Thomas A. Sebeok (ed), *Current trends in linguistics*, Vol. 7, Linguistics in Sub-Sharan Africa. The Hague: Mouton, pp. 367–420.

    1974. Notes on A. Traill: 'N4 or S7?' (with a reply by A. Traill). *African Studies* 33: 243–55.

    1978. Observations on current Bushman and Hottentot musical practices. *Review of Ethnology* 5(2/3): 9–15.

    1980. The age of 'Bushman' languages in southern Africa. In J.W. Snyman (ed.), *Bushman and Hottentot linguistic studies, 1979*. Pretoria: University of South Africa, pp. 59–79.

Wiessner, Polly. 1977. Hxaro: a regional system of reciprocity for reducing risk among the !Kung San (2 vols.). Ph.D. dissertation, University of Michigan, Ann Arbor.

    1980. Hunting and continuity in !Kung San reciprocal relationships. In *Deuxième congrès international sur les sociétés de chasseurs-collecteurs/Second International Conference on Hunting and Gathering Societies*. Quebec: Dépt. d'anthropologie, Université Laval, pp. 766–91.

    1981. Measuring the impact of social ties on nutritional status among the !Kung San. *Informations sur les sciences sociales/Social Science Information* 20(4/5): 641–78.

    1982. Risk, reciprocity, and social influence on !Kung San economics. In Eleanor Leacock and Richard Lee (eds.), *Politics and history in band societies*. Cambridge: Cambridge University Press/Paris: Editions de la Maison des Sciences de l'Homme, pp. 61–84.

    1986. !Kung San networks in a generational perspective. In Megan Biesele, with Robert Gordon and Richard Lee (eds.), *The past and future of !Kung ethnography: critical reflections and symbolic perspectives, essays in honour of Lorna Marshall*. Hamburg: Helmut Buske Verlag (Quellen zur Khoisan-Forschung 4), pp. 103–36.

Wikar, Hendrik Jacob. 1935 [1779]. Berigt aan den Weleedelen Gestrengen Heer Mr. Joachim van Plettenbergh . . . (Report to His Excellency Joachim van Plettenbergh . . .), with translation by A.W. van der Horst. In E.E. Mossop (ed.), *The journals of Wikar, Coetsé and van Reenen*. Cape Town: The Van Riebeeck Society (Vol. 15), pp. 20–219.

Willcox, A.R. 1956. *Rock paintings of the Drakensberg: Natal and Griqualand East*. London: Max Parrish.

    1963. *The rock art of South Africa*. London: Thomas Nelson and Sons.

1966. Sheep and sheep-herders in South Africa. *Africa* 36: 432–8.

Wilmsen, Edwin N. 1982. Exchange, interaction, and settlement in northwestern Botswana: past and present perspectives. In Renée Hitchcock and Mary R. Smith (eds.), *Settlement in Botswana*. Marshalltown, South Africa: Heinemann Educational Books, pp. 98–109.

1983. The ecology of an illusion: anthropological foraging in the Kalahari. *Reviews in Anthropology* 10: 9–20.

1986. Historical process in the political economy of San. *Sprache und Geschichte in Afrika* 7.2: 413–32.

1989a. *Land filled with flies: a political economy of the Kalahari*. Chicago and London: University of Chicago Press.

1989b. Those who have each other: San relations to land. In Edwin N. Wilmsen (ed.), *We are here: politics of aboriginal land tenure*. Berkeley: University of California Press, pp. 43–67.

1990. The political history of minorities and its bearing on current policy. In *Botswana – Education, Culture and Politics*. Centre of African Studies, University of Edinburgh (Seminar Proceedings No. 29).

Wilmsen, Edwin N. and James R. Denbow. 1990. Paradigmatic history of San-speaking peoples and current attempts at revision. *Current Anthropology* 31: 489–24.

Wilson, M.L. 1986a. Notes on the nomenclature of the Khoisan. *Annals of the South African Museum* 97(8): 251–66.

1986b. Khoisanosis: the question of separate identities for Khoi and San. In Ronald Singer and John K. Lundy (eds.), *Variation, culture and evolution in African populations: papers in honour of Dr Hertha de Villiers*. Johannesburg: Witwatersrand University Press, pp. 13–25.

1989. The problem of the origin of the Khoikhoi. *The Digging Stick* 6(1): 2–4.

Wilson, Monica. 1969. The hunters and herders. In Monica Wilson and Leonard Thompson (eds.), *The Oxford history of South Africa*, Vol. I. Oxford: Clarendon Press, pp. 40–74.

Wily, Elizabeth. 1973a. An analysis of the Bere Bushman settlement scheme. Report to the Ministry of Local Government and Lands, Gaborone, Botswana.

1973b. Bere as a prototype for further development. Report to the Ministry of Local Government and Lands, Gaborone, Botswana.

1976. Bere and Ka/Gae. Report to the Ministry of Local Government and Lands, Gaborone, Botswana.

1982a. Botswana's development strategy for its indigenous desert people, the Kalahari Bushmen. In United Nations Institute for Training and Research, *Alternative strategies for desert development and management*, Vol. 4. New York: Pergamon Press, pp. 1108–21.

1982b. A strategy of self-determination for the Kalahari San (the Botswana government's programme of action in the Ghanzi farms). *Development and Change* 13: 291–308.

Winter, Jürgen C. 1981. Die Khoisan-Familie. In Bernd Heine, Thilo C. Schadeberg, and Ekkehard Wolff (eds.), *Die Sprachen Afrikas*. Hamburg: Helmut Buske Verlag, pp. 329–74.

Woodburn, James. 1980. Hunters and gatherers today and reconstruction of the past. In Ernest Gellner (ed.), *Soviet and Western anthropology*. London: Duckworth, pp. 95–117.

1982a. Egalitarian societies. *Man* (n.s.) 17: 431–51.

1982b. Social dimensions of death in four African hunting and gathering societies. In Maurice Bloch and Jonathan Parry (eds.), *Death and the regeneration of life*. Cambridge: Cambridge University Press, pp. 187–210.

Wright, John B. 1971. *Bushman raiders of the Drakensberg, 1840–1870*. Pietermaritzburg: University of Natal Press.

Wuras, C.F. 1920. *Vokabular der Korana-Sprache*. Berlin: Dietrich Reimer.

1929. An account of the !Korana. *Bantu Studies* 3: 287–96.

Yellen, John E. 1976. Settlement patterns of the !Kung: an archaeological perspective. In Richard B. Lee and Irven DeVore (eds.), *Kalahari hunter-gatherers: Studies of the !Kung San and their neighbors*. Cambridge, MA: Harvard University Press, pp. 47–72.

1977. *Archaeological approaches to the present: models for reconstructing the past*. New York: Academic Press.

Yellen, John and Henry Harpending. 1972. Hunter-gatherer populations and archaeological inference. *World Archaeology* 4: 244–53.

Yellen, John E. and Richard B. Lee. 1976. The Dobe-/Du/da environment. In Richard B. Lee and Irven DeVore (eds.), *Kalahari hunter-gatherers: studies of the !Kung San and their neighbors*. Cambridge, MA: Harvard University Press, pp. 27–46.

Yengoyan, Aram A. 1968. Australian section systems – demographic components and interactional similarities with the !Kung Bushmen. *Proceedings of the Eighth International Congress of Anthropological and Ethnological Sciences, Tokyo* 3: 256–60.

1978. Culture, consciousness, and problems of translation: the Kariera system in cross-cultural perspective. In L.R. Hiatt (ed.), *Australian Aboriginal concepts*. Canberra: Australian Institute of Aboriginal Studies, pp. 146–55.

Zeuner, Frederick Eberhard. 1963. *A history of domesticated animals*. London: Hutchinson.

Ziervogel, D. 1955. Notes on the language of the Eastern Transvaal Bushmen. In E.F. Potgieter, *The disappearing Bushmen of Lake Chrissie: a preliminary survey*. Pretoria: J.L. van Schaik, pp. 33–64.

Index

Cambridge Studies in Social and Cultural Anthropology

Editors: ERNEST GELLNER, JACK GOODY, STEPHEN GUDEMAN, MICHAEL HERZ-FELD, JONATHAN PARRY

*Available in paperback

	DATE DUE		
MAY 1 0 2000			